# Arab Human Development in the Twenty-first Century

# Arab Human Development in the Twenty-first Century
## The Primacy of Empowerment

Edited by
Bahgat Korany

*An AUC Forum for International Affairs Edition*

The American University in Cairo Press
Cairo • New York

Exclusive distribution outside Egypt and North America by I.B. Tauris & Co Ltd., 6 Salem Road,
London, W2 4BU

Dar el Kutub No. 22967/13
ISBN 978 977 416 658 7

Dar el Kutub Cataloging-in-Publication Data

Korany, Bahgat
        Arab Human Development in the Twenty-first Century: The Primacy of
    Empowerment/Bahgat Korany.—Cairo: The American University in Cairo Press, 2014
        p.    cm.
        ISBN: 978 977 416 658 7
        Arab Countries—Social Conditions
        Social Change—Arab Countries
        303.4

1 2 3 4 5    18 17 16 15 14

Designed by Sally Boylan
Printed in Egypt

# Contents

**To Margaret**
whose support is always there—and effective

# Tables

# Figures

# Boxes

# Acknowledgments

This book was initially prepared as the tenth-anniversary volume of the well-established Arab Human Development Reports, published since 2002 by the United Nations Development Program (UNDP). For this massive international project that began in March 2010, I incurred many debts. My first debt is obviously to my colleagues who wrote the various chapters. Not only did they work hard to respect strict deadlines, but they also accepted graciously the analytical vision, the conceptual framework, and my frequent demands for revisions. They proved over and over again that productive team work is possible in the Arab world, that it is the wave of the future and indeed the most effective one.

At the administrative level the managers of the AUC Forum kept the team and the deadlines running smoothly from its inception. When Shaima Ragab had to move on, Miriam William took her place to make both the transition and the work continue on track as planned. Dr. Yasmine Farouk, an energetic young scholar at Cairo University, backed me up well as the efficient research assistant. My colleague Dr. Ali Hadi, the distinguished university professor of mathematics at the American University in Cairo, was available to iron out all our problems in making tables and ensure that our statistics were correct, well integrated into our texts, and, as far as possible, accessible to the non-specialized reader.

Special appreciation goes to colleagues who submitted background papers on specific topics. They helped back up many of the chapters with proper evidence. These papers are available—mostly in Arabic—on the AUC Forum website (www.aucegypt.edu/research/forum). I also owe a huge debt of gratitude to members of the Advisory Board appointed by the UNDP, who met twice to comment on the contents of the draft and offer feedback that improved the present book. I would like to thank Dr. Wael Kamal of the University of Massachusetts, who readily agreed to allow his recent artwork, the door of Shaykh Zayed's mosque in Abu Dhabi, to become this book's cover.

This is the fourth publication of the AUC Forum in collaboration with the American University in Cairo Press. My thanks go to Nadia Naqib, Johanna Baboukis, Basma El Manialawi, Neil Hewison, and AUCP's energetic new director, Nigel Fletcher-Jones. Because of the special circumstances surrounding this UNDP project and its publication in book form, Margaret Korany's support for this project, more than with any other of my books, has been very effective, especially when frustration and disillusionment were about to get the better of me. This book is dedicated to her.

Since their inception in 2002, as the UNDP's repeated and written assertions show, these Arab Human Development Reports are conceived as the analyses of independent Arab researchers, not always with UNDP approval of their views. To its credit, the UNDP has continued to finance these projects, this one no exception. From the very start and through more than three years, UNDP involvement was present through research support, travels and meetings of the research team, youth discussion groups, and the Advisory Board. I am extremely grateful for this support, without which this text would not have been prepared in the first place. The official launch was announced to take place in Tunis—the cradle of the Arab Spring—in May 2012. Government dignitaries and regional and international media were sent official invitations and the UNDP website specified the date. However, for reasons that were never made entirely clear, the UNDP suddenly and unilaterally decided not to proceed with the launch and the official publication.

In the end, the UNDP authorized the publication of the work through another publisher. For this, very special thanks go to Dr. Adel Abdel-Latif of the UNDP New York office, Maya Abu Zeid of the Beirut office, and all their colleagues. They contributed to the release of this text from the desk drawers of international bureaucracy, helped us update some of the data after the passage of time, and offered technical assistance so that this book could appear in the excellent form that the AUC Press has produced. Neither they, nor anybody else other than the authors, are responsible for its contents.

This book looks at what Arab countries have achieved over the past decade and looks forward to what remains to be done to reach full development, noting the large gap between the region's potential and actual development. Its publication coincides with the beginning of a new era in the region. The chapter authors come from different Arab countries, from Bahrain in the Gulf to Morocco at the very western end of the Arab world. As a result of their close collaboration, this final published text is not a mere collection of chapters, the usual 'reader,' but a volume in which the expertise of individuals converges into a coherent whole.

# Contributors

**Baqer S. Alnajjar** is professor of sociology at the University of Bahrain. He received his PhD from Durham University (England) in 1983. He has published extensively with both the Center of Arab Unity Studies (Beirut) and Dar Al-Saqi (London) on NGOs in the Gulf and the problems of Arab democratization.

**Najoua Fezzaa Ghriss** holds a PhD in educational sciences jointly from the University of Tunisia and the University of Louvain-La-Neuve, Belgium. She is currently a professor of pedagogy at the University of Tunisia, and a member of several professional associations. She has conducted numerous research assessments, and participated in many national, regional, and international workshops and seminars in the field of education.

**Louisa Dris-Aït Hamadouche** is an assistant professor of political science at University of Algiers 3, an associated researcher at CREAD (Research Center for Applied Economy and Development), and a member of ACM (Assembly of Mediterranean Citizens). She is also a member of the research unit directed by Oulhdj Ferdiou called "Democratization of the Arab World: Chaotic Transitions." She is a consultant for the media about international issues.

**Lina Khatib** is director of the Carnegie Middle East Center in Beirut. Previously, she was the co-founding head of the Program on Arab Reform and Democracy at Stanford University's Center on Democracy, Development, and the Rule of Law. Her research interests include the international relations of the Middle East, Islamist groups, political transitions, and foreign policy. She has also published widely on public diplomacy, political communication, and political participation in the Middle East.

**Mustafa Yousef Khawaja** specializes in the indicators and measurements of corruption. He has worked in the Palestinian Central Bureau of Statistics since 1994. He is coordinator of the National Statistical Monitoring System, supervises the Government and Anti-corruption Unit, and contributes to national, regional, and international projects on governance and anti-corruption measures.

**Bahgat Korany** is professor of international relations and political economy at the American University in Cairo (AUC) and director of the AUC Forum. He is an honorary professor at the University of Montreal, an elected member of Canada's Royal Society since 1994, and has been a visiting professor at various universities, from Paris and Oxford to Harvard (visiting scholar). He has published about 95 articles and book chapters, and twelve books.

**Zeyad Makhamreh** is an associate professor of geography at the University of Jordan. He earned his PhD from Trier University in Germany in 2006. He specializes in applied environmental science, particularly land-degradation assessment and land use change in Jordan.

**Mhamed Malki** is professor of constitutional law and political science and director of the Laboratory of Political and Constitutional Studies, Marrakech, Morocco. He has served as an expert with several regional and international institutions. He has published fifteen books and dozens of articles in specialized periodicals, and has been awarded two Arab Prizes.

**Sabria Al-Thawr** is a lecturer in the fields of international development and linguistics at Sana'a University. She also works as a freelance consultant on gender, education, research, and poverty issues with various international development agencies. Her main fields of expertise include research and surveys, research methodology, training and facilitation, education, gender, and conflict analysis in tribal areas. She has several publications related to various development, gender, and education issues in Yemen and the region.

# Part 1:
# Toward the Twenty-first Century

# CHAPTER 1

# Redefining Development for a New Generation:

## A Political Economy Analysis

Bahgat Korany

## Introduction

According to the World Bank and the International Monetary Fund (IMF), among others, at the beginning of the twenty-first century Tunisia and Egypt were likened to the Asian Tiger countries as Arab models of the success of neo-liberal economics and the Washington Consensus. Indeed, their annual growth rates were the highest among the non-oil-producing Arab countries, ranging from 4 percent to 5 percent per year in the first decade of the twentieth century. Yet it was in Tunisia, soon followed by Egypt, that the massive "Arab Spring" emerged, swelled, and then ultimately toppled presidents in January and February 2011, respectively. These events starkly illustrated that *average* economic growth rates do not constitute development, and that such statistics can even be misleading. After all, the most repeated slogans by the protesting masses demanded equality and social justice.

Although the research for this book started almost a year before the Arab Spring, these uprisings brought Arab (mis)development, philosophy, and practice to light. This is why the research is grounded in the concept of human, rather than purely economic, development. This theoretical foundation regards people as the true wealth of a nation, and the empowerment of the individual and society—that is, the expansion of choices available to people—as the foundation for development. Individual empowerment encompasses more than income, health, and education. Indeed, it primarily encompasses political empowerment, which equips individuals to participate in governance and thus influence decision-making. This makes development a daily participatory process enabling individuals to address their needs.

Empowerment and the primacy of inclusionary decision-making—from the village to the top of the political pyramid—for promoting development are key concepts in this book. Empowerment means increasing the capacity of individuals and groups to choose freely in ways that preserve their dignity and identity as well as the freedom to be proactive, particularly in their relationships with authority. This concept affirms the primacy of coordination and partnership in managing the affairs of state and society, in contrast to a control-based model that relies on coercion and compulsion. Empowerment directly addresses marginalization and the power relations that shape it, giving individuals the capacity to achieve self-realization, through integration into the community, which in turn advances development.

Empowerment is also at the core of the emerging democratic transition, which is at the heart of the relationship between the individual and the governing group and among the institutions of governance. Successful implementation of any development policy is impossible without close interaction between government and those affected by government policies. Empowerment means rationalizing and reforming government, moving from coercion to cooperation, which confers legitimacy on government. This transformation is the most important challenge facing Arab countries, whose people have been kept under political control from the top for far too long. The challenge is: How do we change this entrenched dynamic? To find the answer to such a big and basic question, the methodology adopted here is analogous to that of a medical doctor's: get the diagnosis and the prescription right—major restructuring—then initiate the change by overcoming an adaptation deficit. This diagnosis and the mastering of the societal need for change is at the basis of the book's analytical framework.

After presenting this framework, chapter 1 outlines the organization of this volume in detail.

## The Political Economy Framework

This analytical framework rests on one basic argument: development requires empowerment, especially empowerment of the people at the bottom of the social ladder. As stated above, empowerment is "enablement," measured here by expanding the range of choices for people, widening the range of opportunities open to them, and doing away with barriers to such empowerment. Though the satisfaction of basic material needs in poor and subsistence-level societies is crucial, empowerment is not to be limited to the material level. For Mouhamed Bouazizi, who sparked the mass protests in Tunisia, did not set himself on fire only because he was unemployed. Indeed, he had been unemployed for years. He set himself on fire after he was humiliated by a police officer and dehumanized at the police station—two prime symbols of the state. Didn't the slogans of the masses during the Arab Spring demand human dignity?

At the basis of this framework are two basic premises. First, the source of the crisis in development is not exclusively economic, hence the primacy of a political economy approach, which emphasizes the relationship between wealth and power and the revolving doors between them. This approach places economics in a wider context, for politics and business seem to be one and the same thing in many instances in these countries. The concept of 'crony capitalism' expresses this connection well. Don't people in Syria call Mr. Makhlouf, Bashar Al-Assad's cousin, "Mr. Five Percent"? This sobriquet is an indication of the commission paid to him for any foreign or large transaction in Syria. The same pattern existed in Tunisia with Laila El-Tarabulsi—Zine El Abidine's wife—and her family, and in Egypt with Mubarak's sons and their cronies. Indeed, examples of business and politics overlapping abound. The political regime has not only dominated the economy and monopolized political power, it has hijacked the state itself. Contrary to historical (European) patterns of state formation where the state creates the regime, in many parts of the Arab world, there seems to be a contrary pattern. For instance, the official name of the Saudi state demonstrates the dynastic origin—if not ownership—of the state. It is also an indicator of its present functioning. This is what we call the neo-patrimonial clientelistic state, wherein the distinction between public and private ownership is blurred, sometimes even absent. This political economy approach should be thus interpreted as an addition to and an integration of, rather than a marginalization of, economic analysis. After all, economists will approve the necessity of non-clientelistic 'rational-interest,' rather than private-interest, decision making to attain proper objectives. Moreover, in addition to using some basic economic concepts such as opportunity cost and multiplier effect in this chapter, some other chapters (e.g., 4 and 5) also integrate economic thinking and analysis.

Second—in terms of this book's framework—the crisis is neither exclusively internal nor external; the two are interdependent. I have written at greater length about the centrality of *intermestics*, the organic relationship between the *inter*national and the do*mestic* (Korany 2013:

77–100); this idea underpins the analyses carried out across chapters. For example, many big business people act as bridges, representing multinational enterprises as diverse as McDonald's, Pizza Hut, and Samsung. This could make good business in the economy but intermestics' politics are not always good. The economist's concept of a multiplier effect helps explain the (harmful) interplay between the international and the domestic. For example, internal problems that are initially containable may be aggravated through their interaction with external factors. The invasion of Iraq, intervention in Lebanese crises, or penetration of al-Qaeda in Yemen or Somalia are examples that come to mind.

Thus the failure to achieve development-as-empowerment is not only (or even mainly) due to the absence of resources, for contrary to many sub-Saharan African countries, for instance, the Arab world has plenty of resources. The Arab world is so rich, yet with so many poor. The director-general of the Arab Labor Organization recently affirmed that the number of unemployed individuals in the Arab world is twenty million, a 1 percent increase over the last year (al-Ahram, September 21, 2013). This is at a time when financial resources are increasing as the price of oil and the amount of foreign aid to non-oil-producing countries have been on the rise. Where is the problem, then?

In Egypt, the number of people living on less than two dollars a day has been rising and now includes almost 40 percent of the total population (or more than thirty million people). In stark contrast, the number of air-conditioning units in Egypt has risen from 165,000 in 1996 to three million in 2009, that is, in thirteen years more than fifteen times as many units were counted in use (Egypt's statistics, 2012). The same statistics can be marshaled about the acquisition of televisions, resort apartments, and gated communities around Cairo. Similarly, in an oil giant such as Saudi Arabia, there is an increase in the number of Saudi billionaires, while at the same time the number of the poor and unemployed individuals is growing. Thus, the country's Shura Council affirmed in 2010 that the number of poor people reached 22 percent of the total population (three million Saudis). The balance sheet for Saudi unemployment is even more serious: 46 percent of young people between twenty and twenty-four years old are unemployed, and a striking 78 percent of female college graduates (*Al-Hayat*, 16 May 2010).

What do these statistics tell us? The availability of resources is not the only crucial element in development. Even more important is the pattern of allocation or distribution of such resources; that is, the political aspect, the decision making, and its rationale. Indeed, why has development in the Arab region progressed so slowly? What explains this Arab riddle? It is not a lack of resources that drives this disappointing performance, for the region is rich in human as well as financial resources, which flow in from oil reserves and foreign aid, consolidating the rentier state. In fact, the basis for (mis)development is bad policies and inefficient management of resources. That means that the faltering course of development has to be addressed at the top level of decision making, which will then spark the empowerment of individuals and society.

Hence the emphasis in this book highlights the primacy of addressing the performance of the state's top level of management and its decision-making processes, or what I call—following the medical analogy—the CNS (central nervous system).

## The Riddle of Arab Development

It is the CNS that provides the vision of successful development and the ability to implement it. Successful implementation is strongly related to the nature of the state's authority, its institutions, and the legitimacy of its governance. As elaborated in the introduction to part 1, the essence of state authority can be summed up in an equation: state authority equals legitimacy plus coercive force. That equation expresses an inverse correlation: the weaker the state's legitimacy, the greater is its recourse to coercion.

Despite considerable variations in wealth and government structure, most Arab governments are neo-patrimonial, making no distinction between public and personal property and treating the country and its wealth as a private feudal estate ('*izba* is the most repeated Arabic word in the street, meaning 'a ranch,' 'a piece of real estate,' 'a fiefdom'). The state's representatives exercise all power, demanding complete obedience and allegiance from society, leaving no space for civil society to function as an intermediary, participate in government, or influence decision making.

Three key features of this neo-patrimonial/clientelist governance retard development:

- State institutions are reduced to a façade as power becomes obsessed with security. The state's declining legitimacy renders it suspect to its people. The regime returns the coin, becomes increasingly suspicious of its society, expands its security budget and personnel, and increasingly moves toward a *securocracy*.
- This isolated, barricaded regime/fragile state is unable to manage social, ethnic, or sectarian conflict. Society descends into chronic polarization over such issues as, for instance, whether the country should be a civil or a religious state.

- Civil society organizations are weak—because of widespread tribal or sectarian fragmentation, co-option by the authorities, inadequate local funding—eroding social capital, which depends on trust and interdependence in collective action.

These factors hinder the state's ability to address the growing internal and external challenges. As security concerns override legitimacy, the state's sole preoccupation is to suppress the resulting turmoil and postpone its ultimate explosion, while continuing to exploit the economic system for the ruler's benefit. While many rulers have held on to power for decades, their endurance is not indicative of stability but of media control, dependence on outside alliances, and intimidation of citizens through threats of social fragmentation or disintegration into a failed state.

Governance based on coercion rather than legitimacy becomes the rule. The bureaucracy swells, particularly the state security apparatus, and the state embodies securocracy. State–society relations turn from negotiation and compromise to fiat, crowding out dialogue and public participation.

In short, despite differences in economic models and governmental and social structures, most Arab states incorporate elements of authoritarianism unchecked by fragile opposition parties (where they exist at all) or civil society organizations weakened by decades of neglect and intimidation. This pattern of power concentration must change so that everyone can participate in shaping government policies. Weak participation is a structural problem in people's relationship with the agents of power at all levels in the Arab world. As a consequence, empowerment is related to good governance and to the principles of coordination and partnership in managing state and society relations.

Because of this pattern of political regime primacy (and its restructuring), the CNS becomes all-important. Even international organizations, usually very shy in criticizing their member states, admit the primacy of the political. For instance, World Bank annual reports as well as the UNDP publications now have to deal increasingly with the issue of 'governance.' After initial neglect, these organizations now go to the other extreme and become obsessed with the concept and phenomenon of governance. Everything becomes an issue of governance. However, governance is used in these works mainly in its technical sense: how to manage. Governance is thus divorced from its political context and implications. For even governance as management has to face up to politics, that is, the issue of power relations and potential restructuring, especially in the Arab and the Global South contexts, dominated as they are by inequality. As is now clear, the state—hijacked by the regime—is no longer the incarnation of the 'ideal type' state we read about in political science textbooks or hear about in official discourse and media narratives.

It is true that the state is usually extractive (through taxes), but it is also distributional (by offering services subsidized by monies acquired through taxation). The reality, however, is that the social-welfare sector of this Arab state is very weak. Even in many Gulf countries, which tend to offer advanced social-welfare policies for their citizens, the budget for social services is usually modest relative to the budget of the police and army. As a result, most of these hijacked states tend to become neither distributional, arbitrational, nor developmental, but mainly extractive, clannish, and predatory. Hence the emphasis here on the CNS as the location where change toward development-as-empowerment starts. Not only will democratization and an inclusionary approach at the CNS level have an impact on national decision making, but it will also model democratic processes which can then be adopted at the grassroots level. A snowball effect in state–society partnership could then follow.

The Arab Spring uprisings highlight both the urgency of changing course and the enormous potential for change. Furthermore, they affirm the validity of the book's use of an empowerment lens to examine the shortcomings of the current development path and the demands for dignity and social justice.

The uprisings have exposed another dimension of the widening gap between potential and achievement: the gap—in numbers, perception, and knowledge—between a youthful population (people less than twenty-nine years old make up more than half the population in the Arab world) and an aging ruling elite. While these rulers pursued policies leading to stagnation, society was simmering with discontent after decades of marginalization and social exclusion. As the 2004 Arab Human Development Report predicted: "the maintenance of the status quo, from a lack of development accompanied by oppression domestically to violations from abroad, could deepen social conflict in the Arab countries."[1]

These social conflicts can be resolved only by restructuring political authority as the first step in addressing structural imbalances. That requires empowering people and society to expand their choices, and to bridge the gap between possibilities and achievements. Empowering individuals and society to achieve fair and sustainable development must start from the top and be able to trickle down, by opening the centers of decision making to the authentic representatives of citizens, so that they have a direct role in advancing development.

Such an inclusionary approach will help to eradicate that widening gap between potential and actual results—a gulf that depletes capacities—by investing in productive areas rather than in trying to maintain the current structures. Such an approach applies the economist's *opportunity cost*. For example, what if the large number of young people in Arab societies who are now seen as an economic burden were supported in becoming powerful sources of productive energy and creativity? This would make a sizable portion of the population developmental assets rather than a liability. Furthermore, what if Arab governments endeavored to manage conflict—abroad, with each other, and domestically—to reduce losses and maximize gains, instead of allowing such conflicts to fester and drain the available energies? What if governments could reverse the brain drain of scientists, a trend that wastes huge stores of knowledge capacity built up at such a high cost? What if corrupt practices, political or private, were eradicated before they became entrenched?

In other words, by assessing the total opportunity costs—direct and indirect, intangible and material—that persist in (mis)development's destructive practices and by envisioning productive alternatives, countries can expand their scope for identifying and halting damaging policies and their subsequent outcomes.

Operationally, as shown in the organization of this book, development-as-empowerment can be achieved in two ways:

- eliminating barriers to it, by eliminating draining practices or structures, such as corruption, (domestic) conflicts, and poverty
- promoting favorable structures and processes—for example, rule of law, balanced (if not independent) media, healthy environmental practices, education as a means of social mobility, identity formation, and informed citizenship.

### Empowerment Begins at the Top

This book is not still another of the famous 'readers' that dominate in development studies. Although multi-authored, it is conceived as an integrated text, a complete book based on a framework and a main argument followed through the various chapters. The short introductions to the different parts act as bridges to reinforce the book's unity.

The book has four main parts. Part 1 identifies and analyzes the styles of governance in Arab countries to make clear the context in which empowerment must operate, and thus paves the way for the remaining three parts to explore the main dimensions of disempowerment and empowerment. Part 2 emphasizes that empowerment must be initiated at the top, based on rule of law, integrity in governance, and free media. Part 3 is concerned with strengthening the routes to empowerment, through an invigorated antipoverty strategy, a more effective model for conflict management, and greater responsiveness to environmental challenges. Finally, part 4 is about strengthening the roots of empowerment, which depends on the quality of basic education, specifically the basic but under-researched improvements in religious education. The book offers practical steps on what countries can do to empower individuals and society to advance development.

Mhamed Malki shows in chapter 2 that Arab countries need to shift from the ruler's law to the rule of law. They need to give priority to policy planning, remedy the fragility of the legal environment for governance, and affirm the inevitability of change that begins at the top. The chapter highlights the stark contradiction between the ruling regimes' proclamations about a state of rights and law and the reality of coercive Arab regimes with a monopoly on power. Addressing this contradiction requires a new social contract that engages all of society, especially youth, by redistributing power, reforming society, and embracing the concept of the open public sphere.

Change that leads to empowerment must start at the top with adherence to the rule of law, and a balanced relationship between the ruling power and citizens. Rule of law does not preclude respect for traditions, customs, and the fundamentals of tribal justice but finds ways to integrate their essence in a legitimate pattern of rule.

Accepting the rule of law requires observing two key principles:

- No one is above the law, not even the military establishment, their key role in initiating change notwithstanding.
- Empowerment and a balanced relationship between ruler and the ruled cannot be achieved without a competent, impartial, and independent judiciary to uphold the rule of law.

## Freeing the Media

Although coercion and repression are necessary for the maintenance of authoritarian control, they are not enough. To hold on to power, authoritarian regimes have established complex alliances and networks, with roots deep in society and branches that extend into all facets of governance. As Lina Khatib clearly documents in chapter 3, the state media, for example, have been turned into mouthpieces for the executive power. More perniciously, these state-controlled media can force out alternative voices and become the regime's means of exerting soft violence (i.e., brainwashing, or the reinforcement of a single viewpoint).

The absence of balanced and diverse media also obstructs transparency, as the media fail to expose corruption or even, on the contrary, become complicit in it. Corruption—as Mustafa Khawaja's analysis clearly confirms in chapter 4—is not limited to the political class; indeed, the government's practices serve as tacit approval and implicit legitimization of corruption in the private business sector and even in community relations, and lead to a situation where corruption becomes systemic.

## Curbing Corruption

While corruption is not exclusive to developing countries, in the MENA region it tends to be pervasive rather than sporadic or individual. It flourishes through association with ruling elites, who benefit from the absence of transparency and accountability. The spread of corruption begins with stolen elections, signaling support by the upper echelons for a culture of corruption that soon permeates society from the top down. The culture of state corruption spreads from the political level to the economic level. Eventually, not only the economy but also the state becomes 'privatized.' In this neo-patrimonial system, the state reverts to feudalism, rewarding patrons for loyalty rather than competence, creating a vast web of influence determined by kinship affiliations and personal interests. Basic rational or public-interest calculations in management and economic matters are pushed aside.

On the economic level this culture of corruption encourages people to evade taxes, smuggle capital abroad, and apply non-developmental criteria for investment. Economic growth alone becomes the goal, rather than development aimed at improving the standard of living and quality of life of those who have less, which results in an imbalanced growth. Ultimately, corruption that starts at the top spreads and gains widespread legitimization.

## Poverty Alleviation

Poverty, as Sabria Al-Thawr affirms in chapter 5, encompasses more than low income alone. Poverty is also about social and political marginalization and its correlative disempowerment. It is also related to inequality and the absence of social justice. The most blatant inconsistency is that as wealth has grown in the Arab world, so has poverty, exacerbating inequality in access to education and health care. Both poverty and inequality impede empowerment and threaten social peace.

Despite the international consensus on the urgency to end poverty and the strategy to reduce poverty by 50 percent by 2015, as put forward in the Millennium Development Goals (MDG), the latest statistics show meager results in MENA, with especially deleterious consequences for youth and women. There are two common explanations for this failure.

One view is that countries have been impeded in reducing poverty by relying too much on markets and individual enterprise while distrusting solutions based on subsidizing key commodities to keep prices low.

The second explanation is that poverty alleviation has concentrated on sector-based or partial approaches that deal only with symptoms. As we will see in the introduction to part 4, a rights-based approach to poverty is a prerequisite for development-as-empowerment.

## Conflict Management

This is why the Arab 'nation' needs to contain conflicts before they escalate. In chapter 6, Louisa Dris-Aït Hamadouche explores this under-researched topic and argues that conflict in the region is chronic, devastating, and multifaceted. It occurs with foreign powers, between Arab states, and among communities within states. The numerous intractable conflicts across the region cost numerous lives and drain Arab capabilities and resources. Average military expenditure in the region is more than double the global average, while spending on health is less than half the world average.

Social and political differences are facts of life that should not lead to conflict, but that demand political management. Recognizing this could be the first step toward accepting diversity in Arab societies. Managing diversity requires adhering to the rule of law and abandoning the authoritarian mentality that prefers force, compulsion, and 'othering' over dialogue, tolerance, and inclusion.

## Facing Up to Environmental Risks

Environmental problems—as Zeyad Makhamreh demonstrates in chapter 7—present serious impediments to development, which neither the public nor the ruling class seem to understand, despite mounting international concern about, for instance, climate change and its potential impact on the Arab world. Environmental risks threaten human existence itself.

Two key environmental concerns demand attention. First is the lack of awareness of the urgency of environmental dangers among both citizens and those in power. Ministries of environment are treated as second-tier agencies and marginalized in policymaking processes. Second, policies need to focus on the link between environmental threats and daily life.

Solutions include investing in proper housing and transportation by developing the road infrastructure. Not only is the ordeal of daily life reduced, but the feeling of being treated like a citizen with rights is promoted, and a sense of 'belonging' is heightened.

## Rooting Empowerment in Identity

Arab countries have built more schools to accommodate rising enrollment, but an empowering education goes beyond constructing buildings and filling them with students. Education needs to expand human capacity and develop personal characteristics that are in tune with the requirements of today's world.

I have to admit I had initially hesitated to include chapters on education in this book. In addition to several studies by UNESCO, UN studies on development repeatedly—and rightly—include analyses of education. Moreover, in 2008 the World Bank published a detailed study entied "The Road Not Travelled" by Ahmed Galal, a famous economist who is, at the time of writing, Egypt's minister of finance. This study was focused solely on education in the Middle East. I preferred not to burden the reader with yet more analyses regarding education that would not add much to what is already available. Yet I also felt uncomfortable presenting a quasi-handbook on development issues that does not include an analysis of education and its crucial role in development-as-empowerment.

I wanted to show that to serve this function and empower citizens, schools need to be transformed from the factory model—which does not prepare students to successfully engage in a global economy that demands innovation, initiative, and collaboration——to institutions that produce effective, emotionally balanced, and socially active citizens who are able to innovate, produce new knowledge, and advance development.

Moreover, education is not just about learning facts; it is also about shaping personalities, fostering creative intellects, and encouraging critical thought. The key to a sound education is to empower students by preparing them to work in multicultural and multilinguistic settings while maintaining their own identities. These needs notwithstanding, especially for tolerance- and identity-building in the Global Village and given the proliferation of 'foreign' schools in the Arab world, the massive literature on education shows the marginalization if not absence of serious treatment of religious education. Such a lack of systematic research is indeed an anomaly in a region that saw the birth of the three major monotheistic religions and where religion still plays such a major part in both politics and society. After its establishment on the basis of religion, does not the present government of Israel refer to the country as a "Jewish state"? Isn't Islam the basis of Iran's revolution and isn't the country's official name "The Islamic Republic of Iran"? Don't many Saudis still believe that the Qur'an is their constitution? Doesn't the King of Morocco refer to himself as "Amir al Mu'minin"—the Commander of the Faithful? Too, since soon after its independence in the 1940s, are not Lebanon's "consociational democracy" quotas determined according to citizens' religious affiliations? Moreover, after the Arab Spring, the new regimes' elections showed the power of Islamists at the parliamentary and even presidential levels. Religious belief and values in this region shape society and tend to creep into politics. Religion is still a major component of group identity. How, then, does religion figure into education, *the* major location and shaper of identity formation?

While religion is a major component of shared identity in the Arab world, reforms have largely bypassed religious education, which is rarely addressed when the quality of education and its contributions to empowerment are evaluated. Najoua Fezzaa Ghriss, in chapter 8, and Baqer Alnajjar, in chapter 9, agree that religious education has received neither the academic interest nor the political and financial support it deserves. Most governments have focused instead on controlling curricula and ministries of religious affairs, appointing preachers approved by state security, and influencing the content of Friday sermons—that is, by emphasizing the primacy of the 'political' rather than the 'educational' in the choice and promotion of the preachers.

Reviewing religious-education curricula and pedagogy is thus important for empowerment, especially teaching methods and the links between sharia and the new language of the social sciences and the findings of the natural sciences. Religious instruction, far from resisting change or being unable to adapt to it, can engage with the modern world and its ideals, knowledge, and teaching methods. Problems can be turned into challenges that drive thought, purposeful action, and positive change—for the sake of a modernity that is innovative and consistent with personal and communal identity.

## Where Is the Region Heading?

This book emphasizes the state and its institutions because these entities represent society's compass and thus must set the example for community empowerment through a participatory process that is guided by the law. Failure of this process leads to failure of society and its development—from weakening the rule of law to monopolizing the media, spreading corruption, impoverishing people, failing to manage conflict and ensure a healthy environment, and lowering the quality of education.

Modern Arab history confirms that a preoccupation with security at the expense of public services and broad-based empowerment has led to the deterioration of the state and the well-being of most citizens, who suffer from the spread of corruption, poverty, unemployment, and inequality. The developmental state has been transformed into a predatory state, governed by the logic of feudalism and neo-patrimonialism, and dependent on clientelism and personal loyalty rather than competence. Thus after hijacking the state, the failure of the policies of individual regimes has led to the failure of the state itself.

Giving priority to reforming state power in order to achieve social justice and empowerment does not absolve sectarian and ethnic groups from the need to reform as well. Some groups, in general, suffer discrimination and have difficulty working with others, while some rely too much on foreign funding and priorities.

For more than thirty years, democratization has been on the agenda of the Arab world without making any real progress, while outside the region, democracy has spread. Despite challenges and setbacks, the waves of protests mark the start of a new phase in the region, as the events of the Arab Spring have added momentum and a sense of urgency to the task. Democracy is based on respect for the separation of powers, checks and balances, and the existence of effective institutions at all levels, whether in the apparatus of the state or in opposition parties. Equally important is an effective civil society, capable of monitoring government policies and managing disagreement. All three levels—state, opposition parties, and civil society—must respect transparency in decision making and accountability at all levels.

How can the Arab countries manage the transition to democracy? One starting point would be to guarantee the peaceful transfer of power. The framework would be: rule of law; a political process governed by an amended constitution; codification of democratic standards for decision making characterized by transparency and sound conflict management; balanced media; and an education system that emphasizes the strengthening of identities and freedom.

The literature on democratization identifies two phases: *transition*, or 'transitology,' which entails the collapse of the authoritarian system and the attempt to replace it with a more open regime, and *consolidation*, or 'consolidology,' which entails a deepening, a 'routinization' of democratic practice to strengthen its roots and expand its reach into the workplace, family relationships, and the emerging political parties.

Most of the Arab region is still in the transition phase of democratization. Despite many differences, Tunisia, Egypt, and Libya are attempting to address the failures of the repudiated regimes to adapt to the demands of the people. They differ in the type of alternative offered and especially the means to carry out the change—from comprehensive to partial reform, from replacement of the ruling regime to cooperation with it. Setbacks on this long road nothwithstanding, they seem to share an understanding of the necessity for transformation.

The Arab world cannot purely and simply import a ready-made democracy from a foreign context; rather, it needs to contextualize and develop its own indigenous form of democracy. Transplanting the political structures of the liberal western countries into the very different social contexts of the region, characterized by high levels of social injustice and exclusion, will not work. We will come to the issue of "what to adopt and what to adapt" in the concluding chapter.

Where the Arab uprisings of 2011–12 will lead remains unclear. Some observers interpret the current phase as the dawn of expanded freedoms, heralding deep economic reforms, wider human rights and social justice, and sustainable democracy. Others fear an opportunistic exploitation of the political vacuum and chaotic transition by different forms of religious theocracy. Still others predict continuing severe disorder in the region, as stubborn rulers resist change and disappointment takes hold among the people when the desired economic and political gains are not forthcoming. In this pessimistic outlook, popular grievances could follow the fault lines of sectarian and tribal divisions, plunging countries into long internal conflicts, expanding the list of impotent states, and raising the specter of state failure.

As we will see in the final chapter, it is likely that the consequences of these uprisings will differ across the region—for example, oil producers versus non-producers, or ethnically mixed countries versus relatively homogeneous societies.

Some Arab countries may make the transition to more democratic societies over the next decade. As new leaders and governments emerge, leadership groups will have to consider how to extend democratic change in their particular political context; how to endow the new governance framework with effective constitutional and legal substance; how to encourage pluralism by keeping people involved in the process while building alliances to navigate through the contested political space; how to reform or rehabilitate—or protect, or reinvent—key institutions, such as parliaments, the judiciary, and the police; how to manage relations between the military and civilians and maintain law and order; how to prevent the initial winners from 'stealing the revolution'; how to deal with antidemocratic theorists outside the acceptable political scope; and how to confront the past in constructing a new official record or building 'transitional justice.'

## And What's to Be Done Next?

The Arab world is at a defining moment—and in a race against time. The uprisings of the Arab Spring sounded the alarm indicating that time is running out. Arab countries must either adapt to and institutionalize change or join the countries suffering from deteriorating social capital and political decay, on their way to becoming failed states—countries at the lowest ebb of collective and individual disempowerment.

At the top, most political regimes are fractured. At the grassroots, a long-awaited revolution of accelerating expectations is compelling the masses to resort to parliaments of the street—from Tahrir Square to Habib Bourguiba Street and their equivalents. In common revolutionary fashion, the old order is being destroyed to lay the foundation for the new, which is still taking time to function and mature.

But while the Arab Spring is the clearest manifestation of discontent, the crisis did not begin with those protests. Arab protests—initially latent and sporadic—reflect a long-simmering dissatisfaction with the existing systems of governance. The Arab riddle—the gap between resources and desired outcomes—could not continue indefinitely, even under governments based on control and the strong arm of the security apparatus, the so-called securocracy.

Democratization, in either its revolutionary or its reformist mode (or these two forces in combination: 'refolution'), was inevitable—not just because the region would ultimately catch up with the global pace of change, but also because of internal reasons. The delayed onset of democratic change is part of a larger problem: the inability of countries in the region to adapt to change. That rigidity may be one of the most important challenges facing the Arab region. Resistance to change characterizes government regimes, most opposition parties, civil society groups, and national and regional organizations, the Arab League prominent among them. It had its clearest expression in the inability of most governments to comprehend what was happening in the Arab streets or the gravity of the protests.

## If the Ability to Adapt and Change Is the Key, Where Should the Region Start?

While adaptation and change must ultimately involve all of society in a constantly evolving process, reform must begin with the vision of governance and decision-making style at the top level of political power. Political leaders must transition from a system based on control without accountability to one that prioritizes participation and coordination. The foundation for such change is regular communication and dialogue between the top and the base, consistent with empowerment and development.

Addressing the *adaptation deficit* is all the more vital in today's globalized world, where technology is accelerating change in people's everyday lives and facilitating communication locally and internationally. The challenge is how to adapt to this never-ending change for the sake of empowerment and institution building while preserving identity and citizenship. This book proposes that the best way to do that is to guarantee the partnership between state and society, programmed and systematic. That requires moving away from equating difference of opinion with conflict, media with an official monolithic mouthpiece, corruption with 'business-as-usual,' the environment with neglect and deterioration, education with a production line, and government with control. Democratization requires that all forces—primarily those at the top—learn to adapt to the demands of the others while avoiding polarization that leads to the fracture and paralysis of governance.

This spirit of adaptation and change will require dialogue that integrates the demands for social justice, dignity, and freedoms that ignited the Arab street protests into the concept of Arab democracy. In the concluding chapter, we inventory the basics of the world literature on transitology as well as survey the first-hand experiences of leaders who went through such transitions, so that we can fruitfully reflect on how best to meet the existing challenges and find a way forward.

## Notes

1   UNDP 2003a.

# Part 2:
# Empowerment Begins at the Top

# Introduction to Part 2

Bahgat Korany

Change toward empowerment must begin at the top—at the decision-making center. Our main argument is that this CNS is what makes a difference, that is, it is a necessary and sufficient prerequisite to start and guide the development process. This argument is inspired by the primacy of the question "Who governs?" The crucial function of who decides is accepted by all schools of thought, whatever their ideology or cultural background, in the past and at present.

The complexity of governance can be simplified by Weberian political sociology and even rendered in a straightforward equation:

$$G = L + F$$

where (G)overnance equals a combination of (L)egitimacy or voluntary acceptance of authority by the majority of the population and the use of (F)orce against those who are recalcitrant, usually a minority. There is a basic inference there, as the ratio between L and F is an inverse relationship, that is, the more legitimate a regime, the less need there is for the use of force, and vice versa.

In the present Arab context, the state, especially its coercive security arm, is excessively dominant in its interactions with citizens, repeatedly turning to emergency laws to cement its coercive control. Empowerment thus begins with curbing that heavy authoritarian presence, enabling citizens to strike a balance in their relationship with the ruling authority so that it becomes a relationship free of intimidation, blackmail, and the all-too-familiar threat of chaos, and based more on the rule of law.

Empowerment requires an effective legislative and parliamentary system and strong political parties operating within the rule of law— even if custom, tradition, and tribal justice exist alongside the law. Implementing the rule of law is both the most successful realization of empowerment and its most direct route.

Activating the rule of law to achieve empowerment requires two pre-conditions. First, as previously stated in the general introduction, no one can be above the law, not even the strong businessmen or the military establishment. In some countries, including Egypt and Tunisia, the army was a chief contributor to the fall of oppressive regimes—even if through passive resistance by refusing to fire at protesters to save the regime. As a result, the army has become the de facto guardian of the transition, throwing into stark relief the problematic relationship between civilians and the military in the transition toward more open government. How-ever, as we all know, democratic rule requires subordination of the military to the rule of law, just as it does any other state institution.

Second, empowerment and a balanced relationship between ruler and ruled cannot be achieved without a competent, impartial, and independent judiciary to uphold the rule of law. Appropriate academic and professional training help empower judges and reinforce their independence. The judicial system must be capable of monitoring the actions of the executive power and of resisting attempts at coercion or inducement. Judicial independence is compromised when the execu-tive power controls the finances or intervenes in the appointment, transfer, or dismissal of judges. If judges are underpaid, material temp-tations can sway their decisions.

The simplistic idea that the ruler and his clique are capable of gov-erning single-handedly must be reconsidered. Even before the revelations of the Arab Spring, it was known that in order to hold on to power, authoritarian regimes had established a complex set of alliances and networks, with roots deep in society and branches that extend into all facets of governance—a vast array of clients who are tied to the head of the regime by ideology or interest. To repeat, the media and its principal personnel, for example, had been turned into mouthpieces for the executive power. More perniciously, the media can become the regime's means of exerting soft violence—or "per-suasion"—forcing out alternative voices, even during electoral campaigns. As a trade unionist and anchor on Tunisian TV, Kais ben Meftah, explained, "The content of programs and television's activities and coverage were decided in Ben Ali's Carthage Palace . . . the political issues, the viewpoints, the policy lines. . . . This was the most dangerous aspect of the corruption."[1] Little wonder that one of the first changes made after the fall of the ruler—in Egypt and Tunisia, for example—is to replace, arrest, and try the information minister.

Like all societies, Arab countries need balanced media that draw on diverse sources of information. Without the light of an independent media, corruption thrives in the darkness. It flourishes through connections with the ruling elites, who benefit from the absence of transparency and accountability. Ultimately, corruption that starts at the top spreads and gains legitimacy, expanding political alienation, deepening the crisis in distributive justice, exacerbating social inequality, and entrenching itself throughout society.[2] It becomes a system, a dominant savoir-faire, the almost-accepted norm. The spread and institutionalization of corruption from the top begins with rigged elections, signaling support by the upper echelons for a culture of corruption that then permeates society from the top down. Such codification of corruption becomes the dominant order within a vast, multi-tiered web of kinship affiliations and personal and mutual interests that disempower those outside it. Developing countries have lost $20 billion to $40 billion a year to corruption during the past fifteen years, only $5 billion of which has been recovered.[3]

An Egyptian study laments the detrimental effects of the formalistically pluralist system that is effectively a one-party structure, the most dangerous being election rigging. In addition to undermining the peaceful transfer of power, election rigging bestows key positions on unqualified individuals who exploit their immunity and power for personal gain. When personal criteria prevail, a web of mutual interests expands around a core network of relationships.[4] A culture of 'deals' spreads in the name of the state. Individuals are rewarded for loyalty rather than competence. In the drive for personal gain, both the economy and the state itself are privatized—a dominant characteristic of neo-patrimonialism. The Egyptian case reflects a generalized pattern of this mode of governance in many Arab political systems.

This mode of governance leads to the hijacking of the state for the benefit of a selected few. Then, because people tend to follow the example of their leaders, corruption seeps down through society, causing personal interests to dominate at every level, damaging and disempowering the state and society. When loyalty trumps competence in elections, legislatures, and appointments to public office, political participation is a sham and civil society is reduced to subordination. The state weakens as its legitimacy diminishes and its performance declines. To stay in power, the state responds by becoming increasingly repressive and predatory and neither developmental nor necessarily strong. Indeed, the regime unknowingly contributes to making itself a failed state.

At the economic level, a culture of corruption encourages those loyal to the regime to evade taxes and move their money abroad. Objective standards of investment are disregarded, to the detriment of economic development. Economic growth alone becomes the goal, rather than *development* aimed at improving the standard of living and quality of life for those who have less.

## Notes

1   Al Jazeera TV 2008.
2   Salem 2003.
3   Greenberg et al. 2009.
4   Salem 2003.

# CHAPTER 2

# From the Law of the Ruler to the Rule of Law

Mhamed Malki

U nderstanding the rule of law in Arab countries first requires understanding the concept of the rule of law and its relation to empowerment, identifying the obstacles to establishing and consolidating the rule of law in political practice, and analyzing the reasons behind the lack of empowerment. The weak state of the rule of law in Arab countries is not inevitable; it is liable to reform where the will to change exists. The question is how to foster the rule of law to enable empowerment.

## Rule of Law as a Means of Empowerment

The rule of law is related to such concepts as the legal state (*l'état de droit*) and sovereignty of the law, which share the notion that all agents are subject to the authority of the law and its provisions. The rule of law is also integral to constitutional supremacy: all institutions, agencies, and individuals must comply with the constitution and all laws must conform to its spirit and rationale.[1]

The origin and development of the concept of the rule of law within European culture and civilization create methodological and epistemological difficulties in transplanting it to Arab countries—most notably, the need to adapt the concept to social and political frameworks that differ from those in the originating context. This point raises two problematic issues. Understanding them helps indicate the limits of the rule of law and the potential for embedding it in the political culture of Arab states and societies.

First, because Arab legal and political traditions lack a theoretical foundation for the concept of rule of law, Arab countries have not yet built a solid base of deep, practical knowledge in that field. This absence has kept its roots from being embedded in the political culture. Second, the enabling environment for the rule of law—the set of preconditions that facilitate its adoption and establishment in practice—is not yet in place.

The rule of law does not refer simply to an array of laws and legislation that the state maintains to regulate social relations and compel obedience by individuals and groups. The concept is more profound and comprehensive, going beyond the mandate of a regulatory state. The definition adopted here therefore encompasses more than universal submission to the law, or to rule by law. The rule of law today is not limited to principles and instruments of authority regulation, such as the separation of powers (figure 2.1), criminal and civil liability for state employees, an independent judiciary, and all the tenets and guarantees enshrined in the constitution. The concept encompasses new groundwork of basic rights and freedoms. At the forefront are the rights and freedoms that bring about social security (health, education, and social welfare) and support aspirations to human dignity.

The goal of the rule of law is to achieve welfare, to promote its gains,

**Figure 2.1. Separation of powers in Arab countries, 2012**

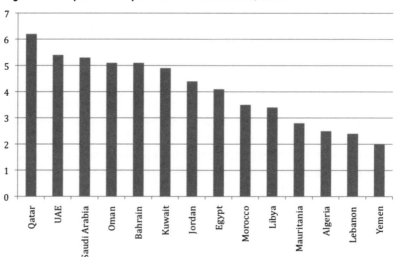

*Note:* The Prosperity Index rates countries on a scale of 1 (weak) to 32 (strong).
*Source:* Legatum Institute. Prosperity Index 2012.

and to make of it a shared social value. But the law will not assume its position of dominance or build a collective awareness of its critical role in achieving stability, peace, and social development without a supportive democratic environment. An enabling democratic environment includes a public sphere open to dialogue and expressions of difference. It also fosters a culture of consensus and mutual agreement that permits shared existence and a balanced relationship between state and society. In addition, representative institutions are founded on democratic legitimacy and an independent judiciary. The enabling democratic environment is strengthened by a social leverage that supports the rule of law and its establishment and consolidation in practice.

### Missing theoretical foundation for rule of law in the region's historical and cultural legacy

Are the components that empower people and enable them to benefit from the rule of law in practice evident in Arab experience, or are they too weak to serve that purpose?

The five previous Arab Human Development Reports agree that the complex and flawed Arab social and political contexts have clamped down on political freedom and prevented the emergence of good governance and the rule of law—the second being a key precondition for the first. [2] Although opinion varies about the relative importance of the individual components of the Arab context, the reports all stress the paradigm of context and use it as a guide in analyzing critical topics relevant to freedom and good governance, such as the Arab state, political authority, systems of rule, the rule of law, citizenship, democratization, reform, and human security.

The Arab context is characterized by two interrelated features that help explain the weak structural receptivity to the concept of rule of law in the Arab political sphere: the pressures of the historical and cultural legacy and the infirmity of the Arab state today—the structure of its authority, its political culture and the type of relationship it has with society, and the international and regional environments.

Religion and the interpretations of religious texts that have shaped the use of religion in politics for decades raise numerous issues of historical and cultural legacy. Most important is the relationship between Islam and politics—or between religion as a revealed text and the political and social order, which requires individual participation and which people should approach with a degree of rationality, efficiency, and accountability. In the west, the birthplace of the rule of law, societies were able to build a space between religion and politics (the secular world)—or at least achieve a compromise between the two spheres—aided by Christian scripture, which encouraged the division. In contrast, in nearly all the Arab countries Islam encompasses both the sacred and the profane worlds. The Muslim experience has not yet yielded many instructive practices for regulating earthly matters, although the foundations of the religious texts (the Qur'an and the Sunna) left the door open to collective thought and reasoned inquiry *(ijtihad)* for ordering people's temporal affairs (the state, authority, and governance).

The issue's complexity is not an unbeatable obstacle to the establishment of freedom, good governance, and rule of law in the Arab–Islamic political realm. But ensuring that religion is not an impediment requires favoring enlightened interpretations of its texts and building support for the spirit of *ijtihad*, which unfortunately came to a standstill centuries ago. The first step is to avoid the political exploitation of religion by regimes already in power and by movements that aspire to domination. One of the chief enlightened interpretations is that individuals have a direct relationship with their creator; thus, there are no religious intermediaries in Islam, no institutionalized religious hierarchy. Similarly, the concept of infallibility has no place in Islam, for all human beings, rulers and ruled, are fallible. As both the object of the rule of law and its foundation, responsibility—political, criminal, or administrative—is fundamental. The depreciation of responsibility in the Arab context, in text and practice, illustrates the tense and uneasy relationship between religion and politics and how that impedes the emergence of the rule of law.

### Missing enabling environment for the rule of law in Arab authority and institutional practices

The second crucial point in the structural resistance to adopting the concept of the rule of law is the current state of Arab authority and its institutional practices. While the historical and cultural legacies have strongly influenced the modern Arab state since its inception, the state bears responsibility for obstructing the establishment of the rule of law within its institutions. Signs of this obstruction are embedded in the concept of the Arab state itself. Its institutional practices reveal structural deficiencies that preclude the establishment of the rule of law and the construction of a sound relationship between the ruling authority and individuals and groups—a relationship that could expand participation and foster citizenship through the guarantees needed to make this relationship a common societal value benefiting all people equally.

With the exception of the riparian state in Egypt and the Sharifi state in Morocco, it is difficult to speak of state formation in the Arab region. In most cases, the Arab state has dissolved either because of the fragmentation of its developmental pattern and stability, triggered by the fragility of the intermediary bodies that once protected its social fabric, or because the impetus for its creation came from colonial powers rather than from internal social demand and consensus. Many Arab states emerged from larger states that were dismantled and reconfigured. More important, because of this troubled evolution, the idea of the state has suffered from being perceived as a foreign import and from insufficient positioning in the collective consciousness.[3] As a consequence, Arabs have had little opportunity to experiment with the institution of the state to gain practical experience of a civic education. Isn't the state, as Abdallah Laroui describes, "the educator of the educated"?

Thus, the Arab enabling environment is fragile and lacks the basic elements that have facilitated the establishment and consolidation of the rule of law in other contexts. Nevertheless, the components of a nascent rule of law exist. All Arab states have embraced constitutionalism,[4] although it came late in countries such as Saudi Arabia (1992), Oman (1996), and Sudan (1998). Arab countries have also adopted a large body of law and legislation on rights and freedoms.

## Impediments to Establishing and Consolidating Rule of Law

Several aspects of Arab political practice impede entrenching the rule of law. The Arab political sphere lacks many of the nine dimensions ascribed to the rule of law by the World Justice Project rule-of-law index.[5] Among the most important conditions are that laws be clear, publicized, stable, and fair and that they protect basic rights, personal security and the security of property, and the right of individuals to engage in private activities. Assessing the rule of law in the Arab countries in light of these indicators yields low rankings for much of the region. This outcome stems not from a lack of law, but from two other obstacles: a set of deficiencies hindering enforcement of the rule of law and the fragility of the institutional environment needed to foster the rule of law, and the inefficacy of its constituent elements.

### Deficiencies in the legal structures

The past two decades have witnessed the spread of constitutionalism in the Arab region even in countries that came late to constitutionalism. In addition, Arab political systems have strengthened laws through amendments and new legislation. These initiatives have codified spheres of activity not previously open for consideration, including freedoms and human rights, gender issues, economics (investment, trade), the energizing of public life, and advocacy of transparency and anticorruption measures in the public and private sectors—even in highly sensitive areas such as defense and security.[6]

The quantitative development of the Arab legal structure over the past twenty years, though uneven across countries, is undeniable. Yet across all the Arab countries, some common elements have prevented the legal system from institutionalizing the rule of law in practice. Two shortcomings, in particular, do much to explain why the rule of law has not taken root and flourished in Arab political culture: the absence of constitutional legitimacy and the gap between the law and its practice.

### Absence of constitutional legitimacy

A remarkable disparity is present in Arab political systems between constitutions, or basic laws, and lower-order laws such as regulations, legislation, and decrees. Arab constitutions consistently recognize rights and freedoms in broad general principles while leaving their elaboration and regulation to implementing legislation. Fundamental constitutional rights and freedoms are rendered meaningless by the laws and decrees issued to regulate them, elaborate on their contents, and specify the conditions and mechanisms for their application (box 2.1).

While all democratic systems share this procedural division between the constituent authority that drafts the constitution and the legislative authority that issues laws, complications are prevented by safeguards and regulations against the infringement of rights and freedoms. Since constitutions in the political tradition of those systems were drafted through consensus between rulers and the ruled, it is not enough to

---

**Box 2.1 Arab constitutions and the protection of individual security**

Constitutions in the Arab countries frequently leave a loophole that gives national lawmakers the opportunity to violate rights and civil liberties: they assign to ordinary legislation the task of regulating what is safeguarded by the constitution. Often the statutory text exceeds the regulatory limits in a way that restricts these rights and liberties and, at times, even usurps them. The outcome is that constitutions are emptied of their core benefit.

—Mohamed Nour Farahat, background paper for AHDR 2009

organize the branches of government and specify their relations to one another. Freedoms need to be positively endorsed and guaranteed in order to become part of the contract.[7]

Arab countries commonly give priority to basic rights and liberties in their constitutional blueprints. The constitutions of all Arab countries provide for freedom of thought, opinion, and belief, in language ranging from brief to detailed. These provisions also provide for the observance of these rights within the framework of the implementing laws and the dictates of public order and tradition, particularly of religious beliefs and worship. Not mentioning freedom of thought and opinion at all is rare. Article 13 of the temporary constitution of Qatar (1972) merely stated, "Freedom of publication and the press is guaranteed in accordance with the law," but this oversight was remedied in the constitution of 5 October 2003, which guarantees freedom of opinion.[8] Some constitutions, such as Yemen's Article 6 and the preamble of the Moroccan constitution, go beyond merely stipulating these freedoms to declaring a commitment to rights upheld in international conventions and charters.[9]

In addition, the constitutions of Arab countries contain provisions on the freedom of peaceful assembly and the freedom to form and join associations. As affirmed by international conventions and treaties, certain economic and social rights depend on freedom of assembly and the freedom to form and join associations.[10] Most important are the right of individuals to form associations of their choice to defend their interests and publicly voice their opinions, the right to found and join political parties, and the right to create professional associations and unions and to pursue all means to support their aims, including the right to strike in all forms.

A marked improvement has taken place in the constitutions of some Arab countries that for decades had a single-party system that impeded the emergence of political pluralism. For example, whereas Algeria's 1976 constitution upheld a single-party system, the 1989 constitution formally adopted pluralism. Other countries that in the late 1980s were forced to abandon the single-party system continued to restrict the exercise of certain rights, rendering pluralism a continuation of the single-party system. Tunisia's Article 66 of the basic electoral law, dated 29 December 1988, limited the number of parliamentary seats allocated to the opposition,[11] effectively invalidating the principle of electoral competition. Provisions on pluralism in other constitutions were ambiguous and open to interpretation, as with Article 5 of Egypt's permanent constitution of 1971. Amendments introduced in 1980 changed Article 5 to read, "The political system in the Arab Republic of Egypt is based on party pluralism."[12]

Nevertheless, the National Democratic Party remained hegemonic until the collapse of the regime after 25 January 2011.

In the sphere of public liberties and human rights, it is clear that although all Arab constitutions recognize citizens' rights to peaceful assembly, political organization, and other basic rights and freedoms, individuals and groups have not been able to exercise these rights. The right to peaceful assembly, for example, has been circumscribed by legal and security restrictions. Many Arab constitutions leave the exercise of such rights to implementing or procedural laws, which, if enacted at all, often restrict rights. In Morocco, for example, the constitution of 1962 mandated the right to strike, but a law regulating that right has not yet been passed.[13] Thus, activating this provision depends on the balance of power among the ruler, individuals, and their professional and union organizations. With little power in the hands of individuals and their organizations, this situation permits the executive power (the Interior Ministry in this case) to control citizens' exercise of this right.

The right to political association is even more circumscribed. The constitutions of many Arab countries do not recognize the right of individuals and groups to form and belong to political parties,[14] and where they do, legislation often restricts the exercise of these rights. Laws regulating the establishment of political parties or associations set strict licensing conditions and even prohibit parties based on religion, ethnicity, language, or region, as in Article 42 of the Algerian Constitution and Article 5 of the Moroccan political parties law (Law 04-36/2006).[15] Although some constitutions recognize party pluralism, legislation restricts this right either by explicit limits on the opposition's share in representative institutions, as was the case in Tunisia, or by practices that favor the ruling party or governing coalition over opposition parties, as has long been the case in Algeria, Egypt, Sudan, Syria, and Yemen.

If the rights referred to above, together with the right to participate in public life and assume office, constitute an indivisible whole, the absence or weakness of freedom of thought impedes the right of individuals to establish parties and associations to express and defend their opinions and prevents them from participating fully in all forms of civil society. Systems that do not guarantee freedoms or observe rights offer little opportunity for professional advancement based on merit, equality, and equal opportunity.

Although the Universal Declaration of Human Rights and subsequent conventions emphasize the right of every person to participate in a country's public affairs without discrimination, the constitutions of

Arab countries do not include provisions consistent with relevant international charters.[16] This is evident in the numerous internal contradictions within constitutional texts. For example, constitutions may stipulate that sovereignty belongs to the people, to be exercised directly through referendums or indirectly through elected bodies. Yet these same constitutions mandate restrictions that prevent free, independent participation, enshrining the single-party system and banning pluralism while conflating the party and state, upholding a pluralism devoid of any real content, or entrenching a dominant-party system and disguising it through the creation of various competing platforms.

The public debate accompanying the transformations that began in Tunisia on 14 January 2011 and in Egypt on 25 January 2011, as well as demands for the reform of political systems in several other Arab states, validates this analysis. There have been persistent calls for an end to the overlap between state institutions and the ruling party, highlighting the party's exploitation of state and public capacities to serve the interests of those dominating decision-making centers. Indeed, the clear discrepancy between constitutional texts and political practice is not limited to participation. Practice has rendered meaningless articles stipulating that the people are the source of sovereignty. This is also the case for all the basic principles of the rule of law, such as judicial independence, separation of powers, equality before the law, and protection of rights and liberties. An enormous gulf exists between enshrining these principles in Arab constitutions—an extremely important step, nonetheless—and safeguarding their implementation.

### The gap between law and legal practice

The gap between the law and its practice is related to the crisis in constitutional legitimacy in the Arab political sphere. Many factors have increased the gap by encouraging manipulation of legal provisions (when enforced) or by fostering the belief that the law is worthless if it cannot be applied properly and fairly. The state is the constitutional and political framework within which individuals learn the fundamentals of citizenship—to exercise their rights, perform their duties, and willingly engage in the public sphere. The weak position of the state in the collective consciousness has supported the inclination to deny the efficacy of the law.

People's recognition of the discrepancy between law and practice and of the negative impact on their rights has profoundly limited their ability to achieve legal empowerment (box 2.2). The course of justice is obstructed and cannot spread through state institutions and society. As

**Box 2.2 "The people want . . . . Did the regime really fall?"**
**—The next day's question**

A follower of the state of affairs in Egypt in the past three decades will understand that the president's ouster, despite its importance, is not enough to move Egypt into a new era. I believe in the 'innate wisdom' of the Egyptian people, as manifested in slogans, jokes, and popular sayings. People sitting in cafés, riding buses, or browsing the Internet will realize that protesters from Aswan in the south to Alexandria in the north and from Shaykh Zuwaid in the east to the New Valley in the west directed their efforts not only at ousting the president but also at toppling the entire system the president created or allowed to exist through negligence, greed, or ignorance. The features of this regime have shaped Egypt's political life for more than three decades.

The regime that was toppled by the will of the majority marginalized the law by ignoring rulings on electoral fraud, subjecting civilians to military courts, exposing professional associations and unions to attacks, and committing others in a long list of violations during thirty years of a tyrannical regime that disregarded citizens' growing desperation as they resorted to litigation as a way to resolve disputes peacefully. The regime was oblivious to the fact that, when the judiciary was impotent in the face of rising injustice, social security would be jeopardized and the concept of the state itself would be at risk.

It was a regime that elevated "politicized law" over "unbiased law," whose officials boasted openly of forging public documents on the pretext of "preventing strife" and whose official investigators complied with these illegal requests. It was a regime that divested its people of everything but despair.

Finally, the people, having lost all hope of ever seeing the law uphold their rights, abandoned efforts to change the regime at the ballot box and called for its overthrow.

—Ayman al-Sayyad, editor in chief, *Weghat Nazar*
(Perspectives) magazine

a result, people lose confidence in the ability of the state and its constitutional institutions to enforce the law—to impose respect for its
provisions and obedience to its authority on equal grounds. Thus,
people unintentionally participate in weakening the law's contributions
to respect for legitimacy and democratization.[17] Arab political practice
is fraught with examples of this disparity between law and its implementation or enforcement.

Discrepancies between constitutions and laws and their application
in practice are just as great for freedoms of expression, opinion, and the
press. International human rights statutes guarantee freedom of expression and the right to access information, and all Arab constitutions
uphold freedoms of thought, opinion, expression, belief, press, and
information—allowing individuals and groups to exercise these liberties
within the bounds of the law and social norms. Yet practice remains
constrained by restrictive legislation and a weak enabling environment.

Despite the limited opportunities for citizens to exercise these
rights, there have been some modest quantitative advances in the Arab
countries over the past two decades in freedom of expression and
opinion in press and audiovisual media. The diversity and number of
media outlets and their ability to exploit the growing potential offered by
the Internet and social media offer some promise of expanded exercise of
these rights. Some Arab countries, such as Morocco, are proceeding cau-
tiously in opening up the media, working to institutionalize
arrangements before moving forward with liberalization.[18] Despite their
importance, however, these steps have not been adequate to firmly secure
these liberties in practice. They have not enabled citizens to harness the
enormous potential offered by new technologies.

Laws in most Arab countries restrict the publication of newspapers
and require licenses for radio and television broadcasts and all forms of
media, making these rights dependent on the approval of state bodies.
Similarly, several Arab countries engage in practices that limit freedom
of expression and the press. People who violate these restrictions are
subject to penalties ranging from fines to detention, imprisonment, and
physical threats. Diverse bodies are empowered to dispense punishment, from the ordinary and administrative judiciary to exceptional and
state security courts.

A quick review of Arab legislation on freedom of opinion, expression, and the press reveals the constraints and tensions in trying to
exercise this set of liberties. These laws position Arab countries apart
from others. With the exception of Comoros, Mauritania, Kuwait,
Lebanon, Qatar, and United Arab Emirates, Arab countries are ranked

**Figure 2.2 Arab countries on the global Freedom of the Press Index, 2013**

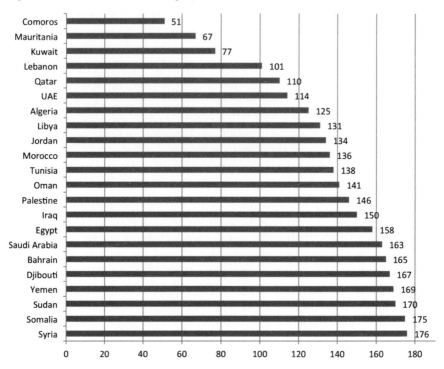

*Note:* The index ranks 179 countries.
*Source:* Reporters Without Borders. Press Freedom Index 2013.
http://en.rsf.org/press-freedom-index-2013,1054.html.

near the bottom of the 2013 Global Freedom of the Press Index for 179 countries (figure 2.2). Arab governments often cite alarming risks to national sovereignty and security or ingrained intellectual, ideological, and doctrinal principles to justify the constant surveillance of freedom of expression, opinion, and the press that restricts these liberties.

Economic, social, cultural, and religious freedoms are integral to political liberties, forming a complementary, indivisible whole. There have been remarkable quantitative and qualitative advances globally in political rights and freedoms, which have been enshrined in international conventions and protocols. Economic, social, cultural, and environmental rights and liberties follow close behind. The Arab region is no exception to the global trend toward entrenching a comprehensive framework of rights and liberties in their constitutions and laws and committing to international conventions.

Arab constitutions assert economic, social, and cultural rights and specify the guarantees needed to exercise them. All Arab constitutions uphold the principles of equality, egalitarianism, social solidarity, and mutual aid and assistance. While important, constitutional principles must be supported by effective laws and institutions and sound practice. Economic, social, and cultural rights have encountered the same obstacles that have obstructed political rights.

*Human Development Report 2010* placed five Arab states (Oman, Saudi Arabia, Tunisia, Algeria, and Morocco) among the ten states that have made the most rapid advances in human development over the past four decades, due to achievements in health and education.[19] A look at the efforts of Arab states in other dimensions of human development, such as empowerment, equality, and sustainability,[20] reveals the limits of these quantitative achievements and the imbalances affecting prospects for economic, social, and cultural development.

The description of the Arab region as one that is "richer than it is developed" still holds,[21] suggesting that there are structural factors that explain the "backlog of policy failures often overlooked by conventional economic analyses." The primary factor among them is "the disjunction between the region's material wealth and its real levels of human development."[22] Had these structural factors been absent, the Arab states would not be experiencing rising unemployment and human poverty and a decline in the components of well-being (box 2.3). This reality, which might be called the "Arab riddle," lies at the core of this study: Why are Arab countries unable to bring actual achievements in the region to the level of exceptional Arab potential?[23]

### Fragility and ineffectiveness of institutional structures

The shortcomings discussed above are not enough to explain the weak position of the rule of law in Arab political practice. Also contributing is the fragility of the underlying institutional structure and the ineffectiveness of its constituent parts, particularly the legislature, as the representative body that drafts legislation on basic freedoms and rights, and the judiciary, as protector of these rights and freedoms and guarantor of their sound practice by individuals and groups. All the Arab countries, to varying degrees, systematically weaken societal forces and institutions, depriving most social forces of any effective influence over the state. This has led to the emergence of a state that intervenes in everything and permits nothing. Confirming this analysis is the very slow unfolding of the transition phase in Tunisia, Egypt, and Libya, as well as current unrest in Bahrain, Jordan, Oman, Syria, and Yemen, which may spread to other countries.

## Box 2.3 Development as freedom

When we move from the direct importance of political freedom to its instrumental role, we have to consider the political incentives that operate on government and on the persons and groups that are in office. The rulers have the incentive to listen to what people want if they have to face their criticism and seek their support in elections. As was noted earlier, no substantial famine has ever occurred in any independent country with a democratic form of government and a relatively free press. Famines have occurred in ancient kingdoms and contemporary authoritarian societies, in primitive tribal communities and in modern technocratic dictatorships, in colonial economies run by imperialists from the north and in newly independent countries of the south run by despotic national leaders or by intolerant single parties. But they have never materialized in any country that is independent, that goes to elections regularly, that has opposition parties to voice criticisms, and that permits newspapers to report freely and question the wisdom of government policies without extensive censorship.

The instrumental roles of political freedoms and civil rights can be very substantial, but the connection between economic needs and political freedoms may have a constructive aspect as well. The exercise of basic political rights makes it more likely not only that there would be a policy response to economic needs, but also that the conceptualization—including comprehension—of 'economic needs' itself may require the exercise of such rights.

—Amartya Sen, *Development as Freedom*
(Oxford: Oxford University Press, 2001), 152–53

### Limited parliamentary power

Due to the dominance of the executive authority in Arab countries, the legislative authority plays a marginal role. Its representative function is minimal, further weakening its authority. This status is reinforced by constitutions that grant extensive legislative powers to the head of the state, including the right to inaugurate parliamentary sessions, address policy directives and programs to parliament,[24] subject laws to popular referendum,[25] dissolve or suspend parliament,[26] demand a second reading of a draft law already approved by parliament, and appoint members of the upper house—as is the case in the constitutions of Bahrain, Jordan, Qatar, and Saudi Arabia, for example. In addition, the head of state may have the right to lead the ministerial cabinet, which reviews and drafts legislation. In practice, more than 90 percent of legislative initiatives are proposed by the cabinet.

The broad discretion granted to the executive branch, particularly the presidency, and the legislature's narrow sphere of authority are a prime factor behind parliament's marginal role in drafting laws to regulate and strengthen the exercise of rights and freedoms. Indeed, in many cases the legislature is compelled to issue or amend laws to curtail rights and freedoms.

### The inferior position of the legislative authority

The legislative authority in Arab countries is weak both in its constitutional prerogatives and in the mechanisms for exercising these prerogatives. Most Arab constitutions heavily favor the executive in the distribution of power. Not only is the executive given an active role in issuing laws, but the legislative authority—the body with the right to originate legislation—is subordinated to the executive.[27] Inspired by the French constitution of 1958, some Arab constitutions (such as those of Algeria, Mauritania, Morocco, and Tunisia) list and limit the prerogatives of the legislative branch while leaving broad discretion to the regulatory or procedural authority of the executive.[28]

The unbalanced constitutional architecture grants heads of state—whether kings, emirs, or presidents—broad powers over legislative action as well as the right to serve as head of the cabinet and oversee its legislative strategy. This structural factor has enabled the executive authority to draft laws bearing on basic rights and freedoms, such as electoral laws; political party laws; laws regulating associations and media; laws regulating freedom of thought, expression, and opinion; and other legislation linked to the exercise of human rights and freedoms, such as criminal laws, criminal procedure codes, citizenship laws, emergency laws, and antiterrorism laws. Although these laws are formally subject to legislative procedure, that does not mean that the legislature has any control over what goes into the draft laws proposed by the executive. Indeed, the executive authority's strong constitutional and political presence permits it to control even legislation that is proposed by the parliament.

Executive dominance in Arab countries springs not only from the broad prerogatives granted by the constitution but also from the composition of parliament. The elected majority is usually loyal to the executive and submissive to its will. This is reflective of the situation in many Arab political systems with a single or dominant party (Algeria, Syria, Yemen, and, until recently, Egypt and Tunisia) and in systems with no political parties, where the dominant affiliation is to tribal, clan-based, or sectarian allegiances (Iraq, Jordan, Lebanon, and the Gulf states). Even in countries that officially revived pluralism decades ago, it is still too shallow to produce the large, strong majorities needed to create a balance between the legislative and executive branches. This is the case in Morocco, for example, whose mosaic-like parliamentary structure does not permit the strongest parliamentary force to hold more than one-sixth of the seats. In the parliamentary elections on 27 September 2007, for example, the strongest force, the Independence Party, took only fifty-two of 325 seats.

### Weak electoral legitimacy

The ineffectiveness of parliaments is not due exclusively to their modest constitutional prerogatives. The fault additionally lies in a deficient electoral process that weakens electoral legitimacy and contributes to the fragile institutional underpinning of the rule of law in Arab countries.

In addition to the many restrictions imposed by electoral laws, and the nature of administrative procedures for electoral apportionment, elections in Arab countries suffer from numerous irregularities that undermine electoral legitimacy and the fairness and credibility of electoral results (figure 2.3). Electoral legitimacy is further weakened by loose or absent judicial oversight of elections and heavy intervention of the administrative authority (usually the Interior Ministry) and polling station committees, whose members are directly or indirectly appointed by the state and in most cases enjoy unauthorized privileges. In a vicious circle, the resultant weak electoral legitimacy creates doubts about the political value of elections and lowers voter turnout. Voter turnout is especially low in populous states such as Algeria, Egypt, and Morocco (figure 2.4).

Diminished electoral legitimacy transforms the legislature from a representative institution to a shell (box 2.4). At best, it turns parliament into a public service utility[29] instead of a space for dialogue, debate, and competition that is capable of producing effective legislation to protect basic rights and freedoms and preserve the rule of law in practice. As a result, although the internal rules of procedure, means of formation, and prerogatives of Arab parliaments vary from state to state, all of them find it difficult to assert their autonomy and all yield to the pressure of the executive authority and the hegemony of its agencies.[30]

## Figure 2.3 Confidence in the fairness of elections, 2012

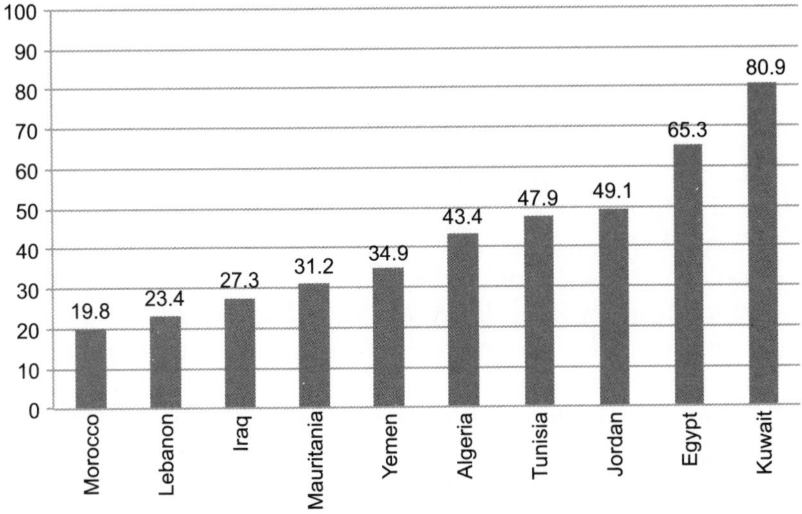

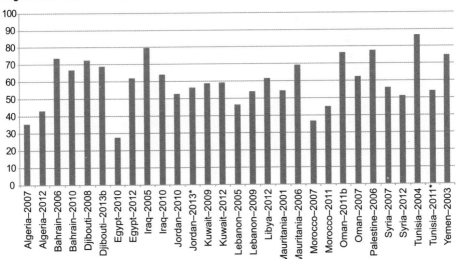

*Note:* Answers based on the question: Do you have confidence in the honesty of elections? (% yes)
*Source:* Legatum Institute. Prosperity Index 2012. www.prosperity.com/.

## Figure 2.4 Voter turnout, 2003–12

*Source:* The International Institute for Democracy and Electoral Assistance 2013.
a www.arabew.org/index/.php/2012-10-13-06-56-03/59-57-12-16-11-2011-1603/-.html
b http://www.electionguide.org/voter-turnout.php

**Box 2.4 A representative parliament**

The first criterion of a democratic parliament is that it should be representative of the people. In the first instance this means that parliament should reflect the *popular will* as expressed in the choices electors make for their representatives and for the political parties in whose name they stand. A parliament that is significantly unrepresentative in this respect, whether through deficiencies in electoral procedure or the electoral system, will to that extent forfeit legitimacy, and be less able to reflect public opinion on the important issues of the day. A democratic parliament should also reflect the *social diversity* of the population in terms of gender, language, religion, ethnicity, or other politically significant characteristics. A parliament which is unrepresentative in this second sense will leave some social groups and communities feeling disadvantaged in the political process or even excluded altogether, with consequences for the quality of public life or the stability of the political system and society in general.

This objective for a democratic parliament of being representative in these different senses is achieved partly through the composition of parliament, which is the result of the election process; partly through fair and inclusive parliamentary procedures, which provide an opportunity for all members to express their views, to take part in the work of parliament on an equal footing with others, and to develop their parliamentary careers.

—Inter-Parliamentary Union, *Parliament and Democracy in the Twenty-first Century: A Guide to Good Practice* (Geneva: Inter-Parliamentary Union, 2006), 13

To illustrate some of the flaws in the electoral process that undermine electoral legitimacy, consider the autumn 2010 elections in three Arab states of varying size: Bahrain, Egypt, and Jordan. All three elections lacked credibility and legitimacy. While the elections in Bahrain (23–30 October) were the least criticized and contested,[31] the organization, management, and results of elections in Egypt (28 November–5 December 2010) were so flawed that an election-monitoring organization described it as "a national disaster."[32] As in Egypt, the elections in Jordan were boycotted by the main opposition group, the Islamic Action

Front, whose participation in the previous parliamentary elections provided an important counterweight to the dominant party.[33] The Egyptian and Jordanian elections resulted in the victory of pro-regime forces and eliminated genuine opposition in parliament.[34] These elections illustrate how the erosion of electoral legitimacy[35] inevitably limits the effectiveness of the legislature and its ability to legislate in harmony with the rule of law. The extremely low representation of women in parliament—less than 10 percent—further weakens electoral legitimacy.

### A subordinate judicial authority

The inability of the judiciary to foster and uphold the rule of law in Arab states stems from two basic factors: a failure to enshrine judicial independence in constitutions and a useless political and social context for the judiciary.

#### Questionable independence

Arab constitutions embrace most of the precepts common in jurisprudence across the world, including innocent until proven guilty, no crime or punishment except by legal text, no punishment but by judicial order, and the right to a fair trial. Arab constitutions also generally uphold judicial independence and affirm that judges should yield only to the authority of the law. This is stated explicitly in the constitutions of Algeria (Articles 138–147), Jordan (Article 97), Kuwait (Article 163), Mauritania (Articles 89–90), Morocco (Section 82), Sudan (Sections 99–101), Tunisia (Section 66), and Yemen (Article 120). Indeed, the Moroccan constitution of 29 July 2011 discusses at length the status of the judiciary, the importance of its independence from the legislative and executive authorities (Section 107), and the rights of litigants and rules of justice (Sections 117–128). In reality, however, gaps in constitutional texts and disparities between text and practice have inhibited the exercise of these rights and principles and diffused any impact that could protect and consolidate the rule of law and enable citizens to experience its influence.

These limits to judicial independence are closely linked to the status of the judicial authority in the constitutional and political order (figure 2.5). A common characteristic of the Arab states is a robust executive that dominates all other constitutional institutions. In states controlled by a ruling party or a majority coalition, such as the presidential coalition in Algeria, or in a nonpluralistic or nominally pluralistic system, the executive controls the channels for passing laws regulating the judiciary and guaranteeing its independence. The executive also supervises judges'

**Figure 2.5 Judicial independence, 2012**

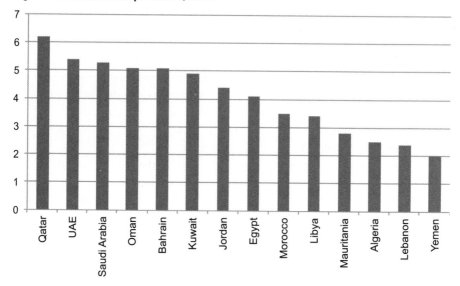

*Note:* 1 indicates extreme lack of independence; 7 indicates full independence.
*Source:* World Economic Forum. Global Competitiveness Report 2012–13.

professional affairs—from appointments, promotions, and transfers to disciplinary measures—using its constitutional and legislated powers.[36] The "exceptional courts" that have been a noticeable feature in Arab countries for decades have eroded citizens' basic rights and freedoms and further undermined judicial independence, integrity, and neutrality.

Some Arab countries (Algeria, Egypt, and Syria, for example) imposed a state of emergency for years and operated through state security courts and military tribunals. These actions threatened rather than reinforced the personal and collective security of the people,[37] minimized their ability to express their choices and act freely, and denied them justice. A state of emergency has persisted for nearly five decades in Syria, three decades in Egypt, and two decades in Algeria (table 2.1). The situation is exacerbated by the expanding role of other state security apparatuses, such as the secret police and intelligence services.[38] The danger posed by this complex web of bodies is that a country ends up with two parallel judiciaries: a civil judiciary that appears to enjoy primacy and an exceptional judiciary that enjoys actual primacy and prosecutes civilians under its own laws and provisions.[39] This is the case for the countries in table 2.1, where emergency laws have been active for long periods.

**Table 2.1. Arab countries under a state of emergency, 1963–2012**

| Country | Years of state of emergency |
|---|---|
| Syria | 1963–April 2011 |
| Egypt | 1981–May 2012 |
| Algeria | 1992–2011 |
| Iraq | 2004–present |
| Sudan (Darfur Province) | 2005–present |
| Palestine, State of | 2007–present |
| Bahrain | March–May 2011 |
| Yemen | March–April 2011 |

*Source for starting years of emergency:* Arab Organization for Human Rights 2008; Internet data for Bahrain and Yemen.

### A corrupt environment

Global assessments of transparency and rule of law find high rates of corruption in Arab countries, though to varying degrees (corruption is discussed at length in chapter 4). Corruption undermines the integrity of the judiciary and is a major obstacle to ensuring justice. In a corrupt environment, the judiciary cannot advance respect for the rule of law and empower citizens to experience its principles in practice.

Certain preconditions are required for credible, independent justice that earns people's trust and respect. For an individual judge, independence requires impartiality and moral and intellectual decency/honesty. This necessitates a system for monitoring professional ethics that protects judges from outside influence, thus allowing their professional advancement without undermining judicial independence. Credible justice also entails a well-ordered and regulated judicial system. The same strict code of professional ethics that binds judges must apply to other legal professionals because judicial rulings are the joint product of judges, lawyers, legal consultants, experts, and jurors.

### Activating the Rule of Law to Achieve Arab Empowerment

The Arab countries have adopted constitutions, established enabling laws, created modern institutions such as a parliament and judiciary, and joined international human rights conventions. While these actions might suggest that Arab countries have advanced far down the path toward the rule of law, in fact more profound and comprehensive changes are required to establish the rule of law and consolidate it in practice (box 2.5). The quantitative advances of the past half-century must be transformed into qualitative advances in thought, management, and leadership that result in legal empowerment—helping citizens experience the rule of law in their daily lives, both in their interactions with the state and its institutions and in their interpersonal relationships. And that will happen only through a far-reaching and consensual reform that embraces the rule of law as a stable, shared social value.

Advancing the rule of law requires a cumulative process of reform. It also requires broad support that includes reform-minded opposition movements and forces, such as parties, trade unions, civil society organizations, intellectuals, and independent reform figures, and that also

## Box 2.5 The desired state

The Arab Spring must overcome fundamental challenges if it is to live up to expectations.

Foremost among these challenges is the need to move forward to complete the transformations in the nature and structure of the political system. The people will not be satisfied with cosmetic or partial changes in the nature of political authority. Therefore, the grassroots movement—composed of youth, women, workers, and the general public—must continue until it achieves the democratic civil state where human rights, the rule of law, and institutions prevail.

The democratic civil state to which the movements of the Arab Spring aspire embraces a constitution that safeguards human rights, ensures separation between the legislative and executive authorities, and grants the judicial authority a realm of autonomy to uphold the law and protect the rights of all citizens alike. The constitution of the democratic civil state also ensures the peaceful transfer of authority and establishes mechanisms for transparency, oversight, and accountability. In short, the democratic civil state is one that strengthens citizenship and the bond of national affiliation and weakens the forces of fragmentation, inferiority, and clientelism.

—Ziad Abdel Samad, Executive Director,
Arab NGO Network for Development (ANND)

extends to power holders who are willing to reform. The more expansive and broadly inclusive the circle of reform, the less resistance it will face and the more successful it will be in meeting the preconditions for democratic change.

Methodologically, two tiers of reforms are needed to create the conditions for Arab empowerment and to embed the rule of law in state institutions and social culture. Both types of reform require mobilizing support and formulating sustainable, methodical, and incremental strategies to advance the rule of law in practice. The first tier calls for enhancing the few constitutional, legal, and institutional reforms that have moved the Arab political sphere closer to the rule of law. The second tier entails structural reforms that target the nature of the state and authority and the redistribution of power and wealth to achieve a balanced relationship between state and society. While the first-tier reforms are feasible given sufficient common will and a set of preconditions, the second tier seems less likely to be achieved over the medium term, although some tentative steps may have been taken as part of the ongoing movement for change begun in Tunisia and Egypt in January 2011. Prospects for the second-tier reforms will be greatly enhanced if the first-tier reforms prove sustainable and bring about the changes needed to institutionalize the rule of law in the state and society.

### Strengthening and deepening ongoing reforms

What steps are necessary to empower Arabs to take advantage of the opportunities made possible by the ongoing reform in the region to establish and consolidate the rule of law in political practice?

The first decade of the twenty-first century witnessed a series of exceptional reform initiatives, some advanced by Arab governments and others triggered by domestic and foreign pressures. Many Arab countries had already begun to develop their constitutional, legal, and institutional systems in the 1990s. Despite these efforts, however, a pressing need remains to extend reforms, implement them properly, and target the next generation of reforms in arenas that remain unchanged. An important step is to reconsider or even replace constitutions with ones that have the consent and approval of citizens and to ratify international conventions and treaties that affirm the full engagement and acknowledgment of Arab states in the universality of human rights. Extending ongoing reforms requires attributing a higher value to citizenship by embedding it in law and practice. Achieving such an array of reforms requires an institutional structure to nurture them, monitor their realization, and ensure their perpetuation.

### Deepening constitutional reforms

Drafting a constitution through consensual dialogue helps to overcome the imbalances inherent in the structure of power and the distribution of authority among the legislative, executive, and judicial branches of government and to embed a productive equilibrium in the new constitutions.[40] The constitution is the supreme document for framing and regulating political life. When a constitution is drafted without consensus—imposed by fiat or a referendum resembling an oath of allegiance more than a free, honest vote—the desired balance becomes elusive, and political life is held hostage to the flaws in the constitutional text. The demand for a new constitution embodying popular legitimacy has been one of the leading rallying cries of the Arab Spring.

The events of the Arab Spring exposed the urgent need to re-evaluate the philosophy underpinning Arab constitutions, all of which were drafted with limited, if any, popular participation (box 2.6). This need is evident in the constitutional debates that accompanied the revolutions in Tunisia and Egypt beginning in January 2011 and the demands echoed in other Arab countries including Algeria, Bahrain, Jordan, Libya, Morocco, Oman, Saudi Arabia, Syria, and Yemen. With the exception of the new Moroccan constitution approved by referendum on 1 July 2011, the nature of the constitutional reforms needed in the Arab countries is still being discussed. On 23 October 2011, Tunisians elected a 217-member National Constituent Assembly in free and fair elections to draft a new constitution. The royal commission in Jordan has completed a set of draft reforms. Meanwhile, debates on drafting a constitution continue in Algeria, Bahrain, Egypt, and Libya.

### Engaging with the universality of human rights

Accepting the universality of human rights can strengthen the rule of law. It is revealing that some of the Arab countries that "quickly joined international and regional conventions formed for fighting terrorism and money laundering"[41] have abstained from joining the eight principal human rights conventions,[42] with the exception of the International Convention on the Rights of the Child and the Convention on the Elimination of All Forms of Racial Discrimination. Most Arab countries have also refused to sign the optional protocols, and four Arab states have yet to join the International Covenant on Economic, Social, and Cultural Rights and the International Covenant on Civil and Political Rights.

Yet even ratification and accession to optional protocols are not enough. More fundamental is the relationship between national and

## Box 2.6 Arab constitutions under review

Constitutional change remains uncertain across the region, except in Egypt, Morocco, and Tunisia, which seem to have achieved some degree of clarity. The constitutional reviews across the three countries vary, depending on the power relationships among the various forces. The power relationships are less stable in Egypt, less certain in Tunisia amid increasing protests, and fairly clear in Morocco.

After the 2011 revolution in Egypt, eight amendments were proposed to the constitution through a referendum. They dealt with reducing the president's term from six years to four, limiting a president to two consecutive terms, easing the requirements to run for president, strengthening election monitoring mechanisms, reviewing the conditions governing member of parliament or citizen sponsoring of candidates presented by political parties, repealing the provision allowing civilians accused of terrorist activities to be tried before a military tribunal, stipulating parliament's approval of any declaration of state of emergency, and extending a state of emergency only after securing approval in a referendum. Based on the 1971 constitution, any principle that does not appear in the new declaration shall be considered to have been repealed.

Parliamentary elections took place after the successful organization of the referendum, and the presidential election in Egypt was held on 23 and 24 May 2012. With regard to the drafting of the next constitution, three influential groups hold different positions: The Islamists and Salafis, the liberals, and the army. To this day, no agreement has been reached on forming a new constitutional commission, and agreement seems unlikely any time soon. The fact that the new constitution has not been drafted yet aggravated the complexity of the situation, whereby the newly elected president would have to operate amid unclarity pertaining to his prerogatives.

In Morocco, the draft constitution outlines a clear separation of powers among the executive, legislative, and judicial branches; expands the remit of the government appointed by the political majority; widens the fields of competence of the legislature; and strengthens monitoring of government performance. Meetings of the Council of Ministers, chaired by the king, will look into the strategic policies, fundamental choices, and issues that guarantee the functioning the state. Reformists insist that the king should serve as both a strategist and an arbitrator. Those who oppose the reforms argue that the proposed reconfiguration would strengthen rather than limit the executive powers of the monarchy. Only events at the next stage will clarify positions.

The draft document has received broad consensus within Moroccan institutions and among citizens. The momentum for political reform seems irreversible. Several factors will shape the future, including how satisfied the people are with the response to their social and economic demands and whether the power base is widened to engage political and civil society players.

In Tunisia, the leading party in the National Constituent Assembly, Ennahda, has decided that the only discussion of national identity and sharia to appear in the constitution will be an extended version of Article 1 of the 1959 constitution ("Tunisia is a free, independent, and sovereign state. Its religion is Islam, its language is Arabic, and its type of government is the republic.") The possibility of applying sharia as the exclusive source of legislation is thus remote, though it may still emerge in the debate.

The 2011 election of the president of the republic and the speaker of the National Constituent Assembly reflected the parliamentary nature of the government. Still to be established is whether the constitution should stipulate direct election (universal suffrage) of the president or, as Ennahda seems to prefer, election by parliament. Also to be addressed later are issues of transitional justice and the role of the constitutional council. The duration of the committee entrusted with drafting the new constitution is also under discussion, given that the current National Assembly is both a legislative and a constituent body. The initial decree set a one-year deadline for electing the constituent assembly. Some concerns have been expressed that the majority may be tempted to hold on to power. Ennahda promised that elections will be held before 2013.

—Abdallah Al Saaf, director of the Center for Studies and Research in Social Sciences (CERSS) international legislation. The trend in Arab countries is to subordinate international law to the constitution, so that national law takes precedence in case of conflict. This makes it difficult to enforce international human rights law in practice, because Arab states often use national sovereignty and the need to respect national particularity as a pretext. One way to prepare for collective engagement with the international human rights regime and foster a legal and moral commitment to the individual and collective consequences of this engagement is to conditionally specify in the constitution that international human rights law takes precedence over domestic law. The Moroccan constitution of 29 July 2011 moves in this direction. It notes, albeit ambiguously, that "international conventions ratified by Morocco, within the scope of constitutional provisions, the laws of the kingdom, and its entrenched national identity, shall take precedence over national legislation immediately upon proclamation."[43]

### Protecting liberties

Practice in most Arab countries reveals how laws restrict freedoms and limit the expression of individual and collective choices. Moreover, ambiguity and loopholes in the law often lead to misinterpretation and misapplication. For example, the laws of the six member states of the Gulf Cooperation Council proscribe the formation of political parties, preventing citizens from establishing political bodies and organizations that represent them and express their choices (figure 2.6). Other Arab states have granted this right with one hand while revoking it with the other through a series of restrictive measures—as in Tunisia, for example, where legislation specified the number of parliamentary seats allocated to the opposition. Even in countries with new laws regulating political parties, such as Jordan and Morocco, numerous loopholes impede the effective and balanced exercise of this freedom.

The same could be said of many other laws that have not been enforced in practice, such as laws regulating economic, financial, and commercial structure, investment, and financial oversight.[44] The new generation of required reforms—strategically important for transforming the rule of law from an empty slogan to a shared social value—includes grounding full citizenship in a common, collective sense of civic equality rather than in affiliation with a geographic territory or in a narrow sense of identity. That is possible only within the framework of a democratic, civil state governed by laws that respect the framework of internationally recognized rights and liberties and that operate through instruments and institutions that guarantee the right of every person to voluntary, honest participation.

## Figure 2.6 Fear of expressing political opinion, 2012

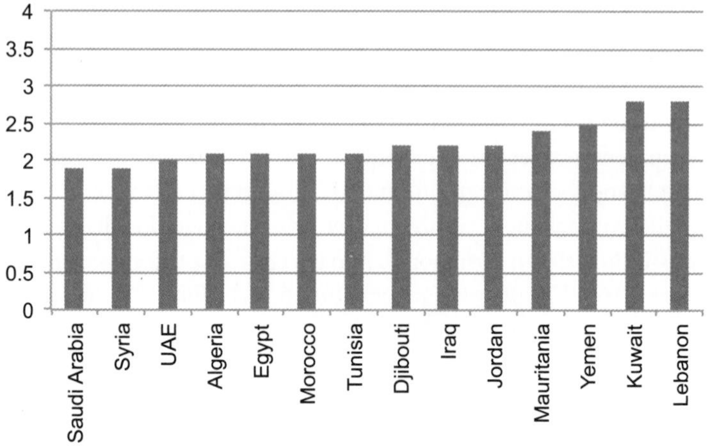

*Note:* A 1 indicates that a majority of people fear expressing opinions, while a 4 indicates that no one does.
*Source:* Legatum Institute. Prosperity Index 2012.

### Becoming a nation of citizens, not subjects

Achieving full citizenship is central to deepening ongoing reforms and embedding the rule of law. The imbalances that characterize the relationship between Arab states and their societies constitute a severe impediment to such progress. During the Arab Spring, collective voices across the region called for affirming the principle of citizenship in constitutions and providing legal and political guarantees for its implementation in practice.

Citizenship must not be a theoretical benefit, but rather the reality lived by people in a civil, democratic state who reap its benefits. Citizenship in the fully civil state must be founded on equality and universality, for human beings are "born into different circumstances, with varied access to options to expand their capabilities, but all are entitled to the same basic rights. The right of citizenship should be identical for all persons living in a given country, regardless of ethnic origin, religious belief, gender, health, culture, wealth, or any other personal attribute."[45]

The Arab countries urgently need to weave the concept of citizenship into their social fabric in order to relieve the tensions disrupting national unity. Imbalances in the social structure (ethnic, sectarian, and tribal), political structure (access to rights and freedoms), and economic structure (equal opportunity) represent a clear danger to the Arab region, though the gravity varies from country to country. The changes experienced by many Arab countries in the first decade of the twenty-first century markedly weakened the idea of coexistence, which the state should protect and preserve legally and constitutionally so that the benefits trickle down equally to all citizens. Only then will full citizenship improve people's circumstances and establish the conditions for a dignified life. The urgency of this need is underlined by the reality of poverty in the Arab region (see chapter 5).

The failure to embrace the principles of equality, egalitarianism, and ethnic, cultural, and linguistic diversity highlights the need to reconfigure the relationship between state and society based on new foundations. Chief among them is the need to openly endorse full citizenship. In Iraq, Somalia, Sudan, and Yemen, conflicts stemming from weak or absent bonds of citizenship have undermined the foundations of the state and put it at risk of disintegration and partition. In many Arab countries, broad segments of society—particularly the most vulnerable, such as women, children, and migrants—feel a sense of marginalization, exclusion, and discrimination. The increasing social incitement in Bahrain, Egypt, Iraq, Morocco, Saudi Arabia, and Tunisia is further evidence of the need to uphold and foster citizenship in Arab political culture.

### Box 2.7 The transition to democracy: Challenges and horizons

Most developing countries share a motto, one that has become the only undisputed political chant: transition to democracy. This mantra conceals the implicit slogan "Democracy is the solution!"

Although the slogan is not new, it is being invoked with the sort of passion that might be accorded to a "magical ring" viewed as capable of solving all problems. However, no one addresses the inherent problems of the "magical ring," which are left completely out of the picture.

"Democracy is the solution!"—the solution to problems pertaining to human rights, public freedoms, civil society, arbitrary abuse of power, exploitation of influence, unemployment, poverty, and on and on. But is democracy the solution to the (lack of) democracy problem—its presence and absence? If partial democracy is achieved, does this lessen the need for democracy as a complete process? Where does democracy begin and end? If it is realized, do other slogans and demands become dispensable? What is the starting point for the transition to democracy?

—Muhammad 'Abid al-Jabiri, *Fi naqd al-haja ila al-islah* (A Critique of the Need for Reform) (2005), 201

### Reforming the institutional structure

The rule of law cannot be consolidated by such reforms alone. That also requires an institutional structure that nurtures laws, promotes respect for enforcement, develops citizens' confidence in state services, and offers equal opportunities and capabilities. By dampening personal and subjective inclinations in favor of objective and public ones, institutionalization makes space for monitoring, evaluation, and accountability. The rule of law requires an enabling environment with institutions that safeguard its observance. However, institutionalization cannot be imposed full-grown; rather, it is the result of an accumulation of practices and experience. Above all, it is a culture fortified by open dialogue and mutual agreement. Without these foundations, institutionalization is merely cosmetic, directed at securing international approval, evading pressures, and manipulating citizens.

Despite efforts to establish, strengthen, and support institutionalization, it still has little traction in the political culture in many Arab countries, as evidenced by the state of the two central constitutional institutions, the parliament and judiciary.

Parliaments are not yet an arena for genuine representation and transparent, impartial mediation or a space for debate and competition over the best legislation for realizing national policy. Electoral laws need extensive reform, and the electoral process requires guarantees to ensure fairness and neutrality; to counteract the influence of primary tribal, sectarian, and clan loyalties; and to check the power of money and the ruling party or dominant presidential alliance. Bold, far-reaching reforms will promote the conditions for the emergence of an Arab parliamentarianism capable of fulfilling its representative functions. Among the demands made during the Arab Spring were calls for reconsidering electoral and party laws; granting the judicial authority power to supervise elections; opening the way for participation by women and young people in parliament; and demanding competence, professionalism, and effectiveness in candidates.

The judicial authority also requires far-reaching reforms to enable it to enforce the rule of law and apply it without discrimination or exception. Numerous attempts have been made to modernize the judiciary and increase its efficiency. Arab constitutions affirm the principle of judicial independence and uphold a set of guarantees protecting judges' independence and the rights and due process of litigants. Nevertheless, the judiciary complains of its inability to serve as a true guarantor and effective protector of the rule of law.

In countries where popular protests have resulted in a change in the head of state, such as Egypt, Libya, Tunisia, and Yemen, as well as in those where popular movements have yet to yield results, such as Algeria, Bahrain, Jordan, and Syria, the judiciary is an object of doubt, suspicion, and recrimination. Still, there is hope that if the judiciary can gain its independence and raise its stature among the public, it can become a leader in the move toward greater democracy. For example, the Moroccan constitution of 29 July 2011 explicitly states for the first time that "the judiciary is an authority independent of the legislative and executive authorities" (Section 107).

### Entrenching the rule of law through structural reforms

Reforms of the kind discussed in this chapter can open doors to qualitative changes that alter the philosophical and political foundations of the relationship between state and society. Structural reforms—changes that bring about a more equitable division and distribution of power among the three constitutional institutions, the legislative, executive, and judicial branches—extend not only to the philosophy of governance and to the constitutional and legal instruments regulating its practice, but also to political culture and social awareness. Thus, the target of these reforms includes all components of society, from political parties to trade unions to civil society organizations, as well as the state and its institutions. For a public movement that advances both state and society to take shape and accomplish its mission, certain social levers have to be in place.

The social groups qualified to lead structural reforms must be linked by a shared conviction of the need for positive change and of the means, strategy, and phases of change. Specifically, this would encompass primarily opposition forces across the political and ideological spectrum that, having remained far from power, cannot be blamed for the current status of the Arab countries—the Islamist movements that advocate peaceful and democratic change, civil society organizations, business groups, and other segments of society. If these social groups can be convinced of the value of dialogue and can identify commonalities, they could forge a consensus that could lead to structural change.

While events in Egypt and Tunisia illustrate the complexity of reaching consensus on the foundations for rebuilding the relationship between the state and society, structural reform is not an impossible result. It is possible if both the political elite and the wider society have the will and determination. There are several pathways to approach opportunities for structural change that would embed the rule of law in Arab political practice; the most important are discussed below.

### Redistributing power in Arab constitutions

The unbalanced constitutional distribution of power is one of the most serious legal and political issues in the Arab countries (box 2.8). The uneven distribution of wealth and the monopolization of power have obstructed progress toward democracy, development, and social justice. The redistribution of power toward the legislature and the judiciary cannot be achieved through technical or gradual reforms but requires a new constitutional architecture that eliminates the imperial presidential dimensions of most Arab constitutional and political systems. The means of empowerment must be extended to the judiciary and the legislature.

Redistributing power requires consensus. Without broad citizen participation, directly and through social groups, and without a clear vision of the philosophy that will underpin and frame constitutional provisions, it will not be possible to draft a constitution stipulating a new distribution of power. The constitutional amendments approved in Egypt in the referendum of 19 March 2011, if supplemented by comprehensive constitutional change, may launch a qualitatively new constitutional allocation that elevates parliament, entrenches judicial independence, strengthens the standing of government, and curbs the powers of the presidency so that it does not transcend other branches of government. The same applies to Tunisia, whose elected national constitutional assembly of 23 October 2011 may, thanks to its electoral

---

**Box 2.8 Arab constitutions and the concentration of power**

The constitutions of many [Arab] countries enshrine the concentration of power in the executive, upholding the right of the king, president, or prince (or revolutionary command council) to legislate. These constitutions grant the head of state broad prerogatives, thus positioning him as the head of the executive branch (and the cabinet), the armed forces, the judiciary, and the civil service. Such provisions may allow the head of state to appoint and dismiss ministers, judges, senior officials, and military officers, and convene and dissolve parliament, if it exists. Laws further entrench the hegemony of the centralized authority over local authorities, permitting the ruler to appoint governors who are responsible to him rather than the citizenry.

—Abdelwahab el-Affendi, background paper for AHDR 2004

legitimacy, be able to draft a balanced constitution that breaks with the tradition of an imperial presidency. In Morocco, the referendum of 1 July 2011 ushered in progress toward redistributing power without fundamentally breaking with the prevailing constitutional philosophy. Current events in Algeria, Bahrain, Jordan, Libya, Syria, and Yemen confirm the pressing need to lay out a constitutional framework for a balanced redistribution of power.

### Establishing a new social contract

Citizens in the Arab countries are near a consensus that it is just as important to deal with unevenly or unjustly distributed wealth as with power that has been monopolized and that arbitrarily restricts people's liberties and rights. The alliance of power and wealth within very narrow circles in Arab political systems over the last thirty years has left Arab countries increasingly susceptible to domestic upheavals and to foreign interferences. A new social contract is thus a priority for creating an environment conducive to the rule of the law. Trust in the state's legitimacy and in the ability of its institutions to serve all the people has been eroded by the state's monopolization of the power to distribute and redistribute wealth; its refusal to employ the standards of merit, competence, and entitlement to determine access to its benefits; and the absence of sound institutions for oversight and accountability.

The first winds of the Arab Spring sprang up in the most marginalized, fragile, and socially impoverished urban and rural regions and provinces in Tunisia before spreading to Egypt, Libya, Syria, Bahrain, Jordan, Morocco, and Yemen. All movements in the Arab Spring emphasized the sources of the social injustice rampant throughout Arab societies—among regions and between urban and rural areas. Re-establishing the legitimacy of the Arab state requires more than reformulating the political relationship between state and society; it also requires reducing social disparities by ensuring equal opportunity. When people see that their share of national wealth is protected by the force of law and efficient institutions, their allegiance to the state deepens and they acquire what Montesquieu called "the peace of mind that comes with security," which is a condition for the emergence and exercise of liberty.[46]

A social contract based on new foundations is a key to empowerment and greater opportunities and a move toward more robust democracy and more comprehensive development. If its conditions are met, a new social contract will throw expressions like the "Arab predicament," the "Arab exception," and the "Arab paradigm" into the trash can.

### Consolidating the public sphere

A free and open public sphere is the most appropriate framework for exercising rights and liberties and expressing choices. The events of the Arab Spring have proven the strategic importance of the public sphere as a space for dialogue and for finding common ground in demands for reform and change. In every Arab country where the people have called for change, their joint efforts to mobilize support and move toward new political and social conditions have occurred in the public sphere.

In Egypt and Tunisia, where qualitative change is just beginning, the importance of the public sphere is evident in its ability to unleash people's energies and spark free expression and responsible engagement with the issues posed by the transition from a closed, undemocratic political system to a democratic one. A direct outcome of this transition has been disentangling the state from the dominant party or dissolving it by legal ruling (as through Tunisia's Constitutional Democratic Rally on 9 March 2011) and reaching consensus on reconstituting the relationship between state and society. The same is true of many other Arab countries (Bahrain, Jordan, Morocco, Syria, Yemen, and to a certain extent, Algeria), where restoring the idea of the public sphere empowered societies to unleash their energies, organize their ranks, and defend their just demands for reform and change.

The increasing embrace of the public sphere and of efforts to consolidate it is of political and practical value. Because the state was not founded on dialogue, consensus, and consent, it lost its neutrality by supporting a narrow segment of society. Lacking the consent of the governed, the state was perceived in the public consciousness as equivalent to coercive power. Thus, the recognition, affirmation, and expansion of the public sphere as a safeguarded space for political practice will restore the standing of its most vital components and agents, such as political parties, trade unions, and civil society. These groups will thus be encouraged to perform their essential functions of mediation, representation, and participation in the decisions affecting citizens' lives.

### Catalyzing positive change through societal reform

Societal reform is fundamental to structural reform that can entrench the rule of law in Arab political practice. Maintaining the primacy of the constitution, guarding the sound application of the law, respecting international conventions as opportunities and not burdens, and complying with the rule of institutions are all aspects of subservience to the authority and rule of law not only by the state and its institutions, but also by society. The state's responsibility to enforce respect for the rule of law is closely tied to society's compliance with its provisions.

The structural faults that have impeded the rule of law in Arab political practice, linked fundamentally to the nature of the modern Arab state and the operating logic of its institutions, are also related to the degree of social awareness and the nature of the culture governing the conduct of its constituent parts—political parties and movements, trade unions, civil society organizations, businesspeople, and citizens. Yet doubts remain about the ability of these social groups to lead the march to positive change. These doubts spring from factionalism, mismanagement of disagreements, absence of internal democracy, and the weak hold of modernity and rationalism in the culture of values. Nevertheless, the profound changes in Egypt and Tunisia, and ongoing changes in other Arab states, have confirmed the ability of society, particularly youth and women (box 2.9), to set in motion political and social dynamics capable of bringing about positive change.

Viewed through the lens of the rule of law, the condition in Arab states is confounding. These states are not lacking in laws or institutions, and their accession to international human rights conventions has increased in recent decades, although ratification still lags. Concepts like the rule of law, a state of law and justice, and a state of institutions have been widely circulated. Yet these countries remain far from the logic and culture of the rule of law.

The rule of law requires more than a constitution and a set of laws, despite their strategic importance; it also requires a culture and a mode of conduct that nurture the rule of law and provide the conditions for its establishment and sustainability. In the absence of a conducive environment, achieving these conditions has proven difficult. As a result, there is a need to revisit concepts such as the state, power, political culture, and awareness of the law and human rights in order to explain the marked resistance to the rule of law in Arab countries. And there is a need to embed and activate the rule of law to empower citizens, distinguishing ongoing reforms in the Arab region from structural reforms.

There are no grounds for accepting the notion of an Arab exception that would make countries in the region incapable of positive change. Change is possible in Arab states under the proper conditions. The events of the Arab Spring confirmed this view, proving Arab societies' need for the rule of law and its important role in changing the rationale of the workings of the state and the performance of its institutions. If the ongoing reforms are extended and their gains consolidated, they may lead to structural reforms, the key to entrenching the rule of law in the Arab region.

## Box 2.9 Arab revolutions and women's rights

The landscape in Arab countries that have witnessed revolutions and popular movements is still chaotic, particularly in countries that saw changes in ruling figures. The situation is even more uncertain for women and their rights. Forces now seeking to rule have taken a stance against past achievements, however modest, and are threatening to renounce them on the grounds that they originated with former regimes, while ignoring or denying the cumulative struggles of women and communities that managed to wrest some rights from the authorities. Moreover, the reformist (or revolutionary) measures needed to guarantee dignity and freedom for every human being and to achieve justice and equal opportunity for all without discrimination, including gender discrimination, have been slow in coming.

If democratic political representation is based primarily on the principle of equal citizenship and the right of people to choose their representatives, human rights is a matter of principles, standards, and foundations not subject to the majority–minority equation. A commitment to human rights should not differ from one political or intellectual current to another, for it is intolerable that a person's dignity and rights should be selectively honored depending on who is in power, their ideologies, or their interests. As victims of repressive regimes that did not respect their human rights and did not achieve development, progress, and prosperity for their countries, it was unimaginable that women would enjoy their rights under such corrupt, undemocratic, despotic regimes. Similarly, it is unimaginable that revolutions and popular and youth movements can achieve their objectives without the fair, democratic, and active participation of women as well as men.

The ability of youth revolutions and popular movements to achieve their objectives and realize the aspirations for change and reform depends on the new leadership's respect for human rights principles, at the heart of which are women's rights. The lives of martyrs, the blood of the wounded, and the sacrifices of all were given for the sake of freedom, dignity, justice, and equality and as a challenge to exclusion, marginalization, discrimination, injustice, and lack of opportunity. It is intolerable that regimes would be reproduced that practice repression, discrimination, injustice, exclusion, and marginalization under a different guise.

An antipathy to or reluctance to fully recognize women's rights and offer full protection for these rights on the basis of equality, justice, and equal opportunity thwarts these revolutions, impedes reforms, denies sacrifices made, and intensifies injustice and discrimination. It perverts the free will of all, women and men, who aspire to a life of freedom and dignity.

—Asma Khader, Secretary-General of the
Jordanian National Commission for Women

## Notes

1  Ghanim 2005.
2  UNDP 2002b, 2003a, 2004a, 2005a, 2009b.
3  Qarni 1987.
4  Libya is the exception among the Arab states. Its constitution was suspended after the fall of the monarchy in 1969, and a constitutional declaration was issued on 12 November 1969, pending a permanent constitution. On 2 March 1977, the declaration of the people's authority was promulgated as a document organizing governance and state affairs. The National Transitional Council, formed after the uprising of 17 February 2011, announced that a new constitution would be written after the fall of the Qadhafi regime.
5  World Justice Project 2011. The index in the 2011 report included sixty-six states, among them four states from the Middle East and North Africa: Iran, Lebanon, UAE, and Morocco.
6  Geneva Center for the Democratic Control of Armed Forces 2003.
7  Leclerq 1994.
8  The permanent constitution of Qatar, published on 5 October 2003, went into effect on 9 May 2005.
9  Article 6 of the Yemeni constitution states, "The state affirms its adherence to the UN Charter, the Universal Declaration of Human Rights, the Arab League Charter, and the generally recognized norms of international law." The preamble of the Moroccan constitution, added with the reform of 4 September 1992 and reaffirmed on 13 September 1996, includes the phrase, "[The Kingdom] affirms its adherence to human rights as internationally recognized." The most recent Moroccan constitution, approved in the referendum of 1 July 2011, preserved this formulation.

10  UN Universal Declaration of Human Rights, Articles 20 and 23 (1948),
    UN International Covenant on Civil and Political Rights, Article 22
    (1966), UN International Covenant on Economic, Social, and Cultural
    Rights, Article 8 (1966).
11  Tunisian Republic, Tunisian Basic Law for the Regulation of Elections,
    Article 6 (144/1988, dated 29 December 1988).
12  Egypt's constitution of 11 September 1971 was amended three times: 30
    April 1980, 25 March 2005, and 26 March 2007.
13  Section 14 of the 1996 constitution upholds the right to strike and defers
    to the implementing law for the regulation of the right, but the imple-
    menting law has not yet been issued. The new constitution, approved on 1
    July 2011, again contained this reference in Section 29. Regardless of
    whether the chronic delay was a maneuver by the state or an implicit
    agreement between it and interested bodies (trade unions), the new consti-
    tution settled the matter by requiring the government and parliament to
    draft and ratify the regulations.
14  The constitutions of fourteen out of twenty-two states recognize the right
    to assembly and association in organized bodies.
15  In the run-up to the parliamentary elections of 25 November 2011, the
    Moroccan parliament discussed a new version of the political parties law.
16  The Universal Declaration of Human Rights 1948 upholds the right of
    every person to "take part in the government of his country, directly or
    through freely chosen representatives" (Article 21). The Covenant on Civil
    and Political Rights (1966) states, "Every citizen shall have the right and
    the opportunity, without any of the distinctions . . . to take part in the con-
    duct of public affairs, directly or through freely chosen representatives."
17  The Venice Commission–European Commission for Democracy through
    Law 1992.
18  See, for example, the High Commission for Audiovisual Communication,
    established by royal edict on 31 August 2002, and the decree limiting the
    state monopoly on audiovisual broadcast, issued on 10 September 2002.
    Law 77–03 on audiovisual communication came into force with its publi-
    cation in the *Official Gazette* on 7 September 2005.
19  UNDP 2010c.
20  UNDP 2010c.
21  UNDP 2002b.
22  UNDP 2009b.
23  See part 1 of this book.
24  This right is a common feature of all Arab constitutions, which give heads
    of state the authority to direct parliaments toward priorities in legislative
    policy. At times, the heads of state present a set of points comprising a
    comprehensive program that the representatives are expected to pursue.
25  For example, this right is granted in the constitutions of Egypt (Article
    152), Tunisia (Article 47), and Morocco (Section 69).

26 However, constitutions do place several formal checks on this right. See, for example, the constitutions of Morocco (Sections 27, 71, 73), Jordan (Article 34), and Yemen (Article 78).

27 Al-Murabit 2010.

28 Parliamentary rationalization seeks to limit the competencies of parliament, or the sphere of the law, in the face of government prerogatives, or the sphere of regulation. France adopted the principle following the experience of the Fourth Republic (1946–58), when parliamentary intervention increased at the expense of the president and government. Rationalization aims to limit, restrict, and check the authorities of parliament. See Malki 2007a.

29 Malki 2007a.

30 Malki et al. 2010.

31 In August and September 2010, the two months leading up to municipal and parliamentary elections, there were individual and collective detentions, as well as curbs on general freedoms. Joe Stork, deputy Middle East director at Human Rights Watch, said, "What we are seeing in Bahrain these days is a return to full-blown authoritarianism. The government has taken over associations and shut down media it doesn't like to silence the loudest critics and intimidate the rest" (Human Rights Watch, "Bahrain: Elections to Take Place amid Crackdown," 28 October 2010, www.hrw.org/en/news/2010/10/20/bahrain-elections-take-place-amid-crackdown).

32 The Independent Coalition for Election Monitoring urged the president to dissolve the parliament as a result. See the press release issued by the coalition after elections, Cairo Institute for Human Rights Studies, 6 December 2010.

33 In Egypt's 2005 People's Assembly elections, the Muslim Brotherhood won eighty-eight seats, becoming the largest political force after the ruling National Democratic Party. The Islamic Action Front in Jordan chose to boycott elections due to the government's failure to provide sufficient guarantees for fair elections, in addition to their objections to the current voting system—the single nontransferable vote—upheld in the most recent amendment in May 2010.

34 Human Rights Watch 2010.

35 Hamzawy 2010.

36 UNDP-POGAR 2007.

37 UNDP-POGAR 2007.

38 UNDP 2009b.

39 For example, the State Security courts in Egypt, established by Law 17/1959 and its amendments and Decree 47 of 28 March 1968 establishing the Supreme State Security Court.

40 International Institute for Democracy and Electoral Assistance 2011.

41 Arab Organization for Human Rights 2010b.

42  Arab Organization for Human Rights 2010.
43  *Official Gazette* no. 5992, 17 June 2011, 2939.
44  Malki et al. 2009.
45  UNDP 2009b.
46  Montesquieu 2001.

CHAPTER 3

# Transforming the Media:
## From Tool of the Rulers to Tool of Empowerment

## Lina Khatib

The Arab media are transforming as a result of their influential role during the reform movements that took off in 2011—the Arab Spring. But challenges remain. When the media can act freely and report from multiple political perspectives, citizens are empowered to become active and effective participants in the political process. Achieving that requires transparency and accountability, with credibility as a shared responsibility of government, media institutions, and media professionals. Political liberalization and expanded freedoms need to be coupled with media owners, journalists, and governments joining forces to create media institutions and a media environment that are credible. Arab citizens, in turn, must learn how to judge and assess the value and credibility of issues raised by media outlets. Achieving these objectives is the challenge facing Arab media today.

### Media Achievements and Challenges
Much has been written about the potential of Arab satellite channels and independent newspapers to promote open debate and raise public awareness—developments that could bring radical change to the Arab public sphere. Private satellite stations have widened the scope for discussing political issues, even those that were once taboo. Indeed, political talk shows, reporting, and live broadcasts from protests have set new media standards and sparked a trend of openness and criticism in the public sphere.[1] But the Arab media also face complex challenges

regarding their potential as a tool of empowerment. The following discussion presents the key elements from both sides of the debate.

### Quantitative and qualitative advances

In the last decade, the Arab media have had major quantitative and qualitative accomplishments (box 3.1). Private satellite channels have become Arab countries' primary media outlets, rising from one hundred in January 2004, to 450 in January 2009, to 1,100 in 2012, at least 600 of which are available to the public free of charge.[2] Satellite channels reach 95 percent of homes in Arab countries, where some 250 million viewers tune in. Technology for viewing programs on mobile devices is rapidly boosting satellite channel penetration. The number of independent Arab newspapers has also grown substantially.[3] Although several newspapers have been shut down, new ones have emerged, bringing the total from 144 in 2003 to 189 in 2009.[4]

Over the last decade the Arab region has also witnessed a large rise in the use of new media, especially among young people (box 3.2). Between 2000 and 2011 Internet use grew 3,458 percent (figure 3.1), and the region now has an estimated 107 million Internet users.[5] In 2007

---

**Box 3.1 Media and the Arab revolutions**

The Arab revolutions—the major headline of 2011—spurred far-reaching transformations in many Arab countries. The media scene witnessed parallel transformations reflecting the extent and thrust of the media's engagement with events as well as their deep effects on each other. In fact, the media provided significant leverage to these Arab events, allowing major leaps forward to take place, just as the media themselves leapt forward. Rather than remaining restricted to the task of traditional reportage, the media became players in their own right in driving transformation. The Arab revolutions took great advantage of this role of the media, especially as third-generation media—spearheaded by satellite channels and the social media networks Facebook, Twitter, and YouTube—had a powerful presence in the Arab mobilizations. In parallel with revolutionizing change in the channels at the level of news-making sources, new media played a major role in the media's leap forward with the emergence of nontraditional media sources such as the citizen journalist and the eyewitness.

The revolution in the sources for the production and dissemination of media messages during the events of the recent Arab transformations has created a new status quo that transcends the professional parameters of traditional media. A multilayered media scene has come into being that comprises numerous, parallel messages and production strands—something that is difficult for governments and traditional censors to control. As government domination of media has weakened, a new reality has emerged that bodes well for those seeking open airwaves and free media. Yet numerous negative ramifications have emerged in parallel, the least of which are the attenuation of media messages, the erosion of news credibility, and the deteriorating ability of traditional media to raise awareness and to enlighten. The abundance of information available sometimes reaches the point of overload, which is accompanied by a tangible falling back in knowledge. This naturally creates worrying cases of confusion and lack of vision when information is not disseminated in a way that meets the requirements of awareness raising.

In addition to inadequate education systems and the waning influence of social and religious upbringing, the media's unfulfilled role in empowering the creation of a knowledge society represents yet another element in the late and underdevelopment of many Arab countries. This situation, overall and in its component parts, fails to respond to aspirations for the building of a knowledge society in the Arab world. In fact, this may be the primary cause of the Arab world's shortcomings.

—Rashed Al-Oraimi, editor in chief, *al-Ittihad* newspaper,
United Arab Emirates

regional broadband penetration stood at 5 percent; by 2010 it had risen to 17 percent and was expected to reach 22 percent by the end of 2011.[6]

The popular revolutions in Arab countries have demonstrated just how vital social media have become to Arab Internet users. Facebook saw its users skyrocket (figure 3.2). An Arabic version of Twitter, launched in October 2009,[7] played a prominent part in the popular movements of 2011.

**Box 3.2 Children of dot.com**

Adults no longer constitute a real source of authority for the rising generation—at least on the level of knowledge. The younger generation knows more than adults and has mastered the rules of information technology, which became an essential part of daily life. The new generation is in the process of replacing adult authority with that of the network authority of the World Wide Web. Adults have become dispensable as youth are more and more connected to the alternative paternity of dot.com.

—Mustafa Hijazi, *al-Insan al-mahdur: dirasa tahliliya nafsiya ijtima'iya* (2005), 206

Figure 3.1 Growth in traditional media and social networking in the Arab countries

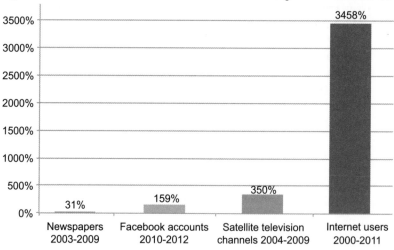

*Source:* World Bank 2012b; Internet World Statistics 2013.

Qualitative improvements have also been impressive. The 2002 Arab Human Development Report noted new media's potential as an alternative to official media and described how nongovernmental organizations (NGOs) could use new media to gather opinions, coordinate activities, and mobilize support.[8] New media, especially social media websites and mobile phones, have been effective for mobilizing Arab protest movements and enabling election monitors, civil society anticorruption groups, and human rights activists, who now rely heavily on the Internet and mobile phones, to document human rights violations.[9]

**Figure 3.2 Facebook accounts in some Arab countries, 2010 and 2012**

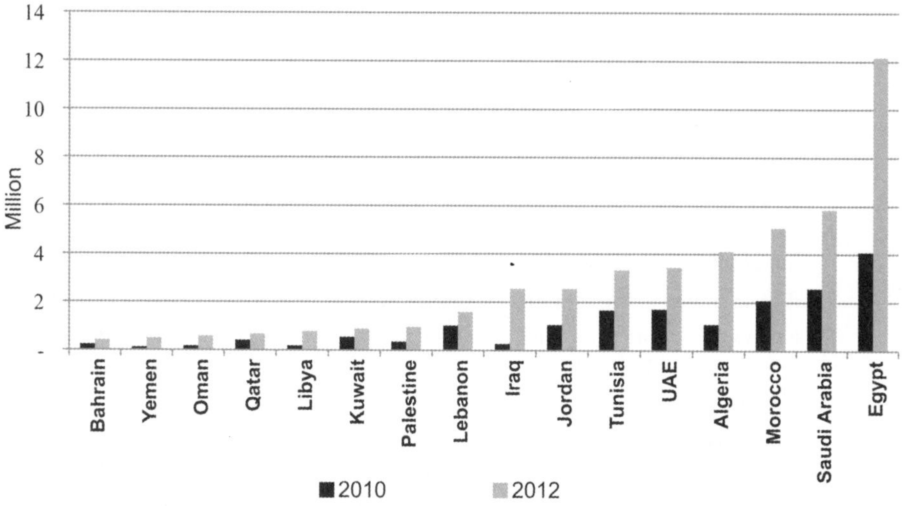

Source: Internet World Statistics 2013; Economy Watch, Economic Statistics
Database 2011.

The press has adopted new media as well, with 85 percent of Arab
newspapers now having websites.[10] There are also many popular online-
only publications. In Egypt, Lebanon, and Saudi Arabia, for example,
news sites constitute the top seven or eight most popular websites.[11]

Newspapers and satellite television have opened up a space for public
debate by providing comment forums on their websites and using the
Internet to elude censorship. In so doing, they provide multiple points of
view and have become competitive with official media.[12]

Arab citizens now have more ways than ever to acquire information
and participate in civil society and political movements.[13] Satellite television stations and new media of all kinds—blogs, websites, social
media—enable Arab writers to reach more people. The stations have created a new space for the transnational exchange and discussion of ideas,
allowing Arab political and civil forces to communicate and expand.

The growing role of the media, especially social media, in political
change is beyond question. New media have helped break the strangle-
hold of the editor-in-chief, allowing youth to liberate media platforms
from the restrictions of private ownership. Anyone can own a website or
social media page. New media have made knowledge products available
to all. They have also supported political emancipation and liberation
from censorship—full government control of this sphere is impossible.

Furthermore, new media have breached the fear barrier, producing a new elite of reformist youth who are willing to stand up for their rights. In an attempt to limit the powerful drive for reform made possible through the Internet, governments have monitored its use, questioned individuals active in the field, and even charged them with crimes. Despite these attempts to silence voices, the flow of information online has continued. The information increasingly available on the Internet over the last five years played a role in sparking the Egyptian revolution in 2011.

### But challenges remain

These major achievements notwithstanding, the Arab media still do not always focus on the concerns of citizens. They continue to suffer from chronic problems, including weak accountability and constraints on freedom of expression,[14] traceable in part to the media's low overall freedom.[15] A few stations with high viewership and advertising revenue dominate the free broadcasting market.[16] Ever protective of this revenue, these stations focus on family entertainment and steer clear of development issues and content that supports freedom of expression.

Censorship, external or self-imposed, remains pervasive.[17] Governments limit freedoms of press and expression under the pretext of national interest and security.[18] Egyptian state television helped the regime conceal from citizens the events following the 25 January 2011 protest in Tahrir Square. Bahraini, Libyan, and Syrian state television distorted the news during the protests in these countries in an attempt to dampen popular campaigns for reform. Dictators use the media to oppress their citizens, as in Libya in early 2011. Regimes control the major stations and use them as platforms for their own views, to the exclusion of opposition voices,[19] as in Bahrain, Syria, and Yemen before and during the popular mobilizations of 2011. The state press continues to use propaganda to silence opposition voices during deepening social crises, as in the 2011 reform movement in Morocco.

These practices undermine the media's role as the 'fourth estate' that guarantees government accountability, and the dearth of independent media intensifies the deficit. Private ownership laws encourage patronage in media production,[20] while constitutional guarantees of freedom of expression are meaningless in the cases where constitutions ban individual ownership of newspapers.[21] Media professionals face multiple challenges in obtaining official information, from a lack of research centers to harassment and intimidation.[22]

Private satellite channels, despite their proliferation, have not played an empowering role in the Arab region overall, neither insisting on government accountability nor supporting civil society. Light entertainment dominates their content, while the share of educational and cultural programming, along with investigative reporting, has declined.[23] And many television stations have defended the ruling regimes.

These problems were exacerbated by the 2008 Arab Satellite Charter adopted by the Arab League (see the section below on "The role of laws and charters"). The 2009 Arab Human Development Report described the charter as "muzzling" the Internet as an outlet for independent and private media channels. Also contributing to the weak independence of Arab media are low levels of media literacy, resulting in passive acceptance of media messages[24] at a time when information exchange between citizens and government has barely started.[25]

The media can contribute to social change by empowering individuals to influence their environment and recognize and solve problems. This chapter focuses on the defining criteria, outlined below, of "empowering media":

- Disseminate credible knowledge and information to all.
- Guarantee the fundamentals of democracy.
- Hold themselves accountable to citizens.
- Guard against political pressure.
- Voice citizens' concerns to others in the public sphere.
- Hold the state accountable.
- Act impartially.
- Express a diverse range of views.
- Exercise freedom of expression and investigation.

## Media and Social Empowerment

The Arab media can contribute to social empowerment by supporting civil society in the public sphere, helping build a knowledge society, strengthening educational institutions, and empowering local communities.

### Empowering citizens and institutions through media–civil society partnerships

The media can be an important tool for civil society organizations (CSOs) in Arab countries. The media can promote civil society's achievements in the public sphere, support its social campaigns, and facilitate communication among CSOs.

Arab CSOs have been on the upswing. During the 1990s the number of CSOs doubled in Kuwait and Saudi Arabia, tripled in Lebanon, and rose 400 percent in Bahrain and 1,000 percent in Yemen.[26] A surge also occurred in Tunisia, Egypt, and Libya following the 2011 uprisings. Yet CSOs still have not developed a strong relationship with the mainstream media. Official media, unwilling to risk political disapproval that would threaten their profits, rarely cover civil society, especially CSO campaigns for politically sensitive reforms. As a result, CSO activities are often relegated to obscurity.

Television stations could change this by allocating more time on news broadcasts and current affairs programs to civil society events and causes, as could the print media by devoting more space to CSO concerns and achievements. A good example is the Lebanese newspaper *an-Nahar*, which has sections on social and civil affairs, in addition to an environment and heritage page that covers government and NGO activities.

To empower citizens, media and civil society must complement each other. The media should acknowledge civil society's role in the public sphere and spread awareness of citizens' rights and duties and of ways citizens can get better social and political representation. In turn, CSOs should increase their media presence by coordinating efforts to create a common space for disclosing their activities and achievements. In Sierra Leone a monthly forum was established in 2008 to bring together journalists, CSO representatives, and government officials in a dialogue on how each could support democracy and good governance.[27] Arab civil society could engage in similar initiatives, creating a two-way relationship with the media based on interaction and dialogue on roles and responsibilities. This kind of dialogue would strengthen the media, especially local media, and reinforce transparency and accountability within CSOs.

The superficial relationships now common between media and civil society reflect the reality in which they function. Numerous limitations, from regulations to state harassment, circumscribe the actions of the media and CSOs, which are sometimes accused of acting for foreign entities when their activities do not align with state policies.

Despite these difficulties, Arab CSOs and social movements are increasing their media presence, many by using new media. In Saudi Arabia, NGOs involved in women's rights have become more active through blogging,[28] and the United Arab Emirates' press is demonstrating greater environmental activism.[29] At Cairo University, engineering students have set up *al-Risala* (The Message), an interactive website that has become the core social support for the poor by collecting and distributing charitable donations. *Al-Risala* now covers fifteen governorates across Egypt.[30]

Nevertheless, technical problems can frustrate these efforts. Arab CSOs seldom update their websites, and poorly designed interfaces make them difficult to use. Some lack vital contact information. Many CSOs and NGOs lack the human and technical resources to produce meaningful news stories on their work or to interact effectively with the media. And many Arab journalists lack the skills to make CSO issues interesting and accessible.[31] Training civil society activists on using media and communications, writing and publishing content, and allocating resources for web management would go a long way toward empowering Arab civil society.

A stronger relationship between the media and civil society would allow organizations to learn about each other's work. Many CSO interests overlap, yet the organizations do not always cooperate. Electronic media can provide a platform for exchanging experience and knowledge and a space for CSOs to garner support and expand their activities.

Both traditional and new media can support civil society by promoting the free flow of information instead of a government monopoly on content (figure 3.3).[32] CSOs could then obtain information from government and from nongovernment sources and transmit it to citizens through the media. CSOs could also convey people's concerns to the government using the Internet, press, television, and radio.

**Figure 3.3 Media—represented by arrows in the figure below—can support civil society organizations by promoting the free flow of information**

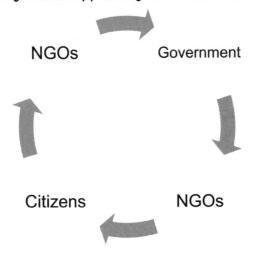

NGOs          Government

Citizens          NGOs

### Using the media to build a knowledge society

The public receives most of its political news from media products (figure 3.4). The 2006 Arab Barometer survey found that, regardless of a country's average level of education, television news is citizens' first source of information about the government, followed by local newspapers (figure 3.5).[33] As such, media bear a major responsibility to their audience regarding the scope and accuracy of information presented.

**Figure 3.4 Percentage of citizens following political news in selected Arab countries, 2005**

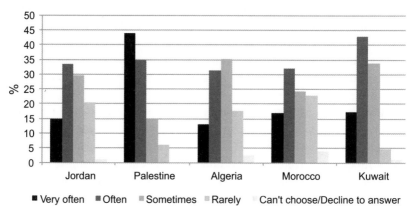

■ Very often   ■ Often   ■ Sometimes   ■ Rarely     Can't choose/Decline to answer

*Source:* Arab Barometer 2006. www.arabbarometer.org/index.html.

Media coverage that raises social awareness on issues such as health and the environment helps make these issues accessible to people.[34] Yet of the nearly 450 Arab satellite channels in 2009, only ten were educational, four produced documentaries, and two focused on health, nutrition, and cooking.[35] There remains a significant gap in media outlets that are serious about supporting knowledge dissemination.

The media have also increasingly become a source of religious education in Arab countries. Some 150 religious channels—most of them Islamic—broadcast throughout the Arab region,[36] and the number is growing.[37] Some are dedicated to religious interpretation, some to religion and social issues, and some to sectarian interpretation. These channels face no content regulation. And some have contributed to sectarian tensions among Islamic schools of thought or have promoted hatred between Muslims and Christians.[38] In 2010 this situation led some Arab governments to shut down some religious satellite channels. The Internet, as another source of religious information, has created similar

**Figure 3.5 Citizens' sources of information on politics and government in selected Arab countries, 2005**

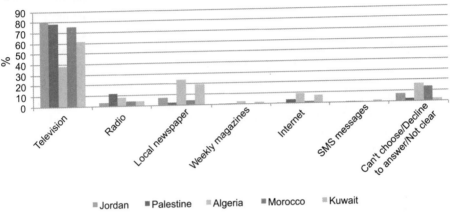

*Source:* Arab Barometer 2006. Available online at www.arabbarometer.org/index.html.

problems. The lack of regulation of religious channels and websites can make it difficult for viewers to differentiate between extremist viewpoints and sound religious exegesis. However, regulation must not be confused with state control.

## Using the media to empower educational institutions

Another way the media can empower Arab citizens is by strengthening their relationship with academia. Knowledge gaps are key obstacles to development. Cooperation among the media, educational institutions, and the government can build the capacities of Arab countries to create a knowledge society.[39]

But knowledge-based media content is not enough; the audience must also be able to engage critically with the content. Arab citizens' general lack of media literacy is rarely a part of public discourse, even in debates on education.

The far-reaching concept of *media literacy* implies an individual's empowerment to critique media content—visual, written, or aural—as a text open to interpretation and challenge, rather than as a text that imposes a single, indisputable viewpoint. Media literacy is especially important today, when people are exposed to so much information. Superimposed audio, doctored images, and unregulated media, especially on websites and charlatan satellite channels that present their content as science, often make it difficult for those without media literacy to distinguish between credible and non-credible content.[40]

Spreading media awareness among youth is especially important in the age of social media. Arab youth use social media and the Internet for all kinds of activities, from entertainment to organizing political protests. The Internet has become part of many young people's daily life.[41] They need to develop a more sophisticated awareness of media that allows them to distinguish credible sources from the dubious.

So how best to increase media literacy in Arab societies? Require media education in school curricula as a resource for lifelong learning. Media education can help students become more cautious and critical. Schools can teach media texts (such as videos, newspaper articles, and excerpts from television programs) alongside traditional texts and encourage students to analyze them critically.[42]

Learning to produce media content, such as writing scripts, directing, and editing, would help students understand how media texts are created and how the creative process shapes final products. Students could learn that such texts are multifaceted, not unified pieces of information or opinion. Students can also be encouraged to express themselves through media, as AmmanNet has been doing since 2000 in a media literacy effort called School Radio. In Jordan, professionals from AmmanNet have introduced "Youth Bulletin," which allows students to create news programs for their peers.[43]

This kind of media engagement can foster individual and collective initiative, yet education curricula in Arab countries remain largely teacher-led, without student input. Schools and universities can provide an ideal environment for strengthening such engagement, encouraging students to use their Internet skills to create educational channels (videos, blogs) for use in schools and universities. In addition to discussing content, students can create written and audiovisual online material.

The growing use of online education, or e-learning, gives students a way to express themselves outside of school hours and empowers them by strengthening their engagement in their own education. Several Arab countries have virtual universities, including Tunisia and Syria, whose virtual university serves about one thousand students. The Mediterranean Virtual University cooperates with Ain Shams University in Egypt, the American University of Beirut, Birzeit University in the West Bank, Jordan University of Science and Technology, and the Islamic University of Gaza.[44]

Virtual education environments have many advantages. The high student–faculty ratios in many Arab universities have reinforced a one-way dissemination of knowledge, from lecturers to students, because there is not enough time to allow students to ask questions or express their opinions. Online discussion forums can help solve this problem, by encouraging discussions in a virtual environment and allowing students to respond to each other.

E-learning environments can also serve as a platform for distance learning courses, making education accessible to students who live too far from schools or cannot afford to attend them. Distance learning can be organized nationally or through open universities that serve multiple countries, such as the Arab Open University, a private institution with its headquarters in Kuwait and branches in Bahrain, Egypt, Jordan, Lebanon, Oman, and Saudi Arabia.[45]

Institutions using e-learning can encourage others in Arab countries to follow suit by exchanging best practices on websites (such as the projects that the United Nations Educational, Social, and Cultural Organization, UNESCO, is undertaking). This kind of exchange would facilitate national and regional cooperation and would enable institutions to provide education materials at reduced costs.

Arab governments can encourage the use of information and communications technology to exchange knowledge by investing in initiatives that increase access to education. Examples include installing Internet-connected computers in public libraries, offering free computer literacy courses, and making e-learning and media literacy part of school curricula.

### Using the media to empower local communities

Media can empower local Arab communities by giving people a platform to express their views, sense of cultural belonging, and individual and collective history, and to develop their sense of inclusion in the greater society.

Film and video have become one way to do this. Events like the Dubai International Film Festival encourage local productions and have become part of the pan-Arab cultural scene. Local electronic media are also growing rapidly, indicative of the Internet's pivotal role. With Arabic one of the Internet's fastest growing languages, it is important that both the public and private sectors support the development of Arabic-language software and content. According to Internet World Stats, Arabic is the seventh most used language on the Internet (its use grew 2,501 percent between 2000 and 2011), yet only 18.8 percent of Arab Internet users consume or produce Arabic content.[46]

The 2009 Arab Knowledge Report found little content on Arab websites that could support social or economic development.[47] An exception was several media initiatives that aimed to empower local communities following the 2006 war in Lebanon by documenting the daily lives of local residents; these could serve as inspiration. One of them, "Lens on Lebanon," equips local communities harmed during the war with the photo and video skills and tools to document their lives.[48] In Jordan the Kharabeesh (Scribbles) company specializes in creating Arabic-language films and animation that draw on local culture. The company's products feature Jordanian characters with local names and dialects and stories illustrating daily life.

In Syria the ReefNet website provides information to rural residents through individual websites for each participating village. Within a year of launch the program had websites for eighteen villages, and more than thirty thousand visits.[49] Dubai holds the Arabesque competition—judged by WordPress—for the best Arabic-language blog dealing with local content.[50] The freedom to create original content is important for empowering local communities through the media, whether by documenting experiences or by producing content to share with other communities.

For technology-based development projects to narrow the knowledge gap and empower people, the project platforms must be inclusive and accessible to members of marginalized groups. For example, making the web accessible to people with disabilities is often overlooked, and media content in minority languages remains limited. Access to information can enable minority groups to participate more effectively as citizens. After years of struggling for linguistic representation, the Imazighen, an indigenous minority group in North Africa, now have numerous websites that address their identity. The Imazighen are also active in Internet discussions on how to use their language in education, science, technology, and media.[51] Ethnolinguistic minorities also use traditional media, including satellite television stations, to assert their rights and celebrate their culture. Official and private media serve Kurdish society in Iraq and Armenian society in Lebanon by offering television and radio programs in their native tongues. All members of Arab societies would benefit from greater access to media that allow them to express their concerns publicly and build an interactive channel with others.[52]

The media's main role is to provide information and to channel citizens' voices into the public sphere.[53] The Arab media already provide a space for citizens to express themselves—for example, through the interactive websites of newspapers such as *Asharq Al-Awsat* and satellite channels like Al Jazeera and Al Arabiya, as well as participation in live television programs by email, telephone, and text message. During the 2009 Gaza crisis, when Israel tried to block media reports out of Gaza,

Al Jazeera enabled people to upload footage filmed on mobile phones, and these recordings were exchanged freely on the Internet and used in Al Jazeera news broadcasts. Al Jazeera later became a partner in the Creative Commons project (http://creativecommons.org), which gives people access to footage belonging to the station.[54] This kind of cooperation increases citizen participation, supports the growth of media capacity, and empowers populations.

Al Jazeera's challenging of the status quo shows how Arab media can use the Internet and mobile phones to encourage citizen journalism, allowing ordinary people to report on events in their setting in real time. Citizen journalism flourished in Syria during the 2011 media blackout (box 3.3).

### Box 3.3 The Syrian revolution and social media sites

If the Egyptian revolution was tagged the "Facebook Revolution," the Syrian uprising can be characterized as the "YouTube Revolution." Because the Syrian government has barred foreign journalists, YouTube has played a pivotal role in transmitting images and information across the country's borders.

Syrian demonstrators have shown extraordinary courage, capturing video footage in an effort to prove that their revolution is peaceful and to bear witness to the horrific torture to which they are being subjected. This coverage has become an effective response to the government propaganda disseminated by official media outlets.

The Syrian revolution—and what citizens are going through—could not have been portrayed accurately without the technological revolution—social media sites in particular. These sites allow citizens to transmit images and to shape the news. In the age of the citizen-journalist formal news correspondents no longer have a monopoly on news coverage; activists are demonstrating, shooting footage, and transmitting the news themselves.

Syrian demonstrators have independently assumed the entire news cycle, from obtaining information to disseminating it. Every day they strive courageously to get out their side of the story, risking sniper fire and torture if captured.

—Radwan Ziadeh, Director of the Damascus Center for Human Rights Studies, 2011

Yet Arab media can go further, granting citizens access to their institutions by enabling them to lead community campaigns on local issues and exercise the right to participate directly in evaluating media performance in covering local issues. In turn, local communities can support their own empowerment through strategies for improving their access to the media and holding media accountable.

## Media and Political Empowerment

The media can encourage good governance primarily by providing information and by holding the government and the private sector accountable for their actions. In providing information, Arab media can intermediate between governments and oppositions during political protests and reforms—by making citizens aware of issues that matter to them and by amplifying their voices so that they reach the government. The media can also enhance people's awareness of their rights and of the mechanisms to secure those rights. As early as 2003 in Somalia, the *Warsan* newspaper was launched to address the lack of information available to citizens following the collapse of the central government.[55] This example can be followed in numerous Arab countries in turmoil today.

Several Arab states have created websites to promote political participation, especially during elections, such as that created by the Lebanese Interior Ministry during the 2009 parliamentary elections. The electorate also uses nongovernmental websites to discuss election issues, such as Al-Qarar Al-Arabi (Arab Decision), whose mission is to provide information on Arab governments, courts, laws, education, and finance.[56] The media have also advanced political empowerment by serving as an outlet for citizens to hold the government and the private sector, including NGOs, more accountable. As the 2011 revolutions have shown, this role is especially important in nascent democracies whose institutions remain weak and susceptible to political pressures. Online forums have opened new horizons for citizens to debate sensitive issues not previously discussed openly, including politics and religion.[57] Some websites allow for cooperation among journalists across the Arab region on human rights, democracy, and development.

The Arab media's involvement in the 2011 protest movements was built on years of effort, if limited in scope, by activists to expose corruption, whether by governments or private companies and from election rigging to illicit trade in human organs.[58] For example, bloggers and activists have used mobile phone cameras to capture evidence of corruption, political oppression, and human rights violations. They have also used software and websites like Ushahidi (www.ushahidi.com)

and Shayfeen (www.shayfeen.com) to monitor and report on elections, as in Egypt in 2010. In 2009 a new independent Egyptian publication, *Wasla* (Connector), began printing blog content, making it accessible to people who do not communicate electronically. Such efforts are ongoing and constitute examples of best practice.

## Media and the challenges of political empowerment

But Arab media still suffer from problems that impede their ability to advance political empowerment. First, not all Arab states have electoral laws that guarantee political parties equal media access, a sign of commitment to strengthening democracy and civil society. And where such laws do exist, they are not always equitably enforced; some television and radio stations work in the interests of particular political parties, granting additional airtime to their campaigns through advertisements or news coverage. Studies have documented extensive violations of equal media access laws in Arab countries,[59] but violators are rarely sanctioned.

Second, Arab media are often subject to political pressure that prods them toward biased reporting. Some media outlets engage in patronage, whether because of ownership connections or financial need. Corruption is also widespread among journalists, who threaten to publish false or scandalous news if not paid bribes.[60] Journalists are often hired by the government and the secret police to blackmail political rivals.

Third, as the 2011 protests made apparent, some media entities continue to distort information and broadcast false information, tricking citizens into making unsound choices. Libyan state media aired false information in an attempt to quell popular movements. Egyptian and Tunisian state media acted as mouthpieces for the authorities and ignored their countries' protesters, while some private television stations followed agendas that stripped their reporting of all objectivity. The Egyptian, Libyan, and Syrian authorities, among others, made numerous attempts to impose media blackouts by interfering with satellite reception, pulling websites off line, and cutting Internet and communication services.

Fourth, the scope for freedom of expression remains limited, even on the Internet. Government authorities try to control the new information media by creating websites that discredit those of the opposition and by passing laws requiring website licensing that curbs freedom of expression and allows the authorities full access to information on Internet users and companies. The authorities also impede access to websites they deem threatening, even those that were established legally. And activists across the region who criticize the government on the Internet are still subject to arrest and can be charged with libel or with threatening national security.

This situation continues a long-entrenched status quo: in 2005, four of the fifteen countries defined as "enemies of the Internet" by Reporters without Borders were Arab states. The governments of Gulf Cooperation Council countries still prevent access to certain websites,[61] while other Arab governments impose censorship through legal pressures, surveillance, high taxes, underdeveloped communications infrastructure, monopoly control of Internet service providers, control of access to hardware and software, and an environment of fear that leads to self-censorship.[62]

Confronting these challenges requires comprehensive reform, beginning with laws, enforcement of those laws, citizen–government communication, and institutions and practices.

### The role of laws and charters: From repression to an open space for free media

Arab media suffer from the abuse of laws, which restricts their freedoms. Press laws generally follow the long-entrenched model of censorship and self-censorship. Newspaper publishing is tightly controlled, as newspapers must be licensed before they can publish.[63] In some countries the authorities have an absolute right to accept or reject applications, without explanation. Some countries allow rejected applicants to appeal to a higher administrative authority, while others grant the right of judicial appeal.

Most Arab countries have press systems with full or partial state ownership. Some grant ownership to the state or to the ruling party; others have mixed private–public ownership. Few grant all citizens the right to practice journalism, without restrictions or conditions. Most require a government license before publishing. And while few limit the right to impose fines and other punitive measures to the judiciary, others grant that right exclusively to administrative authorities. Press systems in several Arab states impose fines on or even incarcerate illegal publishers.[64]

According to the 2009 Freedom House report, satellite broadcasting and digital media, despite their positive impacts in Arab states, continue to suffer unfairly from libel, slander, and defamation laws, as well as emergency laws.[65] The 2010 Press Freedom Index shows these conditions going from bad to worse (figure 3.6). Even Lebanon, the highest ranking Arab country on media freedoms, ranked only 101 globally in

**Figure 3.6 Press Freedom Index rank**

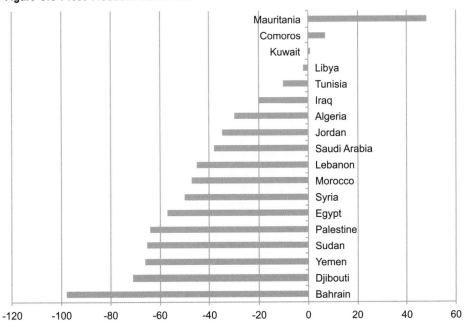

*Source:* Reporters without Borders. Press Freedom Index 2013.

2013, down from 56 in 2002. Other surveys find similar results, including the 2009 report of the Arab Journalists Union on freedom of the press[66] and the 2007 Ibn Khaldun Center report *Civil Society and Democratization in the Arab World*.[67]

Among the most dangerous restrictive press laws is the Arab Satellite Charter (known as the Arab Media Code of Honor) issued by the Arab League in 2008 over objections from Lebanon and Qatar. Article 7, one of its most controversial, states:

Arab media professionals must be committed to credibility and integrity in performing their vocation and must refrain from approaches that directly or indirectly dishonor the people. Respect must be given to the people's national sovereignty and fundamental choices. The people's domestic affairs must not be interfered with, and the media must not be turned into a tool that incites violence. They must not cause damage to heads of state and must remain strictly impartial in debate. This is to safeguard the sanctity and honor of the media's mission.

And Article 5 states:

> Arab media must uphold the principle of Arab solidarity in all that they present to public opinion at home and abroad. They must contribute their full capacity to supporting understanding and cooperation between Arab states and avoid disseminating anything that harms Arab solidarity. They must refrain from directing campaigns of a personal nature.[68]

The Arab media have strongly resisted the charter, weakening its application.[69] But several governments referenced the charter in attempts to black out the media during the protests of 2011. So that the Arab media can function in a more democratic environment, the private sector, civil society, governments, and media institutions need to coordinate regional efforts to repeal the charter officially now that the Arab Spring has essentially repealed it in practice.

Arab media practitioners, media institutions, and civil society activists also need to work together to change laws limiting freedom of expression. There are several examples of best practice in this regard. In Egypt in 2003, the head of the journalists syndicate—an independent opposition party candidate—pressured the government to repeal the 1996 law that permits imprisoning journalists for their reporting. A penal code amendment was introduced in 2006 and eventually passed. In Lebanon a local organization called Social Media Exchange is training civil society groups and NGOs to use social media. In 2010 the organization led a successful campaign to postpone voting on a draft law that would have placed limits on Internet use.[70]

Similar efforts have been made elsewhere in the Arab region, yet in many cases change goes no deeper than public statements that are never fully acted on. An example is the 1996 Declaration of Sana'a, formulated by a coalition of Arab governments, Arab and international press organizations, and media experts under UNESCO auspices (box 3.4). The declaration calls for strengthening the independence and pluralism of Arab media and states that "government tendencies to draw limits/red lines outside the purview of the law restrict these freedoms and are unacceptable." Yet the governments that signed the declaration have not respected it, and its provisions languish, like those of other charters.[71]

The media can foster political empowerment if they act transparently and within the law and if laws are interpreted and applied transparently. Both traditional and new media can be influential here by reporting on cases where media and journalists have been put on trial

**Box 3.4 Declaration of Sana'a**

Arab States should provide, and reinforce where they exist, constitutional and legal guarantees of freedom of expression and of press freedom and should abolish those laws and measures that limit the freedom of the press; government tendencies to draw limits /"red lines" outside the purview of the law restrict these freedoms and are unacceptable.

The establishment of truly independent, representative associations, syndicates or trade unions of journalists, and associations of editors and publishers, is a matter of priority in those Arab countries where such bodies do not now exist. Any legal and administrative obstacles to the establishment of independent journalists' organizations should be removed. Where necessary, labor relations laws should be elaborated in accordance with international standards.

Sound journalistic practices are the most effective safeguard against governmental restrictions and pressures by special interest groups. Guidelines for journalistic standards are the concern of the news media professionals. Any attempt to set down standards and guidelines should come from the journalists themselves. Disputes involving the media and/or the media professionals in the exercise of their profession are a matter for the courts to decide, and such cases should be tried under civil and not criminal codes and procedures.

Journalists should be encouraged to create independent media enterprises owned, run, and funded by the journalists themselves and supported, if necessary, by transparent endowments with guarantees that donors do not intervene in editorial policies.

International assistance in Arab countries should aim to develop print and electronic media, independent of governments, in order to encourage pluralism as well as editorial independence. Public media should be supported and funded only when they are editorially independent and where a constitutional, effective freedom of information and expression and the independence of the press are guaranteed.

State-owned broadcasting and news agencies should be granted statutes of journalistic and editorial independence as open public service institutions. Creation of independent news agencies and private and/or community ownership of broadcasting media, including in rural areas, should also be encouraged; . . .

The international community should contribute to the achievement and implementation of this Declaration.

This Declaration should be presented by the Secretary General of the United Nations to the General Assembly, and by the Director-General of UNESCO to the General Conference, for follow-up and implementation.

*Source:* UNESCO 1996

and by making the public aware of the sanctions the media face, so that the state can be held accountable. Journalists in Arab countries are subject to multiple threats, political pressures, and unfair trials[72]—and they are often targets in war zones. Since the start of the political transitions in 2011, the Arab region has seen politically motivated closings of newspapers and journalists subjected to arbitrary detention and legal action. Governments have imprisoned prominent bloggers and Internet users to halt the rise of online activism.[73]

Civil society can also oppose laws restricting freedom of expression and enabling Internet censorship by coordinating advocacy efforts and raising citizen awareness. To counter such scenarios, Arab NGOs that protect journalists' rights should increase their cross-border cooperation. For example, the Arabic Network for Human Rights Information in Egypt exchanges information and expertise with Iraq's Journalistic Freedoms Observatory. Many CSOs work on these issues, such as the Institute for Professional Journalists in Lebanon, the Center for Defending Freedom of Journalists in Jordan, and Arab Reporters for Investigative Journalism in nine Arab countries.

More initiatives are needed to facilitate their work and improve their communication and coordination, such as a legal framework that protects opposition media and guarantees a right to public information. Electronic media can help by enabling the exchange of information and best practices, joint publishing, and Internet-based dialogue among countries. Electronic media can also coordinate the efforts of journalist syndicates to achieve regional agreements that call for full investigations, by both local courts and the International Criminal Court, into attacks on journalists in conflict areas.

## E-government as a tool of communication between citizens and the state

Efforts are needed to change the culture of government by strengthening communication between citizens and the state. Improved communication would help bridge the gap between state and citizens so clearly exposed during the 2011 protests.

Most information available to the state in Arab countries is withheld from the media and the public on the pretext of preserving public order and national security. Ensuring the right to access public information and facilitating this right are among the pillars of good governance. One way to redress the lack of information is through e-government—government use of digital technology such as the Internet, email, and mobile phones—to communicate with and offer services to citizens, civil society, and private companies, as well as to link to official institutions. Effective e-government requires two-way communication between the government and citizens to foster principles of good governance, including participation, accountability, transparency, interactivity, efficiency, competence, equality, inclusiveness, and rule of law.

In this context, e-government has four benefits:

- It makes information more accessible to citizens.
- It contributes to citizens' democratic representation, such as through communication between citizens and elected officials via email.
- It encourages citizens to participate in the electoral process, such as by providing information and encouraging discussion on websites.
- It solicits comments from citizens, increasing citizen participation in decision making.[74]

As of late 2010, fifteen Arab countries had e-government portals.[75] However, the 2012 United Nations Global E-Government Survey found that a third of Arab states had not shown any improvement over the previous two years in their openness to e-government (figure 3.7).[76] The most frequently used e-government websites in Arab countries are those that provide administrative services, such as renewal of driver's licenses in Egypt or preparations for the Hajj in Saudi Arabia.

**Figure 3.7 Change in world ranking, readiness for e-government, 2010–12**

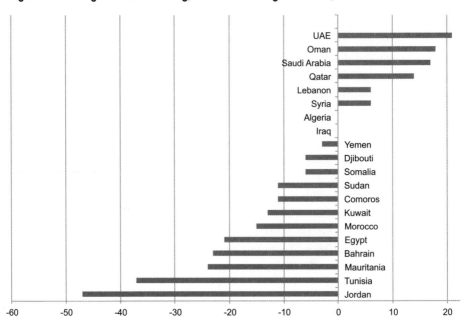

*Source:* United Nations. UN Public Administration Programme. 2012.
Available online at www.unpan.org/egovkb.

Nonetheless, the United Arab Emirates topped the list for improvement in e-government services (up ninety-two places, from
ninety-ninth in 2010 to seventh in 2012), one of the four subindicators
of openness to e-government in the survey. This large improvement
also moved the country from forty-ninth to fifth in overall e-readiness
in Asia. Other Gulf states, including Oman, Saudi Arabia, and Qatar,
also registered noticeable improvements.

There are practical advantages to e-government. E-government
reflects a deep-rooted transformation in how governments manage
their activities. First, it supports political reform. Arab states should be
urged to use electronic media to digitize information and encourage
political participation, actions leading to citizen oversight and greater
government accountability. As the 2009 Arab Human Development
Report noted, constitutions in the Arab region are more ideological
than institutional, and citizens are generally ill informed of their
specifics. Posting the constitution online could stimulate discussion and
gradually expand political freedom.

Second, expanding e-government can also promote institutional reform, including reform of the labor market and public administration. Publishing information on labor laws, for example, could encourage CSOs to press for revisions, while publishing information on government spending and state budgets could lead to reform of public administration and governance and to greater equity. Official information, when easy to access, understand, and monitor, enhances transparency, commitment to the rule of law, and willingness to be held accountable by citizens. In turn, these reforms strengthen civil society, enabling it to become an effective partner in decision making.

Numerous challenges stand in the way, however. Some countries face impediments of insufficient resources and underdeveloped technological infrastructure. Others face the challenge of the enormous disparity in digital capability across countries and social sectors. Illiteracy and computer illiteracy rates are high in many Arab countries.

Countries can overcome these barriers by allocating more funding to e-government and technological infrastructure and to programs for computer literacy. Citizens need civic education to benefit fully from e-government. That can be achieved by revising curricula and by disseminating audio, visual, and print educational material.

Arab countries can learn from other countries how to establish effective e-government. The Netherland's e-Citizen Charter is a model of good practice, with its transparent rights and duties of citizens. It addresses e-government as a means not merely of offering administrative services but also of involving and empowering citizens. The charter calls for accountability and benchmarking, including the public provision of performance data and measures, and it affirms citizens' right to access this information to compare, monitor, and assess state outcomes. The charter further enhances the capacity of citizens to participate in decision making.

Arab states can benefit from good regional practices as well. The 2012 United Nations Global E-Government Survey found that some Arab states—the United Arab Emirates, Oman, Saudi Arabia, Qatar, Lebanon, and Syria—are beginning to use e-government for information dissemination, consultation, and decision making.[77] As another example, Kuwait has a digital repository of legal information (created with help from the United Nations Development Programme) and an electronic library. Oman has programs for teaching computer skills, most of them for women. The United Arab Emirates is developing a 'dictionary' for models of data shared among government agencies, with the aim of creating a unified data framework.

## Empowerment of Media Institutions and Practices

Fully empowering media institutions and practices requires changing the motivation for public and private ownership, moving from media censorship to oversight, supporting a professional and responsible press, and countering gender stereotypes by empowering women through the media.

### Changing the impact of ownership: The predicaments of state-owned and privately owned media

Media development demands transparency in ownership and a diversity of media outlets with a broad range of opinions. Ownership is one of the biggest obstacles to the media becoming an empowerment tool in Arab countries. The party that owns the platform (government, private sector, local community, civil society) influences the content of the news that is reported, how it is reported, and for what purpose. The Arab world needs free media—free of laws restricting expression and free of pressure from the owners or political entities—and journalists with the skills to report impartially without fear of political reprisal, as well as citizens able to access, understand, and assess the information presented.

The media in Arab countries continue to be populated largely by state-owned outlets. In many Arab countries, including Jordan and Yemen, the state owns most television channels, radio stations, and newspapers.[78] The main problem with state media is their tendency to serve as a propaganda tool of the regime, to exclude critical voices, and to ignore the citizens' needs. Ownership also influences the development of media institutions. Although the number of private media outlets is rising steadily, they typically suffer from problems similar to those of state media. In many cases privately owned media are driven by profit motives, presenting content that attracts the most viewers and advertisers—so quality suffers.[79] Some owners distort the truth to broadcast their own opinions or to serve their political interests. Where political pluralism is lacking, private media are allied with the government or 'jointly' owned—that is, owned by members or friends of the ruling party, illegally funded directly through the transfer of public money or indirectly through government support disguised as advertising revenue. Thus, media companies become flexible tools of the political elite, exploited by those who monopolize decision making.[80]

To act as agents of citizen empowerment, media institutions need to present a diverse range of opinions. They need to be free of state control, direct or indirect. Some Arab states have laws that inhibit independent media—for example, by imposing exorbitant licensing fees for radio and television stations.[81] Private media sometimes enjoy a degree of freedom of expression and can criticize local politics if they avoid negative reporting about their hosting and funding government.[82] Governments may permit newspapers more apparent freedom than they do more influential media, such as television, thus masquerading as liberal while covertly silencing any questioning of their authority.

Absent in the media environment in most Arab countries are committed, independent, nonprofit institutions that report free of political and financial influence on issues of concern to citizens and that have strong connections with civil society.[83] Such institutions work with educational and cultural CSOs, operate in a decentralized manner, reach out to weak and marginalized groups, and cooperate in informal networks of independent knowledge producers.[84]

Ownership swayed by political or social biases weakens media credibility. Because it is not always clear who owns a particular media institution or how it is funded, more transparent ownership and finance are essential to enable Arab citizens to become more informed about the factors influencing media coverage and to expand their choices.

### Restructuring the media arena: From censorship to oversight

Arab countries need more open, transparent, and credible media (box 3.5). Achieving that requires restructuring the media arena, amending media licensing laws, regulating media ownership, and establishing norms for accountability and transparency. The political reform movements of 2011 demonstrated the need for major change, while simultaneously creating opportunities to bring about that change. Public debate over freedoms has begun to consider the role of the media. In Tunisia, for example, the Media Ministry was abolished following the 2011 revolution as a bold first step toward creating an independent media arena.

Developing open, transparent, and credible media also requires independent watchdogs to guarantee the soundness of media practices by monitoring media institutions without censoring them—even indirectly. Media institutions are shaped by their context, but countries can still learn from successful media models from around the world, particularly about how to reform official media. An example is public service broadcasting in the United Kingdom, which considers the role of all national media as first to inform, then to educate, and finally to entertain the audience. The licensing and funding of national media outlets depend on their adherence to these principles. Ofcom, an independent, nongovernmental, non-censoring regulator, is charged with safeguarding the right of citizens to file court cases against media channels (box 3.6).

**Box 3.5 Public service broadcasting**

Oppressive regimes continue to control the Arab media and are unwilling to introduce effective regulatory mechanisms to allow the media to function independently. At the same time, the proliferation of regional Arab satellite stations in the 1990s has not resulted in democracy and pluralism. The Arab people, particularly those who are poor, rural, and underrepresented, remain excluded. Yet the popular revolutions begun in late 2010 kindled hope for a reorganization of the media to meet people's aspirations for free, inclusive, and just societies.

The public broadcasting service model offers an alternative to the dual (private–state) system that has proven incapable of meeting the multiple, complex needs and ambitions of Arab societies. Committed public broadcasting serves the entire public, not just political and commercial interests. It aims to meet all of society's needs and desires, regardless of purchasing power, language, ethnicity, or influence. This kind of broadcasting contributes to the growth of free, informed, varied public opinion; represents a spectrum of intellectual orientations, particularly critical opinions; and covers most local affairs in a fair and balanced manner. Moreover, it strengthens national production by insisting that public broadcasting air only high-quality information and entertainment programming.

Developing objective media that serve the Arab people's needs, along with the introduction of regulatory mechanisms to guarantee functionality, should be a top priority for committed Arab revolutionaries in Egypt, Tunisia, and other countries.

—Dima Dabbous, Department of
Communications, Lebanese American University, Lebanon

Adopting a similar model in Arab countries would enrich the television environment, which is dominated by entertainment shows, and regulate the media environment, which generally neglects citizens' political, social, civil, informational, and psychological rights. A 2006 report by the Cairo Human Rights Institute proposed public service broadcasting as the most suitable model for television and radio in Arab countries, and there is growing support for this model among local

**Box 3.6 The mission of Ofcom in the United Kingdom**

Ofcom's main legal duties are to ensure that:

- A wide range of electronic communications services is provided, including high-speed services such as broadband.
- A wide range of high-quality television and radio programs are provided, appealing to a range of tastes and interests.
- Television and radio services are provided by a broad array of organizations.
- People who watch television and listen to the radio are protected from harmful or offensive material.
- People are protected from unfair treatment in television and radio programs and from invasion of privacy.

*Source:* www.ofcom.org.uk/about/what-is-ofcom

CSOs.[85] The Ofcom model is being discussed in Egypt and Tunisia as an appropriate model for transitioning states.[86] In countries swept up by the protests of the Arab Spring, restructuring and strengthening the professional, administrative, and financial competence of the media might be necessary.

### Building media capacity: Supporting professional and responsible media institutions

Establishing public service broadcasting requires building media capacity at the strategic, institutional, and human resource levels.

From a strategic perspective, governments would be more inclined to invest in developing the media and enhancing their capacity if the media were considered "public property"[87] and a "public service."[88] Arab countries urgently need public media that are nonpartisan, supported by public funds, and broadcasting for the benefit of all. Most western European media started broadcasting under public ownership but with strict legal guarantees of independence from government. Increased investment in public media could support transparency in government and media institutions if plans for media institutions' growth were publicly revealed and regularly reviewed to ensure that standards were being met. Media institutions like the Arab Press Network and the Dubai Press Club support the idea that review encourages transparency.[89]

At the institutional level, fostering a culture that encourages media institutions to exchange information and other knowledge resources can support empowerment. Empowerment is strengthened when media institutions have access to knowledge resources that enable them to produce credible, high-quality content. News archives and research centers reduce media dependence on unedited news agency content and allow journalists to fact-check their news stories. Al Jazeera, for example, has an in-house research center. The creation of local news agencies could further empower the Arab media and reduce the region's reliance on western news agencies.[90]

The media also need better information about audiences. Many audience studies are commercially focused and profit-oriented. Depending on them for developing media content reduces variety and quality and is likely to encourage producers to dumb down their content at the expense of richer cultural and educational programming. Better studies are available from Arab universities and research centers, but they fail to reach media institutions. Making these studies of media audiences and their preferences available to media institutions would help them meet the public's needs for cultural, educational, social, and political programming.

At the human resources level, one of the most powerful ways to empower media institutions is to hire ethical and professional journalists and other media specialists. Professionalism in the mainstream Arab media has fallen several notches, even as the number of newspapers and satellite television channels has grown. Only a minority remain committed to professional standards, and still fewer adhere to internationally recognized media standards of conduct despite their stated commitment.

Too often media coverage, including coverage of sports, incites discord between countries or local communities.[91] Bias in covering legal proceedings and domestic and regional conflicts is common and increases tension, making the Arab media participants in political conflict rather than information providers.[92] Arab media need a code of practice that applies to everyone in the field—from journalists to editors to producers—and which is enforced by independent committees of media professionals and civil society members, not by governments.[93]

More attention to capacity building of media professionals can also improve media institutions. For example, the Studies and Economic Media Center, in cooperation with the European Union delegation in Yemen, has a program for developing media skills among young professionals, particularly the media officers of youth groups and coalitions. This program trains its participants in editing, communicating with the media, and using Facebook and Twitter.[94]

The Arab region now offers more specialized university courses in journalism and turns out more media studies graduates than ever, but the programs focus almost exclusively on technical skills and underemphasize media ethics. Only a few high-quality university programs in journalism, such as the one launched at the American University of Beirut in April 2007, offer training in investigative reporting and on covering elections and wars.[95] Arab universities can help empower media institutions by offering more professional training that meets the needs of Arab journalists. The development of investigative reporting is especially important. While bloggers can help expose corruption, they cannot match the depth of analysis of journalists who are supported by media institutions with the resources and infrastructure needed to pursue cases of government and private-sector corruption (box 3.7).

Restrictive editorial policies also impede the work of journalists, transforming them from media professionals to advertising flacks. The blending of journalism and advertising has spread throughout state, opposition, and private newspapers, whether as editorial policy or as nonprofessional endeavors driven by media interests.

Meanwhile, not enough media institutions offer their employees regular training in advanced technologies and professional skills, such as the training offered by the *Gulf News* newspaper in cooperation with Reuters, which would help overcome journalistic biases (against women, for example). The program covers writing, editing, news gathering, and administration, in addition to an orientation program that focuses on employees' writing and editing skills.[96]

---

**Box 3.7 Varying roles of investigative journalism and news websites**
While the new Internet sites and blogs provide enormous breadth and width of information for those with the time and desire to seek it out, they cannot replace one fundamental function of professional journalism that is vital to democracy: scrutiny of those in power. It takes time, effort, money, and knowledge to monitor public affairs and to expose corruption in government and the private sector. Investigative journalism is not cheap, though it is essential to holding those in power to account. Individual bloggers and small news sites do not fulfill this role.

—Peters 2010

Also important are training programs and seminars that exchange information on best practices, as well as regional and international journalism exchange programs. An example of information exchange is the Arab Press Network, an initiative sponsored by the World Association of Newspapers that posts information online for use by Arab journalists and encourages them to interact.[97] Another example is the Arab Newspaper Development Programme, which supports the efforts of independent newspapers in Arab countries[98] to learn from each other and share commercial and editorial strategies.[99] Media empowered through heightened professionalism are better able to distance themselves from political and ideological biases.

### Empowering women through the media: Stereotypical images and pioneering roles

Women have an important role in Arab media today, beginning with their growing presence on television, including as political talk-show hosts and news anchors.[100] During Egypt's 2011 revolution, Arab media highlighted the country's many female activists. Female activists and journalists, such as Nawara Negm, appeared frequently, offering bold commentary on the protests. In a similar vein the Yemeni journalist and activist Tawakkol Karman received broad media coverage for her leadership in the Yemeni reform movement and following her winning of the Nobel Peace Prize. These accomplishments notwithstanding, numerous problems still afflict women's presence in Arab media. Media portrayals of women are frequently exploitative and deepen stereotypes of women as sex objects or as lacking interest in important issues. Many women in the media appear in a context that reinforces traditional images of women as mothers or housewives only. The 2006 United Nations Development Fund for Women report found that nearly 79 percent of a sample of news stories from Arab countries depicted women in traditional roles.[101] The Global Media Monitoring Project found that 78 percent of news in the Middle East reinforces gender stereotypes (figure 3.8 and table 3.1).[102]

Women are also underrepresented in Arab media as news sources and journalists, according to the monitoring project's regional report for the Middle East (covering Egypt, Jordan, Lebanon, Tunisia, and the United Arab Emirates, as well as Israel; figure 3.9).[103] The report found that Arab media rarely feature women as experts or news sources. Women appear mainly in programs that present 'women's' or 'light' issues. While most entertainment news is presented by women, female journalists present less than half the political and economic news. Most

## Figure 3.8 Gender stereotypes in the news in Arab countries, 2010

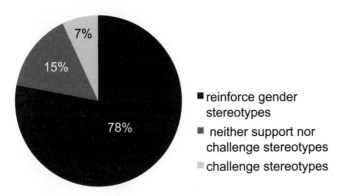

- reinforce gender stereotypes
- neither support nor challenge stereotypes
- challenge stereotypes

*Source:* GMMP 2010.

## Table 3.1. Percentage of news topics that reflect gender stereotypes, by topic

| Topic | Reinforces gender stereotypes | Neither supports nor challenges stereotypes | Challenges stereotypes |
|---|---|---|---|
| The economy | 83 | 13 | 4 |
| Politics/government | 81 | 13 | 6 |
| Crime/violence | 79 | 20 | 1 |
| The girl child | 75 | 0 | 25 |
| Social/legal | 72 | 16 | 12 |
| Science/health | 68 | 18 | 14 |
| Other | 83 | 13 | 4 |
| Celebrity/arts/media/sports | 64 | 19 | 17 |
| **Total** | **78** | **15** | **7** |

*Source:* GMMP 2010.

### Figure 3.9 Women in visual media in the Arab world, 2010

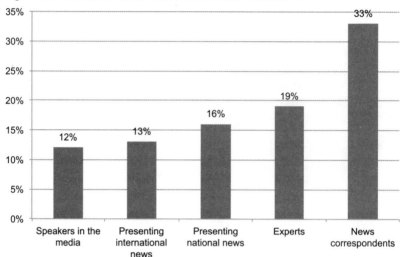

*Source:* GMMP 2010.

news revolves around men as newsmakers. Indeed, only 16 percent of national news items and 13 percent of international news focuses on women, and only 19 percent of experts and 12 percent of discussants in the media are women. Moreover, women make up just 33 percent of news correspondents in the region.

Greater participation of women in all kinds of programming would strengthen Arab television. Women now make up a majority of students in Arab university media programs. Since 2007 women have been accepted into media and international relations courses at Umm al-Qura University in Saudi Arabia,[104] and journalism organizations like the Arab Women Media Center, which trained more than 350 women journalists between 2008 and 2010, offer training to female media professionals.[105] Arab media institutions can thus draw on a growing number of highly qualified women to enrich their programming and make it more representative of women's contributions to Arab society.

More women in editorial and managerial decision-making positions in media institutions could strengthen these institutions, which are still dominated by men, and give women greater political and social influence.[106] Arab countries need mechanisms to help women enter media decision-making circles. One approach is a quota system for management boards. Another is to enable the many prominent female journalists in Arab countries to use their experience to support other women entering the profession by exchanging information and sharing best practices. Female writers and directors can use their television programs to confront gender stereotypes. All journalists, men and women, would benefit from training in gender awareness to avoid gender bias in media reports and confront it in the workplace.

Finally, the development of media in Arab countries toward supporting and empowering women requires improving media practices and the image of women—and increasing their participation. Female journalists continue to face discrimination when gathering material for a story, dealing with officials, and seeking access to public and private institutions. Also, in religiously conservative countries like Saudi Arabia, women journalists face daunting challenges, from restrictions on their movements in public places to bans on attending press conferences.[107] Media syndicates could support female journalists by monitoring such cases and providing opportunities for female journalists to file complaints without fear of reprisal. Female journalists often do not report harassment for fear of losing their jobs. All Arab media institutions and workers would become more productive and the workplace more harmonious if sexual harassment in the workplace had serious consequences for offenders.

This chapter has attempted to provide a broad overview of the challenges and opportunities facing the potential for the Arab media to play a role in empowering citizens in the region. By highlighting examples of best practice, the chapter hopes to illustrate that reform is possible. However, the complexity of achieving reform is illustrated through the presentation of the numerous interlocking issues underlying the media landscape in the Arab world and the persistence of age-old problems. The political transitions that began in 2011 carry with them a degree of hope for the future of the Arab media, but as with democracy, true and meaningful reform is a slow, gradual process that cannot be achieved overnight.

## Notes

1   Zayani 2005.
2   Al Arabiya 2010.
3   UNDP 2003b.
4   World Association of Newspapers 2010.
5   Internet World Statistics 2012.
6   Dubai Press Club 2009.
7   Dubai Press Club 2009.
8   UNDP 2002c.

9   UNDP 2004b.
10  Dubai Press Club 2009.
11  Dubai Press Club 2009.
12  UNDP 2003b.
13  UNDP 2004b, 2005b, 2009d.
14  UNDP 2002c.
15  UNDP 2002c.
16  Dubai Press Club 2009.
17  UNDP 2003b, 2004b.
18  UNDP 2003b, 2004b, 2009d.
19  UNDP 2003b, 2004b.
20  UNDP 2004b.
21  Shaqir 2001.
22  UNDP 2003b.
23  UNDP 2003b.
24  UNDP 2003b.
25  UNDP 2002c.
26  Yom 2005.
27  UNDEF 2009c.
28  Bernardi 2010.
29  Reinisch 2010.
30  UNDP 2009c.
31  el-Mikawy 2004.
32  AAI 2007.
33  www.arabbarometer.org/index.html.
34  See chapter 8 in this volume.
35  Dubai Press Club 2009.
36  Wahba 2010.
37  High Commission for Coordination between Satellite Channels 2010.
38  CAMP and CIS 2010.
39  Schech 2002.
40  See chapter 9 in this volume.
41  Dubai Press Club 2009.
42  Al-Hail 2000.
43  Zaidah 2010.
44  Mediterranean Virtual University, ls-ewdssps.ces.strath.ac.uk/MVU/partners.html.
45  The Arab Open University 2011, www.arabou.org/openedu.htm.
46  www.internetworldstats.com/stats7.htm.
47  UNDP 2009c.
48  Lens on Lebanon 2011, www.lensonlebanon.org/about.htm.
49  Rural Knowledge Network 2011, reefnet.gov.sy.
50  Dubai Press Club 2009.
51  Almasude 1999.

52  UNDP 2006a.
53  Coronel 2003.
54  Al Jazeera 2011, http://cc.aljazeera.net/content/about-repository.
55  Arab Press Network 2005a.
56  Arab Decision 2011, www.arabdecision.org.
57  Hofheinz 2005.
58  Arab Press Network 2009a.
59  Shobaki 2006.
60  Pies 2008.
61  Hofheinz 2005.
62  El Gody 2007.
63  The Arab League Educational, Cultural, and Scientific Organization, www.alecso.org.tn.
64  Bassiouny 1994.
65  Freedom House 2009.
66  Federation of Arab Journalists 2009.
67  Zaki 2007.
68  Website of the Egyptian Ministry of Information 2008.
69  Ayish 2010.
70  Wood 2010.
71  Al-'Abidi 2008.
72  The Global Arab Network 2011.
73  Reporters without Borders 2010b.
74  Rogers 2000.
75  United Nations 2010.
76  United Nations Public Administration Programme 2012.
77  United Nations Public Administration Programme 2012.
78  Sakr 2007.
79  Nasrallah 2007.
80  UNDP 2009c.
81  Thai 2010.
82  Sakr 2007; Reporters without Borders 2008.
83  Thai 2010.
84  Goodman and Shapiro 2009.
85  Ayish 2010.
86  Institut Panos Paris 2011.
87  Peters 2010.
88  Ayish 2010.
89  Arab Press Network 2009b.
90  Deane et al. 2003; Al-Musa 2003.
91  BBC News 2009b; Abu 'Arja 2003.
92  Khatib 2009.
93  Al-Fanik 1998.
94  Studies and Economic Media Center 2012.

95   Arab Press Network 2008,
     www.aub.edu.lb/news/archive/preview.php?id=73880.
96   Arab Press Network 2005b.
97   Arab Press Network 2011.
98   Arab Press Network 2009c.
99   Arab Press Network 2009c.
100  Sakr 2004, 2007.
101  UNIFEM 2006.
102  GMMP 2010.
103  GMMP 2010.
104  Al-Khamri 2008.
105  El Imam 2010.
106  Abu-Fadil 2004.
107  Al-Khamri 2008.

# CHAPTER 4

# Fighting Corruption:
## From Missing Link to Development Priority

Mustafa Khawaja

Corruption has engaged people's attention in Arab countries for some time, though not always with urgency or the desired impact. Combating corruption did not become a pressing priority until the early 2000s, and the push for reform intensified during the "uprisings" of 2011 and the events that followed.

Calls for reform emerged sporadically in the 1990s, led by a few individuals and civil society organizations (CSOs) that argued for the need to oppose and expose corruption. But their narrow efforts failed to overcome the many challenges, from sparse information on patterns of corruption and mechanisms to fight it to limited expertise and no common space for launching an open dialogue. Most governments did not add fighting corruption to their reform programs.

In 2003 the United Nations Convention against Corruption (UNCAC) marked a turning point in official support to combat corruption. National and regional initiatives were launched, but progress remained slight. Then at the end of 2010, the region erupted in unprecedented popular demands for reform and better living conditions, catapulting corruption to the top of the priority list.

As calls for rooting out corruption escalated nationally, regionally, and internationally, institutions developed methodologies for assessing, measuring, and curbing it. This work progressed alongside initiatives within the UNCAC framework. Concern has been especially strong where major societal forces and groups, such as CSOs, have worked to expose corruption and demand that it end, including in Egypt, Libya, and Tunisia.

The global and regional consensus on the need to fight corruption and strengthen enforcement is unprecedented. Public policymakers, leading intellectuals, and reform activists in the region should take up the challenge of curbing corruption, a mission that has assumed strategic dimensions in light of recent developments in the region. This chapter examines corruption—its types, causes, and effects—concentrating on common patterns in the region. It seeks to clarify the reality of corruption in Arab countries and of efforts to combat it and offers ideas for discussion and action.

## Causes and Effects of Corruption

Corruption exists in all countries, though its prevalence and intensity vary. Agreeing on a definition is difficult, as corruption is influenced by many political, economic, social, cultural, legal, and institutional forces. This chapter adopts Transparency International's definition of corruption as the abuse of entrusted authority for private gain (material or not), which aligns closely with global perceptions and includes the private sector as well as the public sector. UNCAC does not define corruption but classifies it by the types of practices considered corrupt and calls on countries to criminalize them. These practices include all types of bribery, particularly the corruption of national and foreign public officials and employees of public international institutions; embezzlement of all forms; abuse of influence and office; and illicit enrichment. UNCAC also calls for criminalizing money laundering and other practices that link concealment and obstruction of justice with corruption.

The simplest categories are *petty corruption*, or practices that affect basic transactions between citizens and public- and private-sector employees and that incur benefits of limited value, and *grand corruption*, or practices that occur on a higher level, which generally involves senior government officials and incurs substantial benefits. These two types of corrupt practice can also be termed *administrative corruption* and *financial corruption*, and they usually take the form of bribery and embezzlement. In addition, *political corruption* or *state capture* is used to describe corruption by high-level government officials who abuse their political power to strengthen their position or to enrich themselves or their associates (box 4.1). Estimating the gains of such corruption is difficult. Most of the time, this type of corruption harms the state and society. Other illegal practices (such as election fraud) usually accompany such corruption; these practices may not fall within the UNCAC's understanding of corruption, although they are connected.

**Box 4.1 Political corruption and state capture**

Studies by nonpartisan Arab and international institutions have looked into the nature of corruption in the Arab region. The research shows the spread of political corruption, whereby a small segment of society seizes control of decision-making positions in the state's institutions: executive (government and its institutions, security, and resources); legislative (parliament); and judicial (the judiciary and the public prosecution). The direct and indirect impacts of these corrupt practices extend to civil society and media institutions. Capture of the state by elite groups has impeded most local and international attempts at reform and fighting corruption.

—Azmi Shu'aibi, general coordinator,
AMAN–Coalition for Integrity and Accountability

Many factors drive corruption, and they are not always easy to identify and diagnose. Individuals might be driven to corrupt activities by personal needs, characteristics, aspirations, or attributes. Structural drivers, such as weakness in legislation and monitoring mechanisms, make corruption easier. The United Nations Development Programme publication *Corruption and Development* identifies the following main reasons for corruption commonly cited by stakeholders: absence of adequate regulation, policies, and legislation; weak implementation and oversight; lack of accountability and transparency; lack of regulations and institutional controls (including institutional weakness in legislative and judicial systems); absence of integrity; monopoly of authority; tolerance of broad discretion; low wages; high reward/risk ratio; and low rates of corruption detection.[1]

Corruption not only depletes government resources, but also weakens the administrative system, slows economic growth, paralyzes the political system, and imperils service delivery, setting back development and threatening national interests and human security. Corruption leads to a loss of confidence in those who govern (figure 4.1) and threatens political stability. It undermines political and judicial institutions as well as people's sense of patriotism by emphasizing competition for power and wealth over welfare for all. Moreover, corruption disrupts the national distribution of wealth, leading to vast income disparities.

## Figure 4.1 Public trust in politicians and CPI in some Arab countries, 2012

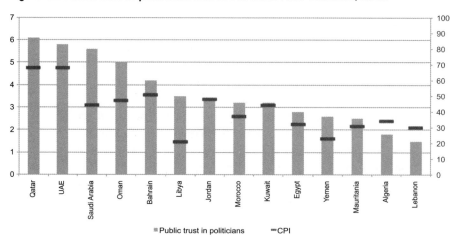

*Note:* CPI: 0 is highly corrupt; 100 least corrupt
Public trust in politicians 1 = very low; 7 = very high.
*Source:* World Economic Forum. *Global Competitiveness Report 2012–2013; Transparency International. CPI 2012*

Corruption also weakens economic growth and destabilizes the investment environment, burdening investors and consumers alike. Businesspeople raise prices to cover the costs of paying bribes,[2] thus passing the costs on to consumers—or to the state budget when the government is the buyer. Corruption increases the total cost for businesses engaged in international transactions by an estimated 10 percent—equivalent to as much as 25 percent of the total cost of purchase contracts in developing countries. The costs of corruption amount to a 20 percent tax on transferring business activities from a country where corruption is low to one where it is medium or high. The components of Transparency International's Corruption Perception Index (CPI) show clearly that corporations use data on the frequency of corruption to guide their investments, resulting in huge losses to developmental efforts in countries with high corruption.

Corruption also reduces public revenues by facilitating tax evasion and capital flight, which slow development by depriving the state of revenue for operating programs and assisting the poor. Corruption also undermines the quality of infrastructure and public services, while increasing poverty and infringing on human rights. In the rentier economies of some Arab states, corruption diverts investment toward nonproductive activities, stimulating competition based on corrupt practices, rather than strong performance.[3] Countries with large reserves of natural resources, such as oil and natural gas, are particularly prone to corruption and illicit enrichment by the elite.[4] Global Witness and other advocacy organizations record violations of regulatory provisions on the use of natural resources in countries the world over.[5]

## Understanding Corruption in the Arab Region

While corruption—its types, causes, and effects—in the Arab region is similar to that in the rest of the world, in-depth studies are needed that delve into specific causes and impacts of corruption and can guide the development of systematic and effective means to prevent and fight it. Among the loudest calls for change in Arab countries today are demands to fight corruption by changing institutional structures and widening political participation, while excluding the powerful elites who have lost the confidence of citizens. The political, economic, and social problems that led to the Arab Spring are widely believed to have resulted largely from the spread of corruption and its infiltration into all levels of governing institutions. In turn, these popular movements exposed many cases of suspected corruption and emboldened people to demand that corrupt practices be disclosed and the perpetrators punished.

Various organizations in the Arab region have defined corruption. The Arab Anti-Corruption Organization defines it as "the illegal acquisition of the two sources of power in society, political power and wealth, in all sectors of society."[6] The Arab Region Parliamentarians against Corruption defines it as "a complex, difficult phenomenon that usually involves individuals from the public (governmental) and private sectors who undertake an activity that is illegal, illicit, and unethical, that reduces a country's economic opportunities, and that taints its social and political institutions."[7] But most activists in the region have adopted Transparency International's definition. The 2010 Arab Convention against Corruption, though noting that "corruption is a multifaceted criminal phenomenon that has negative impacts on ethical values, political life, and economic and social aspects," did not endorse a specific definition. Rather, it followed UNCAC's approach, identifying the practices to be criminalized as corrupt, which largely correspond to those described in UNCAC.

The types of corruption in the Arab region are similar to the types found elsewhere, although political corruption is thought to be a greater problem in Arab countries because of the weak, underperforming state institutions and lack of transparency in public- and private-sector decision making. Political corruption typically brings perpetrators enormous monetary gain through major business deals.

And beyond the money stolen, political corruption undermines the effectiveness of the political system and the executive, legislative, and judicial institutions.

In Arab countries ruling elites tend to remain in power long enough to form close alliances with political and economic elites and security institutions, paralyzing the state's oversight functions and turning the state into the elites' personal property. The exposure of extreme cases of kleptocratic corruption following the Arab Spring supports this perception. Financial and administrative corruption, identified from international indicators, are more prevalent in countries with lower average per capita income.

Despite the extent of political corruption, anticorruption efforts focus mainly on financial and administrative corruption—with the exception of some countries that have experienced radical change in the governing elites since the Arab Spring. Detecting these types of corruption and remedying them can be relatively easy, but in most cases the influential sphere of state elites remains untouched. The amount of lost state revenue from financial and administrative corruption is usually not large, but this type of corruption establishes a pattern of behavior that affects society's value system ('integrity') and reflects directly on prospects for human development.

### Box 4.2 Corruption and democratic change

In a number of Arab states political corruption has impeded democratization and development through rigged elections, whose outcomes are guaranteed and known in advance, and privatization and resource-management policies that enable the ruling elite to commandeer resources for their own benefit and that of their private-sector partners. The ruling elite has been able to act with impunity by securing control over public oversight bodies by hand-picking their heads, controlling the resources allocated to them, and linking the outcomes of their actions to official approval by the government, the head of state, or the official political authority. In many cases these oversight bodies are prevented from holding senior officials accountable without prior agreement from the political authority.

—Azmi Shu'aibi, general coordinator, Coalition
for Integrity and Accountability (AMAN, Palestine)

The driving force behind political corruption is the weakened legitimacy of a political system that enables political leaders to treat the state as their property. Corruption becomes a tool of governance and a parallel system of control. In the absence of legitimate control mechanisms and separation of powers, the ruler makes unilateral decisions that reinforce the loyalty of supporters. This situation is worsened by political instability, political violence, and an absence of political participation, whether because the state curtails individual freedoms or because people are too busy trying to meet basic needs. Other causes for the spread of corruption are the weakness of competing political parties and the fragility of civil society. Traditional structures lend support to this type of corruption, as do traditions of loyalty to family and tribe at the expense of commitment to the nation and the rule of law.

Economic factors can also contribute to the spread of corruption. In a rentier economy, individuals come to focus exclusively on making money, whatever the price or source, weakening support for accountability and facilitating crony capitalism. The economic dependence in a rentier economy also spreads corruption. Even aid, intended to catalyze development, comes to be used to enable corruption among the elite. Multinational corporations, often able to flout rules of transparency and integrity, can spread corruption through their commercial transactions—buying contracts and closing deals—and earmark a huge share of their budget for bribes to the ruling elite.[8] Transparency International's 2011 Bribe Payers Index confirms this pattern in its study of the world's twenty-eight largest economies—representing approximately 80 percent of the global flow of commodities, services, and investments.[9] Privatization offers another opportunity for corruption, through the undervaluing of state assets made possible by inadequate information and transparency, factors associated with weak regulatory and judicial institutions.

The communications revolution has opened new possibilities for gathering information and comparing economic and social conditions across countries. By stirring up envy of other countries' prosperity, these comparisons may encourage corruption.[10] Several studies link corruption with attempts to outsmart regulatory and legal controls following economic liberalization and participation in a globalized economy.[11] Globalization, by increasing trade, has accelerated money laundering and made it easier for expatriates to avoid paying taxes in their country of residence.[12]

## Corruption Impedes Development

There is growing understanding of how corruption stunts development (box 4.3). Research finds that corruption, while prevalent in both developed and developing countries, is usually chronic and pervasive in developing countries, spreading to all levels and hurting the vulnerable more than others. "Corruption harms the poor in an unbalanced manner by way of transferring funds assigned to development to other fields and weakening the government's ability to provide essential services, thus exacerbating inequality and injustice and impeding investments and foreign aid."[13] The German Agency for Technical Cooperation notes that empirical studies demonstrate the link between the spread of corruption and worsening macroeconomic conditions, especially per capita income.[14] One study found that by fighting corruption and strengthening the rule of law, countries can quadruple their GNI over time and reduce infant mortality by 75 percent.[15]

An estimated $1 trillion is paid in bribes each year worldwide—amounting to more than 3 percent of world income in 2002.[16] The amount of money misappropriated or stolen from developing countries each year and diverted from development is more than ten times the nearly $100 billion they receive annually in foreign aid. More than 70 percent of small and medium-size companies in transition economies, forced to pay large bribes to government employees in order to operate, see corruption as an obstacle to their growth and the quality of their goods and services.[17] Tax breaks granted by corrupt government employees reduce tax revenue, hurting service provision. Citizens pay the price of corruption twice—once as a consumer and again as a user of public services.

Consider the construction sector in Saudi Arabia and the lack of strong accountability measures. Many politicians and legal experts say that corruption is rampant in the infrastructure sector and that addressing it requires making officials accountable. As one expert put it: "The destruction to the country's infrastructure wrought by floods reveals the huge extent of financial corruption. Similarly, it makes it clear that holding perpetrators accountable will require genuine political will on the part of the higher authorities in addition to stringent public oversight."[18] Lebanon's energy sector also suffers the effects of corruption: price controls favor private stakeholders, while citizens are forced to accommodate inadequate hours of service and unreliable quality.[19] The bankruptcy of Algeria's largest bank, El Khalifa Bank, because of embezzlement cost the economy some $1.3 billion; during the bankruptcy proceedings it became apparent that the authorities had been aware of the bank's illegal actions for some time but had failed to act.[20]

Corruption also undermines the provision of aid, for both humanitarian assistance and reconstruction. In Iraq, for example, $8.7 billion of the $9.1 billion in reconstruction funds went missing—96 percent of funding just disappeared, presumably into the pockets of Iraqis, occupation forces, and U.S. officials.[21] Billions of dollars of development assistance are lost each year to bribery and misappropriation, and billions more to corrupt international business dealings. Funds stolen from developing countries through corruption are remitted to safe havens, making the UNCAC section on asset recovery one of the most important.

### Transparency International's Corruption Perception Index shows widespread corruption

Transparency International's Corruption Perception Index shows that corruption is a global problem.[22] More than two-thirds of countries ranked in the bottom half on the index in 2012. Denmark, Finland, New Zealand, and Sweden ranked highest, with scores of ninety on a scale from zero (most corrupt) to one hundred (least corrupt). Countries experiencing political instability and conflict ranked at the bottom: Sudan tied for the second lowest position, with thirteen points, and Somalia, the Democratic People's Republic of Korea, and Afghanistan tied for last, with eight points each.[23] While there are concerns about the ability of the index to accurately measure corruption, it remains a valid tool for monitoring general trends in corruption in different countries.

Careful interpretation of the index confirms that corruption in the Arab region is both widespread and severe (box 4.3). Only two Arab countries

---

**Box 4.3 Interpreting the Corruption Perception Index**
Most countries in the Arab region are ranked low (high corruption) on Transparency International's Corruption Perception Index, confirming the common perception that the region suffers from endemic corruption in nearly all aspects of public life: administrative, political, economic, financial, social, and cultural.

Most of the Arab countries in the higher ranks (low corruption) are wealthy oil producers. This might reflect the index's greater sensitivity to smaller cases of corruption since data for the index come from interviews; people involved in major cases of bribery are unlikely to declare their crimes in an interview.

—Abdesselam Aboudrar, president, Central Authority
for Corruption Prevention (ICPC), Morocco

were within the top (least corrupt) quartile of the 176 participating states, while seven were in the lowest quartile, and half were in the midrange.

There seems to be some correlation between corruption and bribery,[24] though the correlation is weaker than might be expected. Considering that bribery is a form of corruption, it seems logical that countries with high levels of corruption would also have high levels of bribery. And that is the case for many countries, but not all. Qatar ranks low for corruption on the CPI and also has a low percentage of people who have encountered bribery (table 4.1). At the other end of the scale, Lebanon, Iraq, and Yemen rank high on corruption and also have a high percentage of people who have encountered bribery. Yet Comoros and Djibouti rank high for corruption on the CPI but have a low percentage for exposure to bribery. And despite the high percentages of people in

**Table 4.1 Correlation between percentage of people who have encountered bribery and scores on the CPI, 2008**

|  | Percentage of people who have encountered bribery | CPI[a] |
|---|---|---|
| Jordan | 5 | 5.1 |
| Qatar | 8 | 6.5 |
| Comoros | 11 | 2.5 |
| Djibouti | 13 | 3.0 |
| Tunisia | 14 | 4.4 |
| Mauritania | 18 | 2.8 |
| Kuwait | 19 | 4.3 |
| UAE | 20 | 5.9 |
| Bahrain | 20 | 5.4 |
| Morocco | 24 | 3.5 |
| Egypt | 24 | 2.8 |
| Syria | 24 | 2.1 |
| Algeria | 28 | 3.2 |
| Saudi Arabia | 29 | 3.5 |
| Lebanon | 30 | 3.0 |
| Iraq | 36 | 1.3 |
| Yemen | 41 | 2.3 |

a: CPI 2008: 0 is most corrupt, and 10 is least corrupt.
*Source:* Transparency International. CPI 2008; UNDP 2010c.

Bahrain and the United Arab Emirates who have encountered bribery, the countries ranked favorably compared with other Arab countries on the CPI. These results suggest that bribery might not be the most common form of corruption, might not have the greatest impact, or might not be considered a form of corruption by many people. Alternatively, the CPI might not give an accurate picture of bribery.

### Inverse correlation between corruption and deprivation in education, health, and standard of living

Corruption's negative impact on development is clear from correlations between corruption and several indicators of development drawn from the Multidimensional Poverty Index,[25] which considers deprivations in education, health, and standard of living. There are strong correlations between corruption and deprivations in health and education and a low per capita share of GNI. High corruption (low CPI) is correlated with rising deprivations in health and education services and falling per capita GNI. The correlation is weaker for standard of living. Mauritania, Yemen, Comoros, and Somalia—which have the region's highest education deprivation—also rank among the most corrupt (see figure 4.2), while the United Arab Emirates, Jordan, and Tunisia have low rates of education deprivation and rank among the least corrupt (high scores on the CPI). However, Tunisia also illustrates the need for caution in interpreting findings based on perceptions: despite its low rate of education deprivation and its strong showing on the CPI, recent events have exposed major corruption.

These trends in the correlation between corruption and development apply strongly to per capita share of GDP, to a lesser extent to health deprivation, and even more weakly to standard of living. There is a fairly strong correlation between the CPI and the composite Human Development Index (figure 4.3), implying that countries need to fight corruption to enable better human development (boxes 4.4 and 4.5).

### Inverse correlation between the Corruption Perception Index and the Prosperity Index

Like development, prosperity is advanced when corruption is reduced, although not in easily quantifiable terms. Trends in the Legatum Prosperity Index (based on eight indicators of income and quality of life)[26] and the CPI for 2011 reveal a general correlation (figure 4.4). Countries near the top on the CPI (less corrupt) also have higher rankings on the prosperity index. The measures share some data sources, though methodologies and rankings differ.

### Figure 4.2 Correlation between CPI and deprivation in education, 2008

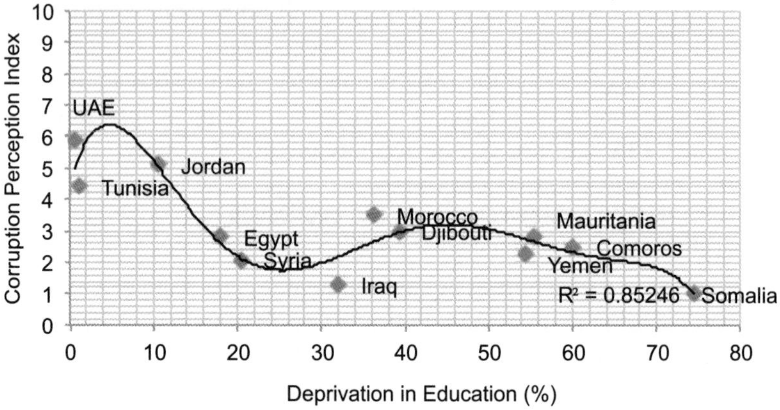

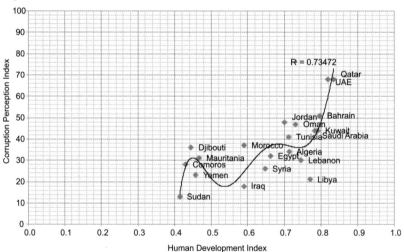

*Note:* For CPI 2008, 0 is most corrupt, and 10 is least corrupt.
Deprivation in Education: Percentage of people who are deprived in education.
*Source:* Transparency International. CPI 2008; UNDP 2010c.

### Figure 4.3 Correlation between the CPI and the HDI, 2012

*Note:* For CPI 2012, 0 is most corrupt, and 100 is least corrupt; for the HDI, a composite index of life expectancy, educational attainment, and income, 0 is low and 1 is high.
*Source:* Transparency International. CPI 2012; UNDP 2013.

**Box 4.4 Don't let corruption kill development**

When public money is stolen for private gain, it means fewer resources to build schools, hospitals, roads, and water treatment facilities. When foreign aid is diverted into private bank accounts, major infrastructure projects come to a halt. Corruption enables fake or substandard medicines to be dumped on the market, and hazardous waste to be dumped in landfill sites and in oceans. The vulnerable suffer first and worst.

—UN Secretary-General Ban Ki-moon
on International Anti-Corruption Day, 2009

**Figure 4.4. Correlation between the CPI and Legatum Prosperity Index, 2011**

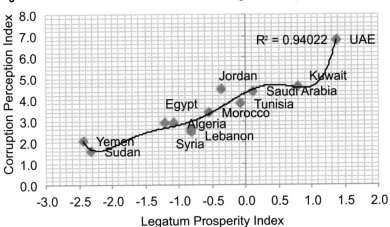

*Note:* For CPI, 0 is most corrupt, and 10 is least corrupt for the Legatum Prosperity Index. It is the average of its sub-indices scores; higher is better.
*Source:* Legatum Institute. Legatum Prosperity Index. 2011; Transparency International. CPI 2011.

**Box 4.5 Strengthening the role of the private sector in fighting corruption to meet development requirements in the Arab region**

There is now an unprecedented Arab consensus on the need to fight corruption. One issue that has not been given enough attention is the role of the private sector in fighting corruption.

Corruption hurts the private sector in many ways: by diverting its resources, distorting competition, weakening efficiency, choking the flow of foreign investment, and worsening poverty and unemployment. Corruption may also create economic elites who monopolize benefits, waste public funds, and distort the distribution of wealth. In recent years, several initiatives have been launched to engage the private sector in fighting corruption. However, these initiatives have not yet been translated into formal strategies in Arab countries. Radical change in the pace of development is hard to imagine without real progress on transparency and accountability in the relationship between the public and private sectors.

Preventive measures against corruption are necessary in public–private sector transactions, as is stricter enforcement of existing laws. However, both sides must also engage in constructive dialogue that takes into account the nature of the private sector in each country, its development requirements, and its role in the national development strategy. The mechanism for reviewing implementation of the United Nations Convention against Corruption could form one of the main channels for this discussion, in preparation for building an honest partnership between the public and private sectors in the region and responding to people's aspirations for a better future.

—Ali bin Fetais al-Marri, chairman, third session of member countries of the United Nations Convention against Corruption

Individual components of the prosperity index can be correlated with corruption and thus with a country's anticorruption efforts. Each component reflects some basic human need, which explains its correlation with resources and their optimal use on communal and individual levels. Beyond meeting citizens' basic needs, countries strive to provide opportunities for citizens to prosper and achieve happiness, and that requires empowering them to support development. Prosperity necessitates fighting corruption and building a strong, supportive society that dedicates its resources to citizens' needs and development.

## Current Efforts to Fight Corruption

Lack of information on the extent of corruption is one of the biggest impediments to combating it. Without evidence on the spread of corruption, it is harder to generate the political will to fight it. The lack of data also makes it difficult to address actions identified as corrupt and to prosecute and hold perpetrators accountable. The lack of data springs from shortcomings in transparency and access to information and from limitations on freedoms of the press and expression. Corruption occurs furtively, requiring effort to uncover. The lack of data also results from inherent difficulties in measuring corruption and from weaknesses in state institutional structures, political systems, and administrative arrangements.

For these reasons, international anticorruption organizations have tried to identify corruption by focusing on the attitudes of citizens, experts, or economic institutions, relying on impressions or opinions rather than objective facts based on evidence. This approach leads to methodological concerns, disregard for local specificity, possible gaps between impressions and reality, and an inability to specify the scale or extent of the problem. But while such approaches preclude comparisons between countries or conclusions based on the extent of corruption in any one country, they can provide useful information on trends.

Many overlapping factors contribute to the spread of corruption. Some can be controlled; others are beyond the scope of national control because of their international dimensions. Cracking down on corruption requires all segments of society to work together and to reach consensus on the need to rise to meet the challenges.

Several features of the context in the Arab region contribute to the spread of corruption and make it difficult to fight. Especially important are the relationships between the political and economic elites and influential figures in the Arab states, which are shrouded in secrecy. An example is the recent revelation that banks in Egypt, Libya, and Tunisia accepted enormous deposits from ousted political elites. While there has been no judicial finding that these vast funds were acquired illegally, the inability to trace them to a legitimate source is at least prima facie evidence of some kind of wrongdoing. Violations of bureaucratic regulations have enabled elites to gain personal advantages through investments, weapons deals, contracts, equipment sales, and implementation of huge projects in the oil, gas, infrastructure, and financial sectors. Aspects of Arab culture also lend themselves to exploitation in ways that facilitate the spread of corruption. For example, gifts and bonuses rooted in social customs have been perverted into corrupt acts, while corrupt acts are excused as expressions of authentic Arab culture. Both Arab and Islamic culture prohibit misappropriation, fraud, bribery, and other forms of corruption.

Responsibility for the spread of corruption is often assumed to rest with the government (figure 4.5). However, many countries that have made progress against corruption have demonstrated that responsibility is rarely one-sided. To achieve a society based on integrity, all parties must work to raise awareness of the damage caused by corruption and assume responsibility for fighting it, from state institutions to civil society organizations, the private sector (box 4.6), and ordinary citizens (figure 4.6). Laws and regulations must be formulated and steps taken to reduce corruption and its root causes.

**Figure 4.5 Diversion of public funds to companies, individuals, or groups due to corruption, 2012**

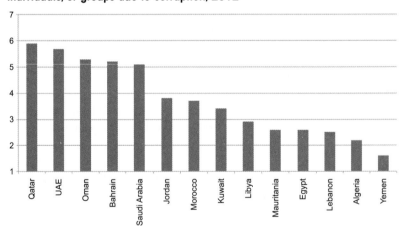

*Note:* One is "very common," and seven is "never occurs."
*Source:* World Economic Forum, Global Competitiveness Report 2012–2013.

**Box 4.6 Some Arab countries have taken action in cases of corruption**

There are many examples in Arab countries of practical action to crack down on corruption and hold perpetrators accountable:

Jordan sentenced several former officials and businessmen to three-year prison terms for corruption. Parliament also opened an investigation into the so-called casino affair, involving a government deal with an investor to build and operate a casino, which is illegal in Jordan. In addition, the Jordanian Anti-Corruption Commission reported that the public prosecutor's office reviewed 122 cases in the first half of 2010—101 of which were referred to judicial authorities for suspected corruption. The commission is also monitoring several unpublicized corruption cases, such as the illegal sale of animal feed subsidies, and some sixty municipal cases; new cases surface daily.

The examining magistrate of Algeria's capital court placed the secretary-general of the Ministry of Public Works and the secretary-general of the Ministry of Fisheries in temporary custody for suspected corruption. An examining magistrate ordered the head of Sonatrach Petroleum Corporation, an Algerian government-owned company, to appear before him to respond to allegations of corruption related to tenders and contracts. The El Khalifa Bank embezzlement case was also pursued by the courts.

In Bahrain, a minister of state was arrested for money laundering.

Egypt's parliament stripped fourteen deputies of immunity to investigate accusations of misuse of state-funded medical treatment—intended for people too poor to pay for treatment—for their own enrichment.

A survey by Yemen's Anti-Corruption Commission indicated that 141 cases were reported to the commission, nineteen of which had been pursued by mid-2008.

The Audit Bureau in Lebanon detected malpractice in value-added tax refunds at the Ministry of Finance and referred the case to the judiciary.

**Figure 4.6 People's engagement in the fight against corruption, by region, 2010**

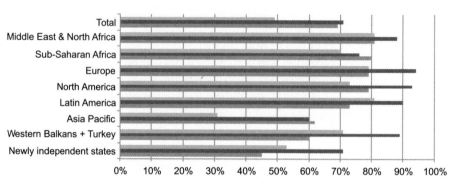

■ Could imagine themselves getting involved in fighting corruption
■ Would support their colleagues or friends if they fought against corruption
■ Think that ordinary people can make a difference in the fight against corruption

*Source:* Transparency International 2010, Global Corruption Barometer 2010.

Sixteen Arab countries have joined UNCAC to combat corruption, and four others have signed but are not yet members. By joining UNCAC, countries proclaim their interest in establishing a more effective, global mechanism to combat corruption and assess implementation and progress. As UN Secretary-General Ban Ki-moon remarked in a message on International Anti-Corruption Day in 2009, "From now on, states will be judged by the actions they take to fight corruption, not just the promises they make."[27] The global financial crisis of 2008–2009 created additional incentives to continue anticorruption efforts and strengthen governance reforms, while offering important lessons on the need to promote integrity and transparency.[28]

In addition, many countries in the Arab region (Iraq, Jordan, Morocco, Saudi Arabia, and Yemen, among others) have formulated national anticorruption strategies. Official anticorruption bodies have been established, and courts have been formed to prosecute cases of alleged corruption (in Palestine and Yemen, for example). Amendments have been introduced to reform governance, parliamentary elections, and municipal and local councils; expand freedom of the press; promote the participation of civil society institutions; criminalize corruption; and hold perpetrators to account.

High-level conferences have dealt with the challenges of fighting corruption and publicized the damage corruption causes in loss of resources and setbacks in human development. The Arab Anti-Corruption and

Integrity Network was formed in 2008 as an official regional network, joining the unofficial network of Arab Parliamentarians against Corruption, which also works to keep abreast of developments in UNCAC implementation. Branches or offices of Transparency International were also established in several Arab countries. The UNDP Regional Bureau for Arab States has noted Arab states' progress in developing legal and administrative frameworks, enhancing political will, and expanding the scope of anticorruption activity officially and through civil society institutions.[29]

Many countries have opened investigations against senior officials and prosecuted those found to be involved in corruption. There have been many complaints, however, that action has been slow and that the authorities have allowed wide latitude to accused perpetrators. Cases have also halted abruptly, without reaching any conclusion. Some people charge that anticorruption efforts have been a sham, sacrificing minor corrupt officials while protecting those at the top. Despite the charges, there have been some prominent cases of influential figures put on trial (box 4.7).

During the changes in political system launched in Egypt, Libya, and Tunisia following the 2011 uprisings, hoards of money were uncovered that had been hidden by members of the elite. Steps were taken to recover the funds, and senior government officials and businesspeople were detained pending investigation for corruption and abuse of power. Similar cases have been uncovered in other Arab countries, and there have been declarations of intent to bring about radical reform. These actions reflect a desire for less corrupt societies and a trend toward a

---

**Box 4.7 Corruption and conflict of interest**

The participation of major businesspeople in official political or party posts without any clear methods for preventing conflict of interest has provided ample opportunities for corruption and facilitated the abuse of office and exchange of benefits between centers of influence and officials. Those involved have taken advantage of the ineffectiveness of legislation and officials' lack of awareness of the principles of transparency, accountability, and integrity.

—Azmi Shu'aibi, general coordinator,
AMAN–Coalition for Integrity and Accountability

social culture that holds offenders accountable and focuses on institution building for better governance.

Although some people see these promising starts as falling well short of what is needed, they could be a springboard to more systematic anticorruption efforts and actions to promote development. Stripping immunity from those under suspicion is fundamental to accountability; the elite of the former political systems in Egypt, Libya, and Tunisia could not have been prosecuted had they not first been stripped of institutional cover.

Multiple challenges remain for minimizing corruption and achieving greater human development in the Arab world (box 4.8). Arab countries need a comprehensive approach based on a diagnosis of the types, manifestations, and causes of corruption within a rentier state whose political structure enables members of the elite and their cronies to usurp state resources. True reform requires reformulating the political system and reconsidering the individual's role in society and the relationships among individuals and institutions in the government, civic, and private sectors.

Comprehensive anticorruption efforts can empower citizens who are now systematically excluded from the political system to participate in public affairs, the economy, and other social realms. That would allow citizens to contribute to building the state and its institutions,

---

**Box 4.8 Fighting corruption requires broad cooperation**

Fighting corruption requires more than changing the regime. It requires comprehensive and persistent efforts by all stakeholders in the fair distribution of public resources, the creation of job opportunities, and other reforms. It requires establishing a culture of transparency and accountability and avoiding conflicts of interest in the management of public funds, government bids and purchases, and management of state lands and natural resources.

These efforts can succeed if a comprehensive system of legislative, institutional, and policy reform is adopted. This starts with a dialogue between all parties to set a national strategy for combating corruption.

—Azmi Shu'aibi, general coordinator,
AMAN–Coalition for Integrity and Accountability

including the economy, social structures, political parties, and civil society institutions.

## Fighting Corruption More Effectively

Despite laudable aspirations and efforts in the right direction—signing UN conventions and regional agreements and implementing a framework of innovative policies and legislative programs, regulatory laws, and anticorruption monitoring mechanisms—actions still fall short. More is required of all actors at all levels and in all areas.

Diagnosing the causes of corruption touches on the structure of the political system, which holds the keys to change. The foundation for progress is the political will to expand participation in public policymaking by institutions and individuals—increasing opportunities for individuals, which is the traditional definition of human development. Political will in this context refers to the commitment of all parties in society to face up to corrupt practices and their causes and to minimize or eliminate them. This commitment should be exhibited first by elected officials or appointed leaders, who should launch comprehensive initiatives to fight corruption, and second by all stakeholders, who should demonstrate a deep understanding of the causes of corruption and mobilize against it. An effective system of sanctions is also required.

Political will involves a continuous and cumulative process of committing to and insisting on progress at all levels, including state institutions, the private and civil sectors, and individuals.[30] The fundamental expression of political will is progress on changing the system that governs institutional activity even if that conflicts with personal interests or—assuming good intentions—the force of ingrained habit. Comprehensive strategies are needed that prioritize reform as part of a broader anticorruption effort.[31] To achieve these aims, Arab countries need to rebase their constitutions in a new social contract. (See chapter 2 for a discussion of the rule of law in Arab countries.)

The primary expressions of this approach are reflected in a new integrity and credibility of elections and the possibility of robust input from citizens and organizations. It requires transparency and openness of the state and its institutions to enable citizens and organizations to reach informed positions. This transparency can be achieved only by expanding freedom of the press and other media, which in turn requires freedom of information based on clear laws and regulations that guarantee access to accurate, timely information at reasonable cost. (See chapter 3 for a discussion of the role of the media in empowerment.)

Given that corruption—by definition—involves the government, civil society, and private sectors and—by diagnosis—is prevalent in all these sectors to varying degrees and effects, governments must engage all stakeholders in formulating policies and measures to combat corruption and guide anticorruption efforts. Each state must create the appropriate formulas to achieve the highest level of participation.

Effective policies and programs to fight corruption require more than formal compliance with international obligations to raise scores on various indicators or to appease opposition parties and civil society advocacy groups. Strategies and legislation need to move beyond abstract plans to specific measures that can advance development.

Ratifying international anticorruption agreements remains relevant, however. Self-assessment of progress implementing UNCAC and other international accords is an important step, enabling countries to track their progress and observe changes linked to specific efforts. It boosts official support for fighting corruption, highlights strengths and achievements, reveals vulnerabilities, and encourages participation in a national process of discovery.[32] This process ensures the broadest participation of institutions involved in anticorruption efforts, raises awareness of efforts at the national level, and promotes dialogue and cooperation among all parties. It also expands options for international cooperation and exchange of experience,[33] providing policymakers and decision makers with detailed information for formulating plans to achieve development goals.

Anticorruption efforts should focus at the sector level and include regional and geographic priorities to achieve a balance between marginalized rural areas and areas of urban prosperity. Priority attention should go to the sectors most susceptible to corruption—foreign and major capital investments, weapons, infrastructure, and oil and other natural resources. Taking a sectoral approach is likely to increase opportunities for spending on education and health and to draw attention to oversight of the volume and mechanisms of spending, with the goal of improving services. The UNDP's Anti-Corruption and Integrity in the Arab Countries project supports links among national anticorruption strategies, development programs, and the Millennium Development Goals by incorporating integrity benchmarks and practices into basic service provision.[34]

Countries need codes of conduct and regulations clarifying all laws so that differences in interpretation do not create openings for abuse. The concepts of rule of law and judicial independence should be reinforced, emphasizing the principle that all citizens are equal, regardless of their legal, family, political, or financial status.

A joint study by Morocco and the Organisation for Economic Co-operation and Development (OECD) produced a legal framework, including implementation and accountability guidelines, to promote integrity and fight corruption in public procurement.[35] In Iraq, a similar study developed draft legislation and implementation mechanisms for public procurement practices that included guidelines for public-sector employees on how to crack down on corruption.[36]

Case studies of policy reform in public administration in nine Arab states were prepared to show what countries were doing to fight corruption and build supportive institutions, with the intention of attracting investment and supporting the economy.[37] International conventions were used to identify areas of governance that needed more attention. The report noted accomplishments in public administration and governance in human resources and public finance management, integrity, labor regulations, administrative procedures, e-government, public–private sector partnerships, gender issues, and management of water resources. Researchers addressed each area by discussing public strategies in each country over the first decade of this century.

All stakeholders in the Arab region need to strengthen their technical and administrative capabilities to combat corruption and to raise awareness among citizens of the dimensions of the problem and the implications for development (box 4.9). Ties should be strengthened among Arab countries through networks for exchanging experience, sharing methods of communications with institutions within and across countries, promoting joint efforts, and cooperating in prosecuting wrongdoers. Laying the foundations for communication and dialogue across institutions is an important part of an anticorruption system. The United Nations Development Programme (UNDP) has provided technical and financial support and facilitated networking among Arab countries and with global parties. The UNDP has also helped build national partnerships among stakeholders and has promoted the Arab Anti-Corruption and Integrity Network.

To properly identify and diagnose corruption, countries need to develop national measurement methodologies and processes that take into account Arab national and cultural characteristics and social values. Having these tools would boost the credibility of corruption assessment; motivate national reviews of policies, programs, laws, and related measures; and help raise awareness of the importance of combating corruption.

**Box 4.9 Corruption and the Arab Spring**

In 2011, young men and women in the Arab world rose up against tyranny calling for dignity for all people. They put combating corruption at the top of their list of demands, confirming a grave flaw afflicting the region and its people, which was diagnosed by the first Arab Human Development Report of 2002.

The Arab Spring radically altered the conversation about corruption, giving it new urgency and prominence and emphasizing the strong connection between anticorruption activities and democratization efforts. It mobilized citizens to monitor and question officials responsible for managing public funds at every level and to demand greater oversight and punishment for corrupt practices and the recovery of stolen assets. All these factors promote integrity and good governance.

The Arab Spring also carried warnings. Demanding an end to corruption, however vociferously, is not enough to actually end corruption. People need to participate directly in preparing programs, supporting institutions, and creating mechanisms for identifying and remedying all points of failure in state and society. Fighting corruption must be a long-term effort to change attitudes and actions; results in the short term will be incomplete and imperfect because the problem is extensive and complex. Ambitious programs are needed to enhance integrity and consolidate the bases for good governance that will enable diligent, patient endeavors that can achieve results over the medium to long term. Efforts are needed on all fronts: supporting and encouraging official anticorruption bodies to perform to their promise and potential, exerting popular pressure through civil society and representative bodies, and benefiting from international mechanisms for monitoring and oversight under the United Nations and other international organizations.

—Abdesselam Aboudrar, president, Central Authority for Corruption Prevention (ICPC), Morocco

The Arab Spring exposed many of the shortcomings in laws and procedures that have enabled corruption to spread and impede development (box 4.9). Now, the focus needs to shift to establishing cultural, legal, and procedural systems that are more resistant to corruption. Recovering from the capture of the state by elites who have turned the state and its institutions into a personal fiefdom calls for a new social contract for a modern state founded on the broadest possible participation, respect for human rights, and a democratic system of governance marked by fairness, transparency, and accountability.

Taking advantage of the new political and popular will to fight corruption and the growing understanding of corruption's detrimental effects on development, Arab states should include combating corruption among their long-range development goals. Mongolia, for example, with the help of the UNDP and other agencies, is dedicated to the new development goal of "democratic governance," which is consistent with the commitment of the international development community to achieve prosperity and growth by realizing the Millennium Development Goals by 2015. Fighting corruption can empower Arab citizens to achieve development, shifting them onto a path to a stable society of healthy, educated, and prosperous citizens.

## Notes

1   UNDP 2008.
2   Moody-Stuart 1999.
3   Limam 2011a.
4   U4 Anti-Corruption Resource Center 2011.
5   http://www.globalwitness.org/news-and-reports.
6   Arab Anti-Corruption Organization 2006.
7   Muhsin 2010.
8   Limam 2011a.
9   Transparency International 2011.
10  Salah 2003.
11  Muhsin 2010.
12  Limam 2011a.
13  UN Secretary-General 2009.
14  GTZ 2004.
15  Nazario 2007.
16  World Bank 2004.
17  World Bank 2000.
18  Abdullah 2010.
19  Hobeika 2010.

20   Limam 2011a.
21   Bowen 2013.
22   Transparency International's Corruption Perception Index evaluates and ranks states according to how corrupt state officials and politicians perceive the states to be. It is a composite index based on corruption data gathered through specialized surveys that gauge the opinions of businesspeople and analysts worldwide, including specialists and experts from the country being evaluated. The index focuses on corruption in the public sector and defines it as abuse of public office for private benefit. Surveys used to prepare the index ask questions about abuses of power to achieve personal benefit: government personnel accepting bribes during procurement, misappropriation of public funds, and the efficacy of anticorruption efforts, for example. Sources do not distinguish between administrative and political corruption. This index is based on Transparency International's calculation of the degree of corruption on a scale of zero to ten, with zero being the most corrupt and ten being the least corrupt.
23   Transparency International 2012.
24   Bribery data are from UNDP 2010c.
25   UNDP 2010c.
26   The Legatum Prosperity Index is the foremost global tool measuring the degree of prosperity and how countries can achieve it. A special feature of the Index is that it does not focus on income alone, but takes into consideration citizens' quality of life. The Index consists of eight sub-indices, each of which represents a fundamental aspect of prosperity.
27   UN Secretary-General 2009.
28   OECD 2009.
29   UNDP–PACDE 2011.
30   Brinkerhoff 1999.
31   Limam 2011a.
32   The third session of the conference of the state signatories to UNCAC in Doha in November 2009 decided that all state signatories subject to review would prepare replies to the convention's self-assessment checklist through broad consultations at the national level with all relevant stakeholders, including the private sector and institutions outside the public sector.
33   UNDP 2010b.
34   ACAID.
35   OECD 2009.
36   OECD 2008.
37   OECD 2010.

# Part 3:
# Supporting Empowerment Processes

# Introduction to Part 3

Bahgat Korany

P overty is about more than income; it is multi-dimensional. It is about social and political marginalization—in a word: disempowerment. But determining how many people are poor, even at the measurable material level, is still problematic. It depends on the poverty line used ($1.25 or $2 a day), and measuring real purchasing power can be more problematic as it is usually dynamic, changing with prices and inflation.[1]

Chapter 5 presents the essential statistics on poverty in the Arab world and discusses their implications, especially for youth and women. Despite the international consensus on the urgency of ending poverty, results have been meager. There are two common explanations for this failure.

One is that poverty-reduction efforts have been impeded by too much reliance on markets and individual enterprise and a distrust of government solutions based on keeping prices low by subsidizing key commodities. These arguments rest more on the inefficiency of government interventions than on their insufficiency. For example, as stated above, the energy subsidies of many Arab countries primarily benefit the business interests of regime loyalists, adding to budget deficits without reaching those in need.

The second explanation is that poverty-reduction efforts have concentrated on sector-based or partial approaches that deal only with symptoms. Focusing on economic growth instead of development emphasizes numeric indicators rather than the context in which subsidies are allocated. To reiterate, entrenched poverty cannot be regarded independently of the development model and the possibility of creating an empowerment-based social contract. Poverty policies have to be part of a new social contract that views the poor as citizens with rights who are deprived of a decent life by multiple factors. Policies need to address the obstacles to empowerment—unemployment, illiteracy, health, and social impediments that increase inequality—as part of a comprehensive development strategy.

As mentioned above, this type of rights-based approach to reducing poverty looks not only at the lowest acceptable level of poverty but also at the highest acceptable level of wealth and luxury—through a progressive tax system, for example. The just distribution of wealth is an important component of an empowerment-based social contract that reduces the causes of internal tension and helps confront external threats. Empowering society in this way slows the proliferation and mismanagement of disputes and conflicts that exhaust development resources and capabilities and provoke foreign intervention under the guise of humanitarian assistance. The mushrooming and intensification of conflicts—especially the social protracted ones—add to negative energy and drains society's potential rather than building on it.

In this region, as in some others of the "global South," conflict is pervasive, for example, with Israel and other foreign powers. However, intentionally or not, its inter-Arab aspect is overlooked and consequently under-researched. Yet this type of conflict is chronic, devastating, and multifaceted and can be even more draining. It is not limited to bilateral relations but could involve foreign powers as well as other Arab states and their communities. Numerous examples illustrate such inter-Arab conflicts: the Egyptian–Saudi conflict in the 1960s over Yemen; the Algerian–Moroccan "guerre de sable," also in the 1960s, and the present tension over the Western Sahara; the Syrian civil war that began in 2012; the so-called Shi'a–Sunni conflicts; the tribal–political conflicts in post-Qadhafi Libya and post-Saleh Yemen; and emerging warlordism of different types. The many intractable conflicts across the region have increasingly become an enormous drain on Arab capabilities. As has already been mentioned, average military expenditure is more than double the global average.[2]

The Center for Systemic Peace counted 315 episodes of armed conflict (twenty-six of them ongoing) that took place around the globe sometime between 1946 and 2009, involving a total of 110 countries.[3] One or more of the fourteen member countries of the United Nations Economic and Social Commission for Western Asia were involved in fifty-nine of these conflicts, with an estimated human cost of close to 3.5

million people. Some 90 percent of the people who died as a result of conflicts in the Arab region were civilians, half of them children.[4] By the time the civil conflict ended in Lebanon in the 1980s, it had claimed 150,000 lives. At the time of writing, Syria's civil war goes on with catastrophic effects, including the desperate efforts of refugees and internally displaced persons to secure appropriate shelter. For the protagonists, defeat is not retreat but exile and even death. We haven't yet started to estimate the economic consequences of the eventual 'peace,' from rebuilding basic infrastructure to reinstituting health centers to provide physical rehabilitation services to those in need of such therapies. But it is already estimated that Syria will need thirty-seven years to return to its 2010 development level. The psychological rehabilitation across generations will take much longer. A similar story can be told about Iraq, Yemen, Sudan, or even Libya, which will hopefully escape the trap of Somalization.

How can Arab countries halt this epidemic?

At the global level, there is an increasing awareness of the devastating costs of conflict, especially the domestic ones. The end of the Cold War helped in restraining superpower motivation to intervene in and inflame local conflicts. As recent data by *The Economist* (9–15 November 2013) demonstrate, more conflicts ended in the fifteen years following the fall of the Berlin Wall than in the preceding half century, with conflict-plagued countries declining to 12 percent. Moreover, negotiated settlements have jumped from 10 percent to 40 percent—an increase of 300 percent. Can the Arab world learn to escape from the destructive trap of the draining lose–lose downward spiral?

Differences need not inevitably lead to conflict. Ethnic, religious, and sectarian diversity is the rule around the world; in more than two-thirds of countries the largest ethnic group does not exceed 65 percent of the population.[5] The problem is not diversity but how it is managed at the clan, tribe, or other sociopolitical level. Here again, the most important contribution to manage existing conflicts and prevent them from flaring up depends on the CNS. In some cases the problem is authoritarian regimes or ideologies that cannot accommodate pluralism, whether social or political. In others, misguided nationalist policies have ignored social and political diversity, looking at the Arab region as monolithic. Social and political differences are facts of life that require political management. Recognizing this could be the first step toward accepting social and political differences in Arab societies. The starting point for managing diversity is to adopt the rule of law and abandon the authoritarian mentality that resorts too easily to force, compulsion, and 'othering' over dialogue and tolerance.

The authoritarian mentality is shortsighted. Such shortsightedness in major policies is also characteristic of the thinking concerning environmental problems. These issues are typically overlooked even though their impact constitutes another serious impediment to development, one that neither the public nor the ruling class seems to understand, despite mounting international concern about climate change and its impact on the Arab world. Chapter 7 shows that environmental risks threaten human existence itself.

The Arab region has contributed much less—historically and structurally—to atmospheric pollution than the industrialized countries and China and India. The onus thus falls on the major industrialized countries to reduce pollution and carbon emissions. In addition, these countries should offer developing countries scientific and material support to help them avoid making the same mistakes in a rush to development at any cost. All parties need to strengthen the mechanisms for transforming early warning into early action on environmental threats. Developing countries will need an estimated $100 billion a year by 2020 to mitigate the deleterious effects of climate change[6]—a large sum but one that pales in comparison to the enormous military budgets at the global and regional levels.

The focus is on the link between environmental threats and daily life—from the proliferation of slums and informal housing to the toll of inadequate transportation systems—all aggravated by accelerating urbanization. The outcomes include overcrowding, bad air quality, land degradation, and rising levels of greenhouse gases.

In many Arab countries the number of private cars is growing by 7 percent to 10 percent a year, yet governments have no plans to slow or adapt to this expansion. The toll on people's health and the economy is immense. The Arab transportation sector is an enormous, inefficient consumer of energy: It accounts for 32 percent of energy consumption and 22 percent of greenhouse gas emissions in the region. Estimated health-care costs arising from air pollution totaled $10.9 billion in sixteen Arab countries in 2008, some 1.2 percent of GDP.[7] The shortcomings of the transport sector impose a massive burden on economic productivity, estimated at 3 percent to 10 percent of GDP, while the absence of mass transport systems worsens social inequality and exclusion.[8]

Arab countries need to invest in transportation, by developing the road infrastructure, upgrading vehicles, and building public transport systems. Such investments will lead to a healthier society while generating savings of some $61.8 billion in national budgets over the medium to long term.[9]

# Notes

1   Arab League and UNDP 2010.
2   World Bank 2012b.
3   The United Nations *Economic and Social Commission for Western Asia* cites data collected by the Center for Systemic Peace in its study "Major Episodes of Political Violence, 1946–2009." According to the center's latest data (up to 2012), the number of conflicts has reached 326, thirty-two of which are currently ongoing.
4   ESCWA 2010d.
5   Mossaad 2008.
6   *Failed States Index* 2013b.
7   Qaisi and Sha'ban 2011.
8   Qaisi and Sha'ban 2011.
9   Qaisi and Sha'ban 2011.

# CHAPTER 5

# Ending Persistent Poverty:
## Pathways to Reform and Empowerment

Sabria Al-Thawr

D espite intensified efforts to reduce poverty, deprivation and inequality still force millions of people to endure harsh living conditions due to their limited options and the elites' control of wealth, resources, and productive assets. Unequal access to opportunities excludes a broad sector of society, preventing them from participating and making their own choices. Fair, balanced, and sustainable development will be achieved only when all dimensions of empowerment receive equal priority.

Following the Millennium Summit of the United Nations in 2000, 192 states agreed to cooperate to achieve eight Millennium Development Goals. Foremost among them are eliminating hunger and cutting poverty rates in half by 2015. But results have fallen short of international aspirations; high levels of poverty and powerlessness persist in many Arab societies.

Despite the region's wealth in resources, broad swathes of Arab countries' populations continue to suffer from the multiple effects of poverty and deprivation. And despite acceptable economic growth rates since 2000, the overall poverty rate is still high and even increasing in some countries,[1] with 65 million Arabs under the poverty line of $2 a day.[2] Poverty reduction is affected not only by economic growth but also by the flow of aid, which has shrunk in recent years. Unemployment rates are rising in the context of a major decline in foreign aid and a rise in violence and instability.

Countries have not adopted development policies that support and protect the poor and their rights and which translate into real change.

Successive Arab Human Development Reports have revealed the failure of the current development model, with its almost exclusive focus on economic growth, to achieve just and sustainable development. The 2009 report *Development Challenges in the Arab States* identifies six inter-related challenges: reforming institutions, providing nearly 51 million job opportunities by 2020, reinforcing and financing pro-poor growth, reforming education systems, diversifying the sources of economic growth, and increasing food security and self-sufficiency within existing environmental constraints.[3] Addressing these challenges calls for a new, comprehensive, freedom-based model of human development.

The Arab model of development has proved incapable of achieving true gains in living conditions, accomplishing political and social reform, and building a state that guarantees freedoms and true citizenship. Rather, it has burdened Arab populations with a legacy that threatens stability and perpetuates insecure living conditions. The popular uprisings that swept the region in 2011 came as a spontaneous reaction to worsening living conditions and the failure to address the problems of society's poorest, most vulnerable groups—groups that continue to grow larger.

### The Dilemma of Increasing Wealth and Worsening Poverty

Despite gains in health and education, inequality and acute class differences are still marked features of Arab societies. With the large disparities in living conditions and community well-being, the middle class has begun to disappear in some Arab states.[4] Poverty, endemic in rural areas and inseparable from illiteracy, continues to spread. The number of poor people in the Arab states has risen since the mid-1980s despite the oil boom and economic growth. More than two-thirds of the population (220.2 million people) live in medium- and low-income countries.[5] More than 15 million people suffer from malnutrition. Close to 10 percent of the total population is unemployed, and more than 23 percent of the youth population is unemployed.[6]

Poverty has become endemic in countries of strategic importance—countries that are channels for half of the world's trade and which possess vast natural wealth in oil, gas, precious metals, water, and fertile land. Some analysts blame the spread of corruption, bad resource management, and highly uneven income distributions for worsening the impact and spread of poverty.[7] The Arab region does better than other regions on income poverty (figure 5.1). But the change over 1999–2008 was not very strong: extreme poverty ($1.25 a day) fell five percentage points, while the share of people living on $2 a day fell eleven percentage points.[8]

**Figure 5.1 Fall in income poverty percentages, world regions compared, 1999–2008**

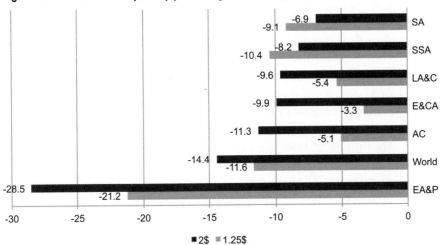

- 2$  ■ 1.25$

*Source:* Calculations based on World Bank POVCAL data sets (in 2005 PPP).

Comparisons with other regions do not reveal the huge disparity between the countries of the region, between rural and urban areas within countries, or for geographically or politically isolated communities. Six Arab countries, among the poorest in the world, suffer from high poverty rates and a growing food deficit as a result of unstable economic, political, and social conditions: Comoros, Djibouti, Sudan, Somalia, Mauritania, and Yemen. Meanwhile, three Gulf states— Kuwait, Qatar, and the United Arab Emirates—are among the wealthiest in the world.[9] So the true poverty indicators for the Arab region might well be catastrophic if the oil-producing countries, for which accurate poverty statistics are not available, were excluded.

Two aspects of disparity across Arab countries may shed light on the problem of poverty and wealth: the uneven distribution of abundant resources and disparate development conditions.

The Arab region possesses ample human resources, with young people making up the highest proportion of the population. It also enjoys tremendous wealth; the Gulf states and Iraq, for example, possess half the world's oil reserves. But the poverty and inequality experienced by large segments of the population are inconsistent with this rosy picture. Economic structures, demography, and the distribution of benefits reflect further inequality. The oil-producing countries hold almost a seventh of the region's population (14.1 percent) but more than half its GDP (62.1 percent). Mixed-economy states hold almost half the region's population (49.3 percent) but nearly a quarter of its GDP (23.1 percent; see figure 5.2). So per capita GDP reaches more than $30,500 a year in the oil-producing states, with average per capita consumption that ranges from $43 a day (United Arab Emirates) to $10.50 a day (Saudi Arabia). Compare that with annual GDP per capita of $1,284 in states that rely on raw material exports, and average consumption ranging from $1.50 a day (Mauritania) to $2.10 (Djibouti).[10]

Development conditions also differ widely. The oil-producing states are capable of reaching the Millennium Development Goals without difficulty. Four Arab countries—Oman, Saudi Arabia, Tunisia, and Algeria—recorded the fastest progress in human development and in non-income-related dimensions (health and education), though recent events in Tunisia require clarification of the type of progress and who has benefited. Revenues from natural resources such as oil have enabled the oil-producing countries and some mixed-economy countries to expand services and improve infrastructure to realize long-term development gains. The least developed countries, however, trail far behind, particularly those torn by unrest and political conflict—like Palestine, Somalia, and Yemen.

**Figure 5.2 Population shares and GDP per capita shares in the Arab states, 2011**

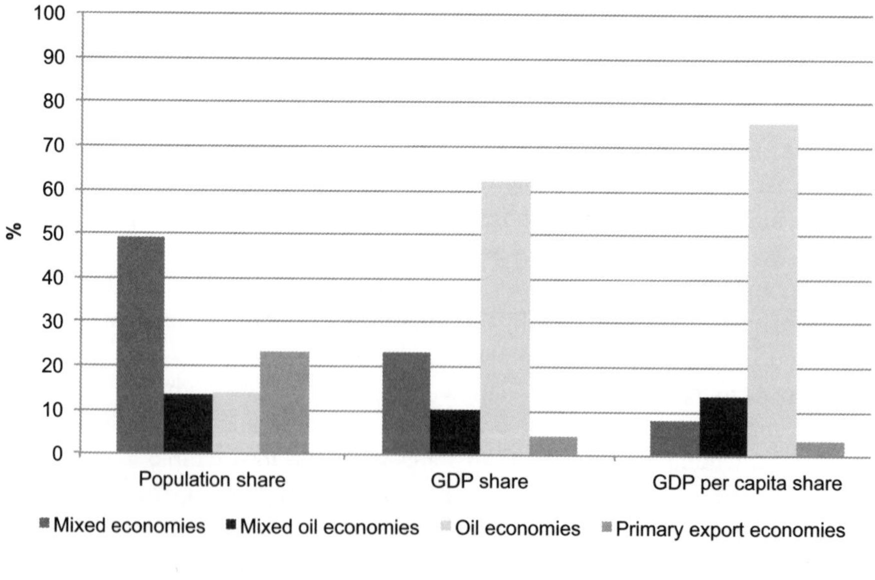

*Note:* Excluded countries: Iraq and Palestine
*Source:* Calculations based on UNSD 2012 and World Bank 2012b data.

The real problem lies with the least developed countries—such as Djibouti, Mauritania, Somalia, Sudan, and Yemen. Poor countries dependent on raw material exports, whose prices have plummeted in recent years, cannot possibly achieve a level of economic growth that will enable them to reduce extreme poverty. Add to that rising food prices and falling oil prices and reductions in international development aid as a result of the global economic crisis, and prospects look dim for poor people in these countries.

## Understanding Poverty in the Arab Region

If the $1-a-day poverty measure is used to compare poverty in the Arab region with that elsewhere, rates in the Arab region appear low. The shortcoming of this poverty measure is that it is more appropriate for the least-developed countries, which suffer from extreme poverty, than for medium-growth countries or countries with high rates of development such as the Gulf states, where a different level of poverty exists. So, relying solely on this measure gives a misleading picture of the reality of poverty in the Arab region and of how it varies across countries. Moreover, data based on the $1-a-day measure do not include the Gulf countries. For that reason many recent studies have adopted the $2-a-day measure, which experts consider more appropriate for the region. By that measure, the poverty rate jumps from 2.5–3.5 percent to 31.5 percent.[11]

The understanding of poverty has evolved beyond material poverty to include other aspects of deprivation, such as marginalization, the inability to access resources and productive assets, the inability to exercise freedom of choice, the inability to access or benefit from services, and the lack of a sense of security. The human poverty metric thus attempts to measure aspects of deprivation related to health, education, and capacity by introducing the concept of rights and capabilities into an understanding of poverty that is more inclusive than low income.

The Multidimensional Poverty Index (MPI) expands the concept of poverty by incorporating deprivations in health, education, and standard of living. It uses all the indicators from household surveys to categorize family members as poor or not according to the number of aspects of deprivation they suffer. The household data are then gathered into a measure of poverty on the national level.[12] A family is categorized as living in multidimensional poverty if it suffers deprivation on one-third or more of the indicators.[13] The MPI differs from the Human Development Index (HDI) in that it measures aspects of deprivation on the family level and is therefore more detailed; the HDI tends to be a more global measure and less detailed in its dimensions.[14] Multidimensional poverty varies considerably across the Arab region (figure 5.3).

### Figure 5.3 Multidimensional Poverty Index across the Arab region

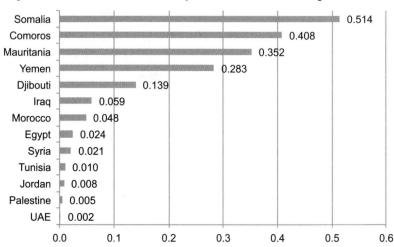

*Note:* The MPI indicates the extent of poverty the poor experience as a ratio of the potential weighted deprivations the society could experience. For example, in Somalia, the poor experience 51.4 percent of the potential weighted deprivations the society could experience.
*Source:* UNDP 2011a.

People in Arab countries living in multidimensional poverty make up 2.2 percent of the 1.6 billion people in the world living in multidimensional poverty. The highest rates of incidence of multidimensional poverty are in Somalia (81.2 percent) and in Yemen, Mauritania, and Comoros (all above 52.5 percent; see figure 5.4). The incidence is below 6 percent in Egypt and Syria.

Somalia suffers from severe fragmentation, which has negatively impacted the living conditions of most of its people. Mauritania and Yemen also registered very high percentages of the population suffering multiple deprivations, particularly in education and health. Sometimes, as in Morocco and Tunisia, the percentage of people in danger of falling into multidimensional poverty is greater than the percentage living in multidimensional poverty. The lower the HDI, the more likely the MPI is to exceed the income poverty index.[15]

A regional comparative analysis of the indices for human poverty and multidimensional poverty—based on a division of the Arab states into the Levant, North Africa, Gulf States, and the least developed countries—shows that the majority of Arab countries had higher rates of deprivation than the mean expectation based on their incomes. But when the MPI is

### Figure 5.4 Percentage of population living in multidimensional poverty in the Arab region, 2011

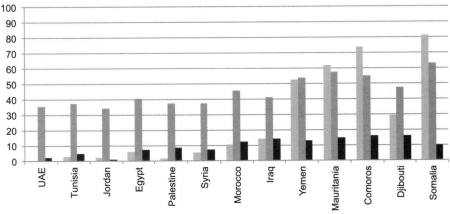

*Note:* Headcount is the percentage of the population that is multidimensionally poor (weighted deprivation score of at least 33 percent). Intensity of deprivation is the average percentage of deprivation experienced by people who are multidimensionally poor. Population vulnerable to poverty is the percentage of the population at risk of suffering multiple deprivations (deprivation score of 20–33 percent).
*Source:* UNDP 2011a.

used, human poverty rates appear to conform to the situation in these countries.[16]

Much work has been devoted to formulating indicators that reflect the varying manifestations of poverty in Arab countries.[17] But questions remain: Which measure best reflects the reality of poverty in the Arab region? Are new measures needed that are capable of revealing the actual level of deprivation and human poverty in the Arab countries? The recent popular uprisings clearly demonstrate that the populations of these countries have lost patience with practices that sugarcoat reality, such as using indicators that do not reflect the true levels of deprivation and exclusion experienced by broad sectors of Arab societies.

What can be said about poverty in the Arab region is that it primarily affects three groups: residents of rural areas, youth, and women.

### Poverty among residents of rural areas

Rural poverty stands out in several Arab countries (table 5.1), due largely to a lack of diversity in economic activity and a reliance on agricultural productivity to drive growth. Agricultural productivity has declined

**Table 5.1. Rural poverty rates in selected Arab countries, latest year available**

| State | Percentage of rural who are poor | Percentage of poor in rural areas | Percentage of urban who are poor |
|---|---|---|---|
| Algeria | 15 | 52 | 10 |
| Djibouti | 83 | 31 | 39 |
| Egypt | 27 | 78 | 10 |
| Mauritania | 50 | 78 | 30 |
| Morocco | 15 | 68 | 5 |
| Sudan | 85 | 81 | 27 |
| Syria | 15 | 62 | 8 |
| Tunisia | 8 | 75 | 2 |
| Yemen | 40 | 84 | 21 |

*Source*: World Bank. *Improving Food Security in Arab Countries*. 2009.

steadily as a result of climate change, reductions in cultivated area, and deteriorating environmental conditions. The agricultural sector absorbs most of the workforce in the least developed countries: the percentage of people employed in agriculture reaches 50 percent in Yemen, Sudan, and Mauritania, 36 percent in Morocco, and around 27 percent in Egypt.[18]

The likelihood of being poor is high for those living in rural areas—for example, the incidence of poverty is more than fifteen times higher in rural areas of Sudan than urban areas (figure 5.5).

The disparity is heightened by the weak service provision and poor infrastructure in rural areas, which make it more difficult for rural communities to diversify activities and generate jobs and growth. Perhaps the clearest indicator of rural poverty is the rapid rate of migration to cities, which strains the ability of urban centers to provide basic services. Slums also suffer from high unemployment and overcrowded schools, contributing to the deterioration of living conditions in urban areas as well.

### Poverty among youth

The region has 121 million children and 71 million young people,[19] who together make up more than 20 percent of the population in more than twelve countries (including heavily populated Algeria, Egypt, Iraq, Morocco, Sudan, and Yemen). These numbers reveal the enormous

**Figure 5.5 The likelihood of poverty for rural residents compared with urban residents, 2009**

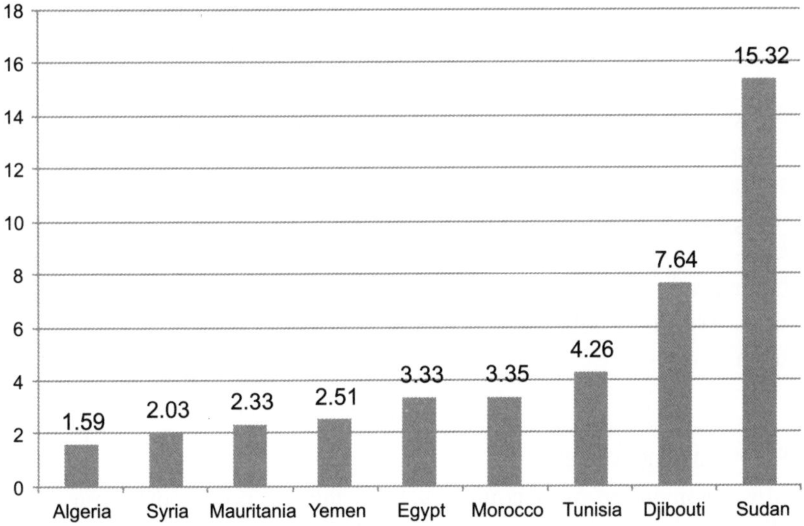

*Source*: Based on data from the World Bank report *Improving Food Security in Arab Countries*, 2009.

challenge of providing education, training, and employment now and in the future. The unemployment rate in the Arab countries is 9.7 percent, more than 50 percent higher than the global rate of 6 percent.[20] Young people make up 54.4 percent of the unemployed, by far the highest percentage in the world. Around 40 percent of secondary school and university graduates (15–25 years old) cannot find jobs,[21] leading to intensive migration.

Three factors explain much of the low employment indicators for young men and women in the Arab countries:

- Slow economic growth linked to the world economic crisis and the stagnant labor market, leading to shrinking job opportunities in the public sector in countries implementing structural reforms.
- A small, weak private sector unable to create diverse job opportunities.
- A mismatch between education and training and the requirements of the labor market, with little focus on technical and vocational skills.

Globalization has had an impact as well, causing many groups to be excluded from the job market because of rising competitiveness and the advances in knowledge that shape many new job opportunities but that the great majority of young people in Arab countries lack. Indeed, broad segments of Arab youth, especially those who come from poor or low-income families, are not well educated. They have fewer chances to find jobs in the formal labor market, which requires sophisticated knowledge and skills. They are forced to seek employment in marginal or seasonal jobs in the informal sector, jobs with no fixed wages and no reasonable chance to develop professional skills, improve labor productivity, raise the level of wages, or improve living conditions. Getting a job, then, does not necessarily mean freeing oneself from poverty, since the working poor make up a high proportion of the poor. [22]

### Poverty among women

Most women in Arab countries have few or no opportunities and choices. Traditional poverty measures based on income greatly underestimate poverty among women because they tend to use the family as a unit of analysis, thus obscuring intrafamily gender discrimination. Even so, some family expenditure surveys have highlighted the depth and breadth of poverty in families supported by women. In Egypt, Lebanon, and Syria, widows with more than three children who are the sole breadwinners in their families make up a large percentage of the poor. Divorced women in Jordan are also more likely to be poor than are women in family groups. [23]

Unemployment rates for women in Arab countries are the highest in the world, sometimes nearly three times those of young men. [24] Added to stagnant labor markets is discrimination against women due to the cultural structure of society, which prevents women from working in many professions or circumstances (figure 5.6). Women are concentrated in the informal sector (such as agriculture and handicrafts) and work in low-wage jobs without social security benefits. In Egypt, Morocco, and Yemen women make up 40 percent to 50 percent of the informal agricultural workforce. [25]

There are also distinctions related to capacity. Some 80 percent of girls are not expected to enroll in school, compared with 36 percent of boys, and in remote rural areas of Egypt and Yemen, girls who do go to school remain enrolled for less than four years. [26] Limited education means low capacity and weakens women's ability to compete for jobs. Women's poverty is worsened even more by societal discrimination

**Figure 5.6 Women's Economic Opportunity Index in Arab countries, 2012**

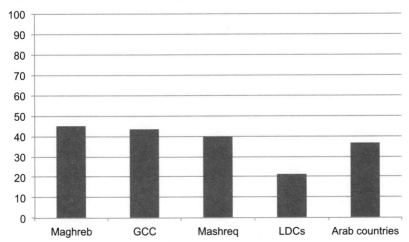

*Note*: Scale of 0 to 100 scale; higher is better.
*Source*: Calculations are based on EIU 2012 data.

that deprives women of access to vital resources such as health insurance, social security, property ownership, and inheritance, and thus lowers their chances of owning productive assets.[27]

Women's poverty must be addressed from a realistic perspective based on social and cultural conditions in the region. That means treating women's poverty as a deprivation of basic rights, which requires providing greater opportunities for freedom, dignity, and a better quality life to women as partners in the development process rather than as recipients of assistance.

## What to Do? Pathways to Reform and Empowerment

Global progress toward the Millennium Development Goals—particularly the goal of eliminating extreme poverty and hunger—has been uneven. Several factors have impeded gains in Arab countries:

- *Shrinking role of the state as provider of basic services and social welfare,* in response to current economic conditions locally and internationally and as a result of free-market economic policies. These policies were not accompanied by measures to prepare and empower individuals and communities to persevere with less state support, leading to a state of crisis in relations between the state and citizens.

- *Lack of economic diversity on the local level*, where traditional agriculture and services have remained the two largest sources of employment over the past three decades. The lack of economic diversity coincided with a decline in agricultural productivity because of a failure to upgrade technology and to respond to changing climate conditions.
- *Impact of global crises*, particularly financial and food crises. Global economic indicators have improved, but employment opportunities have declined, and the global labor market is expected to remain stagnant until 2015.[28] That will increase unemployment and reduce opportunities for migrant labor and remittances.
- *Political and security challenges that stand in the way of redistributing Arab labor from labor-exporting countries* such as Egypt, Jordan, and Morocco. Challenges include difficulties relocating and obtaining work visas and sponsors, as in the Gulf states. Arab youth lack the requisite qualifications and skills to compete with migrant laborers from Asia, especially in the Gulf states, which import more laborers than any other country in the region.
- *Underfunding of comprehensive poverty-reduction programs*, especially compared with areas such as defense. Making conditions even worse are the limited capacity of government institutions in many Arab countries to reach the poor and their failure to adopt comprehensive social policies.
- *The weak contribution of the private sector to employment creation*, in the inhospitable business environment in countries plagued by instability or corrupt rulers.[29]

Empowering individuals and building their capacity to participate and choose freely are the cornerstones of human development. They require reducing poverty, advancing social welfare, and expanding the choices available to members of society. The focus is on investing in education, collaborating meaningfully with development partners, and empowering the least represented groups, such as youth and women.

### Investing in education and human capital

Investing in human capital is the surest route to growth in the age of the knowledge economy. Education indicators in high-poverty, low-development countries such as Djibouti, Mauritania, Somalia, Sudan, and Yemen are shockingly low—and well below what their per capita incomes would predict.[30] One conclusion is that there is not always a direct correlation between education and per capita income, though low educational levels tend to go along with low per capita income. There are nearly four million adolescents in Arab countries, 59 percent of them girls, many not enrolled in school. Moreover, some countries—including Egypt, Lebanon, Mauritania, the State of Palestine, Sudan, and Yemen—have begun to experience a high male dropout rate as young men try to find work to improve their families' living situations.[31]

The quality of education continues to be a challenge. Despite the resources invested in education, students are not gaining the skills needed to earn a living (see chapter 8). In particular, flexible alternatives are needed that provide good-quality, short but intensive educational programs for people unable to enroll in regular schools. These might include people in isolated communities or marginal social groups and people living in conflict zones who have been unable to enroll in school for social, political, or economic reasons. Programs could be flexibly delivered to such communities through homeschooling, mobile schools, or other innovative approaches. The programs should use standard evaluation criteria and issue formal diplomas.

### Investing in youth: Arab societies' hidden capital

Arab countries and societies are transitioning into a new knowledge-based world that is evolving at an ever-accelerating pace. Graduates of the traditional education system lack the knowledge and skills to operate in this new knowledge economy. That calls for a new approach to investing in education and human capital.

Making up more than 60 percent of the population in Arab countries, young people must be at the forefront of any reform and empowerment efforts (box 5.1). Opinion polls conducted for the 2002 Arab Human Development Report found that young men and women felt a positive sense of belonging to their country and were aware of the social and economic issues their country faced. Their commitment was reaffirmed by the Arab youth uprisings in early 2011. Countries need to build on these values by expanding capacity—providing young people with skills that match labor market requirements, empowering them politically, and opening the way for them to participate in their country's development.

Prior generations of Arab youth—those growing up before the 1980s—enjoyed opportunities for free state-funded education. Such educational opportunities are decreasing, particularly in rural areas. Today's youth suffer from high unemployment, lack of skills, and a

## Box 5.1 Arab youth and the future of development

A "youth bulge" in the population in many Arab countries has been a concern of policymakers for more than a decade, particularly the resulting pressures on the labor markets. Over the past ten years, the region's labor force has grown at an unprecedented rate of nearly 3.3 percent a year—or more than three million people a year. For more than two decades youth unemployment rates have averaged around 25 percent—persistently higher than in any other region.

As this large cohort of young people enters the workforce, the resulting higher employment rates offer the potential for increased savings, domestic investment, and job-driven growth. Moreover, young people—likely to be engaged with technology and global issues—bring with them the potential for innovation and positive change, in both the economic and the civic spheres. To take advantage of the economic and social potential of their youth, governments of the region need to create opportunities in education, job creation, self-employment, and community engagement.

So far, countries have not fully capitalized on this youth population. While they have accommodated the incoming cohorts of young people in their education systems by building more schools and classrooms, education quality has suffered. Furthermore, education systems have proven resistant to reform, failing to inculcate the skills and experience needed to make youth competitive in today's global labor markets. Growth in public-sector employment has not kept up with the large numbers of new labor market entrants, while job creation in the private sector has been stifled by restrictive regulations—despite strong economic growth over the past decade.

Most new jobs are in the informal sector and fail to meet expectations or to provide decent wages, benefits, job security, and opportunities for career advancement. Youth from marginalized backgrounds are particularly disadvantaged. Unable to supplement their education through tutoring and private education, poorer youth are less likely to achieve high enough grades on national exams to secure places in public higher education institutions—a key entry point to a formal job.

As the youth bulge enters adulthood across the region, the supply pressures on education systems and labor markets are expected to decline sharply. This will provide countries of the region with an opportunity to focus on improving education quality. Successful education system reform would, in turn, create a higher-skilled workforce able to spearhead economic growth—but only if governments introduce the regulatory flexibility that would encourage business development, growth, and high-skilled job creation.

Realizing this bright future requires a fundamental change in the relationship between citizens and the state. The Arab Spring allowed young people to see themselves as the primary architects of their own and their countries' future. This political awakening should be accompanied by an economic spring that encourages young people to seek out economic opportunities to create their own careers. However, the revolutions in Egypt, Libya, Tunisia, and Yemen have led to a return to public-sector hiring, more worker protections, a reliance on traditional public works programs as the main social safety net, and a wider role for government in the economy, all of which bode poorly for long-term economic prospects for youth in the region.

The old social contract remains intact. Turning entrepreneurial spirit into better economic outcomes for youth requires new thinking to bolster private-sector development, incentivize firms to invest in job creation, encourage entrepreneurs to establish and grow their businesses, and design social safety nets that focus on service-based skills development.

—Tarik Yousef, founding dean, Dubai School of Government

dearth of opportunities. The governments of Arab states acknowledge the need to marshal resources for investment in youth development, but the lack of political commitment and a preoccupation with economic, political, and other challenges have prevented translating these pronouncements into action. Youth unemployment rates are at an all-time high, while their knowledge and skills are at an all-time low.

## Collaborating with development partners

Countries need to find better ways to collaborate with key development partners: civil society organizations and the private sector.

### New roles for civil society

Civil society organizations (CSOs) play a mediating role among the state, individuals, and the market.[32] An active civil society may be a sign of a freer political environment. CSOs can respond more flexibly to local development needs than can a large bureaucracy. And they are known for the low costs of the services they provide and their proximity and access to the poor; 55 percent of CSOs in Arab countries are engaged in charitable work. Despite the many volunteer human rights organizations and scholarly establishments that contribute effectively to Arab countries, most CSOs make only negligible contributions to human development. Charitable CSOs are concentrated in urban areas, while grassroots organizations are weak in the countryside, where poverty is greatest.[33]

Most CSOs engage in charitable work because it requires little institutional capacity or strategic vision. Therefore, their work stalls if funding is cut. Few evaluation studies of these organizations have been conducted. A 2004 report by the Arab nongovernmental organization Network for Development on poverty alleviation affirmed the contribution of numerous CSOs in drawing up antipoverty strategies and administering rural education and development programs. Some pioneering regional CSOs have adopted a development approach, and their numbers have grown in recent years. Among them are the Mohammed bin Rashid Al Maktoum Foundation, Qatar's Silatech Foundation, and others whose activities have expanded to more Arab and Islamic developing countries.

Determining whether partnerships of government, CSOs, and the private sector are effective and efficient requires further assessment. Research is also needed on ways of developing and strengthening such partnerships to lighten the burden on the state, particularly in providing social services and implementing development projects in local communities. It may be possible to galvanize civil society institutions by updating their development approach and building capacity. Part of the success of loan associations, which are proliferating, comes from their clear vision and purpose, their highly specialized training in the mechanics of lending and in ways of relating to local communities, and the existence of pioneering global and regional models that have made it easier to learn lessons and improve performance. Adopting a similar approach could create a new generation of CSOs with a development orientation to support local community development.

### The private sector and social responsibility

Private corporations are no longer assessed only on the basis of their profit, nor do they build their reputation solely on their financial status. The private sector, as a prime generator of national income and a source of job opportunities in the informal sector, has begun to focus on social responsibility, the obligation to incorporate social and environmental concerns in addition to profit-based production. As defined by the World Business Council for Sustainable Development, these include economic growth, social progress, and environmental protection. The private sector has begun to contribute to social services and to projects that create jobs in local communities. Major Arab companies are contributing to banks for the poor, microfinance activities, and charitable and development projects. But these trends need to be integrated with national and regional strategic development visions to have real impact.

The private sector has had only a minor role in creating job opportunities in most Arab countries. Reasons include the lack of initiative, risk avoidance, reliance on the state, and falling investment, despite government attempts to liberalize the economy and reduce spending. Too many bureaucratic restrictions, weak labor protection legislation, and a growing mismatch between education and the needs of the market inhibit the private sector's ability to create jobs.[34]

Also impeding a more robust role for the private sector are the limited capacity of government institutions and the absence of supporting nongovernmental organizations and private-sector institutions capable of implementing efficient and innovative development and investment programs. The lack of freedoms and the spread of corruption have resulted in a crisis of confidence between the state and the private sector. The private sector in the Arab countries has also failed to put the concept of social responsibility into practice.

So building and strengthening an effective partnership between the state and the private sector should accelerate economic growth by reducing unemployment, creating jobs, alleviating poverty, and creating a supportive base for development and reforms.

### Building pathways to comprehensive reform

Economic, political, and social conditions in the Arab region call for accelerating reforms and empowerment. Demands are intensifying for reforming government institutions, combating corruption, and supporting and diversifying national economies. The popular uprisings in many Arab countries are a response to the slow pace of reform.

The ruling regimes in Arab countries need to implement genuine reforms, consolidate the bases of good governance, and begin to decentralize development-related decision-making and administrative powers. Taking these steps could revive local community development and reduce geographic, demographic, and economic disparities within countries.

There are two tracks for effecting political and economic reforms:

- *Regional.* Economic cooperation and integration among Arab countries must be pursued to achieve vital resource diversity and to consolidate regional and local stability.
- *National.* Political, economic, social, and security reforms need to be accelerated. Comprehensive, pro-poor policies are needed that aim to achieve justice and equality and favor disadvantaged sectors. Equal citizenship that respects the specificities and diversity of each country and community should be stressed.

Stepping up and diversifying economic activity, reducing dependence on a single source of income (oil or raw materials), and creating a climate that encourages local and foreign investment are pivotal to economic reforms that will increase private-sector effectiveness and accelerate growth. That requires building trust among the state, civil society, and private development partners. The main role here belongs to governments, to expand opportunities for participation and to grant civil-society and private-sector partners the necessary facilities and powers within an integrative framework.

Poverty alleviation should be the aim of general and economic policy, including the following:

- *Reconsidering the methodologies for measuring poverty and for monitoring and tracking poverty indicators.* The intent would be to obtain more accurate measures that reflect regional and national variations.
- *Basing economic reforms on realistic national visions.* Those visions would support economic growth, income redistribution, rural development, creative solutions to declining production and resource shortages (particularly water), and restructuring of local labor markets through public–private partnerships that can create real job opportunities for youth and the poor.
- *Expanding the availability of integrated, comprehensive policy packages and pro-poor growth programs.* Such programs must accommodate

the divergent needs and circumstances of vulnerable groups, poor people, and the distinctive features of their communities.

- *Boosting investment in human capital.* Countries should reform their education system, increase the amount and quality of resources allocated to education, and focus on knowledge and technology gaps.
- *Evaluating the social protection nets that have accompanied structural reforms in Arab countries.* Periodic impact assessments of reforms and improvements in their mechanisms should focus on empowerment rather than welfare, which fosters dependency.
- *Broadening participation.* Civil society institutions, parliaments, local municipal councils, and organizations of the poor should be involved in monitoring, assessing, and gauging the effectiveness of poverty-reduction policies.
- *Encouraging nontraditional partners, such as CSOs, to play a complementary role.* CSOs can work with poor people and local communities to implement empowerment-based development programs and broaden the base of popular participation by including community organizations, such as school and student councils, and neighborhood or village organizations and councils in targeting and coordinating local development solutions.
- *Opening the way for the private sector to develop and reform vocational and technical education.* The goal would be to match vocational and technical education outcomes to private-sector and market needs and economic trends, as occurs in advanced industrial nations.
- *Changing sociocultural attitudes toward manual, semiskilled, and skilled labor.* Young people need encouragement to become productive and autonomous in many different sectors rather than competing exclusively for public-sector jobs (box 5.2).
- *Instilling positive attitudes about the role of women in Arab societies, particularly their economic contributions, and empowering women to acquire resources, assets, and property.* Social and religious leaders have an influential role in changing such attitudes.

## Combating Poverty: A Collective Responsibility

Combating poverty is a collective responsibility of multiple political, social, and economic parties, with the state as the leading player. No single player can solve all the problems of unemployment and poverty alone, especially in light of the current economic, political, and material circumstances in the Arab region.

**Box 5.2 Changing society's negative view of vocational work**

Despite the great need for skilled labor in the industrial, technical, and other fields, society takes a dim view of such work, which means it is not young people's first choice when they look for work, even though it is more lucrative than the public sector. The demand for skilled labor intensifies when economic activity is thriving and diverse.

A massive media campaign was launched in Egypt during Ramadan 2007 to reinforce the value of work. The campaign message was broadcast on television during prime time for the purpose of creating a positive, inspiring image of industrial and skilled work, and complete information was provided on how and where young people could obtain such jobs. In response to the campaign, 110,000 Egyptian youths went for interviews, and 87,000 of them were actually employed. This campaign was accompanied by the implementation of pre-employment pilot programs. Such programs corresponded to the requirements of vacant positions in private-sector establishments which pledged to hire the trainees.

—UNDP 2010a

### Socialization institutions

Socialization institutions, such as the family, school, and places of worship, have a variety of responsibilities:

- Changing negative attitudes toward work by instilling a strong work ethic and a culture of striving hard and rejecting dependency.
- Changing society's view of work in the public sector, which continues to be the aspiration of many young people.[35]
- Changing negative perceptions of vocational and technical education, which is viewed as less prestigious than academic education.

### The local community

Local communities can do much to improve conditions for poor people and help them help themselves:

- *Empowering the poor to organize themselves* into community pressure groups to participate in policymaking and the fair distribution of resources and development gains, and to propagate and reinforce a culture of community accountability. These mechanisms might include establishing quotas to ensure that the poor have a voice on local and representative councils and in civil society institutions for development, agricultural cooperatives, and other bodies, and setting up organizations for the poor to participate actively in the community.
- *Moving toward cultural and social reform with the aim of ending stereotypes* that impede modernization and the emergence of creative thinking and that breed a culture opposed to sociocultural change. Such a culture elevates negative values of social discrimination, glorifies the role of the state and ruling regimes, and stifles freedoms on the pretext of obedience to authority and one's elders. These rigid stereotypes are transferred across generations, with each new generation reproducing the oppressive culture in which they were raised.
- *Creating community-based organizations for youth and the poor.*

### Institutional measures
Arab countries need to introduce several institutional measures to support change:

- *Intensifying regional cooperation in development and investment projects.* Such projects might involve Arab and international partnerships with civil society, the private sector, and Arab financial institutions.
- *Balancing the traditional development approach of most Arab governments*—by investing in infrastructure and basic services, activities that frequently suffer from mismanagement and bureaucracy—*and the human development approach*, which is concerned with building human capacity; increasing welfare, education, and training; fostering a climate of freedom; and empowering the poor politically, legally, and socially.
- *Adopting income redistribution policies* to treat the multiple dimensions of poverty and inequality (box 5.3). The goals are to improve poor people's access to productive assets, invest in social infrastructure, expand loan projects, implement tax reforms, apply investment incentive policies in rural areas, and impose progressive taxation to redistribute wealth[36]—all while fostering and supporting self-employment and income-generating work opportunities.

**Box 5.3 The new roles for the state**
Some of the state's new roles have to do with managing the "struggle over distribution." This means building the capable state, strengthening the business sector so that the state can prevent elite and capitalist forces from monopolizing the market, and expanding public services to the largest possible extent. This approach has achieved successes in East Asia and some Latin American states, where the strong, capable state has set the balance between the various components of the market, society, and state. Getting the balance right is helped by the presence of civil society institutions that can mediate between state and society—as in Indonesia, where such institutions pressured the state to expand political freedoms and to adopt poverty reduction programs after the 1997 financial crisis.

—UNDP 2010c, 62–63

## Toward a New Social Contract

The state's shrinking role in social service provision and its gradual abandonment of a caretaker role, together with a move toward a free-market economy over the past two decades, have left a vacuum not yet filled by other organizations. Economic policies to boost growth and alleviate poverty do not appear to have created an environment conducive to sustainable development. Weak spots have become visible in the social policy that accompanied structural reforms and thus prevented real gains in poverty reduction:

- *State priorities that no longer cover all groups in society as a result of reforms and elite groups' monopolization of resources.* Efforts to compensate for this imbalance involve targeting specific groups instead of providing social services and fundamental social rights to all, as called for in the Millennium Development Goals. Those closer to service providers, such as people in urban areas, and those who know how to access services benefit more than others.
- *The weak effect of these targeted policies to empower poor people to escape the cycle of poverty because too many other aspects of daily life are overlooked.* The poor may not be able to benefit from meager cash

assistance or partial subsidies of health and education services because of fees, poor-quality services, or rampant corruption and mismanagement.

- *Failure to integrate these policies*, together with economic policies, into a comprehensive strategy.
- *Dependence on services without regard for empowerment*, with the exception of programs for funding microfinance programs that include capacity building.

## Integrating Social Policy and Renewing the Social Contract

As the basis of a new social contract, some countries have tried to expand the understanding of social policy as having to go beyond providing fundamental social services, such as health and education, or meeting basic needs, because progress in these areas has not been accompanied by equitable social development. Wide inequalities remain, requiring further efforts to realize sustainable and structural social gains for all and to narrow the gaps among social groups, especially with poverty rising.

Integrated social policy stresses the inclusiveness of society and a universal right to comprehensive social services that enhance well-being and expand the capacity to contribute to society's development. Such policies ensure equal opportunities to participate in society and the economy, to meet the needs of the poor and vulnerable, and to empower institutional mechanisms to eliminate barriers to inclusion and participation.[37] Integrated social policies reinforce development from a rights perspective, helping to end exclusion, deprivation, and marginalization. Such policies require a participatory democratic climate where people are the basis for social policy formation and where elite groups are not allowed to monopolize power in a way that biases policies in their favor.

The experience of countries that have integrated social policies shows five common elements that contribute to high levels of social well-being.[38]

- *The adoption of a set of attitudes, principles, and values* reflected in decision makers' vision and political commitment to social welfare, social rights for citizens, collective responsibility, stability, social and political cohesion, and social justice.
- *The pursuit of strategies for social welfare*, such as gradual reform in social policy, integrated social and economic policies, investment in human capital, recourse to productive welfare and the social development model, and reliance on universal coverage of social services and benefits.

- *Measures that support social welfare*, such as public backing for social policies, an effective role for labor unions and pressure groups, public participation in decision-making processes, government responsiveness to citizens' demands, solidarity agreements between employers and employees, a public administration with competence in planning, and supremacy of the principles of transparency and accountability.
- *An effective role for the state* in boosting economic growth, an effective taxation system, structural reform, and a mixed macroeconomy.
- *The presence of 'pressure factors,'* including demographic characteristics, regional differences within society, the influence of experts and technocrats, modernization processes, women's empowerment, and efforts to reduce unemployment.

On this basis countries can be assessed on how well they are following integrated social policies:

- *Formulating and implementing social policies integrated with economic and general policies* based on fairness, equal opportunities, and the provision of adequate resources to implement the policies. Within these approaches, comprehensive, effective social policies for poverty alleviation should be based on rights and freedoms.
- *Expanding the institutional and social base of participation* to formulate a comprehensive vision of integrated social policies and to create supportive pressure groups and effective coordination mechanisms by forming political alliances on several levels.
- *Harmonizing and integrating political, economic, and social reforms* to assess the capacity of the poor to participate meaningfully in political activities and to build alliances with organizations and institutions on various levels so as to form pressure groups.
- *Reducing factors that lead to emigration* by generating job opportunities (figure 5.7).

These policies need to be consistent in their development orientation and supported by subsidiary reforms concerned with specific sectors and groups. The programs should include a variety of interventions and alternatives to overcome disparities among social groups and to treat all aspects of deprivation and exclusion that afflict specific groups or classes. A program might, for example, aim to eliminate pockets of poverty or address needs in outlying rural areas.

**Figure 5.7 Brain drain, 2012**

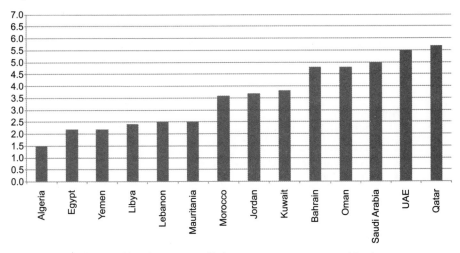

*Note*: 1 = The best and brightest normally leave to pursue opportunities in other countries; 7 = there are many opportunities for talented people within the country.
*Source*: World Economic Forum, Global Competitiveness Report 2012–13.

The revolutions in Egypt, Libya, Syria, Tunisia, and Yemen mark the beginning of an era in which the people have announced their rejection of the policies that have been imposed on them by elites and that neither serve their interests nor meet their needs. These were not revolutions of the poor, but revolutions inspired by a longing for dignity and for ending the suppression of freedom, the looting of wealth, and the policies that impoverished entire segments of the population.

Arab governments need to agree with their citizens on a new social contract based on equality and participation. Such contracts may represent a way out of the impasse created by the failure of previous policies to meaningfully reduce poverty. But the material and institutional capacities (as well as the sincere commitment) of the Arab countries to follow this approach, particularly countries with average or low economic growth, need to be fully addressed nationally and regionally.

Investments in segments of society that have been excluded—such as youth, women, and the poor—help create economic, political, and social stability. Policies must promote fairness, justice, and all avenues of human development. As is evident by the popular demands for change in many countries in the region, temporary solutions—such as the placatory cash grants offered by some Gulf states or the belated political concessions proposed by the governments of Egypt, Syria, and Yemen—are not the answer. A lasting solution requires comprehensive, immediate, and genuine reform on the national level, reinforced by regional economic integration, with states pursuing systematic, strategic economic growth in a coordinated fashion.

## Notes

1  UNDP and the Arab League 2009a.
2  UNDP and the Arab League 2009a.
3  UNDP and the Arab League 2009a.
4  al-Faris 2001.
5  UNDP 2010c.
6  ILO 2012.
7  al-Juhni 2010.
8  The Middle East region also includes other states, such as Turkey, Iran, and Israel. Consequently, such a comparison should be treated with caution.
9  Mirkin 2010.
10  UNDP and the Arab League 2009a.
11  UNDP and the Arab League 2009a.
12  The MPI is derived by multiplying the percentage of families who suffer from multidimensional poverty and the severity of the poverty.
13  For more details on how to calculate the indicator, see UNDP 2010c, Technical Notes, 225.
14  Abu-Isma'il, Ahmad, and Ramadan 2010.
15  UNDP 2010b.
16  "Khulasat tahlil muqaran li mu'ashshirat al-faqr al-bashari wa muta'addid al-ab'ad" (Summary of a Comparative Analysis of Indicators of Human and Multidimensional Poverty). Abu-Ismail, Ahmad, and Ramadan 2010.
17  ESCWA 2009.
18  ESCWA 2009.
19  Mirkin 2010.
20  ILO and UNDP 2012; ILO 2013.
21  UNDP 2009b.
22  Arab Labour Organization 2010.
23  UNDP and the Arab League 2009.
24  World Bank 2010.
25  UNDP 2009b.
26  ESCWA 2010.
27  Faiz 2009.
28  ILO 2010.
29  Arab Monetary Fund 2010.
30  ESCWA 2010.

31   Arab Monetary Fund 2010.
32   Adli 2005.
33   ANND 2004.
34   al-Mutlaq 2008.
35   UNDP 2010a.
36   ESCWA 2009.
37   ESCWA 2008.
38   ESCWA 2007a.

CHAPTER 6

# A New Approach for Managing Conflicts

Louisa Dris-Aït Hamadouche

Numerous conflicts riddle the Arab region. Some are intensely violent, others less so, and still others are dormant. Some are between states; others are internal, but with cross-border repercussions.

This chapter focuses largely on the internal conflicts, although some of them arise from clashes between states or from foreign interventions. It investigates how Arab states have managed these conflicts and how their management affects human development. To what extent have the conflicts drained human and material resources, disrupted development, further fragmented society, and weakened Arab countries? What can be done to escape the vicious cycle of violence and coercion and redirect energies toward development?

Understanding conflict requires understanding relations among and between countries as well as social groups. Some political philosophers see conflict as pathological and irrational—inconsistent with innate human nature and harmful to humanity.[1] Others believe that conflict is natural, a mirror of humanity's selfish and aggressive nature, and existing in all places and times.[2]

Conflict does not necessarily entail armed confrontation, which is war,[3] because opposition and disagreement can be confined to symbolic violence expressed through threats, boycotts, or sanctions. But the hostile intent remains, perhaps leading to strained relations or to armed force. Advocates of the realist approach argue that international players should seek not so much to end conflict as to manage it better.

One way to transcend these different conceptions and embrace the multiple facets and stages of conflict is to define it as a clash between individuals and groups over ideas, values, or material ends.[4] This definition also permits entertaining a concept that is the opposite of conflict—defined "not [as] the absence of war (in the form of armed conflict), but rather [as] a set of mechanisms that allow actors to build the foundations for lasting peace" (box 6.1).[5]

**Box 6.1 About peace**
Humanity's feeling of responsibility to create a decent life and make it worth living with dignity has always been stronger than the will to kill life. Despite great battles, the survival of the human race is the clearest expression of a yearning for reconstruction, not for destruction; for progress, not for regression and death. This tendency is strengthened day after day thanks to the rapid and astonishing development of information technology and the communications revolution. Walls between human societies have fallen down, and the lives and destinies of societies have converged, marking the emergence of a new phase—a phase where peoples are not only residents of a small village, as they say, but members of one family, despite differences in nationality and race or in culture and language. All the members of this one family interact in all corners of our planet and share the same aspirations and fears. Despite all its missteps, humanity will go on in its march toward what is "beneficial to the people" and will make different cultures, identities, and specific characteristics of civilizations come closer to each other on the road toward positive convergence and interaction, both in taking and in giving. Thus, understanding will gradually replace dispute, cooperation will replace conflict, peace will replace war, and integration will replace division.

Our contemporary world is marching with confident steps toward a new and positive world with human prospects and globalization that will guarantee the values of freedom, truth, justice, and cooperation to all human beings. It will be a world where all relationships, dealings, and laws will be based on the prohibition of all forms and practices of exclusion and enslavement. This will mean a globalization with no policies of injustice, oppression, discrimination, or tyranny and a world full of partnership and cooperation, dialogue and coexistence, and acceptance of others. This will mean a globalization where resorting to the law of power and its might, against groups, peoples, and nations in order to deprive them of their liberty and human dignity, will disappear, once and forever. Am I dreaming too much?

I see on the horizon a glimpse of a new world, of a shining and flourishing globalization. I certainly see the end of a vicious and black history in which so many peoples and nations had experienced horror, tragedies, destruction, and disaster. I certainly see the beginning of a humane, prosperous, and generous history full of love and fraternity.

Peace within one country is no less important than peace between countries. War is not just a conflict between states. There is another type of war, which is far more bitter; that is the war of despotic leaders who oppress their own people. It is a war of those to whom people have entrusted their lives and destinies, but who have betrayed that trust. It is a war of those to whom people have entrusted their security, but who directed their weapons against their own people. It is the war which today people face in the Arab States.

Peace does not mean just to stop wars, but also to stop oppression and injustice.

—Tawakkol Karman, 2011 Nobel Peace Prize laureate, www.nobelprize.org/nobel_prizes/peace/laureates/2011/karman -lecture_en.html

The majority of internal conflicts are of the type that has been termed third-generation conflicts,[6] typified by their society and their intractability. Edward Azar, an early theorist on this type of conflict, held that modern conflicts were protracted social conflicts characterized by blurred boundaries between internal and external causes and internal and external players. He identified five variables that impact conflict escalation: group identity, human needs, governance, the state's ability to satisfy the needs of individuals, and international links based on economic and political relations.[7]

Conflict management is the mustering of moral and material means to direct and control conflict, bringing to bear the following strategies:[8]

- *Confrontation:* Resorting to various means to impose one's will, prompted by vital interests. The conflict management strategy is to create conflict to promote one's interests.
- *Avoidance:* Ignoring the conflict and not attempting to solve it, because the time is not right or because sufficient means or information are not available.
- *Accommodation:* Catering to the demands of the adversary because the relationship is more important than the issue under dispute.
- *Collaboration:* A solution that satisfies both sides.
- *Compromise:* A solution partially satisfactory to all sides due to the balance of power between them, applied where there are interests of medium importance.
- *Neutrality:* A strategy for third parties. Active neutrality refrains from supporting any of the conflicting parties while striving for a solution. Passive neutrality also refrains from supporting any party, but the neutral party, rather than helping resolve the dispute, simply ignores it.

## Classifying Arab Conflicts

The Arab region has experienced numerous and various conflicts since the middle of the last century, using diverse means and methods to handle them. Some of these conflicts have preoccupied regional players more than others; such disputes can be referred to as central conflicts, as opposed to peripheral ones. Central conflicts have riveted the attention of most, if not all, Arab states; peripheral conflicts are no less intense but are implicitly deemed marginal, whether due to the desire of certain players to restrict the range of parties involved in handling them or the lack of direct repercussions on influential powers in the Arab region. The classification of conflicts has adopted the criteria of central and peripheral, because these variables reflect the degree of importance that Arab countries accord to some conflicts as opposed to others.

More significantly, these criteria offer a key to understanding the conflict management strategies employed and to making more accurate predictions about the outcome of conflict resolution efforts. They also reveal the divergence in the agendas and priorities of Arab countries.

## Figure 6.1 Arab countries as a share of population and world conflicts

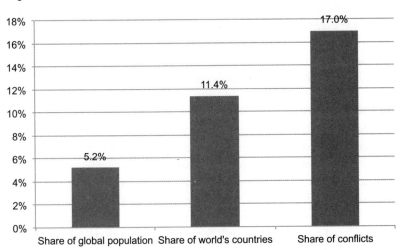

*Source*: Conflict data are from the PRIO-Uppsala Armed Conflict Database 2012; World Population Prospects, the 2010 Revision.

- Central conflicts: Acute and protracted conflicts that concern and affect all or most Arab countries and are managed by a large number of parties.
- Peripheral conflicts: Conflicts managed by only a few countries and ignored by most others, despite their being far from marginal in terms of their powerful impact within their subregional sphere.

This chapter focuses on conflicts that are still ongoing, as well as on those that have subsided in a way that has produced an ongoing effect—particularly on human development. It looks at the role of Arab actors, although impacts from the outside environment are inevitable. In view of the pivotal role played by the ruling regime—in its capacity as a central nervous system—there will be a focus on this entity as a primary player. The conflicts are discussed chronologically, from the oldest to the most recent.

Conflicts in the Arab world, even domestic ones, must be analyzed from a regional perspective. The rivalries and antagonisms between Arab states have an impact on the course of a conflict and how it is resolved or settled, especially in cases where several governments are competing to monopolize the role of mediator. It is also important to take into consideration the fact that the Arab region lacks a regional power or powers that work collectively to forge acceptable understandings and which the majority of regional parties support.

## Central Conflicts

Certain conflicts display different characteristics: some are regional, others are essentially internal, and yet others would rank as conflicts between states. Among these conflicts are those that have dragged on for years, while others are relatively recent, although they are eruptions of tensions that have long been dormant.

### The Arab–Israeli conflict and its offshoots

The Arab–Israeli conflict has stood at the forefront of the central conflicts since the 1940s. Although it cannot be classified as an internal conflict, the Arab–Israeli conflict contains many elements that have affected internal Palestinian politics and its relations with the region. Because of this feature, the Israeli occupation has implications at different levels, from the internal to the international. It must, therefore, be considered as a kind of hybrid, because it fuels regional and domestic conflicts while creating tensions at the global level. That said, the essential root of the conflict is the Palestinian people's deprivation of their legitimate right to statehood and their lack of the empowerment necessary to obtain this right. The Arab–Israeli conflict is governed by an array of legal, historical, religious, economic, strategic, regional, and international factors. As currently framed in legal terms, the conflict revolves around the territories that fell under Israeli control in 1967 and that are deemed occupied territories in accordance with UN Security Council Resolution 242, which covers the Occupied Palestinian Territories (OPT) (including East Jerusalem) and the Syrian Golan Heights. The conflict has affected the lives of millions of people in the Arab region—causing the displacement of close to five million Palestinians and the dispersion of refugees to Jordan, Lebanon, and Syria—and claiming hundreds of thousands of lives. The conflict has led to the continuous illegal exploitation of resources and the destruction of infrastructure. As a result of the conflict, 124 Jewish settlements have been established all over the West Bank, with another twelve in the East Jerusalem area, all of them recognized by the Israeli government. In addition, nearly a hundred smaller settlement outposts dot the West Bank; these are not officially recognized by the Israeli government, although they were established with the aid of the Israeli authorities.[9] Above all, the conflict has precluded the establishment of a genuine, effective Palestinian state.

Among its most salient regional repercussions, the conflict has divided the Arab world, fueled inter-Arab discord, and generated lines of confrontation within some states (Jordan in 1970 and Lebanon from

1975 to 1990). It has engendered disturbances in neighboring states as the result of the expulsion of Palestinians after Israel's creation and expansion. The displacement of large Palestinian communities following the 1948 and 1967 wars altered the demographic composition of neighboring countries, especially Jordan and Lebanon (box 6.2). The resultant tensions manifested themselves in violent confrontations with Palestinian organizations in Jordan in 1970 and during the Lebanese civil war between Palestinian organizations, Lebanese factions, and Syrian forces, which had originally entered Lebanon with a political cover from some Arab countries.

### Box 6.2. Palestinian refugees: An overview

Estimates vary for the number of Palestinians refugees displaced from within what became the borders of Israel in 1948. In 1949, the United Nations Conciliation Commission put the number at 726,000; the newly established United Nations Relief and Works Agency estimated 957,000 in 1950. The Israeli government has in the past suggested numbers as low as 520,000, while Palestinian researchers have suggested up to 850,000. Regardless of the specific number, it is clear that around 80 percent of the Palestinians residing within what became Israel were forcibly displaced by the creation of the Jewish state. Of these, approximately one-third fled to the West Bank, another third to the Gaza Strip, and the remainder to Jordan, Syria, Lebanon, or farther afield.

In 1967, another 300,000 Palestinians fled from the West Bank and Gaza, to Jordan (200,000), Syria, Egypt, and elsewhere. Of these, approximately 180,000 were first-time refugees ("displaced persons"), while the remainder were 1948 refugees uprooted for the second time. Estimates put the worldwide Palestinian population at over 8 million today. In January 2010, UNRWA data showed some 4,766,670 refugees registered in its "area of operation" (West Bank, Gaza, Jordan, Syria, Lebanon).

The population of 1967 displaced persons stands at approximately one million (many of whom are also 1948 refugees). The overwhelming majority of these are in Jordan.

**UNRWA registered refugees (January 2010)**

|  | In camps | Not in camps | Total |
|---|---|---|---|
| Jordan | 341,494 | 1,642,239 | 1,983,733 |
| West Bank | 197,763 | 581,230 | 778,993 |
| Gaza | 502,747 | 603,448 | 1,106,195 |
| Lebanon | 226,533 | 199,107 | 425,640 |
| Syria | 127,831 | 344,278 | 472,109 |
| Total | 1,396,368 | 3,370,302 | 4,766,670 |

The situation of Palestinian refugees varies widely.

- In the **West Bank**, refugees are stateless due to continued Israeli occupation and the failure to establish a Palestinian state. They live under a combination of Palestinian Authority and Israeli civil–military administration, in partial accordance with past peace agreements. Three-quarters of the refugees live outside of camps, and use both UNRWA and PA services. The standard of living of West Bank refugees is similar to that of the non-refugee population.

- In **Gaza**, refugees are also stateless because of the failure of the peace process to establish an independent Palestinian state. The area is administered by the local Hamas-controlled government. Although Israel disengaged from Gaza in August 2005, it retains direct control over Gaza's airspace, coast, and most of its borders, and severely restricts access. The current Egyptian–Israeli embargo against Gaza has caused severe economic decline, requiring substantial humanitarian assistance (largely channeled through UNRWA).

- In **Jordan**, most Palestinians (except refugees who arrived via Gaza, and some who arrived after 1967) are full citizens, and enjoy a standard of living generally equivalent to other Jordanians. Fewer than one in eight Palestinian refugees in Jordan lives in a camp, and most camps have effectively become urban neighborhoods.

- In **Syria**, Palestinian refugees are non-citizens, but are provided with full access to employment and social services. Only one-quarter of the refugees still live in a camp. Their condition is generally similar to others in the country.
- Conversely, stateless Palestinians in **Lebanon** face numerous employment restrictions and are barred from owning property. Consequently, they generally live in adverse circumstances, often in poor and overcrowded refugee camps. Because of this, many have left the country, and the actual number of refugees in Lebanon is likely to be much lower than UNRWA figures—probably around 250,000. There have been some changes in Lebanese government policy since 2005, and some minor reforms were made to employment restrictions in August 2010.
- Palestinian refugees living outside of these areas are dealt with by UNHCR, rather than UNRWA. In Kuwait, most Palestinians fled or were forced to leave after the 1990–91 Gulf War. In 1995, Libya expelled many of its Palestinians in a bizarre protest against the peace process. In Iraq, many refugees faced attacks after 2003, and fled the country. In Egypt and the Gulf states, Palestinians are typically treated as foreign visitors/residents.

*Source:* Palestinian Refugee Research net,
http://prrn.mcgill.ca/background/index.htm

This conflict has also caused acute polarization between Arab states over how it can be resolved. The Palestinians themselves are sharply divided in opinion over this dilemma. The Arab–Israeli conflict has snowballed, growing in size and accumulating side effects in the form of conflicts and polarizations. If Palestinians have been its chief victims, other Arab peoples have also suffered as a direct consequence. For example, the Arab–Israeli conflict has become a factor that threatens the national security and unity of neighboring countries, by aggravating internal divisions within those countries.

### The conflicts in Sudan

One year before the independence of Sudan in 1956, fighting broke out between the north—the seat of the country's political, economic, and military weight—and the south, against a backdrop of administrative arrangements and power centers that worked to marginalize the south's inhabitants. Fueled by religious, cultural, ethnic, and tribal factors, hostilities escalated into a civil war that lasted until 1972 and resulted in thousands of casualties and displaced persons. The 1972 Addis Ababa Agreement,[10] which brought an end to the seventeen-year civil war, scored a major political achievement in that it created the kernel for autonomous rule for the people of the south. However, the agreement was fragile and did not last more than ten years. In 1981 the parliament of the south was dissolved, and two years later (in June 1983) then-president Jaafar Nimeiri abolished the system of autonomous rule for the south. Soon afterward, in September 1983, he issued a decree imposing sharia law throughout Sudan, thereby reigniting the north–south civil war. From 1983 onward, fighting raged between the Sudan People's Liberation Army (SPLA) and the Sudanese Army, leaving a toll of vast numbers of dead, wounded, displaced persons, and refugees.

The civil war lasted until 2005, when the SPLA, led by John Garang, and the government of Sudan concluded a Comprehensive Peace Agreement (CPA). The agreement, signed in Nairobi on 9 January 2005, established the most important principles and arrangements for the interim phase, which lasted until 2011. In that year, the south seceded from the north on the basis of a popular referendum (held from 9 to 15 January 2011), bringing an official close to a series of wars that had lasted more than thirty-four years and that directly affected human development and human security in a country that possesses a wealth of human capacities and natural resources. Nevertheless, the seeds of conflict continue to exist in the border areas between the north and south. Specifically, 80 percent of the oil wells are located along the border between the north and the south, or in the south itself, which threatens to undermine the delicate peace.[11]

In Darfur, brutal conflict flared up in 2003 due to tribal and ethnic tensions between inhabitants of diverse ethnic origins, and international, African, and Arab efforts have so far failed to end it. The causes of the Darfur conflict are similar to those that precipitated the conflict between the north and the south, in addition to deliberate marginalization and exclusion, and poor economic, human, and political development. The conflict was further stoked by resource scarcity, desertification, and rapid climate change, which diminished water resources and pastureland and generated waves of internal migration in search of these resources.

In February 2003 the Justice and Equality Movement (JEM) and the Sudan Liberation Army (SLA), taking advantage of the conflict with the south and tensions in Darfur, attacked military centers subordinate to government forces in Khartoum. The subsequent intensification of the conflict reached horrifying proportions, causing hundreds of thousands of deaths.

The United Nations Security Council hastened to intervene, dispatching UN and AU peacekeeping forces (UNAMID) to ensure the safety of 1.8 million displaced persons and to prevent further massacres. Nine years after the outbreak of this conflict, armed tensions remain unabated (box 6.3).

### Box 6.3. Sudan: A test for the African Union

The partners in Sudan's Government of National Unity, the northern National Congress Party and the Sudan People's Liberation Movement (SPLM), which has been in power in southern Sudan since a 2005 peace accord, agreed on 23 June 2010 that "negotiations on post-2011 referendum issues and arrangements shall be facilitated by AUHIP [the AU's High-level Implementation Panel for Sudan] supported by IGAD [the Inter-Governmental Authority on Development, a regional grouping], the IGAD partners' forum and the UN."

Formed in 2008 by the AU's Peace and Security Council to investigate the Darfur crisis, AUHIP is led by former presidents Thabo Mbeki of South Africa, Pierre Buyoya of Burundi, and Abdulsalami Abubaker of Nigeria. According to the same memorandum of understanding, signed after talks in Mekelle, Ethiopia, the negotiations will be divided into four themes, each with its own working group: citizenship; security; financial, economic, and natural resources; and international treaties and legal issues.

**Contradictory role.** Thus the AU, whose Constitutive Act enshrines as a founding principle "respect of borders existing on achievement of independence," now finds itself in the somewhat contradictory position of overseeing arrangements that will probably culminate in the breakup of an African state. As the International Crisis Group points out in *Sudan: Regional Perspectives on the Prospect of Southern Independence*, the AU is a signatory and guarantor of the 2005 Comprehensive Peace Agreement. "International actors can play a pivotal supporting role, though the trust and confidence of the parties is essential for any third-party engagement to bear fruit. Thus, while it has an obligation to do everything in its power to make unity attractive in Sudan, it is also bound to respect the right of self-determination. If it were to renege, the credibility of the institution would suffer in the region and beyond. It is in some degree torn, and divisions among its member states in response to the referendum result could be disastrous. The way the body responds will be important not just for Sudan, but for the AU itself."

**International response.** Since the CPA was signed in 2005, several international fora have sought to coordinate international involvement in its implementation, with varying degrees of success. The Assessment and Evaluation Commission (AEC) was established in October 2005 in accordance with the CPA, while other ad hoc bodies have emerged more recently. The "E6" group, for example, is comprised of six special envoys representing China, the European Union, France, Russia, the United Kingdom, and the United States. The E6 has begun meeting regularly—notably in Moscow in October 2009 and in Sudan in May 2010—and issuing statements, which harness the collective political and diplomatic pressure of the nations and international bodies the six envoys represent.

In January 2013, on the fifth anniversary of the signing of the CPA, two men who had a critical hand in the peace process—Lt. Gen. Lazarus Sumbeiywo, the chief mediator, and former US Special Envoy John Danforth—argued that "unless international support is dramatically increased to help north and south agree on the foundations of their future, the elections and referendum may throw Sudan back into civil war." But as ICG analyst Zach Vertin pointed out, the onus for a smooth CPA endgame lies not only with the AU. "Coordinating international engagement is crucial, but it's also important to remember that, first and foremost, it is Sudan's two dominant parties that will be responsible for resolving the outstanding CPA agenda and preserving the peace," he told IRIN. "International actors can play a pivotal supporting role, though the trust and confidence of the parties is essential for any third-party engagement to bear fruit."

*Source:* IRIN Africa, humanitarian news and analysis, UN Office for the Coordination of Humanitarian Affairs, http://www.irinnews.org/report/89669/sudan-a-test-for-the-african-union

### The conflict in Lebanon

Since its declaration as an independent state in 1943, Lebanon has suffered from internal instability, fed by the surrounding regional climate and the repercussions of the Arab–Israeli conflict. At times this condition not only threatened Lebanese national security but also jeopardized the survival of the state as a multidenominational entity.

In addition to political assassinations and recurrent Israeli aggressions, the causes of Lebanon's instability include regional (Arab and non-Arab) and international interventions, which have become intertwined in the fabric of the Lebanese conflict.

The seeds of conflict began to sprout in the 1950s. In 1958 an acute domestic crisis, exacerbated by interwoven Arab and international interests, escalated from a political into a military conflict between the various Lebanese factions, leading to a direct foreign intervention by US Marines, at the behest of then-president Camille Chamoun. Not long afterward, Lebanon was sucked into the eddy of international and regional conflict, with the result that internal conflict erupted once again in 1975 and escalated into a fifteen-year civil war that led to the factionalization of the Lebanese Army and drew in Palestinian, Israeli, and Syrian forces to varying degrees. A range of regional, international, and domestic changes helped usher this war to a close in 1990. Shortly before this, in 1989, most Lebanese parties, factions, and denominational authorities had met in the Saudi Arabian city of Taif, where they reached an agreement on a new formula for power sharing between Christians and Muslims, known as the Taif Accord.[12]

In the course of the civil war, Lebanese factions and parties fought against one another, with the support of factions of the Lebanese military, with or against Palestinian groups (which had established their headquarters in Beirut and then carried out military operations against Israel from Lebanese territories), and the Syrian and Israeli armies on Lebanese land. The years of civil war also brought interventions on the part of an Arab multinational deterrent force in 1976, and a French, US, and Italian deterrent force in 1982. During these years, too, Israel carried out two interventions. The first took place in 1978, when it occupied southern Lebanon up to the Litani River on the pretext of needing to protect inhabitants of al-Jalil (Galilee) from Palestinian resistance operations. In response the UN Security Council issued Resolution 425 calling on Israel to withdraw and, at Lebanon's request, established a temporary UN force in the country (UNIFIL). The second Israeli intervention occurred in 1982, when Israeli forces invaded southern Lebanon and swept into Beirut with the aim of purging Lebanon of Palestinians.

Following the end of the civil war in 1990, Lebanon experienced a period of relative stability, in spite of the continuation of resistance operations carried out by Hezbollah against the Israeli occupation in southern Lebanon which, in turn, led to the Israeli Operation Grapes of Wrath in 1996. Four years later, on 25 May 2000, the Israeli Army withdrew from southern Lebanon (with the exception of the Shebaa Farms and the hills of Kfar Chouba). However, only six years later, in the summer of 2006, it launched another war against Hezbollah and the Lebanese army, which lasted thirty-three days. Since 2005 Lebanon has been rocked by a series of political assassinations, the first and most notorious being the assassination of former prime minister Rafiq al-Hariri on 14 February 2005. This event precipitated the withdrawal of Syrian forces from Lebanon on 25 April of the same year, ending Syria's nearly thirty-year military presence in the country. The Hariri assassination entered into domestic and regional political equations, with political forces in Lebanon splitting into two chief factions known as the March 14 bloc, which opposes the Syrian regime, and the March 8 bloc, which supports it. Domestic tensions continued to mount, reaching a peak in May 2008, but regional interventions prevented further escalation and possible civil war. In the 2008 Doha talks, brokered by Qatar, the disputants agreed to create a national unity government and to elect a president and hold parliamentary elections. The accord was dubbed the Doha Agreement.

## The conflicts in Iraq

Over the past three decades, Iraq has been gripped by an almost uninterrupted succession of wars and internal conflicts, wreaking enormous death and destruction and severe harm on human development.

The Iraq–Iran war lasted eight years (1980–88), after which Iraq invaded Kuwait in August 1990, triggering an Arab and international military drive in 1991 to force Iraq's withdrawal. The train of armed conflict also included violent and bloody clashes between the central government in Baghdad and some domestic opposition groups. This internal conflict can be divided into two phases, separated by the US invasion in 2003. The conflict effectively began in 1982 and manifested itself in clashes against the Shi'a opposition in the south (the Supreme Islamic Council in Iraq, the Army of the Mahdi, and other militias), which sometimes resorted to armed force, and in the conflict with the Kurds in the north, the political, humanitarian, economic, security, and development repercussions of which continue to be felt today.

With the fall of Saddam Hussein's regime following the US invasion, Iraq was plunged into internal chaos. The numerous parties involved were divided on the basis of their political, ideological, sectarian, and ethnic affiliations, and motivated by hatreds and resentments that had accumulated under the iron fist of Hussein's authoritarian regime. Since that year, more than 100,000 people have been killed, more than 2 million have fled to neighboring countries, and more than 2 million have been internally displaced.

The war on terrorism began with the US invasion of Iraq in 2003 and its repercussions continue to unfold. Indeed, the war on terrorism waged by the Iraqi government and the international coalition encapsulates the post-Saddam phase in Iraq, in which the country's cities and religious sites have been victims of terrorist operations that have claimed thousands of lives so far.

At the end of December 2011, US forces withdrew from Iraq, ending eight years of occupation. The situation that arose in Iraq after the US invasion and in the course of the occupation galvanized the attention of all regional players. Many regional powers saw this war as an opportunity to strengthen their sway and to influence the course of political and security developments in Iraq.

## Terrorism

The war against terrorism in the Arab region is another conflict that has attracted regional attention and occasioned serious cooperation. Governments have waged war against organizations that resort to violence to achieve political ends. The 1998 Arab Convention on the Suppression of Terrorism defines terrorism as "any act or threat of violence, whatever its motives or purposes, that occurs in the advancement of an individual or collective criminal agenda by seeking to sow panic among people, causing fear by harming them, or placing their lives, liberty, or security in danger."[13]

This definition overlooks—and conceals—the political ends that motivate terrorist groups. On the other hand, the convention made a point of drawing a distinction between terrorism and resistance, stating, "All cases of struggle by whatever means, including armed struggle, against foreign occupation and aggression for the sake of liberation and self-determination, in accordance with the principles of international law, shall not be regarded as an offence. This does not apply to any act that jeopardises the territorial unity of any Arab State."[14]

Terrorism and development are closely related, yet terrorism in Arab countries is generally handled from a strict security perspective, producing temporary solutions that are unable to control the pattern and evolution of terrorist operations.[15] During the past three decades in particular, most Arab countries have been victims of waves of terrorist operations of varying degrees of force, violence, and scope, perpetrated by extremist organizations that use Islam as the basis of a manipulated rhetoric that justifies their actions and their violence.

Iraq ranks first among Arab states in terms of the number of terrorist operations carried out in it—more than 6,400 in the 1970–2010 period.[16]

## Popular uprisings

At the outset of 2011, the Arab region underwent an enormous upheaval: "The people want the fall of the regime!" proclaimed the slogan that was echoed from the Atlantic to the Gulf. In Egypt, Tunisia, and Yemen, the uprisings evolved into popular revolutions that succeeded in toppling regimes.

The repercussions continue to weigh on other countries, notably Bahrain, Morocco, Algeria, and Saudi Arabia, which can therefore be added to the list of regional hotspots. In other countries, the social uprisings turned into domestic armed conflicts, as occurred in Libya and as is still in progress in Syria. These social uprisings should not be viewed as incidental accidents that will wither away once the "status quo" is maintained either by a security grip through repressive measures or incentives offered to the people. The current social uprisings are structural phenomena that reflect the fragility of the institutional and political edifices of paternalistic rentier states that proved incapable of establishing a social contract (see chapter 2 on the rule of law).

While the neoliberal reforms that were undertaken in some Arab countries—including Algeria, Morocco, Egypt, and Jordan—were instrumental in aggravating the fragility of these political structures, clampdowns in the political realm and restrictions on free expression have been a greater factor still. The violence and protests in these states are an epoch-making culmination of the policies and behavior of the Arab nation-state. Neither the caretaker state nor the rentier mode of social control has succeeded in sustaining a sociopolitical contract that binds the ruler and the ruled.[17]

Indeed, the ongoing social protest movements developed into political revolutions that truly epitomize the collapse of the political contract that Arab regimes had imposed on their peoples. More ominously, ethnic, religious, and tribal antagonisms are probably inflaming these uprisings. The attacks on Copts in Egypt (in December 2010 and October 2011) are a harbinger of this looming precipice in several states.

## Libya

Some Arab uprisings escalated into fierce armed confrontations, as occurred in Libya, and in Syria where the situation is becoming increasingly critical. Events in Libya began in mid-February 2011 in the form of a peaceful grassroots uprising in Benghazi, in the eastern part of the country. The demands there were no different from those voiced by dissidents in other Arab countries. Protesters asserted the right of the Libyan people to freedom of opinion and, simultaneously, their right to peaceful protest. However, events soon took a different turn when Libyan, regional, and international parties adopted a strategy of escalation. Muammar Qadhafi opted for violent confrontation, using heavy weaponry against civilians and extremely belligerent rhetoric. As the regime's repression of demonstrators grew more and more brutal, armed engagements flared, one city after the other left the authority of the central government, and the political opposition turned into an armed uprising after demonstrators succeeded in seizing arms and ammunition.

Meanwhile, regional and international reactions shifted from condemning the violence to increasingly serious measures. On 22 February 2011 the Arab League suspended Libya's membership. Then, less than three weeks later, it called for the imposition of a no-fly zone. Accordingly, the UN Security Council passed Resolution 1970, imposing a set of sanctions on Libya. Then, on 17 March 2011, it issued Resolution 1973, authorizing the use of force in order to protect civilians. The violent confrontation between the revolutionaries and the regime concluded with the killing of Muammar Qadhafi on 20 October 2011. Since then, Libya has been in the throes of a transitional phase, and the contours of its new political order remain unclear.

## Syria

The Syrian uprising also began in February 2011; since then, clashes with security forces have steadily mounted and loss of life and destruction have spiraled.[18] In Syria, too, the popular uprising developed into an armed conflict, between the army and security forces, on the one hand, and protesters and the Free Syrian Army on the other. On 15 March, demonstrators took to the streets in Damascus to demand political freedoms and the release of some political prisoners. The fever soon spread to Daraa, Hama, Homs, Deir al-Zor, Aleppo, and other governorates. The regime unleashed excessive military force against civilians in order to quash the uprising, driving some soldiers in the regular army who refused to fire on civilians to break away to form the Free Syrian Army for the defense of civilians.

In spite of the thousands of defenseless civilians being killed, wounded, and arrested, Arab, regional (mainly Turkish), and international efforts have so far failed to halt the violence in Syria. Moreover, the UN Security Council was unable to pass a resolution toward this end because of the vetoes exercised by Russia and China. The crisis in Syria has sparked regional and international polarizations, which have helped the ruling regime preserve significant room to maneuver when using excessive force against the uprisings, some of which have become armed. The situation in Syria contrasts with the Libyan case, which drew a high degree of regional and international consensus. Interestingly, the polarization in Syria has given rise to a new diplomatic channel for resolving Arab conflicts, whereby a joint Arab League–UN envoy is selected.

### Conflicts on the verge of eruption: The case of Bahrain

In the context of the uprisings which began in 2011, some Arab countries are undergoing domestic developments of a severity that has yet to reach its peak in a government–opposition confrontation. Without a doubt, the crisis in Bahrain is one of these open-ended situations. Bahrain, which obtained independence in 1971, is one of the most advanced Arab countries as gauged by the Human Development Index. Despite this success, Bahrain is still lacking in equal opportunity and equality between the two major components of the Bahraini popula-tion, in which regard the demographically larger component—the Shi'a—is at a disadvantage.

At the beginning of this century, when Bahrain began to implement a policy of political liberalization, the Shi'a demographic majority suc-ceeded—through al-Wefaq National Islamic Society, the largest Shi'a party in Bahrain—in securing several parliamentary seats in the legislative elections of 2006 and 2010. Nevertheless, the reverberations of the events of the Arab Spring of 2011 propelled large portions of the Bahraini popu-lation to take to the streets with demands for radical changes in the system of government. Prime among these demands were calls for a constitutional monarchy and democratic elections. On 14 February 2011, clashes erupted between the police and the Bahraini opposition in Manama, which led to talks between the government and the opposition. However, after a month of continuous violent demonstrations, the government declared a state of emergency and mandated the army to take the measures necessary "to protect the safety of the country and its people." At the same time, the government appealed to the GCC's Peninsula Shield Force to help restore order. On 14 March, a large contingent of Saudi forces together with units from some other Gulf countries entered Bahrain. In the course of the clampdown, the government of Bahrain and the security forces were accused of recourse to excessive force, disregard for human rights, arbi-trary detention, torture, and systematic intimidation.

What heightens the delicacy of this internal situation is that Bahrain is one of the Arab countries most vulnerable to the influence of regional politics and the polarizations in the Gulf. Particularly since the 1979 Islamic revolution in Iran, Bahrain's vulnerability has heightened with the political changes in Iraq following the US invasion, on the one hand, and the growing sensitivity among the GCC members, on the other, toward outside attempts to intervene in their domestic affairs by exploiting the factor of sectarian diversity. A royal edict was issued in July 2011 that created the Bahrain Independent Commission of Inquiry, a fact-finding commission tasked with preparing a report on the events of February and March 2011 based on international human rights stan-dards. The commission submitted its report in November 2011. The report stated that the violence in Bahrain "was the result of an escalating process in which both the Government and the opposition have their share of responsibility in allowing events to unfold as they did." The report recommended forming a national committee to implement the recommendations of the report, in which the opposition parties and civil society organizations are represented, in addition to the cabinet.

## Marginalized Conflicts

The second group of conflicts vary in severity—some are static, and others are of moderate or low intensity—but they share the trait of intractability. These conflicts have persisted for decades, if not since the establishment or independence of the states involved, defying all attempts at resolution or settlement.

### The conflicts in Yemen

Yemen has been in a condition of unstable equilibrium since the emergence of the modern state at the beginning of the 1960s and particularly since the southern portion of the country gained independence from Britain in 1967. From that time forward, the two halves of the country have experienced several civil wars. The north was embroiled in civil war for several years following the establishment of the republic; in 1979, armed clashes erupted between the north and the south; and in 1986, South Yemen was plunged into civil war. Today the internal situation in Yemen is inflamed on several fronts. Above all, tensions continue to seethe between the north and the south as an extension of the partition and civil war; confrontations flare against the Houthis in the north; and a war against al-Qaeda continues.

Various regional, international, and internal factors combined to permit the unification of the Yemen, creating the Yemeni Republic, which was declared on 22 May 1990. From then on, the fragile unity plus regional and domestic changes, as well as tribal, political, religious, economic, and climatic factors, combined to delineate the future of the conflicts in Yemen. The rush of events inside Yemen and abroad translated into an unfolding political and military panorama that opened with the economic, political, cultural, military, social, and religious merger of the north and south. Fallout from the 1991 Gulf war followed, and then the eruption of civil war between the north and south in 1994, which culminated a tense period in which the southerners complained of exclusion and marginalization and lashed out at the economic policies of the government headed by former president Ali Abdullah Saleh. The war threw into relief the problem of citizenship and equality of all citizens before the law, especially in the framework of a state grounded in tribal and clan affiliations. Tribal and sectarian conflicts intensified the wars with the Houthis in the north and with al-Qaeda in central and southern Yemen in particular, aggravating the fragility of the Yemeni regime and leaving more than forty thousand dead. In the north, the Houthis, who portray themselves as an ideological movement, demand the right to be recognized as a political party, especially since the movement's leader, Hussein al-Houthi, sat in parliament from 1993 to 1997. They also demand the right to establish cultural and educational facilities in various fields for the dissemination of Zaidi Shi'a Islam. These conditions propelled the Yemeni government into a military, economic, religious, and political conflict with the Houthis that has generated five wars, the most recent being in 2011.

Yemen was marginalized from the Gulf Cooperation Council (GCC) due to radical political and economic differences between the wealthy oil-producing states with high national incomes and low population densities, and Yemen itself—which is permeated with tribal, revolutionary, secessionist, and terrorist currents; which does not possess great oil wealth; and which is further disadvantaged by a low national income and scarcity of natural resources. Yemen officially applied for GCC membership in 1999. However, the GCC's sole concession, which it made in 2001, was to partially include Yemen in some of its subsidiary organizations and agencies. Nevertheless, credit is due to the GCC, which, backed by the Arab League and the United Nations, achieved the peaceful transfer of power from President Ali Abdullah Saleh to his vice president, Abd Rabbuh Mansur Hadi, on 23 November 2011, in the framework of what has become known as the Gulf Initiative.

### The Western Sahara conflict

Upon Spain's withdrawal as a colonial power from the Western Sahara in 1975, fighting erupted between Morocco and the Polisario Front over the status of this region. Polisario demands the right of self-determination, and independence by means of a popular referendum organized by the UN Security Council. Rabat, for its part, regards the Western Sahara as part of the political entity of the Kingdom of Morocco in accordance with the Madrid Accord of 1975. Arabs, Africans, and Berbers make up the tribal, cultural, and social fabric of the Western Sahara, the very last nonautonomous African territory. The fact that tribal affiliations in this area interweave with those in Morocco, Mauritania, and Algeria lends a regional character to this conflict. Yet, as intense as it has been in the Maghreb region, the conflict has never become central for most of the other Arab countries; control and mediation have been restricted to the UN framework and the African Union. In 1991 the United Nations sent in the UN Mission for the Referendum in Western Sahara (MINURSO) to monitor the ceasefire and organize a popular referendum that would enable the Sahrawi people to choose between self-determination and full integration into the Kingdom of Morocco (box 6.4). The conflict remains pending, with no likelihood of a solution in sight in view of the Moroccan refusal to organize the referendum.

**Box 6.4 MINURSO facts and figures**

Current authorization until 30 April 2014: Security Council
resolution 2099 of 25 April 2013
Authorized Strength
- 237 military personnel
- 6 police officers
Current (30 September 2013)
- 233 total uniformed personnel:
  - 26 troops
  - 6 police officers
  - 201 military observers
- 95 international civilian personnel*
- 167 local civilian staff*
- 13 United Nations Volunteers
* Statistics for international and local civilians are as of 31
  August 2013
Country contributors
Military personnel: Argentina, Austria, Bangladesh, Brazil,
  China, Croatia, Egypt, El Salvador, France, Ghana,
  Guinea, Honduras, Hungary, Ireland, Italy, Malawi,
  Malaysia, Mongolia, Nepal, Nigeria, Pakistan, Paraguay,
  Peru, Poland, Republic of Korea, Russian Federation,
  Sri Lanka, Togo, Uruguay, and Yemen

Police personnel: Chad, Egypt, Jordan, and Yemen

Fatalities
- 5 troops
- 1 police
- 1 military observer
- 3 international civilian personnel
- 5 local civilian personnel
  15 total

Financial aspects
Method of financing: Assessment in respect of a Special Account
Approved budget (1 July 2013—30 June 2014): $60,475,700

## The conflict in Somalia

In 1969 Siad Barre staged a military coup d'état to overthrow the democratically elected government in Somalia. By the end of the 1970s and early 1980s, the clan system, dominated by the Marehan clan in particular, had consolidated its grip over political and civil life, driving the other clans and tribes to take up arms and wage war on the Barre regime. When the regime lost power in 1991, Somalia was sucked into a nightmarish vortex of violence and civil war, leaving hundreds of thousands of dead, wounded, displaced persons, and refugees. In 1992, prompted by the ferocity of the military operations and by the massive deterioration in human and food security, the United Nations, pursuant to UN Security Council Resolution 794, deployed an African–international peacekeeping mission, in the name of "humanitarian intervention," to monitor and safeguard ceasefire operations and to supervise humanitarian assistance operations. US forces played the leading role in this mission. As the humanitarian and security circumstances deteriorated further, a second Security Council resolution was issued at the behest of the UN Secretary-General.

Resolution 814 invoked Chapter VII of the UN Charter, which authorizes international forces to use armed force to carry out an international resolution. However, reality on the ground as shaped by the Somali militias proved so overwhelming that the United Nations was forced to end its operation in Somalia in 1995. The tribal and civil conflicts and their repercussions on human security and development defined the last decade of the twentieth century in Somalia. The events of 11 September 2001 in the United States engendered a new construct for the Somali conflict. "Somalia" now became a byword for a breeding ground for terrorism due to the nation's lack of a central power strong enough to bring the domestic situation under control. The year 2004 was pivotal; a group of warring forces succeeded in reaching an agreement in Kenya to form a parliament and a transitional federal government, whose president appealed to the African Union for an international peacekeeping force to help restore peace to Somalia. The African peacekeeping mission did not last long. Following the withdrawal of its forces in 2006, fierce clashes erupted between the central government and the Islamic Courts Union. As Mogadishu appeared on the verge of falling into the hands of radical Islamist groups, Ethiopia was galvanized into mounting a military intervention that same year, which defeated the Islamic Courts. In 2007 another African peacekeeping force—the African Union Mission in Somalia (AMISOM)—was created with a UN-authorized mandate to restore security in Somalia. However, the Shabaab movement, which had previously formed a faction of the Islamic Courts, is still fighting and threatening the transitional government.

The Arab countries did next to nothing to help solve the Somalian civil war; there has been no serious Arab League initiative to resolve the crisis. The Arab countries did not participate in the UN peace processes, choosing instead to leave the war to African and international management. The Arab League's attitude[19] can best be demonstrated as follows: the civil war had virtually no repercussions on Arab countries, except for Djibouti. Reasons include Somalia's geographic location, its nonassimilation into the global economy, and low levels of Arab communication and trade with Somalia. Arab countries began to change their attitude once the conflict spilled beyond Somalia's borders, with the spread of piracy in the Gulf of Aden and the Mandab Strait threatening international trade, Arab trade included.

## The Cost of Conflict: Deep Disempowerment

Conflict is severely detrimental to human development, exacting a high toll by deepening disempowerment. The impacts can be studied at the social, economic, and environmental levels.

### The social cost

Conflicts in the Arab region have had enormous human and social costs, in the numbers of civilians and combatants killed or wounded (table 6.1) and of displaced persons and refugees (figures 6.2 and 6.3). Conflicts have separated large segments of the populace from basic services. And they have resulted in the deterioration of social and health services, the concentration of government spending on security and defense, and the forced migration of civilians during and after combat, leading to more deaths. According to a recent World Bank study on conflicts in the Middle East and North Africa, there are three noncombatant deaths for every combatant death during armed confrontations.[20]

The three Arab–Israeli wars, with standing armies against standing armies, claimed forty thousand to eighty thousand lives—more than twenty thousand people were killed in the Lebanon–Israeli wars and ten thousand in the two Palestinian intifadas.[21] In Iraq 114,000 civilians died from 2003 to 2011.[22] Recorded suicide operations from 2003 to 2010 were responsible for about 19 percent of Iraqi civilian casualties, 26 percent of the civilian wounded, and 11 percent of civilian deaths.[23] Terrorism has cost Algeria more than two hundred thousand dead and missing.

Conflicts are harmful to all areas of life, not least to education. In Iraq education has collapsed since 2003, with the flight of more than three thousand academics and the emigration of 30 percent of primary and secondary school students and 40 percent of university students. In Lebanon

**Table 6.1 The human costs of major wars in the Arab region, 1948–2007 (civilian and military deaths)**

| Country | Minimum | Maximum |
|---|---|---|
| Saudi Arabia | 29 | 29 |
| Kuwait | 2,000 | 5,000 |
| Jordan | 7,000 | 7,000 |
| Syria | 5,000 | 11,500 |
| Egypt | 24,009 | 41,009 |
| Palestine | 46,131 | 47,731 |
| Lebanon | 136,190 | 136,190 |
| Iraq | 580,625 | 741,700 |
| Total | 800,984 | 990,159 |

*Source*: Strategic Foresight Group. The Cost of Conflict in the Middle East. 2009.

**Figure 6.2 The rise in displaced persons**

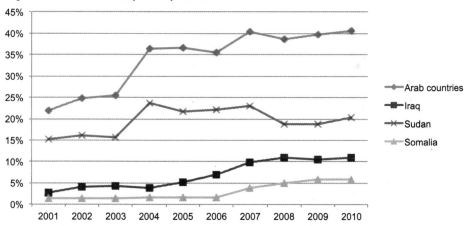

*Source*: World Bank 2012b.

forty thousand children had their education interrupted due to the war in 2006.[24] More than 1,300 schools in the State of Palestine had to shut their doors because of curfews and sieges. For refugees the Palestinian plight remains a special case: in 2011 there were around five million Palestinian refugees, 29 percent of them living in fifty-eight camps.[25]

## Figure 6.3 Refugees from Arab countries, 1990–2010

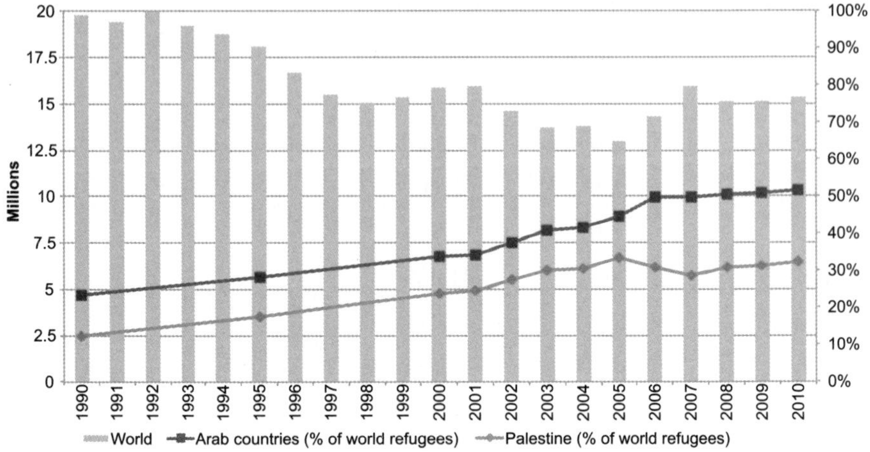

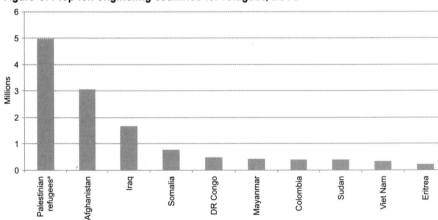

*Source:* World Bank 2012b; UNRWA In figures (from 2000 to 2011), and the numbers of Palestinian refugees 1950–2008.

Arab countries make up four of the top ten states that suffer most from the refugee phenomenon (figure 6.4). These rankings are indicative of the gravity of the conflicts in these states, given that the refugee problem carries a high probability of the same conflicts spilling over into neighboring countries that receive refugees. Lebanon and Somalia are vivid examples of this phenomenon.

## Figure 6.4 Top ten originating countries for refugees, 2010

a. UNRWA in figures 2011
*Source*: World Bank 2012b.

## The economic and security cost

Conflicts destroy economies. The per capita income in countries free of conflict is more than three times that in countries involved in conflict and around twice that in countries that have just emerged from conflict.[26] The Arab region has been hit particularly hard.[27]

Jordan spends 7 percent of its GDP on refugees, who make up a third of its population.[28] The Lebanese–Israeli war of 2006 cost Lebanon $3.6 billion, or 8 percent of its GDP.[29] Civil wars and terrorism have reduced economic growth in Iraq, Somalia, Sudan, and Yemen.

Iraq's invasion of Kuwait in 1990 had economic repercussions for Yemen, due to its support for Saddam Hussein's regime. An estimated eight hundred thousand Yemeni immigrants working in Saudi Arabia and other Gulf countries were expelled. As a result, Yemen lost remittances, which drove the poverty rate up by 47 percent as of 1996.[30]

The persistence of domestic and regional hotspots also sours commercial relations, making inter-Arab trade a leading economic casualty. Inter-Arab trade remains much lower than internal trade in other regional blocs, such as the Asian states, the European Union, and North America.

Military expenditure comes at the expense of economic and human development in Arab countries. Among the world's top ten countries in the percentage of GDP allocated to military spending in 2005, half are Arab: Jordan, Oman, Saudi Arabia, Yemen, and Syria. And the regional arms race has intensified as never before. Between 1995 and 2005 Saudi Arabia's arms purchases soared from $18 billion to $30 billion.[31] The trend shows no sign of easing: arms spending in Egypt and the Gulf countries is expected to climb 10 percent annually until 2019.

Compounding the problem of arms spending is the increasing militarization of society, as evidenced by the rising number of people enlisted in the military, engaged in state security agencies, or working for private security firms (figure 6.5). The State of Palestine is now the Arab region's leader in the number of security bodies, armed forces, and paramilitary groups.[32]

The security cost may be attributable largely to allocating resources to the fight against terrorism and to the inclination of Arab countries to manage this threat individually rather than regionally. Uncertainty about security has become a justification for Arab states to maintain high military spending. Most Arab countries spend more on arms than on education or health (figure 6.6), as opposed to such countries as Brazil, South Africa, and Turkey, where education spending is two to five times greater than military spending.[33]

**Figure 6.5 Enlistment in armed forces and security agencies, 1985–2011 (% change)**

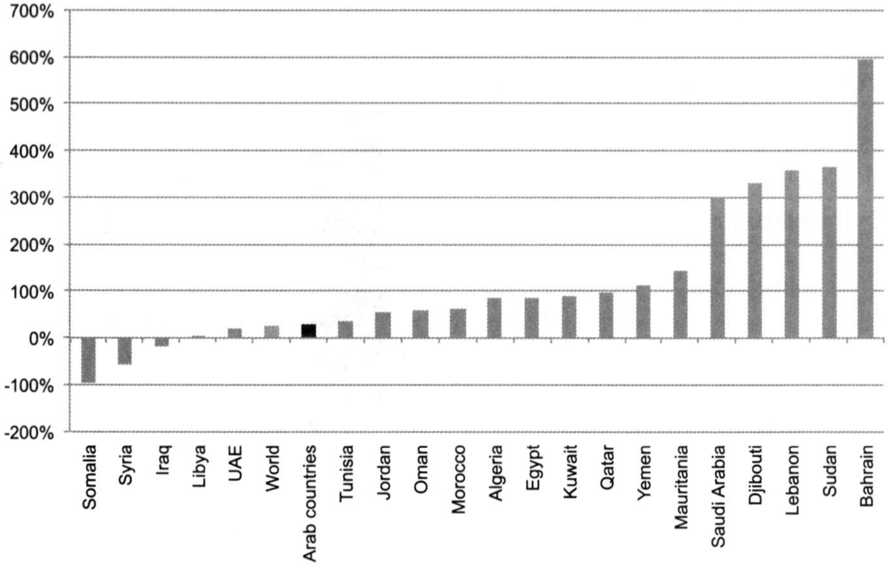

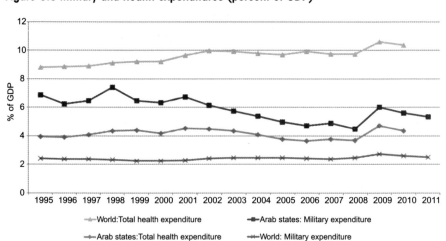

*Source*: Calculation based on World Bank 2012b.

**Figure 6.6 Military and health expenditures (percent of GDP)**

*Source*: World Bank 2012b.

## The environmental cost

Warfare has taken an enormous environmental toll in Arab countries. Of the twelve United Nations Environment Programme assessments on the effects of conflict on the environment, five were for Arab countries, acknowledging the problem in Iraq, Lebanon, the State of Palestine, Somalia, and Sudan. The Arab country most vulnerable to conflict-related environmental damage is Iraq, whose people have suffered decades of virtually uninterrupted warfare—from the war with Iran, through the invasion of Kuwait, to the US invasion. Recall, too, that Iraq was subjected to intensive aerial bombardment during the interval between the liberation of Kuwait and the US occupation. The environmental damage wrought in Iraq by the 2003 war alone is estimated at $6.4–$11.0 billion.[34]

Kuwait sustained heavy losses in the Iraqi invasion, with environmental damages estimated at $40 billion.[35] More than six hundred oil wells were blown up—producing 500,000 metric tons of pollutants a day, pouring 25 million to 50 million barrels of oil onto the land, and creating the largest oil slick in history (estimated at six million to eight million barrels), which severely damaged the Gulf marine environment.

In Gaza, in the State of Palestine, conflict has exacted a direct environmental cost of more than $50 million and an indirect cost of $830 million, extremely high losses in view of the area's meager resources.[36]

The 2006 Israel–Lebanon war caused major environmental damage, the most serious from the targeting of an oil refinery that spewed 10,000 to 15,000 tons of oil, polluting ninety miles of the Lebanese coast and thirty miles of the Syrian coast. In addition, damage to the Litani River hurt agriculture, which also bore the brunt of aerial bombardment, with 62 percent of the bombs falling on agricultural land.[37]

Darfur, with 1.8 million displaced persons, has suffered the most severe environmental impact of human displacement, in view of the area's arid and marginal land.

## Possible Solutions: Four Levels of Empowerment

This section discusses solutions that have been applied and proposes ideas that can empower Arab societies to reduce conflicts and their detrimental effects on human development—empowerment that is political, economic, judicial, and secure.

### Political empowerment: Democratic and political reforms

Arab government approaches to conflict management have been led by narrow interests. Needed instead are political reforms that can resolve existing conflicts and forestall future outbreaks. Democratic systems produce mechanisms that can contain and prevent conflict and safe-guard peace.[38] Most important are institutional reforms,[39] including reform of the judiciary.[40] Political alliances and coalitions can rebuild confidence and help ensure the broadest representation of forces.[41] Note that 86 percent of Arabs associate democracy with such political criteria as pluralism, equality under the law, the rotation of power, and the rejection of hereditary succession.[42]

It is impossible to incorporate principles of good governance without bringing civil society actors—associations, political parties, the media—on board to raise awareness of the dangers that threaten the Arab region. Education system reform is also essential (see chapter 8). Curricula and pedagogy can be revised to foster citizenship, tolerance, and acceptance of the other, all of which are prerequisites for development. The under-lying aim of education reform is to produce a citizenry that knows its rights and duties and understands the challenges facing society.

Some analysts refer to two forms of past democratization in the Arab region, neither of them desirable. The first is epitomized by the Algerian experience, where political liberalization gave rise to unstable political forces, some of which espoused an extremist discourse. This situation triggered a breach of the constitution, precipitating terrorism and a shutdown of political life. The second form is apparent in Iraq, where the idea of imposing democracy from abroad led to the fall of an authoritarian regime, followed by the collapse of the institutions of the state and the eruption of politico-sectarian conflicts and terrorism. In contrast, consider how Arab popular uprisings of recent years have set the course for democratic transition based on confidence building through inclusion.[43]

### Economic empowerment

Internal conflicts, especially armed ones, leave huge human and mate-rial losses. Thus, reconstruction should be the first stage of resolution and recovery. In Darfur and Somalia, states pledged financial aid for reconstruction, but the promises never translated into action, especially in Somalia, which lacks the government apparatus even to oversee reconstruction. To establish a link from the outset between reconstruc-tion and future regional integration, it is important to encourage economic actors in the Arab world, especially from the private sector, to invest in the countries targeted for rebuilding.

In any attempt at regional integration, transcending the country perspective helps minimize regional power struggles and can sometimes transform such rivalries into constructive competition that benefits all.

Administrative and communication networks need to be put into place to encourage trade exchanges, which gradually evolve into free trade zones, customs federations, and, at a more advanced stage, a common market. But if this course is to succeed, all available country and regional resources must be mobilized, and there must be a genuine political will to translate words into deeds. Two-thirds of Arab respondents believe that inter-Arab cooperation is less than it should be.[44] And three-quarters favor lifting travel restrictions for Arabs, free movement of goods between Arab states, a joint Arab military force, and a unified currency system.

The customs federation is scheduled to go into effect in 2015, on the condition—as yet unfulfilled—that the Arab free trade zone is fully operational. Another regional project involves construction of a road and rail network from Casablanca to Cairo. And the 2009 Arab Economic Summit called for expanding the regional electricity grid to meet shortages in some Arab countries, doubling natural gas pipelines, making peaceful use of nuclear energy, increasing solar power, deregulating air transport, and investing in modern communication technologies. Other projects are possible, such as developing communication networks of university scholars, researchers, intellectuals, and cultural actors to bridge opinions, generate interwoven interests, and strengthen the sense of belonging to a group.

Such integrative approaches can resolve conflicts—as in Europe (between Germany and France, for example) and in South America (Brazil and Argentina)—and in preventing the escalation of conflicts—as in Southeast Asia (China and Japan) and Northeast Asia (Russia and Japan).

### Judicial empowerment: Transitional justice

Transitional justice is a means of resolving conflict and remedying its consequences by addressing the human rights violations of the parties in conflict. It is based on the principle that resolving a conflict so that it does not reoccur is impossible without administering legal, moral, economic, and restitutional justice. In this process, responsibility is attributed, the guilty are punished, and compensation is paid. The application of transitional justice involves the following steps:[45]

- *Prosecution, with an emphasis on senior officials.* The aim is to deter the repetition of abuses, to stem hatred and the desire for revenge, and to rebuild trust in the state. There are few Arab models of transitional justice, except in Iraq; a spirit of vengefulness has prevailed instead.

- *Involvement of national, international, or joint courts.* Resorting to national courts is difficult when the crimes are systemic. Joint national–international courts that applied national legislation were set up in East Timor, Kosovo, and Sierra Leone. Recourse to international courts is available in countries that apply the principle of universal jurisdiction (which include many countries in Europe and South America) or through the International Court of Justice (ICJ). Prosecution through the ICJ requires that the state in which the crimes were committed be a member of the ICJ or that the UN Security Council issue a resolution calling for prosecution (as with Sudanese president Omar al-Bashir).
- *Inquiries by truth commissions.* Whether national or international, under the auspices of the United Nations or nongovernmental organizations (NGOs), truth commissions focus their investigations on victims; recommendations come after a set period that can range from eighteen to seventy-two months. Successful examples include the commissions established in Argentina in 1983, in South Africa in 1995, and in Morocco in 2004.
- *Material and moral reparation.* Under the 2005 UN General Assembly Resolution 60/147, "Basic Principles and Guidelines on the Right to a Remedy and Reparation for Victims of Gross Violations of International Human Rights Law and Serious Violations of International Humanitarian Law,"[46] Algeria and Morocco extended reparations to families of terrorism victims and missing persons.
- *Institutional reforms in the security apparatus and judiciary.* The most common reforms are dismissing security personnel who have committed abuses, creating new institutions to protect human rights, promulgating legislation to safeguard the rights of the individual, and introducing vetting systems for prospective personnel. Such measures were introduced in Algeria in 2004, leading to the dismissal of many senior officers.

Despite reservations about amnesty, no provisions in international law explicitly prohibit recourse to it for violations against human rights. Moreover, the declarations and resolutions intended to deter the use of amnesty are not binding. But there are provisions that encourage amnesty (Protocol II of the Geneva Conventions), although the intended beneficiaries are combatants, not criminals.

### Security empowerment: Regional and international cooperation in combating terrorism

Arab countries remain cautious about exchanging intelligence and coordinating efforts to fight terrorist groups. With the exception of a few bilateral agreements, regional cooperation on terrorism is still inadequate. Arab multilateral mechanisms and practical solutions include the following:

- *Drying up material resources.* 'Material resources' refers to logistical support, such as arms and funding. Eliminating them starts with heightening surveillance on money laundering, fighting organized crime that branches out to include terrorist groups, and criminalizing payment of ransom money.
- *Drying up moral resources.* Clerics and preachers need to be involved in refuting the sources of inauthentic religious authority and legitimacy on which terrorist movements rely. Awareness-raising campaigns can address the segments of society that might willingly or unwillingly offer support to terrorist groups.
- *Stepping up intelligence exchanges and coordination.* Success in reducing terrorism depends on the accuracy and density of information on active and sleeping terrorist networks and the areas and parties they target. The need for better intelligence spurred Algeria, Mauritania, Mali, and Niger to establish a regional intelligence center to combat al-Qaeda in the Islamic Maghreb.
- *Avoiding the visible presence of foreign influence* that furnishes terrorist movements with an additional pretext for fighting the current regimes in the name of jihad against foreign powers and their allies. The US presence in the Gulf since 1990 and US intervention in Somalia in the early 1990s demonstrate how such a presence furthers the recruitment of 'volunteers.'
- *Avoiding the security-solutions trap.* Countries need to resist the tendency to prefer security remedies over institutional reforms and political legitimacy, particularly in circumstances conducive to the growth of violence[47] when people look to security agencies for protection.[48]

Stability in a regional system is possible with a hegemonic power—a dominant power endowed with legitimacy—that safeguards the system's rules, values, and equilibrium.[49] At its base is the assertion that international relations are founded on mutual interests and the division of profit and loss. Countries opt to resolve conflicts not because of their love for peace, but because they believe that a particular settlement serves their interests. Accordingly, a system based on a hegemon permits international cooperation that takes into account cost–benefit calculations.[50]

Can some Arab states create an alliance that would achieve stability that rests on their relative regional, economic, and political weight?

Arab conflicts have sometimes led to illegitimate military interventions, some by neighboring states (box 6.5). Rather than helping, the intervening neighboring states have worsened the security situation. Meanwhile, some UN interventions have had profoundly adverse effects, and some have failed to yield the desired results.

### Box 6.5 Humanitarian intervention

*Humanitarian intervention* was a term traditionally used, particularly during the nineteenth and early twentieth centuries, to justify military intervention by a state or group of states (always European or western) in another state's territory (the Ottoman Empire or China, for example). The pretext was to prevent massacres (now designated as grievous violations of human rights) by the other state's authorities or by a section of its population against some of its subjects from religious or racial minorities or, in some cases, foreign communities.

The theory of humanitarian intervention as a justification was used in political or moral discourse and was not formulated into a legal principle with customary content and conditions, although some efforts were exerted in that direction. Humanitarian intervention flourished at a time when the resort to war was not forbidden, and of course "he who can do more can do less," meaning that humanitarian intervention was a political and moral justification for the use of a power legally mandated in general.

The UN Charter introduced a totally different legal system. Article 2, Paragraph 4 imposed a total ban on the individual or unilateral use of force (by either a single state or a group of states) with the sole exception of legitimate self-defense (Article 51). This action, of course, is apart from the "collective measures" by the United Nations itself in the name of the international community. Consensus exists on the imperative character of this ban.

The Kosovo crisis raised the matter anew since "humanitarian intervention" was one of the legal justifications put forward by NATO for the use of military force against Yugoslavia without a Security Council Resolution.

Following the Kosovo crisis, the independent International Committee on Intervention and State Sovereignty was formed to investigate the topic. Its report, "The Responsibility to Protect," issued in 2001, resonated widely.

The report contains many constructive suggestions, such as broadening the scope of "collective measures" through UN mechanisms and encouraging resort to the General Assembly in the event of a paralyzed Security Council. However, it also provoked strong opposition for its failure to deal frankly with unilateral intervention (either by a state or group of states) outside the UN framework. It implicitly opened the door to such a possibility by mentioning two cases where it suggested that the use of force also applied to unilateral use of force without UN authorization: large-scale loss of life and ethnic cleansing.

Some may ask what is wrong with the unilateral use of force to prevent or stop such atrocities when perpetrated on the widest scale. In reality, the danger lies in using force in the name of humanity, or under the humanitarian banner, while refusing to be subject to the judgment and evaluation of this humanity.

When the Security Council is paralyzed by a veto, the General Assembly can be more open and representative of humanity at large. However, unless two-thirds of the General Assembly agree that the situation represents a case of need (or a humanitarian emergency), how can any agency claim a need for military intervention without stirring the strongest doubts over its true intentions—that it aims to serve its own interests in the name of serving humanity?

—George Abi Saab, professor, international law; former judge, International Criminal Tribunal for the Former Yugoslavia; and member, Appeals Board of the WTO's Dispute Resolution Mechanism

**Figure 6.7 Current UN operations in the Arab region and their authorized strength, 2012**

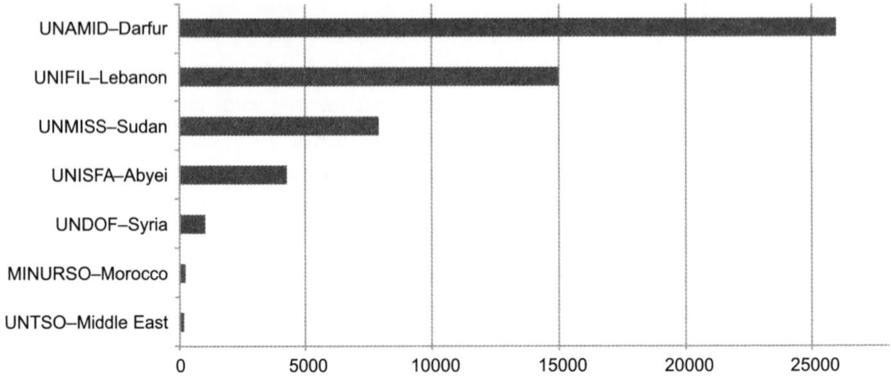

Source: United Nations Peacekeeping Operations 2012.

The United Nations has led many operations to settle conflicts in the Arab region. Arab participation in these operations has been limited mainly to Egypt, Jordan, and Yemen (figure 6.7).

Iraq's invasion of Kuwait in 1990 triggered a fracture in the Arab order because of the rift between the supporters of Iraq and the coalition forces (thirty-three countries) supporting Kuwait, and between supporters of an Arab–Arab solution and supporters of US intervention. The fracture was aggravated by the war's eventual extension to the invasion of Iraq in 2003. The lack of an institutionalized and legally codified Arab conflict-resolution system explains why the 2011 flight ban over Libya was imposed by NATO rather than by Arab states and without their broad participation.[51]

Article 5 of the Arab League Charter states that member states should settle conflicts by peaceful means and that disputant state parties should appeal to the Arab League Council to settle their conflicts. Article 6 urges a state that is under attack or threatened with attack to appeal to the council for immediate intervention. The council is to determine, by unanimous decision (without the input of the aggressor state), the measures necessary to deter or stop the aggression. Despite the poor success rate (table 6.2), the charter encourages recourse to the Arab League for arbitration and judgment, which requires the consent of the parties to the conflict.[52]

**Table 6.2 The outcomes of Arab League mediation**

| Type of intervention | Failures | Successes |
| --- | --- | --- |
| Mediation/reconciliation | | Jordan and neighboring countries, 1950 |
| Nonintervention | Sudan–Egypt, 1958 | |
| Mediation, emergency forces | | Iraq–Kuwait, 1961 |
| Mediation | Morocco–Algeria, 1963 | |
| Mediation/reconciliation | | North and South Yemen, 1972 |
| Deterrent force | Lebanon 1976–83 | |
| Mediation/ceasefire | | Egypt–Libya, 1977 |
| Mediation | Qatar–Bahrain, 1986 | |
| Mediation | Iraq–Iran, 1987 | |
| Mediation | Iraq–Kuwait, 1990 | |
| Mediation/contact group | Somalia, 1992–2006 | |
| Mediation | Lebanon, 2007 | |
| Mediation/reconstruction | South Sudan, 1985–2008 | |
| Mediation/reconstruction | Darfur, 2003–2008 | |
| Mediation | Hamas–Palestinian Authority, 2009 | |
| Mediation | Yemen, 2009 | |
| Mediation | Algeria–Egypt, 2010 | |
| Request flight embargo | | Libyan conflict, 2011 |

*Source:* Synthesis by the author

The Arab League could become more effective in resolving conflict by adopting several reforms (box 6.6):

- Reactivating its Joint Defense and Economic Cooperation Treaty and its military annex.
- Reconsidering the voting and decision-making system.
- Rotating the office of the secretary-general to promote a spirit of shared responsibility.
- Creating a joint Arab rapid intervention force along the lines of the African Union's.
- Introducing a post responsible for security and peace affairs in the Arab world.

## Box 6.6 The Arab League and its prospective role

What takes place in the aftermath of the Arab Spring will continue to have a serious impact on the status and the emerging responsibilities of the League of Arab States. One urgent challenge is that the Secretariat must stop equating Arab states exclusively with Arab governments. The Secretariat needs to recognize that "the state" is both government and civil society. This entails a redefinition of the league's mandate, and a review prior to introducing amendments to its charter, which accommodate the profound changes necessary to meet the Arab people's heightened expectations. These changes must adjust to the rapidly growing expectations of newly empowered people—especially youth and women—and promote opportunities in human security, sustainable development, and the ongoing, expanding definition of human dignity.

Along with this must come clarification of the term "Arab." It must refer to anyone who is a citizen of an Arab state irrespective of ethnic and religious considerations. In other words, different ethnic or religious groups must be treated equally as part of the culture of pluralism. It is crucial that the term "Arab" not imply any form of discrimination, to avoid the system that led, for example, to the separation of South Sudan.

Since the transformative changes of the past few years, the League of Arab States has sought to take stronger initiatives, as it did in Syria. The United Nations and most of the international community have welcomed its enhanced role. This opening can lead the Arab League to become a viable instrument in fulfilling the objectives and policies recommended by the Arab Human Development Reports.

—Clovis Maksoud, professor of international law,
American University, Washington, DC

## Empowerment by Preventing Conflict

Conflict prevention is complex, involving more than the United Nations.[53] Frequently, preventive action is not intended to avoid the outbreak of conflict but to alleviate its severity and limit its scope. Even so, pre-emption is the stated aim of any preventive policy, whether its focus is practical or structural. Practical prevention consists of short-term efforts to lessen the severity of a conflict or crisis by employing peaceful or coercive instruments. Because of the demonstrable shortcomings of practical prevention—it comes too late—it is necessary to resort to structural prevention, which functions over the long term and focuses on intervening as soon as the circumstances or dynamics of conflict arise. This is why an early warning system is necessary.[54]

### An Arab early warning system

The objective behind the proposal for an Arab early warning system is to preclude reliance on any imported intervention model that, implemented elsewhere, produces new realities on the ground and leads to a redrawing of the social and political blueprints of some states. This was the ultimate aim of the US military operations in Iraq and Afghanistan. Setting up an early warning system in the Arab region would help bring stability to states plagued by internal conflicts—and could reduce the tensions that mar some bilateral Arab relations. Other countries have successfully used early warning systems, which are founded on a set of rules and principles, to prevent some conflicts. These guidelines could be adapted to the Arab situation by taking into account social, historical, and cultural rivalries that reflect how the development of the state in the Arab region followed a different path from that taken by European, American, and Asian societies. Three measures could be considered for this approach to conflict management:

1. *Creating an Arab Conflict Prevention Center*[55] staffed by Arab conflict analysis specialists to compensate for the region's lack of risk assessment and pre-emptive forecasting. The center's tasks would include:[56]
   - Tracking signs of latent conflict.
   - Creating a set of indices to help predict potential outbreaks of violence.[57]
   - Issuing warnings.
   - Planning responses before and after the outbreak of violence.
   - Monitoring existing conflicts daily.
2. *Creating an information network.* This network would include NGOs with detailed knowledge assembled through close involvement with society; the media, to transmit events as they occur; and research centers that specialize in producing in-depth studies on sensitive subjects.
3. *Creating a link between early warning and early response.* Early response is contingent on the will of states, which, in turn, depends on their interest in averting violence.

Due to the difficulties of this task and the increasing frequency of flare-ups of conflict, the UN is contemplating a shift from a strategy of early warning to a strategy that incorporates changes to mechanisms and planning. The idea is to foster permanent readiness for crisis management in the regions and states that are structurally and institutionally deficient. Analysts believe that such intervention will be lighter and more flexible, especially since it will focus on realistic, realizable aims and be grounded in security for citizens, justice, and effectiveness.[58]

## The philosophy and mechanisms of mediation

Islam enjoins mediation in disputes and conflicts, in application of the strictures of the Qur'an and Sunna. Mediation requires the influence of a third party to facilitate negotiations and propose solutions satisfactory to the disputants, but on the condition that the solutions safeguard the group interest, which takes precedence.[59] To achieve this overriding interest, the issue under dispute is isolated and separated into its parts to enable the parties to transcend secondary allegiances (such as tribal and clan bonds).

Multiple options are proposed to alter the perceptions of the disputants. The aim is to steer them away from a distributional view of power, which reflects a zero-sum mentality, and toward an integrative perspective that views goals and interests as more important than the center of power and that understands that the interests of the part are impossible to attain independent of the interests of the whole. If a rational proposal (based on a cost-benefit assessment) conflicts with the interests of the whole, those interests should prevail.

The paradigm for the art of mediation is the early Islamic Constitution of Medina between the city's Muslims, Jews, Christians, and pagans. It established the principle of equal citizenship in Medina and recognized its pluralistic society. A set of basic rights laid out in the charter confirms this approach. The groups themselves emphasized equality before the law; the sovereignty of the law over all, without discrimination on the basis of gender, color, or origin; and freedom of belief.[60] This constitution implies that the aim of mediation is to promote the group's welfare—to lay the basis for a pluralistic state.

Arab culture assigns great responsibility to the mediator. Contrary to the standard view, a mediator is not a neutral party in a conflict but rather a member of the community who enjoys good relations with the disputants. On this basis, it should be possible to boost the role of such Arab players as the Arab League, the Organization of the Islamic Conference, the Gulf Cooperation Council,[61] and the Arab Maghreb Union, letting them assume the mantle of a supranational authority whose will transcends that of member states, disputants included. For example, in 2009, the Organization of the Islamic Conference launched an initiative to reform its structures and methods of operation and to create a peacekeeping force.

NGOs and individuals can also engage in mediation. Some NGOs in the west have demonstrated their effectiveness within the framework of multitrack diplomacy. Arab NGOs may be able to perform the same role, perhaps in reforming curricula in religious schools and reconciling points of view to lessen acrimony. Among the NGOs that have aspired to such a role are the League of Muslim Women in Sudan, the Civil Society Network for Peace in Sudan, and the National Association for Social Mediation in Morocco.

## Genuine Reconciliation

Reconciliation processes must take into account the psychological, social, and moral aspects of conflict resolution, as well as certain properties specific to Arab culture: the commitment to family relations and paternal authority, tribal allegiances, traditional codes and conventions, and a strong ethos of honor and chivalry.[62] As a result, citizens in Arab societies see themselves less as fellow members of a nation bound by the laws of the state and more as members of a community to whose influence they accede in order to safeguard social and moral integration and cohesion.

Reconciliation proceeds from the premise that resolving conflict is impossible without addressing the victims' feelings of fear and hatred and their desire for revenge. Therefore, restoring civic peace also entails the payment of compensation by the least harmed state or tribe to the state or tribe that suffered the greatest harm so that the parties can start afresh. Reconciliation comes only through a profound and gradual process that begins with an agreement to compromise. The process passes through confession, repentance, pardon, and compensation—and ends with reconciliation.

### An exemplary model

The model for reconciliation is that applied in the Republic of South Africa. To overcome the legacy of the apartheid system and forge a new relationship between blacks and whites, it was clear that reconciliation had to be based on two non-negotiable principles:

- Total and public truth leads to reconciliation, pardon, and compensation.
- Not telling the truth or confessing only partly leads to trial and punishment.

The public meetings between victims and their families and criminal perpetrators served as moral trials of the perpetrators and a starting point for the victims' psychological recovery. At the same time, efforts were made to deter revenge campaigns against whites and to prevent threats to state institutions and the economy. Less than two decades after the reconciliation process, South Africa, a G20 member state, has emerged as the strongest economy and the only stable democracy in Africa.

### Arab examples of reconciliation

In Lebanon, after the end of the civil war, peacemaking and reconciliation were applied more in the interests of security than in a spirit of reconciling past enemies. The system of consensual democracy that was chosen as a basis for reconciliation has three characteristics:

- Society is divided into religious, ethnic, and ideological minorities.
- These divisions are sharp, and the cohesion within each of them is strong. As a result, each minority follows its own elites.
- Leadership and administration of the affairs of state are conducted through negotiations between the elites of each minority.

At the social level, cultural diversity was affected by the ferocity of the civil war and the spread of sectarianism. Among the consequences were proliferating bribery and nepotism, migration, legislative paralysis, extension of the president's term, two constitutional amendments, and conflicts between forces despite Syria's withdrawal.

Morocco offers the only instance in the Arab region of political reconciliation followed by the creation of a reconciliation commission.[63] The process included a fact-finding inquiry and dialogue involving all disputants and compensating all victims. It concluded with amnesty for all opposition members and a set of political reforms that cleared the way for an active civil society.

In Algeria reconciliation took place within the framework of the Algerian Charter for Peace and National Reconciliation, which required neither admission of guilt nor repentance. The state offered reparations equally to terrorists who handed over their weapons, families of the victims of terrorism, families of terrorists, and families of the disappeared. The amnesty, applied after a popular referendum, was general: 7,540 terrorists, including eighty-one "emirs," turned themselves in and benefited from the amnesty provisions. Ongoing terrorist attacks are the work of an al-Qaeda-affiliated group that rejects any reconciliation initiative from the Algerian authorities.

In Somalia the procession of settlement attempts and reconciliation initiatives has included the 1996 Sodere Agreement, the 1997 Cairo Declaration, the Djibouti initiative of 2000, the Intergovernmental Authority on Development initiative of 2003, the 2005 Kenya agreement, and the 2008 Arta conference, which laid the foundations for a new regime. While the dissolution of the Islamic Courts Union may have opened a window to reconciliation, the Shabaab movement's insistence on full implementation of Islamic sharia law ultimately cast Somalia back to the situation before January 2009 (the Djibouti agreement).

### Tribal arbitration

A tribal social system continues to prevail in many Arab societies. Tribe and tribal rules and values thus figure in how these societies are organized and resolve conflict. The modern approach to tribes, by incorporating them into civil society, proceeds from the premise that civil society consists of all institutions that emerge voluntarily, function institutionally, choose their bodies and leaderships democratically, work to achieve their aims through active participation and peaceful and democratic means, and operate within the framework of systems, rules, and principles agreed on by their members.[64]

Conflict resolution based on tribal authority continues in countries with a high prevalence of primordial allegiances and tribal solidarity. Social stability is contingent on the tribe, which constitutes a moral space in which to regulate matters of violence, justice, and honor in accord with codes and conventions that may either conform to or conflict with the laws of the state or sharia. The recent popular uprisings worked to affirm the role of the tribe in Libya and to strengthen it in Tunisia.[65]

In Yemen the tribe has been important in sustaining social cohesion during difficult times.[66] When the central authority has collapsed, the tribe has stepped in to oversee the evacuation of cities and markets, to protect roads, and to shield noncombatants (women, children, religious leaders, professionals, and non-Muslim minorities).[67] Relations between tribal courts (which fall under the authority of the tribal elites) and official courts (which fall under the authority of the religious elites) swing from cooperative to antagonistic, depending on the strength or weakness of central state authority. The harder the state tries to impose official arbitration over tribal arbitration, the more tensions rise. But a compromise solution can be found in most cases.

Conflict resolution has six principles—compensation, punishment, repentance, pardon, the satisfaction of both parties, and the involvement of the tribe as a whole—and culminates in reconciliation between the disputants.

To a large extent, tribal arbitration in Yemen has been instrumental in preserving social harmony and cohesion, for it fulfills two essential functions: justice and solidarity on the societal level. And while state institution building remains incomplete, it also serves to preserve national unity and prevent total collapse on the political level.

Tribal justice also reduces violence. A 2007 field study of armed conflict in three Yemeni governorates (Ma'rib, al-Jawf, and Shabwa) over 2001–2005 identified 158 conflicts involving more than two hundred tribes, with only 6 percent resolved. Establishing development projects in one area rather than another usually triggered these conflicts, and the disputants deployed all manner of weapons.[68]

The current sociopolitical uprising in Yemen has not diminished the influence of the tribe. Indeed, one factor that weakened President Ali Abdullah Saleh was the withdrawal of the support of the Bakil and Hashid tribal federations.

### Attrition stemming from conflict management strategies

Conflict management has many dimensions, including assessing benefits and costs and long-term against short-term interests. For the Arab–Israeli conflict, the bargaining strategy pursued by some parties might appear to have been rational because it enabled some people to regain their occupied territories while giving others the international recognition that enables them to emerge from international isolation. But in the medium and long terms, this strategy concentrated the power to resolve the situation in the hands of outside parties. It also fragmented the Arab position and divided the Palestinian front and was instrumental in precipitating internal conflicts in Lebanon and the State of Palestine. And it facilitated moves by extremist groups to appropriate the Palestinian cause and use it as a shield to acquire legitimacy.

For internal conflicts, the confrontational strategies pursued by the ruling regimes in Libya, Somalia, and Sudan were instrumental in expanding and intensifying disputes and their human, material, and development costs. The secession of South Sudan from the north is an object lesson in the ultimate price for failing to resolve a conflict in a mutually satisfactory way before it is too late. Arab states have yet to apply the principle of democratic peace that has been so effective in Asia and Latin America.

Meanwhile, the strategies of indifference, avoidance, and passive neutrality that have characterized some conflicts (Somalia, Western Sahara, Yemen) reduced the number of intervening parties, which might suggest that the conflict would become easier to resolve. But these strategies also failed to resolve the conflicts, dooming the regions to geographically confined violence or perpetual tensions. The cost of this approach is high, for it has partitioned the Arab region into subregional orders (the Gulf, the Maghreb, the Mashreq, the Horn of Africa), each tending to ignore the others. If it has permitted the rise of pivotal states (Saudi Arabia, Egypt), they have not been hegemonic powers— able to secure stability and promote regional economic cooperation.

### Settling rather than solving

Settling conflict by addressing the immediate causes has taken the place of solving conflict by dealing with its root causes. That might end the violence but not the animosity because it only partially satisfies the parties. Settling may lead to coexistence but not to a sustainable resolution based on a spirit of cooperation over mutual interests.

Terrorism is frequently addressed through security measures and military means. However, the complex nature of terrorism and the political dimension inherent in any terrorist group demand that political solutions be part of any strategy. Algeria and Iraq tried to put this principle into practice through a policy of reconciliation. Their approaches greatly reduced the level of violence but did not end it completely because of the lack of political reforms.

Also unresolved are the border disputes in the Gulf. Indeed, some observers have come to suspect "a collective will among the leaders of the [Gulf Cooperation Council] states to keep the border conflict alive as part of the inducements that are sometimes required in political and economic haggling."[69]

The consequences of settling rather than solving a conflict depend on the nature of the conflict. In central conflicts settling can lead to the re-eruption of a conflict (Lebanon) or to less violence (terrorism). In marginalized conflicts settling can generate such a charged climate as to preclude any joint development project. For the Palestinian–Israeli conflict, attention should focus primarily on empowering the Palestinians and, in tandem, empowering Arab countries.

Today, attention is focused on the new circumstances and political outcomes that will arise from the social protest movements. Where regimes have already collapsed, the evolution of these movements is linked to how the interim governments handle them. Confrontation and repression can turn peaceful protests into armed uprisings and precipitate political and security instability, with national and regional dimensions. Conversely, regimes that bow to the inevitability of change and opt for negotiating can set in motion a process of political and economic liberalization. Resorting to avoidance and playing for time—the most likely choice for wealthy states—may contain the protests temporarily through economic enticements and partial concessions, but these strategies simply postpone the day of reckoning.

The Palestinian–Israeli conflict remains the main gauge of progress toward regional stability. The first step is reaching agreement between the Palestinian parties. If the transition phase in Arab countries continues to stall, it is difficult to imagine active, unanimous Arab backing for the Palestinian cause.

## Notes

1   Among the exponents of this thinking are Erasmus and Montaigne in the sixteenth century, Immanuel Kant in the eighteenth century, and such pioneers of the peace-building school as Boulding, Galtung, and Burton.
2   Viewed as a means of survival in the Darwinian and Malthusian sense of the term; Bouthoul 2007.
3   War as a continuation of politics through other means involves the systematic and planned use of armed force to compel an enemy to bow to one's will; see Freund 1976.
4   Tardy 2009.
5   UN 2005.
6   Kaldor 1999.
7   Abdel-Ghafar 2003.
8   The Foundation Coalition (foundationcoalition.org/publications/brochures/conflict.pdf).
9   B'Tselem 2011.
10   Signed between President Jaafar Nimeiri and Joseph Lagu, the leader of the southern liberation movement, Anya Nya.
11   Marchal 2010.
12   Chamber of Deputies n.d.
13   Arab Convention on the Suppression of Terrorism 1998.
14   Arab Convention on the Suppression of Terrorism 1998.
15   Dris-Aït Hamadouche and Zoubir 2013.
16   National Consortium for the Study of Terrorism and Responses to Terrorism 2012.
17   Catusse, Destremau, and Verdier 2009.
18   ICG 2012.
19   "Somalie: La Ligue Arabe est totalement absente" 2007.
20   World Bank 2011b.
21   Strategic Foresight Group 2009.
22   Iraq Body Count 2012.
23   Iraq Body Count 2011.
24   Strategic Foresight Group 2009.

25  UNRWA 2012.
26  Gates, Hegre, Nygård, and Strand 2010.
27  Gates, Hegre, Nygård, and Strand 2010.
28  Strategic Foresight Group 2009.
29  Strategic Foresight Group 2009.
30  IOM and LAS 2004.
31  Strategic Foresight Group 2009.
32  Strategic Foresight Group 2009.
33  World Bank 2012b.
34  Strategic Foresight Group 2009.
35  AFED 2008.
36  Strategic Foresight Group 2009.
37  AFED 2008.
38  Haéri 2008, Lomborg 2004.
39  World Bank 2011b.
40  World Bank 2011b.
41  World Bank 2011b.
42  Arab Center for Policy and Research Studies 2011.
43  World Bank 2011b.
44  Arab Center for Policy and Research Studies 2011.
45  Freeman 2007.
46  UN 2005.
47  World Bank 2011b.
48  World Bank 2011b.
49  Landau 2006.
50  Côté 2006; Kebabjian 1996.
51  Brahimi 2011.
52  al-Mukhadimi 2004.
53  Brahimi 2000.
54  Semien 2009.
55  The concept of this center could be compared to Boulding's idea to create sociological "weather stations" to gauge social temperatures and sociopolitical pressure levels.
56  Abdel-Ghafar 2003.
57  Briefly, the indices would consist of: structural upheavals (both social and political); political indicators (legitimacy of the regime, human rights); economic indicators (distribution of wealth, food security, military expenditures); social indicators (demographic composition, social relations); environmental indicators; historical indicators (precedents); and external factors (relations with neighboring countries, international political and economic status)
58  World Bank 2011a.
59  Abu-Nimer 1996.
60  Bassiouni 2003.

61   Pinfari 2009.
62   Irani and Funk 1998.
63   Irani and Funk 1998.
64   Sa'id 2008.
65   Bu Taleb 2011.
66   al-'Alimi 2000; Burgat 2008.
67   Sa'id 2008.
68   NDIIA 2007.
69   Damon News 2010.

CHAPTER 7

# Urbanization, Climate Change, and the Environment

Zeyad Makhamreh

S tudying and understanding the origins and nature of environmental problems in Arab countries is the first step in learning to
conserve and sustain resources and boost economic growth. This
chapter analyzes the environmental degradation in Arab cities and the
challenges to Arab human security resulting from climate change, with
an emphasis on empowering Arab citizens to cope with these issues.

These challenges are interrelated. Rapid population growth, changing
lifestyles, and rising energy consumption have led to high population concentrations in urban centers. This has accelerated environmental
degradation in Arab cities, increased pressure on infrastructure, and raised
energy consumption. The increase in energy consumption produces more
air pollution domestically and accelerates climate change globally. The
rising temperatures and frequent droughts accompanying climate
change exacerbate water shortages and desertification, lower agricultural
productivity, and thus further increase energy consumption. This
chapter discusses these difficulties and the scientific and practical solutions that can alleviate their impact. The chapter also suggests ways to
empower people to meet these challenges.

## Urbanization and the Environment

Urbanization refers to the growth of urban populations relative to rural
populations, accompanied by extensive economic, political, and cultural
development in urban areas. Measured by the ratio of city residents to

the total population, urbanization is a natural process in most countries, stimulating economic growth through industrialization.

### Population growth and urbanization

There were almost seven billion people in the world in 2010; 82 percent of them lived in developing countries. Approximately 359 million people, or 5 percent of the global population, live in Arab countries. Although the rate of population growth in the Arab countries has declined in recent decades—from 2.8 percent per year in the 1970s to 2.1 percent at the end of 2010—it remains among the highest in the world; the average is 1.4 percent in developing countries and less than 1.2 percent worldwide.[1] The population of the Arab world nearly tripled between 1970 and 2010, jumping from 128 million to 359 million. Some projections see the total population of the Arab countries reaching 598 million by 2050 (figure 7.1).

Urban areas make up about half the total population today. By 2050 the urban population is expected to approach 432 million, or around three-quarters of the population in the region. Contributing factors are high fertility rates, central economic and administrative planning, and an imbalance in development policies between urban and rural areas.

**Figure 7.1 Projected population growth in Arab countries, 2010 to 2050**

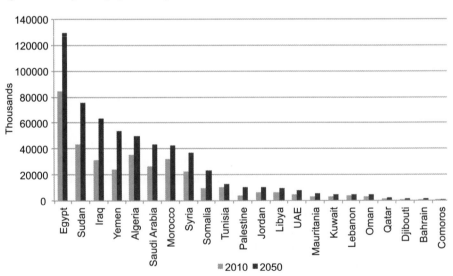

*Source*: UNDP 2010d. AHDR research paper series. Population Levels, Trends, and Policies in the Arab Region: Challenges and Opportunities.

## Urbanization and the environment

The population in Arab countries is concentrated in large and small cities of one to five million people. Cairo, with a population of more than ten million, is the only megacity in the Arab region. The urban population is 98 percent in Kuwait and Qatar, 82 percent in Saudi Arabia and Jordan, 43 percent in Egypt, 33 percent in Sudan, and 32 percent in Yemen (figure 7.2). Rapid, unplanned urban growth in Arab countries has led to deteriorating habitat, failing infrastructure, expanding slums, and rising air pollution and traffic accidents.

### Figure 7.2 Urban and rural Arab populations, 2010

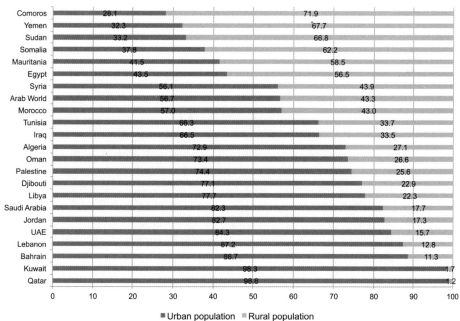

■ Urban population   ■ Rural population

*Source:* World Bank. WDI 2013.

## Slums and missing services

With urbanization in developing countries has come a rapid increase in the share of the urban population living in slums. World population is expected to increase by two billion people by 2030, with much of this increase occurring in built-up areas of developing countries. About half the increase is expected in slum areas, doubling the slum population from one to two billion. In many Arab countries more than half the urban population lives in slums (figure 7.3).[2]

**Figure 7.3 Percentage of population in Arab countries living in slums**

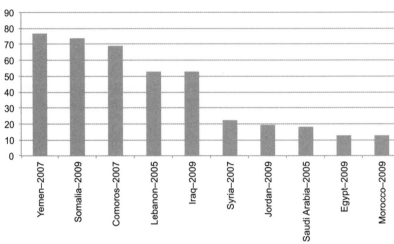

*Source:* Millennium Development Goals Database 2013.

Slums have spread noticeably in Arab countries that have suffered internal or external political crises. Slums, with their high population density and poor infrastructure, are linked with high poverty, rapid population growth, and political crises.[3] They lack basic services such as clean water, sanitation, electricity, road networks, social services, schools, and health-care centers.[4] They are also marked by informal businesses, unlicensed and often in violation of laws, codes, and regulations.[5]

Some Arab countries have increased the supply of affordable housing through targeted programs. Morocco reduced the number of slums by 65 percent between 1990 and 2009,[6] cutting the numbers of people living in slums by more than half. Egypt and some other countries have made progress in managing slum areas, but slum populations remain high.[7]

In other countries the situation has worsened or failed to improve. Poor neighborhoods are large and growing in Iraq, Mauritania, Somalia, and Sudan. The slum situation in Syria and Libya is worse, especially after the political crises in both countries.

Slums are not simply marginal, poor, unrecognized areas. They are a reality here to stay for some time. Policymakers need to focus on developing and improving slum areas and minimizing the problems they face. Designing and planning interventions requires assessing environmental and social conditions to provide appropriate assistance, whether from inside or outside the community. The government can work with the private sector and civil society organizations to provide suitable housing for the poor and improve economic conditions in slums.

Approaches that have worked include sharing land, refurbishing buildings and infrastructure, and rebuilding residential areas. Approaches need to be tailored to the circumstances and social characteristics of the slum area. Slums spring up primarily because of weak economic and social development and policies that create imbalances between supply and demand in residential areas. Providing reasonably priced housing of suitable quality helps prevent people from resorting to informal housing solutions.

## Air pollution

The accelerating rates of urbanization, energy use, and technological advance have worsened air quality, especially in major urban centers. Concerns about health have also grown, as the incidence of respiratory diseases has risen. Air pollution is responsible for approximately 3,400 deaths annually,[8] in addition to about 15,000 cases of bronchial infection, 329,000 cases of respiratory tract infection, and numerous cases of asthma. The costs of air pollution total about 2 percent of GDP in developed countries and 5 to 20 percent in developing countries.[9] Reducing exposure to this environmental danger would have large economic and health benefits.

Air pollution in the Arab region is linked primarily to rapid urbanization, increased vehicle use, the spread of industry, and rising fossil fuel energy consumption. Larger Arab cities including Amman, Baghdad, Cairo, Damascus, and San'a have levels of air pollution that exceed World Health Organization standards.[10]

Transportation is the primary cause of air pollution in cities. The huge increase in the number of vehicles—around half the vehicles in Arab countries are concentrated in cities—has produced a notable rise in the levels of air pollutants. The transportation sector is responsible for 70 percent to 80 percent of all hydrocarbon emissions, and vehicles emit more than 1.1 million metric tons of nitrogen oxides annually. In addition to these greenhouse gases, the lead additives in petrol and many other fuels in Arab countries account for more than half the region's lead emissions, again concentrated in urban areas.

The consumption of fossil fuel for generating electricity, refining oil, desalinating water, and other industrial uses also worsens air pollution. These activities reduce air quality by releasing carbon dioxide, methane, volatile organic compounds, and nitrogen and sulfur oxides.

In Bahrain, Jordan, Lebanon, Syria, and Yemen, air pollution is concentrated in major cities and results primarily from heavy use of transport. In Lebanon more than 1.4 million motor vehicles are registered, and about 55 percent of them are more than fifteen years old. Lebanon's total carbon dioxide emissions for 2008 led to atmospheric lead and suspended particulate levels several times higher than global standards. But since the 2003 ban on the use of diesel fuel in vehicles and lead additives in fuel, there has been a gradual improvement.[11]

In Syria, the transportation sector is responsible for around 70 percent of air pollution in cities. The concentration of respirable suspended particulates (PM10)[12] is high in the region (figure 7.4). In Damascus PM10 concentrations are estimated at 749 micrograms per cubic meter ($\mu g/m^3$) in areas of heavy traffic, and 333 $\mu g/m^3$ in residential areas.[13] (The level permitted by the World Health Organization for PM10 is 50 $\mu g/m^3$ ).[14] This high concentration is traceable to factories burning fossil fuels, aging vehicles, low fuel quality, and heavy reliance on minibuses for public transport.[15]

In Algeria, Egypt, Morocco, and Saudi Arabia, air pollution is also concentrated in major cities and results primarily from industry, energy production, and transportation. Algeria's air pollution is linked to transport, the burning of refuse, and industrialization in such cities as Algiers and Wahran. The annual concentration of PM10 in the capital is about 50 $\mu g/m^3$, with an ozone concentration of 180 $\mu g/m^3$, sulfur dioxide concentration of 360 $\mu g/m^3$, nitrogen oxide concentration of 400 $\mu g/m^3$, and a carbon monoxide concentration of 10,000 $\mu g/m^3$. (The average permitted level by the World Health Organization for ozone is

**Figure 7.4 Fine particulate matter (PM10) concentrations, 2010 (micrograms per cubic meter)**

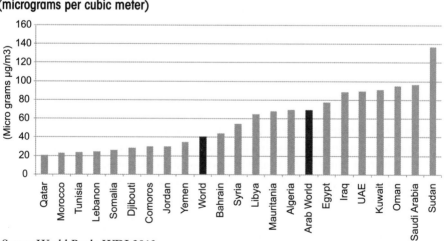

*Source:* World Bank. WDI 2013.

100 µg/m³; for sulfur dioxide, 20 µg/m³; for nitrogen oxide, 200 µg/m³; and for carbon monoxide, 10 µg/m³).[16] In addition, 180 metric tons of lead are released every year in the capital's streets.[17]

Egypt's greenhouse gas emissions are estimated at 0.6 percent of the global total. Pollution levels are high in industrial zones and urban centers, sometimes reaching six to eight times nationally permissible levels. Average sulfur dioxide concentrations in Egypt are about 69 µg/m³, above the WHO standard of 50 µg/m³, and far higher during rush hours.[18] In addition, high concentrations of sulfur compounds point to the burning of fossil fuel, with suspended particulates reaching 580 µg/m³ in Cairo.

Air quality is also affected by meteorological factors, including temperature and wind. Climate change (see below) will have a direct impact on air quality and thus on the health of the population, through ground-level ozone and suspended particulate matter. Increased carbon dioxide concentrations have led to higher concentrations of tropospheric ozone and airborne particulates. Global death rates have risen 1.1 percent for every 1°C increase above the baseline. Extreme heat increases tropospheric ozone, along with nitrogen dioxide and other air pollutants. Temperature, wind, and solar radiation influence the production and emission of ozone.[19] Concentrations of tropospheric ozone are expected to increase throughout the world, particularly in Arab countries. High exposure to ozone is correlated with an increased incidence of lung infections, asthma, and allergies affecting the respiratory tract.[20]

A wide range of options and regulatory strategies can reduce air pollution:

- Increasing citizen awareness and empowerment to improve the condition of vehicles through periodic maintenance and inspection programs.
- Educating decision makers and citizens on fossil fuels and the environmental risks they pose—to improve fuel quality and to minimize the pollution and health risks arising from fuel combustion.
- Developing environmental policies, laws, and standards for clean air. That requires setting national and regional specifications for acceptable levels of air pollution and making these standards known to citizens and decision makers.
- Fostering cooperation among the private sector, civil society organizations, and the public sector to modernize the transport sector and to reduce reliance on minibuses by constructing electrically powered railways.

- Prohibiting the import of old vehicles and introducing fiscal incentives to encourage the replacement of old cars with new, more efficient and less polluting vehicles, such as electric and hybrid vehicles.
- Reducing fuel consumption by rationalizing consumption and halting fossil fuel subsidies in countries that provide them, including Egypt, Syria, and the Gulf states.
- Minimizing dependence on fossil fuels and shifting to less polluting energy sources, such as natural gas, electricity, and renewable resources. It may be possible to compensate poorer citizens harmed by the discontinuation of petroleum subsidies by supplying energy from renewable resources[21] at reasonable prices.
- Conducting environmental impact assessments for different industries and issuing and enforcing directives for industrial zones located near residential areas.

## The Impacts of Climate Change

The arid and semiarid regions in the Arab countries are highly vulnerable to the effects of climate change because of their dry climates.[22] Rising temperatures and lower average rainfall will intensify the pressure on natural systems and water resources.[23]

The majority of Arab countries are already experiencing scarce water resources, high evaporation rates, and volatile average yearly rainfall. Arid and semiarid regions make up 81 percent of the land area, with 52 percent receiving average rainfall of less than 100 millimeters (mm) a year, 30 percent receiving 100–300 mm a year, and 18 percent receiving more than 300 mm a year (figure 7.5). Rainfall reaches more than 1,500 mm a year in the elevated regions of Lebanon, Syria, and North Africa, the coastal regions, and southern Sudan. Of the Arab region's 13.8 million square kilometers (km²) of land, 40 percent is capable of supporting agriculture (5.5 million km²).[24]

Human behavior plays a significant role in climate change through increased production of carbon dioxide and other greenhouse gases and particulate matter. The Arab countries contribute 4.8 percent of global $CO_2$ emissions. The Gulf countries and other oil-exporting countries, as well as Egypt, have higher than average emission rates for the region (figure 7.6).

Despite this modest contribution to worldwide levels of greenhouse gas emissions, the anticipated effects of climate change on the Arab region are severe. Surface temperatures in Arab countries are projected to increase 2.0° to 5.5° C by the end of the twenty-first century, and average rainfall is expected to decline 20 percent.

**Figure 7.5 Climate zones in the Arab region**

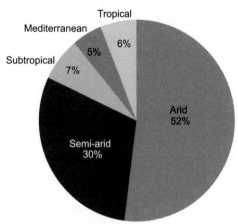

*Source*: ACSAD 1997.

**Figure 7.6 Carbon dioxide emissions in the Arab region, 2009 (percent of global total)**

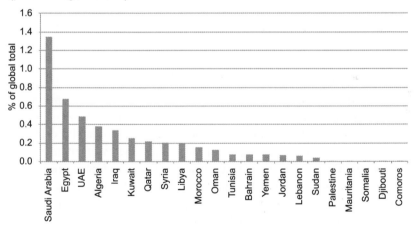

*Source*: Calculations based on World Bank WDI 2013.

Climate change is intensifying water scarcity, drought, and desertification and increasing energy consumption in the Arab countries. These countries are extremely vulnerable to drought, lower rainfall, and a marked increase in temperatures, which threaten food security and living standards through their negative impacts on agricultural productivity, energy consumption, economic growth, and environmental degradation.[25]

## Climate change and water scarcity

Climate change in Arab countries cannot be considered in isolation from accelerating population growth, industrial development, and increasing demand for irrigation water, all of which are contributing to increased natural, social, and economic pressures. Rising demand for water and food—a result of population growth and higher living standards—has increased pressure on already scarce water resources. The availability of water is thus one of the most important factors influencing growth and development in Arab countries. Any decline in rainfall and rise in temperature will greatly reduce the water available for human consumption.[26]

Most Arab countries view fresh water as a rare and valuable resource. Water resources fluctuate widely because of the heavy dependence on rainfall, which is low, and because renewable water supplies come from external sources. Total available supplies of water stand at approximately 262.9 billion cubic meters (m³), of which 226.5 billion m³ is surface water, 36.4 billion m³ is groundwater, and 11.9 billion m³ is nonrenewable groundwater.[27]

The distribution of water resources differs greatly by country. The most abundant annual supplies are in Egypt (58 billion m³), Iraq (65 billion m³), and Sudan (75 billion m³). Next are Algeria, Lebanon, Mauritania, Morocco, Syria, Tunisia, and Yemen, with annual supplies of 5–30 billion m³. The remaining Arab countries have annual water supplies below 5 billion m³.

Per capita water availability in the Arab region is among the lowest in the world (figure 7.7)—and declining due to climate change (with diminishing annual rainfall and rising evaporation rates[28]), limited amounts of renewable water, rapid population growth, and accelerated urban development, accompanied by rapidly increasing demand for water in urban areas. With the population of the Arab countries on the rise, the urban population is expected to increase from 60 percent to 75 percent of the total. Urban water requirements for domestic use will rise by more than 20 percent over today's levels.

With the exception of Iraq, which enjoys annual per capita water availability of more than 2,400 m³, all Arab countries face a critical water situation. Morocco and Syria are facing water stress, with annual per capita water availability of slightly less than 1,000 m³. Other Arab countries are experiencing water shortages, with annual per capita water availability far below 1,000 m³. Some countries, such as Jordan and the Gulf states, have per capita water availability of less than 200 m³ a year. Warmer weather is expected to intensify water stress everywhere. The annual per capita water availability in Iraq is predicted to decline by

**Figure 7.7 Annual per capita renewable water available in Arab countries**

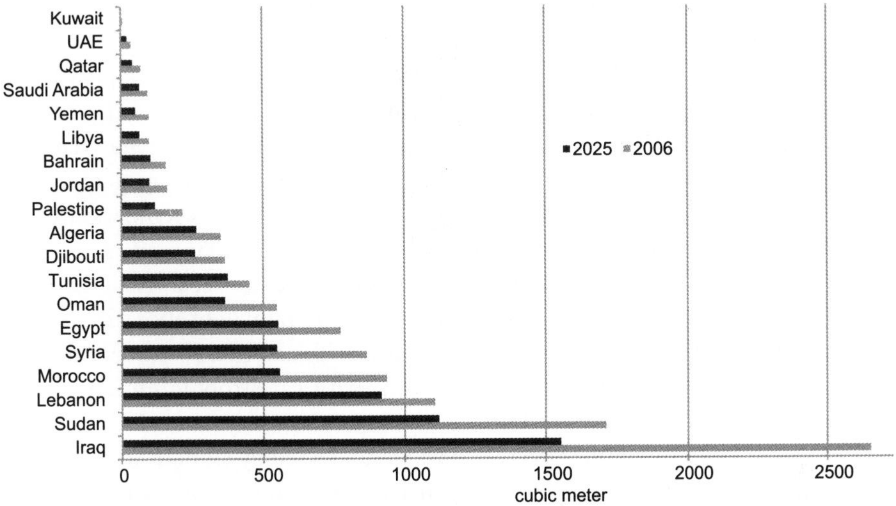

Source: Arab Forum for Environment and Development. Annual report 2010. Arab Environment, water: Sustainable management of a scarce resource.

half—to as low as 550 m³ by 2050.[29] Algeria, Egypt, Morocco, Syria, and Tunisia will experience acute water shortages by 2050; other Arab countries will face severe water crises as well.[30]

Jordan and the State of Palestine have the poorest water availability because of their heavy reliance on rainwater and the difficulties of sharing water sources with Israel. Mounting water-related political problems, together with climate change, will make the situation worse.

Future scenarios depict further declines in rainfall of up to 20 percent in some countries, increasing the pressure on water resources. According to some forecasts, the water shortfall will increase from 28.2 billion m³ in 2000 to 75.4 billion m³ in 2030. Changes in surface flows depend mainly on temperature and rainfall. An average temperature increase of 5°C by 2030 will shrink the snow-covered area of the Tigris and Euphrates watershed from 170,000 km² to 33,000 km², causing a 40 percent decline in the flow of these two rivers since 1999.[31]

Nearly all Arab countries on the Mediterranean Sea will be affected by climate change. Rainfall is expected to decline 20 percent to 25 percent in North Africa and some parts of Egypt, Jordan, Saudi Arabia, and Syria, where temperatures are expected to rise 2° to 2.75°C. These countries may be the most affected by climate change since they depend almost entirely on rainfall. Libya is an exception, since it relies on the

Great Man-made River, but this is expected to run dry by 2050. Climate change can be expected to increase the incidence of extreme weather events, exacerbating water scarcity.

The Nile River is very sensitive to rainfall in the Ethiopian highlands. A 20 percent decline in rainfall there could reduce the natural flow of the Nile to as little as 20 percent of the usual average. Temperature fluctuations also affect natural flows, though not by as much. In the Equatorial Lakes and Bahr al-Ghazal sub-basins, a temperature rise of 2°C could cut the natural flow in half.[32]

The Tigris and Euphrates Basin is projected to see a rise in temperature of no less than 2.5°C and reductions in rainfall of about 25 percent by 2070 (since 1999).[33] These changes will lead to a 50 percent decline in these rivers' annual surface flows, with catastrophic impact on the availability of water in Iraq and Syria.

The subregion expected to be least affected by climate change is the Arabian Peninsula, whose internal water resources are extremely limited, with little to no rainfall. The effects of climate change on water resources for these states will be positive, albeit quite limited. The exception is Yemen, which relies heavily on rainwater for its water needs and so will be more affected.

### Climate change and agricultural resources

The Arab region's agricultural area makes up about 8.5 percent of global agricultural area.[34] By 2011, the average in the Arab region was about 1.15 hectares per person, twice the global average of 0.68 hectares per person. However, the agricultural land per capita is shrinking every year because of rapid population growth.[35]

#### Variable rainfall and higher temperatures

Agricultural land in Arab countries is divided into irrigated crops, rain-fed crops, and pastoral areas; arid desert regions make up the rest (figure 7.8). Rain-fed agricultural land area is four times that of irrigated agriculture. Rain-fed crops are more likely to have variable yields, because of volatile rainfall and climate change. Pastureland, the greater part of agricultural land, is more sensitive than other types of land to climate change and human intervention. In addition, half the area of the Arab countries consists of arid or extremely arid regions considered unsuitable for agricultural production due to their harsh climate and water scarcity. These natural conditions, the impact of climate change, and the large increase in population in Arab countries threaten food production and food security.

**Figure 7.8 How agricultural land is watered in Arab countries**

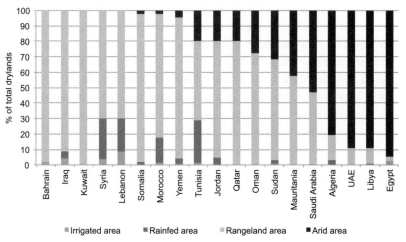

*Source*: Proportions calculated on the basis of data in Tables 1-a and 1-b in H.E. Dregne and Nan-Ting Chou, *Global Desertification Dimensions and Costs.*

Drought, the result of too little rainfall and high temperatures, can lead to environmental disasters in the Arab region. Climate change is likely to have a clear impact on water systems in the Mediterranean region and the Arabian Peninsula. The period of winter rainfall is expected to be shorter than usual, while summers become drier and hotter and include more long heat waves, altering ecological zones and agricultural production.

These regions will also become more vulnerable to drought or to unfamiliar climate events, such as floods and an unprecedented rise in maximum and minimum temperatures.[36] Higher evaporation rates from bodies of water and more transpiration from plants and crops will increase the quantities of water needed for plants to grow. Waves of drought will reduce agricultural production of rain-fed crops and water supplies—and speed the desertification of agricultural land.

Declining food security

Agricultural production and food security in Arab countries are closely tied to water availability. Globally, climate change will have only a minor impact on agricultural production, but with important regional differences. By 2080 agricultural production in developed counties is expected to increase around 8 percent due to lengthened growing seasons. In the developing world, however, agricultural production will fall 9 percent, with the greatest percentage decline around African desert regions and Latin America.[37]

In the Arab world studies indicate that climate change may cause severe damage to agricultural production and a decline in the yields of most basic crops[38] unless adaptive measures are taken. Climate change may increase water needs as much as 16 percent for summer crops and 2 percent for winter crops by 2050. Moreover, climate changes in the Arab region could increase the quantity of water needed for irrigation anywhere from 5 percent to 18 percent in countries such as Egypt and Jordan.[39]

The main dangers of climate change in North Africa and the Middle East are weather volatility and the frequency of long droughts. The decline in available water may have a major impact on food security. Forecasts indicate that a medium-range increase in temperature will affect river flows, leading to flow reductions of 30 percent in the Euphrates River and 80 percent in the Jordan River by the end of this century.[40]

Most agricultural crops grown in Arab countries are rain-fed; the total area of irrigated crops is less than 28 percent.[41] Agricultural production is expected to fluctuate widely from year to year, and average annual production is expected to decline. Recent studies estimate that agricultural production in the Arab region as a whole will shrink 21 percent by 2080, with a decline of nearly 40 percent in some countries, including Algeria and Morocco.[42] Annual agricultural productivity and food security are closely bound with annual variability in rainfall, particularly apparent over recent decades.[43]

Some Arab countries—Comoros, Mauritania, Somalia, and Yemen, for example—still depend on subsistence agriculture. But the greater frequency of droughts will slow the growth in yields and reduce food production, increasing malnutrition, famine, and death. In northeast Africa, repeated severe droughts and curtailed wet seasons may change river systems. The Blue Nile in Sudan would suffer from an acute water deficit—with negative impacts on agriculture and forestry throughout the region.[44]

As for irrigated agriculture—which is widespread in Egypt and the Arabian Peninsula, representing 95 percent and 100 percent, respectively, of their cultivated land—climate change will increase water consumption, particularly in countries with limited water resources, rapid population growth, and rapid development.[45] For example, total annual irrigation requirements in Egypt are expected to rise 6 percent to 16 percent by 2100 as a result of increased water consumption.[46]

Climate change in Arab countries will reduce productivity and quality in rain-fed, irrigated, and pastoral agriculture—and worsen food security. The increased demand for food as a result of population growth will also widen the gap between food production and consumption, possibly increasing internal social pressures.

## Extreme weather conditions

Climate change is expected to result in a rise in extreme weather conditions, increasing the frequency and severity of related disasters and exposing more people to the threat of droughts, floods, and sandstorms.[47]

The Arab countries' desert climate promotes the movement of sand, creating sandstorms. Rising temperatures increase soil erosion, making the soil less cohesive and more susceptible to movement when storms occur. Sandstorms in the Arabian Peninsula and the Sahara have increased notably over the past five years: those in Khartoum in 2007 and 2009 and in Dubai in 2009, for example, led to traffic accidents, delayed flights, and health problems. Major economic losses from sandstorms in North Africa and the Middle East are estimated at up to $12.7 billion.[48]

Arab countries have recently recorded an increase in the frequency and severity of extreme weather events, particularly droughts, flash floods, and sandstorms. Coastal states such as Djibouti, Somalia, and Sudan live under constant threat of drought due to unpredictable rainfall coupled with high temperatures. Some North African countries, especially Algeria and Morocco, are suffering drier conditions than before, with repeated droughts during 2001–10.

The Gulf states have been experiencing a large increase in rainfall, producing flash floods. With climate change, cyclones and floods are expected to become more frequent and more severe.

Some of the major extreme weather events linked to climate change in the Arab countries have been Cyclone Gonu, which hit the Sultanate of Oman in June 2007, the floods that swept over the Hadramawt in Yemen in 2008, and the flash floods that inundated Jeddah in Saudi Arabia between 2009 and 2011. Cyclone Gonu, which left 49 dead and affected nearly 20,000, is one of the most powerful ever to strike the Arabian Sea region.[49] The floods in Yemen left 180 dead and 10,000 homeless, destroyed 2,000 homes, and damaged infrastructure networks. Similarly, the flash floods in Jeddah in 2009, 2010, and 2011 caused heavy property losses because the city's infrastructure was unprepared.[50]

In Algeria, a month's worth of rainfall fell in just a few hours in 2001, accompanied by 120-kilometer-per-hour winds.[51] Damage was concentrated in the capital city of Algiers, with 750 people dead, 24,000 people displaced, more than 7,500 homes seriously damaged and property losses of around $300 million. All told, floods may have affected up to 10,000 families (40,000 to 50,000 people).

The extreme weather phenomena, together with ongoing heat waves (such as the one that occurred in 2010), have had a major impact on energy consumption and the production of agricultural crops in the Middle East and the Arabian Peninsula. Accordingly, they have drawn Arab citizens' attention to the deleterious effects of climate change on people's daily lives. Moreover, these phenomena are expected to increase markedly in the future.

### Energy consumption and energy security

Climate change and energy security, two of the most serious challenges facing Arab countries, are tightly linked. Warmer winters and hotter summers will boost energy requirements for cooling and heating, increasing greenhouse gas emissions and organofluorines (chlorofluoro-carbons and hydrofluorocarbons). The higher incidence of storms and floods will also damage energy infrastructure.

Electrical loads have reached their limits in some countries, resulting in power outages. In addition, higher temperatures are expected to reduce the effectiveness of power stations and the efficiency of gas turbines between 20 and 25 percent.[52] Reduced river flows will slow hydroelectric production, especially important for Egypt, Iraq, and Syria.

Oil and gas account for almost all (97.5 percent) energy consumption in Arab countries. Average annual per capita energy consumption in the region comes to around 1.7 tons of oil equivalent (TOE), falling between consumption of 1.8 TOE in some developing countries such as China and 3.9 TOE in some advanced economies such as Japan. But per capita energy consumption varies widely depending on climate, income, living standards, and urbanization—from 0.29 TOE in Yemen to 12.8 TOE in Qatar.[53] Industry is one of the most energy-intensive sectors, accounting for 45 percent of total consumption, followed by the transport sector at 32 percent. The domestic, commercial, and agricultural sectors consume most of the remaining energy. Energy consumption is expected to increase about 90 percent by 2040, and oil prices are also expected to rise.

#### Prospects for developing renewable energy

Reducing reliance on oil as an energy source is necessary to reduce pol-lution and slow climate change. Arab countries should put clean-energy security high on the agenda and develop technologies that rely on renew-able energy sources—sources of energy that can produce clean, environmentally safe energy without depleting natural resources. Wind, solar, water, and bio-energy can all generate electricity, both on and off the national grid.

The Arab states possess a fair supply of wind power; most countries have average annual wind energy capacity of nearly 1,400 continuous hours a year, economically viable in the long run (figure 7.9). Some countries, such as Egypt and Morocco, have a good supply of wind power, with wind speeds of 8–11 meters per second.[54]

**Figure 7.9 Estimated average annual wind energy capacity in the Arab region, 2010**

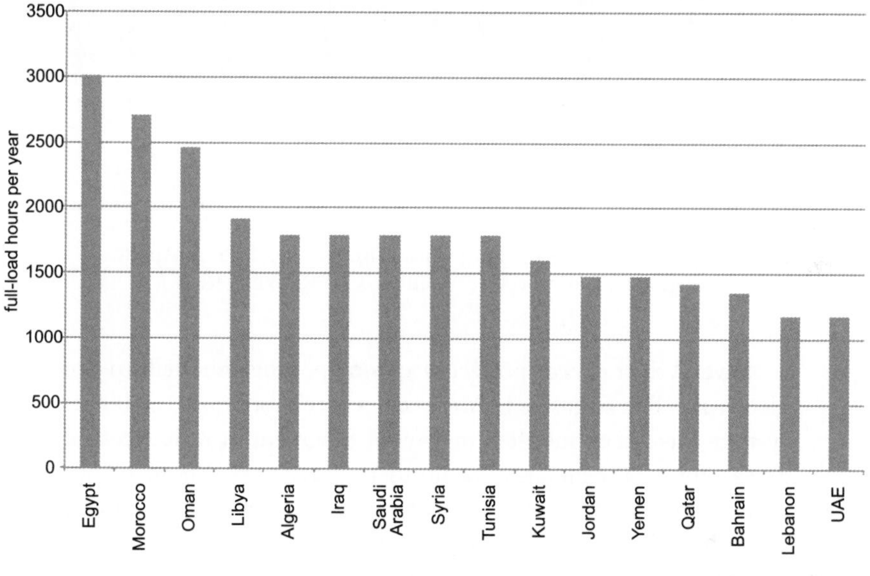

*Source:* ESCWA 2010c. "Promoting Large-Scale Renewable Energy Applications in the Arab Region: An Approach for Climate Change Mitigation."

This potential wind energy is not being exploited, however. Only Jordan and Tunisia have installed a few traditional wind power projects, and Egypt and Morocco have recently invested in wind energy at the commercial level. Installed wind energy capacity in Morocco came to 54 megawatts in 2005, 1 percent of total capacity, and wind farms are now being constructed with an overall capacity of 500 megawatts. Lebanon published the first national wind atlas in January 2011.

Arab countries also possess a tremendous potential for producing solar energy at an annual rate of 4–8 kilowatt-hours per square meter. The region's direct solar radiation and clear skies give it a latent capacity to generate concentrated solar power as well as photovoltaic power (figure 7.10).[55]

## Figure 7.10. Average solar radiation intensities, 2010

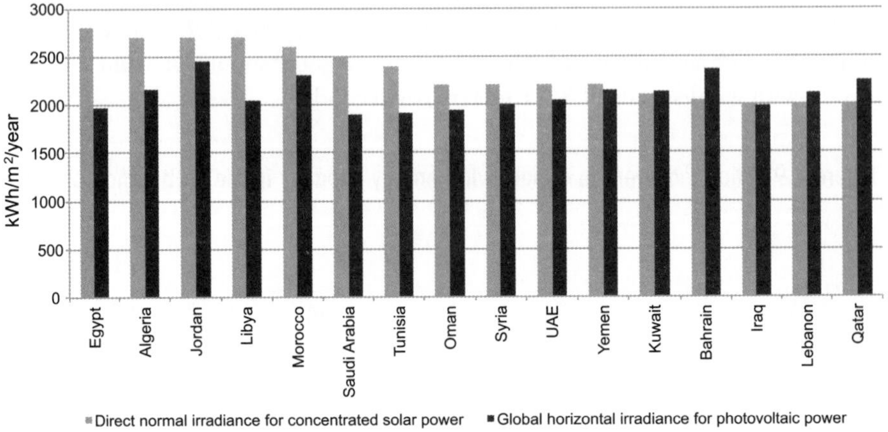

■ Direct normal irradiance for concentrated solar power   ■ Global horizontal irradiance for photovoltaic power

*Source*: ESCWA 2010c. "Promoting Large-Scale Renewable Energy Applications in the Arab Region: An Approach for Climate Change Mitigation."

Several solar energy projects are using photovoltaic cells to generate electricity. The largest is in Morocco, where more than 160,000 energy systems have been installed in around 8 percent of residences in rural areas—for total generation of up to 16 megawatts. Photovoltaic-powered water pumping applications have been developed in Tunisia, with a maximum capacity of up to 255 megawatts.[56]

Solar energy is expected to play a large role in the production of clean energy in the non-oil-producing countries in the Arab region. Projects in Algeria, Egypt, Jordan, Morocco, and the State of Palestine have productive capacities of 30 to 250 megawatts.

But energy generation from renewable sources is still far below potential.[57] Renewable energy's share of energy production capacity in the Arab region remains small, at no more than 7 percent in 2007, mostly hydropower in Algeria, Egypt, Iraq, Lebanon, Mauritania, Morocco, Sudan, Syria, and Tunisia.

Solar and wind energy production have not exceeded 442 megawatts, the equivalent of 0.5 percent of aggregate energy consumption, limited to Tunisia, Egypt, Jordan, Morocco, and the State of Palestine.[58] Egypt is the leader, with a capacity of 2,842 megawatts in hydropower and 305 megawatts in wind and solar in 2008.[59] In 2012, the wind energy production in Egypt increased to reach more than 965 megawatts. Several Arab countries have introduced solar and wind power to their strategic energy plans, to provide 1 percent to 42 percent of basic electrical power by 2020, with Morocco the highest.[60]

- Renewable energy resources represent important economic options for producing electricity, as they contribute to energy security, economic development, and environmental sustainability:[61]
- Renewable energy is a particularly promising option for non-oil-producing Arab countries and countries suffering from structural economic problems, since it offers a way of obtaining the energy needed for economic advancement at a reasonable cost. It would also enable Arab countries that subsidize energy to redirect the funds to other development-related and economic projects, improving living standards.
- Renewable energy makes it possible to separate economic development from greenhouse-gas production. Safe for the environment and for human health, it conserves natural and human resources and saves money.
- Renewable energy in rural and remote areas can promote agricultural development, create new jobs, and sustain economic growth. The result is greater economic and social development in remote areas, minimizing pressure on urban areas.
- Renewable energy sends a clear political message to the international community about the Arab region's commitment to global policies that aim to counter climate change.

## Strategic Solutions for Energy Security

There have been numerous plans for establishing electricity links among Arab countries, but the plans have been plagued by technical, political, or financial problems. With climate change and energy security among the biggest challenges facing Arab countries, they need to focus on a strategic response to energy security that incorporates these elements:

- Developing renewable energy to generate electrical power at competitive prices, improving regulation of the sector, and raising individual and institutional awareness of the importance of renewable energy.
- Increasing the efficiency of current energy sources by developing equipment and techniques to reduce leakages and losses.
- Integrating electricity grids across the Arab region to save energy and facilitate electricity exchange and flow between Arab states.
- Strengthening regional cooperation in formulating strategies for achieving energy security and coping with climate change.[62]
- Because the agriculture and water sectors in Arab countries are particularly vulnerable to climate change, they must be given

high priority in plans for adaptation. Only modest steps have been taken so far.

Some of the most important areas for adaptation to climate change include:

- *Using the media to raise citizen awareness and education on climate change and its impact*, including deterioration of the urban habitat, in ways that are simple to understand. This requires developing skills, techniques, and media awareness on all levels, from decision makers to the public. Effective partnerships are needed between relevant institutions, local and regional media, civil society institutions, and educational institutions.
- *Coordinating the work of farmers and academics* to study options for changing the timetable for sowing crops to adapt to changes in temperature and growing cycles. Agricultural inputs can also be changed in accord with emerging climate conditions. For example, farmers might modify crop varieties, fertilizer use, and irrigation and water management practices.
- *Managing water supply and demand* to encourage rational and more efficient use. Countries should apply the virtual water principle and implement an optimal water productivity strategy to improve the productivity and efficiency of agricultural water use to achieve the largest water saving per unit of production. Countries should encourage development of modern technologies that save water in agricultural, industrial, and domestic uses and that exploit nontraditional water resources, such as waste water, water harvesting, and saltwater desalination.
- *Encouraging innovation and research and development*, which requires modernization and specialized national and regional research centers, as well as increased cooperation and coordination among them. Research would aim to develop crops better suited to dry climate conditions and water scarcity. Regular, ongoing evaluation of land resources, especially agricultural and water resources, would also be conducted, along with investigations of the causes of their degradation.
- *Preserving natural and environmental resources and guaranteeing social justice.* Government and nongovernmental bodies should establish sustainable development policies, develop a system of cooperatives and community organizations in agricultural resource management, and apply scientific methods to these approaches.

- *Focusing on collective and institutional performance in managing adaptation strategies.* One way to do this is to invite the participation of the largest possible number of government institutions, civil society organizations, and local residents in developing and implementing strategies to guarantee popular, political, and financial support.

Clearly, climate change in Arab countries cannot be considered separately from rapid population growth, industrial development, and demand for water and energy sources. All these factors intensify natural, social, and economic pressures, making the Arab region more sensitive to the effects of climate change and less stable. All this makes it essential to increase citizen and decision-maker awareness of the problems and of measures to minimize their impact.

Arab countries enjoy a great variety of renewable and environmentally clean energy sources that promise a better future if these sources receive the strategic priority they deserve and are put to use in an economical and sustainable way. Developing a culture of environmental awareness among Arab citizens is also crucial.

## Notes

1   UNDP 2010d.
2   Arima 2010.
3   UN-Habitat 2003.
4   UN-Habitat 2003.
5   Sheuya 2008.
6   UN-Habitat 2012.
7   Khalifa 2011.
8   Anwar 2003.
9   UNEP 2007; UN-Habitat 2009.
10  ESCWA 2005; UNEP 2006.
11  AFED 2008.
12  Suspended particulates are a type of solid particle small and light enough to remain airborne for long periods. The most widespread forms are fine particles with an average diameter of less than 10 μm (PM10), as well as ultrafine particles with an average diameter of less than 2.5 μm (PM2.5).
13  Haffar 2004.
14  WHO 2005.
15  Naeas 2008.
16  WHO 2005.
17  AFED 2008.

18   ESCWA 2005; UNEP 2006.
19   Nilsson et al. 2001.
20   Chen et al. 2004; Ebi and McGregor 2008.
21   The use of renewable energy in Arab countries is discussed in detail in the second part of the chapter.
22   IPCC 2007.
23   AFED 2009.
24   World Bank 2012b. Data refer to 2005.
25   UNDP 2010d.
26   World Bank 2007a.
27   AFED 2010.
28   IPCC 2007.
29   IPCC 2007.
30   FAO 2008a.
31   AFED 2009.
32   AFED 2009.
33   AFED 2010.
34   FAO 2010.
35   World Bank WDI 2013.
36   Nicholson 2005.
37   IPCC 2007.
38   AOAD 2008.
39   Eid and el-Mowelhi 1998.
40   AFED 2009.
41   FAO 2008b.
42   World Bank 2007a.
43   Abou-Hadid 2006.
44   UNFCCC 2007.
45   Medany and Attaher 2007.
46   Nagano et al. 2007.
47   IPCC 2007.
48   UNDP 2010d.
49   al-Nahdy 2007.
50   BBC News 2009a.
51   UN Resident Coordinator's Office in Algiers 2001.
52   Daycock et al. 2004.
53   World Bank. WDI 2013.
54   Chedid and Chaaban 2003.
55   al-Karaghouli 2004.
56   Abdel Gelil 2008.
57   Patlitzianas, Doukas, and Psarras 2006.

58  OAPEC 2009.
59  EEHC 2008.
60  ESCWA 2010c.
61  Renewable energy, solar energy in particular, will continue to grow globally due to the greater environmental security it provides over nuclear energy, particularly in light of events in Japan in 2011.
62  al-Dageli 2010.

# Part 4:
# Rooting Empowerment
# in Identity

# Introduction to Part 4

Bahgat Korany

A s in many other post-colonial and deregulated societies into whose structures the colonial legacy penetrates deeply, the issue of identity in the Arab world is paramount. The speedy rise to power of Islamists in the post–Arab Spring context is due not only to their organizational power and the corruption of former regimes, but also—and mainly—due to their emphasis on defending or reclaiming a threatened identity. To be effective, the convincing argument affirms, development has to be 'authentic'; development does not mean satisfying material needs only, but also spiritual and moral ones, at both the individual and national levels. This is why such simplistic slogans as "Islam is the solution" have been both seductive and mobilizing. Education is certainly the most privileged sector where the satisfaction of both material and spiritual needs harmoniously meet. Education becomes then the epitome of development at the various levels; it is indeed the essence of empowerment. This is why, as explained in the general introduction, this volume could not be conceived as complete without an analysis of education, its challenges, and how to overcome them.

By expanding choices for development, education becomes the passport to sustainable development and empowerment. Education is the main agent of change in a knowledge society—and the key tool for adjusting to it. Knowledge of one's rights and duties, leading to effective political participation, is the first pillar of personal empowerment and a means to influence decision making. Education is also the mainstay of national empowerment, as a major component of the power to persuade (soft power) that increasingly determines a country's global standing.

Quantitative indicators of education reveal considerable progress in education in the Arab world. For example, between 1999 and 2007 the average net enrollment ratio in primary education rose from 78 percent to 84 percent. While a noteworthy advance, this rate is still slightly behind the global average, which rose from 82 percent to 87 percent. And many Arab countries regressed on this index, with Oman dropping from 83 percent to 72 percent and the State of Palestine losing more than twenty percentage points, slipping from 99 percent to 77 percent.[1]

While quantitative data can build a general picture, the quality of instruction may be more important. Education is not just about learning facts; it is about shaping personalities, fostering creative intellects, and encouraging critical thought. The key to a sound education that builds productive, content human beings is to support students in constructing their own identities. In an ever more integrated world, countries need to guard against education systems that train individuals to be insular and hostile to those who differ from them. It is also crucial to resist systems that encourage individuals to assimilate into the other and therefore lose their identity, as this constitutes another form of disempowerment.

Religious education is especially important as a foundation for shaping identity, but it has been neglected in many Arab countries, shielded even from assessment and criticism. It seemed as if conservative religious authorities and governments were in cahoots to keep these institutions under control rather than support their development. As the two following chapters demonstrate, in schools that provide religious education the curricula are kept traditional and unchanged, buildings are deteriorating, and teachers are extremely ill paid. It looks as if the institutional cultures among these schools have not evolved since Taha Hussein, Egypt's minister of education in the early 1950s—himself a product of religious education and dubbed "the dean of Arabic literature"—criticized their state. In efforts to improve education overall, countries have failed to give religious education the attention and political and financial support it merits. As stated in the general introduction, most governments have focused on controlling ministries of religious affairs, appointing preachers approved by state security, and influencing the content of Friday sermons. Such practices could impede efforts at renewal at a time when many associations and private schools have responded to people's increasing attachment to their faith as a means of confirming identity. The Sharia Society in Egypt produces preachers who tend to be conservative and has more than five thousand proselytizing centers and mosques. Private Islamic schools are proliferating in some of Egypt's upscale neighborhoods, such as Qattamiya near the American University in Cairo. Notably, more and more women are seeking training as preachers.

After the Arab Spring, more explicit criticism has come to the fore, including that from well-established religious institutions such as Egypt's al-Azhar and Tunisia's al-Zaytuna. For instance, in addressing the ministers of basic and higher education, the dean of al-Azhar insisted that students of religious institutions should study the Qur'an as well as modern sciences and contemporary knowledge. In Tunisia, there is a lot of criticism against the diffusion of non-authentic fatwas and their impact on bolstering religious fanaticism and social strife. On the contrary, fatwas and the respect of religious basic principles such as hard work, honesty, anticorruption, and best practices can be harnessed to contribute effectively and massively to the effort of development. In highly religious societies in the Arab world, the potential contribution of religion to development is still very much neglected.

In religious education, as in all parts of the education system, acquiring modern knowledge for empowerment and preserving identity is crucial. For instance, efforts to advance the Arabic language, both in terms of pedagogy and in finding Arabic equivalents for new terms and scientific discoveries, could reinforce the reform of religious education. New information technologies offer many avenues to develop the Arabic language to ease its acquisition at home and its spread abroad and to take advantage of the knowledge gains of the modern age.[2] Through new technologies, Arabic can help transform the region from a consumer to a producer of knowledge: as Arabic scholars publish their findings in Arabic, the Arabic language will become more recognized internationally, helping to reinforce identity.[3]

## Notes

1   Arab League and UNDP 2010.
2   UNDP 2009c.
3   The Executive Council of the League of Islamic Universities resolved at its meeting in November 2011 to launch a project that uses technology to modernize Arabic language instruction. The language laboratory project will use computers for language instruction and to trace the development of the Arabic language through Arabic texts (al-Ahram, 24 November 2011).

# CHAPTER 8

# The Role of Education in Individual and Sustainable Development

## Najoua Fezzaa Ghriss

The changes in economic, social, and cultural aspects of life shaped by recent scientific and technological advances have motivated education authorities worldwide to rethink their choices regarding the systems they oversee. They are seeking new pedagogical approaches that are better able to respond to the demands of an ever more competitive world that needs human capital capable of driving development.

The main focus is on basic education, not only because it is a fundamental right, but also because "it is the entry point for lifelong learning and the primary path to building an essential human capability, namely, knowledge."[1] Basic education is an essential pillar of individual development and empowerment. The importance of basic education also lies in the profound impact of learning at that stage on all subsequent phases of a person's life. How people live tomorrow depends on how the young are raised today.

Therefore, a basic rule for safeguarding the future is to prepare upcoming generations; the only way to do that is through education, the formal system that has the greatest impact on society. This process is essential for creating the human capital and energy needed to drive cognitive, technological, economic, and social development, which demand well-trained minds and bodies. This preparation requires a system of diverse values to bolster it and ensure that it is used for the benefit of individuals and society.

This chapter focuses on the importance of educating and raising children on the basis of a set of higher values—religious in particular, that contribute to human development—and on understanding the factors conducive to doing so. Acquiring spiritual values, like gaining knowledge and skills, is not a genetic endowment. It is a gradual process of formation in which schools play a fundamental role in shaping children's ethical values and behavior. This in turn influences their ability to contribute to the realization of a knowledge society and to the advancement of civilization.

What is the state of education in Arab countries? How successful have education systems been in preparing youth intellectually and ethically? How successful has education generally, and religious education in particular, been in raising moderate citizens with the intellectual and spiritual capacity to encompass modernity without jeopardizing their own authenticity?

To answer these questions, this chapter proceeds from basic education to religious education, looking at the current state of the subject, at its shortcomings and their causes, as well as at prospects for change and development. The objective is to establish an education system that can integrate mind and spirit and help prepare balanced individuals capable of contributing to sustained, comprehensive development.

## The State of Arab Education at the Turn of the Century

Despite the resources devoted to basic education and advances in many aspects of the education systems in Arab countries, progress has been slow and imbalanced, with outcomes below expectations. The Arab region lags behind East Asia and Latin America on many education indicators, including cognitive attainment, analytic and creative skills, literacy rates (writing and reading skills), and average years of schooling. The prevalent pedagogy in most schools in the region emphasizes learning by rote rather than the development of higher cognitive skills. The Education for All Global Monitoring Report characterizes education in the Arab region as "extremely poor."[2] Among the several causes mentioned is the inability of the Arab educational philosophy "to grasp the new concept of education, limiting it to the acquisition of knowledge, to the exclusion of its spiritual, moral, and psychological dimensions." Similarly, reforms have focused on improving quantitative aspects of education while overlooking qualitative development. As a result, many graduates are unqualified to contribute to the development of society.[3]

Based on the 2010 Education for All Development Index, a composite index of four goals that ranges from zero to ten (perfect attainment),[4] only Qatar and Kuwait came close to achieving the four goals, and Mauritania was the furthest from these goals.[5]

The Arab countries also fared poorly on all the key pillars measured by the Knowledge Economy Index compiled by the World Bank. On the education pillar, only Bahrain made it to the upper third, and six countries—Oman, Algeria, Lebanon, Jordan, Saudi Arabia, and United Arab Emirates—made it into the upper half (five to ten) of the scale (table 8.1). And while their scores nearly equaled the average for Latin America, they were still below the European and Central Asian averages.

**Table 8.1 Results on the Knowledge Economy Index for Arab states, 1995 and 2012**

| | Knowledge economy | | Economic incentive and institutional regime | | Education | | Innovation | | Information and communications technology (ICT) | |
|---|---|---|---|---|---|---|---|---|---|---|
| | 1995 | 2012 | 1995 | 2012 | 1995 | 2012 | 1995 | 2012 | 1995 | 2012 |
| Djibouti | 3.01 | 1.34 | 3.94 | 1.85 | 0.35 | 0.73 | 2.66 | 1.44 | 3.01 | 1.33 |
| Sudan | 2.08 | 1.48 | 0.71 | 0.48 | 1.27 | 0.84 | 2.17 | 1.44 | 2.08 | 3.16 |
| Mauritania | 2.32 | 1.65 | 1.43 | 2.05 | 1.17 | 0.71 | 1.92 | 1.68 | 2.32 | 2.18 |
| Yemen | 2.44 | 1.92 | 1.85 | 2.91 | 1.38 | 621 | 2.03 | 1.96 | 2.44 | 1.17 |
| Syria | 3.49 | 2.77 | 2.05 | 2.04 | 3.11 | 2.40 | 3.07 | 3.07 | 3.49 | 3.55 |
| Morocco | 4.17 | 3.61 | 4.60 | 4.66 | 2.44 | 2.07 | 4.79 | 3.67 | 4.17 | 4.02 |
| Egypt | 4.68 | 3.78 | 4.14 | 4.50 | 4.64 | 3.37 | 5.08 | 4.11 | 4.68 | 3.12 |
| Algeria | 3.50 | 3.79 | 1.85 | 2.33 | 3.88 | 5.27 | 3.41 | 3.54 | 3.50 | 4.04 |
| Tunisia | 4.54 | 4.56 | 4.65 | 3.81 | 3.57 | 4.55 | 4.29 | 4.97 | 4.54 | 4.89 |
| Lebanon | 5.38 | 4.56 | 4.29 | 4.28 | 6.65 | 5.51 | 4.26 | 4.86 | 5.38 | 3.58 |
| Jordan | 5.55 | 4.95 | 5.67 | 5.65 | 4.48 | 5.55 | 6.17 | 4.05 | 5.55 | 4.54 |
| Kuwait | 5.71 | 5.33 | 5.36 | 5.86 | 4.51 | 3.70 | 5.50 | 5.22 | 5.71 | 6.53 |
| Qatar | 5.86 | 5.84 | 5.64 | 87.6 | 5.52 | 3.41 | 4.79 | 6.42 | 5.86 | 6.65 |
| Saudi Arabia | 5.02 | 5.96 | 4.45 | 5.68 | 4.11 | 5.65 | 5.00 | 4.14 | 5.02 | 8.37 |
| Oman | 5.34 | 6.14 | 6.33 | 6.96 | 3.65 | 5.23 | 5.48 | 5.88 | 5.34 | 6.49 |
| Bahrain | 6.97 | 6.90 | 6.95 | 6.69 | 6.49 | 6.78 | 6.93 | 4.61 | 6.97 | 9.54 |
| UAE | 6.39 | 6.94 | 6.90 | 6.50 | 4.46 | 5.80 | 6.59 | 6.60 | 6.39 | 8.88 |

*Note:* Zero is poor, ten is strong.
*Source:* World Bank 2012a.

Students in Arab countries also rank low in math and science on the periodic assessments supervised by the International Association for the Evaluation of Educational Achievement (IEA) such as the Trends in International Mathematics and Science Study (TIMSS) assessment (figure 8.1). Arab states' averages fell below the international average in all the completed assessment periods.[6] Less than 1 percent and 2 percent of Arab students taking the TIMMS reached the advanced international benchmark in math and science respectively, and more than 40 percent reached the low international benchmark, the minimum score required to achieve an acceptable performance level (table 8.2). In 2007, Jordanian and Lebanese students scored highest in the Arab region (Jordanians in science and Lebanese in math) and made the most rapid progress in international rankings. In 2011, eighth-grade students from the United Arab Emirates scored highest in math and science but fell eleven points short of the global average.

Results are similarly low on the Programme for International Student Assessment (PISA).[7] On the 2006 cycle, Arab students lagged behind the international average and scored especially low on ability to use scientific knowledge in problem solving related to daily life (table 8.3). The scores of the participating Arab countries were close to the bottom of the international range in all the targeted skills, with Jordan higher than the other two.

Scientific thinking—the ability to understand phenomena and use scientific knowledge to solve problems and improve conditions in the real world—appears to be a weak spot for students in Arab countries. Furthermore, they have an inability to understand written texts and to

**Table 8.2 Percentages of Arab students achieving international benchmarks on the Trends in International Mathematics and Science Study (TIMSS) assessments, 2011**

|  | Mathematics benchmarks | | | | Science benchmarks | | | |
|---|---|---|---|---|---|---|---|---|
|  | Advanced | High | Average | Low | Advanced | High | Average | Low |
| Fourth grade | 0.9% | 5.4% | 19.3% | 43.0% | 1.6% | 7.7% | 22.7% | 42.6% |
| Eighth grade | 0.7% | 6.6% | 25.1% | 53.3% | 1.5% | 10.4% | 33.4% | 62.6% |

*Source:* TIMSS 2011 International results in Science; TIMSS 2011 International results in Mathematics.

**Figure 8.1 Arab student scores on the Trends in International Mathematics and Science Study (TIMSS) assessments, 2003, 2007, and 2011**

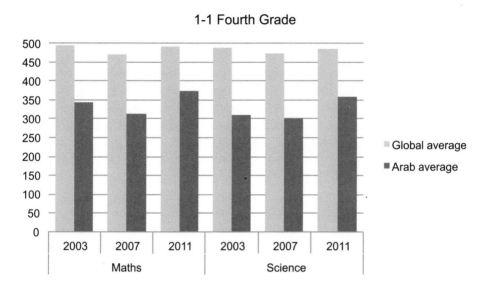

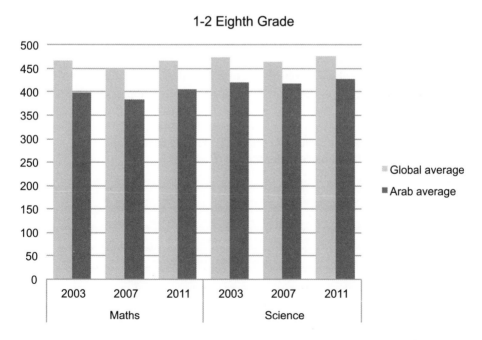

*Source:* Source: TIMSS International Database Explorer (IDE) 2013

**Table 8.3. Results of participation for three Arab countries on the Programme for International Student Assessment (PISA), 2006**

| | Scientific literacy | | Identifying science issues | | Scientific interpretation | | Using science facts | | Mathematical literacy | | Understanding written texts | |
|---|---|---|---|---|---|---|---|---|---|---|---|---|
| | Score | Rank | Score | Rank | Score | Rank | Score | Rank | Score | Rank | Score | Rank |
| Jordan | 422 | 45 | 409 | 47 | 438 | 42 | 405 | 48 | 384 | 51 | 401 | 45 |
| Tunisia | 386 | 54 | 384 | 54 | 383 | 54 | 382 | 53 | 365 | 55 | 380 | 52 |
| Qatar | 349 | 56 | 352 | 56 | 356 | 56 | 324 | 56 | 318 | 56 | 312 | 55 |
| International[a] | 563 | 322 | 555 | 321 | 566 | 334 | 567 | 288 | 499 | 311 | 556 | 285 |

a. The lowest and highest internationally recorded scores.
*Source*: OECD. 2007. PISA 2006 Science Competencies for Tomorrow's World. Part II, Data. OECD Programme for International Student Assessment.

process (comprehend, analyze, and evaluate) information they have read—another cognitive gap revealed by the 2009 PISA cycle results. It is clear how far behind Arab students are in mastering the tools of knowledge (figure 8.2).

The Arab Human Development Reports are consistent with other regional and international reports in their assessment of the deteriorating state of Arab education. The 2003 report, *Building a Knowledge Society*, traced the root of the problem of Arab education to the preschool level and the family. Arab societies are predominantly paternalistic, demanding absolute obedience to male elders, who tend to control and engage in all issues. Child rearing typically suppresses questioning,

**Figure 8.2 Performance of Arab students and OECD students on the Programme for International Student Assessment (PISA), 2009**

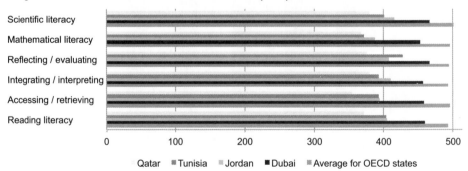

*Source*: PISA 2009. Performance of 15-year-old Students from the US in Reading, Mathematics, and Science Literacy in an International Context.

exploration, and initiative. Together, these practices drain individual motive, negatively impact self-confidence, and weaken inquisitiveness, creativity, and independent thinking. School frequently reinforces these deficiencies by overemphasizing discipline and obedience, stifling the spirit of critical thinking and independent, objective analysis.[8]

While the Arab Human Development Reports acknowledge the progress that Arab countries have made in increased spending on education, steadily growing enrollment rates, and rising literacy rates, they do not overlook the worrisome decline in the quality of education. The 2002 report observes: "Despite the scarcity of available studies, complaints concerning the poor quality of education abound. The few available studies identify the key negative features of the real output of education in the Arab countries as low level of knowledge attainment, and poor and deteriorating analytical and innovative capacity."[9]

The *Arab Knowledge Report* of 2009 finds that one of the chief shortcomings of basic education in the Arab region is the great disparity in time allocated to each subject area. As the report points out, "Science and technology instruction and foreign language instruction seem fated to get the shortest end of the stick in the distribution of class time."[10] These are precisely the key subjects for acquiring, developing, and adapting knowledge.

The Arab Human Development Reports have warned that the decline in education quality not only threatens the scientific and cultural development of Arab countries but also jeopardizes economic and social development and Arab national security. All the reports have strongly affirmed the need for radical reforms and have consistently linked economic growth with the quality of education. The reports argue that the intellectual and cognitive development of an individual—child, youth, or adult—through education and training is a vital form of capital that needs to be constantly improved and developed in the interests of the individual and society.

In sum, children's upbringing and education have received considerable attention in all the Arab Human Development Reports. Together, these reports constitute a rich quantitative and qualitative information base that can enable accurate diagnoses of education's problems and point the way to viable solutions. Observers find that Arab education systems have been suffering from the same problems and deficiencies and that the occasional cosmetic fix has not addressed the flaws. The question is whether these problems are intractable or whether some structural constraint has inhibited addressing them more effectively.

## How Religious Education Fits into the Basic Curriculum

Discussions of human development must also cover religious upbringing, which affects people's ideological and intellectual orientations and their attitudes and behavior concerning what are private and what are public matters. Without denying the influence of other institutions on religious upbringing, this chapter focuses on the school as the official social institution responsible for bringing education policy to life and shaping the characteristics and behavior of future generations.

### How international conventions and reports view the importance of religious education

A special edition of the United Nations Educational, Scientific, and Cultural Organization (UNESCO) International Bureau of Education journal *Perspectives*,[11] dedicated to "Education and Religion: The Paths of Tolerance," observed that until the end of the twentieth century, education theories were heavily rationalist, and educational aims centered on filling young minds with "knowledge." In the twenty-first century, education theory called for striking a balance between the rational and the affective aspects of learning by empowering individuals to obtain knowledge and add meaning to their lives at the same time.

The journal also drew attention to two changes in religious education. Some countries with a completely secular education system were incorporating (or contemplating doing so) religious dimensions in their curricula and familiarizing students with the history of religions and religious symbols. And some countries where religion has long dominated curricula (Islamic countries, for example) have begun to imbue religious education with a stronger emphasis on tolerance and respect for other religions. A global survey by the Centre International d'Études Pédagogiques in France found that the education systems in most countries, whatever their political system, have some form of religious education, although the amount of attention it receives and the quality of the education varies.[12]

All international declarations and conventions on human rights and the rights of the child are unanimous in affirming freedom of religion and the right to practice one's faith in an atmosphere of respect, tolerance, and peaceful coexistence among all faiths (box 8.1). The 2004 Human Development Report, *Cultural Liberty in Today's Diverse World*, affirmed cultural liberty as "a central aspect of human development" and stressed the "profound importance of religion to people's identities."

**Box 8.1 Education and personal development**
Several international conventions touch on the relation between education and personal development.

"Education shall be directed to the full development of the human personality and to the strengthening of respect for human rights and fundamental freedoms. It shall promote understanding, tolerance, and friendship among all nations, racial or religious groups, and shall further the activities of the United Nations for the maintenance of peace."
—Universal Declaration of Human Rights, Article 26.2

"States Parties shall respect the right of the child to freedom of thought, conscience, and religion."
—Convention on the Rights of the Child, Article 14

"In those States in which ethnic, religious, or linguistic minorities or persons of indigenous origin exist, a child belonging to such a minority or who is indigenous shall not be denied the right, in community with other members of his or her group, to enjoy his or her own culture, to profess and practice his or her own religion, or to use his or her own language."
—Convention on the Rights of the Child, Article 30

"The States Parties agree that the education of the child shall be . . . directed to the preparation of the child for responsible life in a free society, in the spirit of understanding, peace, tolerance, equality of sexes, and friendship among all people, ethnic, national, and religious groups and persons of indigenous origin."
—Convention on the Rights of the Child, Article 29(d),
www.agfund.org

In keeping with this spirit, the 2005 Arab Human Development Report, which focused on the empowerment of women, states:

No political power can ignore the fact that religion, and especially Islam, is a crucial element in the cultural and spiritual makeup of the Arab people. However, the reopening of the door of independent jurisprudential thinking, its encouragement and affirmation, remain a basic demand if the creative marriage between freedom in its contemporary, comprehensive definition and the ultimate intent of Islamic law (Sharia) that is required for the society of freedom and good governance, is to be achieved.[13]

The 2009 Arab Human Development Report compares the class time allocated to various subjects, including Islamic education. The comparison revealed large variations at two levels:

- *Among school subjects:* "A study on the time allocated to school subjects in basic education in Arab countries during the last decade shows considerable variation between these countries in the proportion of class time allotted to religious education and foreign language instruction; a moderate variation in the class time dedicated to science and technology, social studies, the arts, and physical education; and general conformity in the amounts of time allotted to Arabic language and math instruction."[14]
- *Among Arab countries:* After noting a discrepancy between Arab and other countries in the amount of class time allotted to religious instruction (12 percent in the Arab region compared with 5 percent globally), the report reveals differences among Arab countries in time allotted to Islamic education: "The quota for Islamic religious instruction reaches 28% in Saudi Arabia, followed by Yemen (20%), Sudan (18%), and Oman (17%). In Tunisia and Algeria, the time ratio for Islamic religious instruction is around the global average of around 5% for religious education."[15]

Despite these general observations, no previous Arab Human Development Report has explicitly examined the content of religious education, how it influences children's upbringing, and whether it contributes to achieving balance between authenticity and modernity, topics addressed in this chapter.

### Paucity of data on religious education in Arab countries

Objective data on formal religious education in Arab countries are scarce. Well-researched studies are few and far between, and many are outdated.

There are at least two possible causes. One, the first generation of development approaches focused on material aspects and per capita income, which led to an emphasis on intellectual qualifications and practical skills and on contributions to economic, political, cultural, and social activities. Marking a turning point, the 2004 Arab Human Development Report established a comprehensive concept of development, defining it as the expansion of the scope of human liberties and stressing the importance of religion in the formation of a people's identity. Additionally, no deep religious conflicts threatened the interests and security of the great powers until the events of 11 September 2001. Those attacks were the major catalyst that turned attention to religious education (especially in Islamic countries) and positioned reform of religious education programs as an urgent 'outside' demand.

Despite the diversity of sources, all the reports and studies that touch on the subject acknowledge flaws in religious education in Arab schools. For example, the Saudi writer and scholar Abdul Hamid Abu Sulayman holds that conceptual, methodological, and behavioral distortions have transformed Islamic thought into an abstraction that receives only superficial treatment in schools.[16] He complains that religious education rarely goes beyond rote learning, repetition, and imitation, and relies on stuffing children's heads with religious knowledge while neglecting their psychological and emotional upbringing. He believes that the religious concepts selected for instruction are inappropriate to children's mental and emotional makeup, such as verses from the short suras of the sixtieth *hizb* of the Qur'an, which are filled with images of hellfire and torture on Judgment Day. The prevalent discourse is one of intimidation and retribution, rather than love, tolerance, and disciplined freedom. Abu Sulayman argues that ignorance of the nature of childhood and the failure to devote sufficient attention to children's education have crippled children's capacity to perform well and be creative. The only way out of this dilemma, he believes, is to develop "critical Islamic social thought and liberate the Muslim intellect."[17]

This view is echoed by Mustafa Bokran,[18] a Moroccan professor of Islamic education and scholar of Islamic thought, who also complains of the backwardness of Islamic educational curricula. Why instruct preparatory-school children, he asks, on the *zakat* (alms tax) levied on livestock and gold at a time in their lives when they desperately need to develop spiritually? Bokran calls for renewing Islamic fields of learning and staffing schools with teachers who can be effective role models: living testimony to what they teach and a concrete translation of theory into genuine, real-life behavior.[19]

Yahya Abu Zakariya, an Algerian scholar and journalist, contends that religious education at the secondary school and university levels "has become an intellectual luxury; the focus is exclusively on the historical side, with no relation to the present day, as though Islam was a cultural legacy of the distant past that has no bearing on shaping all the details of the present and future."[20] Asma bint Abdul Aziz al-Hussayn, professor of psychological health at the Girls College of Education in Riyadh, criticizes religious education curricula for devaluing critical thought and constructive dialogue and promoting rote learning and cramming, which encourage superficial thinking.[21] Her conclusion that Islamic educational programs have failed is seconded by Ibrahim Mohammed al-Shafi'i, a professor at Cairo University, who attributes the failure to two chief flaws.[22] First, the subject is divided into too many branches, thus obscuring the unity and integrity of religious knowledge. Second, the logic of the topic itself rather than the interests of learners determines the curriculum at each grade level, which stifles student interest.

### Religious education in the curricula of various Arab countries

This section, based on a review of religious education curricula in eight Arab countries, finds them to be largely disconnected from reality and dominated by a narrow concept of knowledge.[23] Most religious education curricula are organized linearly, converting a selected set of aims and topics into textbook form. Religious topics are detached from contemporary concerns, with an emphasis on historical issues and legacies and religious precepts and prohibitions. Teachers are expected to convey that information to students, who are expected to memorize it so they can repeat it on exams. In this traditional memorize-and-recite method, religious education has minimal impact on their skills, values, and behavior. Religion becomes a form of cultural heritage with no relevance for today.

The curricula present concepts and experiences as unrelated, separate units. No effort is made to deepen the understanding of religion by stimulating the higher faculties of analysis, synthesis, and evaluation through critical thinking, debate, and dialogue or to engage learners' cognitive, emotional, and psychodynamic experiences· This approach is driven by an outmoded, intimidating discourse. Students become passive recipients of knowledge who store pieces of unconnected bits of information that have no real meaning or practical use, reinforcing the separation of religion and rational thought. The effect is to reinforce passivity and dull inquisitiveness and to weaken the ability to reach objective judgments. This method of teaching encourages students to form a fragile relationship with religion based on emotional reactions, making children easy victims of erroneous ideological teaching.

### Algeria

Religious education is included in the public education curriculum in Algeria as part of social studies instruction. Its aim is "to complete the development of the learner and shape his personality ideologically, intellectually, emotionally, physically, aesthetically, and morally in accordance with the Qur'an and the Sunna."[24] The curricula cover the Qur'an, Islamic creed, jurisprudence, Hadith, the life of the Prophet, stories of the prophets, morals, and ethics. The primary-school program has four parts: "I know my religion," "I behave myself," "I love my family," and "I respect others." The middle-school program also has four parts: performance of duty and appreciation, tolerance and magnanimity, social interaction, and diligence and perseverance. Islamic education continues into the secondary level as "Islamic sciences," with the addition of two subject areas: Islamic thought and Islamic culture.

The concepts treated at the primary and intermediate levels range from those directly connected to Islamic beliefs and rites of worship (more coverage) to those more closely associated with daily life in general (less coverage). For example, the Islamic-studies curriculum for grade three comprises twenty-five units taught over forty class periods.[25] Eight units treat topics related to good behavior, relations with parents and others, not being wasteful, and "sowing and planting" (appreciating the value of plants). Approved textbooks for Islamic education in the primary grades give little attention to values related to democratic outlooks, such as cultural plurality and modernity (figure 8.3). The curriculum for the third year of middle school has nearly the same distribution, with religious concepts that have a bearing on daily life making up about 47 percent of the material.

Textbooks emphasize practices of Islamic worship, with little focus on cultural pluralism and democratic practices.[26] Disparities are evident across grades in attention to values. Tolerance receives the greatest

**Figure 8.3 Percentage of curriculum devoted to different values in Islamic education textbooks, grades 3–5, in Algeria, 2011**

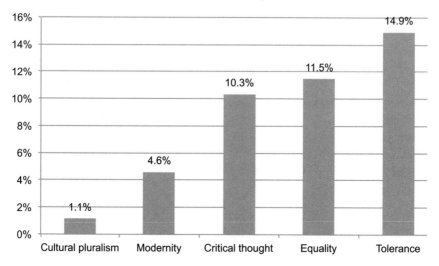

*Source:* Sika 2011. "al-Tarbiya al-diniya fi-l-'alam al-'arabi". Background paper.

coverage, although for the most part the value is associated with relationships among Muslims rather than with others. Equality is next, including gender equality and equality among people in general. Still, the analysis and illustrations in the textbooks reveal a strong male-centered tendency. The relationship between modernity and religion is barely touched upon (5 percent coverage in the entire curriculum), broached in a discussion of the importance of science and knowledge to the consolidation of faith.

### Egypt

Egypt has two official religious curricula, Islamic and Christian. Instruction begins at the primary level. Analysis of the values covered in the textbooks reveals wide differences in the attention accorded each value (figure 8.4).[27]

Very little instruction occurs on the values of modernity and cultural pluralism. Modernity is not even mentioned in the Christian education curriculum, and it does not appear in the Islamic curriculum until grade six. The concept of cultural pluralism, restricted to the grade four curriculum, makes a brief appearance. Equality and tolerance receive the most emphasis in the Christian curriculum, while critical thinking and equality receive top rank in the Islamic curriculum.

**Figure 8.4 Coverage of selected values in Islamic and Christian religious education textbooks in Egypt, 2011 (percent)**

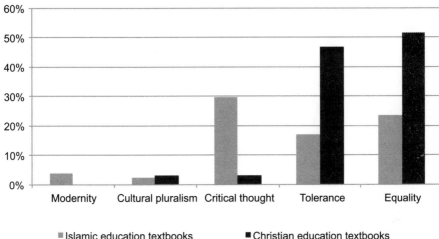

Islamic education textbooks    Christian education textbooks

*Source:* Sika 2011. "al-Tarbiya al-diniya fi-l-'alam al-'arabi." Background paper.

The Islamic religious studies curriculum emphasizes equality among all Egyptians, regardless of religious affiliation, and the need to respect the prophets. Gender equality is brushed upon indirectly, through the stress placed on obedience to parents and the mother's importance in the family. Although the value of tolerance is affirmed, the curriculum evidences some prejudice against other faiths.

The Christian religious studies curriculum presents the concept of equality as embracing all members of society, through an affirmation of the importance of civic participation in national affairs, and nondiscrimination on the basis of ethnic or religious affiliation. Gender equality is ignored. Tolerance is broached through an appeal to love the other and the encouragement to respond to others' offenses by praying for them.

### Jordan

In line with Jordan's Ministry of Education's philosophy and objectives, which are based on Islamic thought, religious studies are part of basic education and are among the core secondary-school courses. Islamic studies syllabi cover a diversity of topics, with considerable disparity between the number of lessons on purely religious concepts (Qur'an and Hadith studies, Islamic doctrine, and jurisprudence) and on subjects related to daily life and contemporary concerns and values (table 8.4).

**Table 8.4 Distribution of Islamic studies topics at the basic education level in Jordan, 2011**

| | | Number of lessons | |
|---|---|---|---|
| Grade | Total | Purely religious subjects | Subjects related to contemporary concerns and values |
| 1 | 59 | 48 | 11 |
| 2 | 65 | 58 | 7 |
| 3 | 72 | 62 | 10 |
| 4 | 82 | 70 | 12 |
| 5 | 51 | 41 | 10 |
| 6 | 58 | 44 | 14 |
| 7 | 12 | 10 | 2 |
| 8 | 12 | 10 | 2 |
| 9 | 12 | 10 | 2 |
| 10 | 61 | 45 | 16 |

*Source:* Adillat al-mu'allimin li-jami' al-sufuf. Department of School Curricula and Textbooks, Jordanian Ministry of Education.

Only about 27 percent of required topics are directly related to individual character and behavior and to daily life in general. They focus on higher human values (such as mercy, honesty, sincerity, and modesty) and manners (conversational etiquette, public courtesy, table manners, polite ways of asking permission). Curricula also demonstrate concern for the family (marriage, brotherhood, kinship bonds) and social relations (cooperation, social solidarity) and attention to social ills (gambling, monopolies, cheating). In addition, there is a slight treatment of topics with universal dimensions, such as environmental protection, kindness to animals, international relations, and Islam's attitudes about other faiths. The Islamic perspective on science and knowledge receives little attention, however—just four of the required lessons. These relate to the ethics of the quest for knowledge, the role of the intellect, Islam's concern for science, and the status of scholars.

### Lebanon

Lebanon is unique among Arab countries for being home to eighteen recognized religions. Because of this religious pluralism, Articles 9 and 10 of the constitution stipulate the need to respect other faiths and the right of each religious community to choose the religious education material it deems appropriate.

Therefore, state schools in Lebanon adopt a range of methods and curricula to teach religion. In schools with students of different faiths, students are usually separated during religious instruction and taught the concepts of their religion or sect without reference to the beliefs of other faiths. This isolation feeds the tendencies to deny the validity of other beliefs and plants the seeds of religious and sectarian division. Somewhat diminishing the impact of religious instruction is students' dismissal of it because it is not an exam subject.[28] Neither Islamic nor Christian private schools require students of other faiths to attend religious classes, though students may do so with parental permission.

The values addressed in religious textbooks fall into three primary areas: knowledge about the faith and its rights and duties; morals, general manners, and proper behavior; and history and lives of the Prophet and saints.[29] There is no explicit or intentional negative reference to other faiths, although little information is provided about other faiths. While the religious curricula stress the values of tolerance and respect for other faiths, the transmission of these values is impeded by the poor training received by religious education teachers.[30]

### Syria

Like Egypt's, Syria's education curriculum includes two strands for religious education, Islamic and Christian. Muslim and Christian students are taught in separate classes. Separating students for religious instruction has recently stirred controversy, with some people arguing for its continuation and others advocating for change, including replacing the courses with one on "general morals."

Official textbooks for Islamic and Christian religious education vary greatly in their attention to contemporary values, both between and within Islamic and Christian religious education classes (figure 8.5).[31] The values most stressed are critical thinking, tolerance, and equality, with some disparity between the two curricula. The values of modernity and cultural plurality barely receive any attention.

**Figure 8.5 Coverage of selected values in Islamic and Christian religious education textbooks in Syria, 2011**

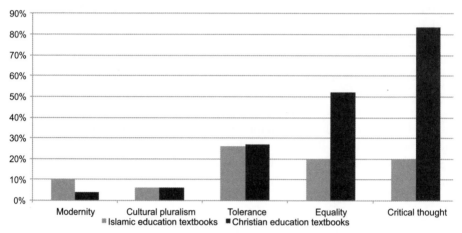

*Source:* Sika 2011. "al-Tarbiya al-diniya fi-l-'alam al-'arabi." Background paper.

A qualitative analysis of the ideas appearing in the textbooks reveals several other characteristics:

- Tolerance is treated broadly and not restricted to Syrians or core-ligionists. The Islamic textbooks stress that tolerance is an inseparable element of the faith.
- A male-centered outlook prevails (quantitatively and qualitatively) in both the Islamic and Christian textbooks, despite some attention to the value of gender equality.
- The presence of the same values in both curricula does not preclude differences in presentation (in the lessons and drills, in exercises in thinking, in the contents of textual information).

## Tunisia

Religious studies are compulsory in first through ninth grade in Tunisia. In secondary school, religious studies are part of the humanities curriculum, covered under the rubric "Islamic thought." In official curricula, religious education is presented as a component of social upbringing, "in view of the role it plays in building a balanced personality and equipping the person to take initiative and act."[32] Taught in three integrated branches—Qur'anic guidance, the creed, and morals—the study topics are distributed as illustrated in table 8.5.

**Table 8.5 Distribution of Islamic studies topics at the basic education level in Tunisia, 2011**

| Grade | Hours per week allotted to Islamic education | Percentage of topics related to contemporary issues and values |
|---|---|---|
| First | 1 out of 20 | 38% |
| Second | 1 out of 22 | 48% |
| Third | 1 out of 25 | 50% |
| Fourth | 1 out of 25 | 44% |
| Fifth | 1 out of 30 | 43% |
| Sixth | 1 out of 30 | 44% |
| Seventh | 1.5 out of 32 | 43% |
| Eighth | 1.5 out of 31.5 | 40% |
| Ninth | 1.5 out of 32 | 46% |

*Source:* Tunisian Ministry of Education. 2006. "al-Baramij al-jadida li-l-tar-biya al-islamiya" (New Programs for Islamic Education). Directorate for Academic Programs and Textbooks.

Islamic studies' share of total weekly school time at the basic level does not exceed 5 percent. The program focuses on multiple issues. Some pertain to religious doctrine and observances, such as faith, divine unity, prayer, and fasting, and others to the affairs of daily life—the relationship with the other and with the surrounding environment. A substantial portion of this last set focuses on morals (sincerity, loyalty, honesty, altruism) and manners (conversational etiquette, table manners, polite ways to ask permission). Family and social relations (kinship bonds, respect for parents, sociability, social solidarity) also receive attention. Topics related to contemporary phenomena and humanitarian issues include the rights of the child, environmental balance, generational interdependence, respect for differing beliefs, and human interaction. Somewhat less attention is paid to knowledge, with a focus on the value of knowledge and the student's duty toward the teacher.

### United Arab Emirates

An Emirati report acknowledges that the Islamic education curricula are improvised, are inconsistent in their values, and exhibit a strong male bias, and that methods of instruction are based primarily on memorization and

**Figure 8.6 Values covered in the sixth-grade Islamic studies textbook in the United Arab Emirates, 2011**

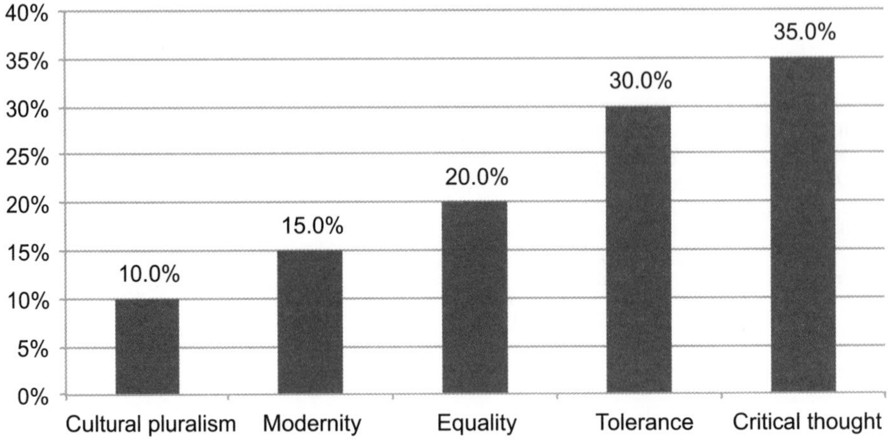

Source: Sika 2011. "al-Tarbiya al-diniya fi-l-'alam al-'arabi." Background paper.

do little to instill religious concepts and values.[33] The topics covered have little bearing on daily life and contemporary issues. No attention is given to pedagogy or to preparing teachers. The report recommends a comprehensive overhaul of the Islamic studies curriculum to adjust to developments in the world today.

The sixth-grade Islamic studies textbook addresses several contemporary values, but they receive uneven attention (figure 8.6). Although critical thought receives the most attention, it generally features only in questions raised at the end of the lesson. Equality is commonly taught by highlighting the value of women and their ability to benefit others. The values of modernity and tradition are touched on in the assertion that the quest for knowledge means more than religious knowledge for imams and shaykhs.

### Yemen

The education curricula were extensively reformed at the time of the political reforms following unification of South Yemen and North Yemen in 1990. However, a large number of religious schools continue to operate outside the reform and beyond the reach of the supervisory authorities. The pluralistic political climate following unification facilitated the emergence of religious institutions of diverse outlooks and programs in several southern and eastern governorates.

The distribution of Islamic education topics at the basic education level vary enormously across grades between topics of a purely religious character (tenets of the faith, Islamic jurisprudence, the biography of the Prophet, and rites of worship) and topics related to contemporary issues and values (character formation, social relations, and daily life issues). Topics related to contemporary issues and values range from 18 percent to 36 percent of the total (table 8.6).

Aspects pertaining to behavior (table manners, public courtesy, polite conversation, and personal hygiene) and personal morality (promoting virtue; avoiding deceit, injustice, and mistrust) receive the most attention. Aspects of religion with a bearing on science and knowledge are limited to references to the value, pursuit, and tools of knowledge as well as a deepening understanding of the faith. Religious topics with a bearing on contemporary life are entirely absent, apart from two references to environmental concerns (kindness to animals and economizing water consumption). Values covered in the curriculum range from personal values (honesty, sincerity, modesty, and self-restraint) to social values (cooperation, humility, and social solidarity) and universal values (tolerance, justice).

**Table 8.6 Distribution of Islamic education topics at the basic education level in Yemen, 2011**

| Grade | Number of classes | Number of topics | Percentage of topics related to contemporary issues and values |
|-------|-------------------|------------------|----------------------------------------------------------------|
| 1 | 88 | 30 | 30 |
| 2 | 88 | 33 | 33 |
| 3 | 88 | 32 | 28 |
| 4 | 118 | 36 | 22 |
| 5 | 118 | 34 | 18 |
| 6 | 118 | 32 | 28 |
| 7 | 118 | 74 | 22 |
| 8 | 118 | 66 | 24 |
| 9 | 118 | 59 | 36 |

*Source:* Yemeni Ministry of Education. Department of Curricula and Guidance. Scholastic Requirements for Islamic Education 2009–10.

## How Education Systems Impede Development

In the absence of a comprehensive, long-range vision for education in Arab countries, successive reforms have been largely contradictory and disruptive, neither complementing nor completing what came before and depending entirely on the support of the initiating authority. Thus, the lifespan of reform efforts and the amount of human economic effort invested in them depends on the authority's remaining in power. The history of Arab education reforms exhibits no cohesive thread, and their features are hard to define. There are several explanations for this discontinuity.

### Lack of political will for change

Lack of political will is the most serious obstacle to change, for it provides an opening to a host of potential ills (such as nepotism, corruption, and negligence). If education reform means reforming minds and equipping them with an awareness of people's rights and duties and the capacity to criticize, hold accountable, and oppose exploitation and injustice, the authorities might have little enthusiasm for solidifying new education programs.

Although increased spending on education in some Arab countries may indicate a will to change, some of the world leaders in education quality are not the highest spenders. The bigger impact comes from the management of resources. While the Arab education scene is not short on reform initiatives, the legislation, institutions, and resources needed to transform theory into action are absent.

### Dependence on western education philosophies

Foreign education reform projects—especially those originating in France (for the Maghreb countries) and the United Kingdom and the United States (for the Mashreq and the Gulf countries)—remain the primary inspiration for Arab ideas on reform. Little thought is given to the mechanisms needed to generate reform and create an education system compatible with the characteristics and needs of Arab countries. One failure after another has resulted from depending on western education philosophies without considering the local context—including economic, social, and cultural constraints and pressures—or the changes in intellectual and material structures (content, methodology, and pedagogical approach) needed for the program to take root and thrive.

Instead, education decision makers in Arab countries need a comprehensive perspective and an integrated systematic approach that considers the local context and the diverse internal and external interactions governing the system's equilibrium and the quality of its outputs. Simultaneously, the new strategy for education must remain open to experiences from the outside, regionally and internationally, borrowing intelligently in the expectation that the relationship will develop into reciprocal exchanges of expertise and joint production.

### Incomplete diagnosis of the problems in the education system

Diagnosing the problems in the education system without understanding their origins and causes leads to superficial remedies with minimal impact. Reformers can treat only the symptoms but never eliminate the causes. Reforms have proceeded as a series of experiments tested one after the other by trial and error—a far cry from solutions based on accurate diagnosis and objective, systematic evaluation.

The crux of the problem may be that Arab educational reform is short on perseverance; it seeks immediate results, whereas investments in human capital demand patience and resolve to overcome entrenched obstacles. Because investments in human capital pay off only in the long run, education projects that appear promising initially may fade away soon after implementation begins when the effects are not immediate or the first major difficulty surfaces.

### Inadequate information about the state of the education systems

Information is fundamental to evaluation, follow-through, and progress. To monitor development, assess gains, diagnose difficulties, and guide strategies for reshaping education programs, policymakers require accurate information.

Gaps in information systems in many Arab countries make it difficult for policymakers to make the right decisions.[34] A 2004 study of education and training in Arab countries found multiple gaps, including a disconnect between data collected and data needed, especially for analyzing links among inputs, processes, and outputs; lack of information on teaching and learning practices and mechanisms; and overloading of decision makers with irrelevant information.

In addition, the usefulness of information depends on its quality. Quality is the product of a selection process that adheres to rigorous methodological and technical guidelines recognized by the research community. Education decisions are frequently made in haste, which can put pressure on information providers to cut corners to meet decision makers' immediate needs. That process undermines the credibility of information, the validity of the deductions derived from it, and the soundness of the decisions based on it.

But even when high-quality information is available, as from comparative international reports, it is rarely used to diagnose education problems or to reach objective, constructive conclusions that can advance development. In most cases national reports derived from international studies tend to justify shortcomings (by pointing to differences in methodology or means of assessment, for example) or to focus on Arab country rankings more than performance or the causes of shortcomings.

### Lack of transparency and accountability in handling education problems

Although the concept of the open school or open academy has made its way into the lexicon of many pedagogical circles in the Arab region, it has not yet made its way into the classroom or the highest levels of decision making in the education sector.

The academic environment in Arab countries is insular and does not easily accept outside intervention. Aside from periodic assessments of teachers (inspections), and administrative reviews of school heads, and, occasionally, the Ministry of Education's provincial branches, most Arab countries have no system of accountability in the public sector. The absence of oversight and accountability paves the way for multiple ills that further weaken the education system, qualitatively and quantitatively. A system of incentives linked directly to outcomes is needed to motivate greater effort.

### Religious education's failures are a product of contradictory tendencies

The reasons for the failure of religious education may vary by Arab country, but the root cause is the failure to provide an environment that promotes the development of a balanced, reflective character. Religion is a mode of conduct and a way of life, and affiliation with a religion or sect does not preclude respecting and coexisting with those whose beliefs differ.

Religious education is undervalued, viewed as being of secondary importance, so inadequate attention is devoted to constructing curricula, selecting teachers, and choosing pedagogical and evaluation practices. The subject is approached from a closed, one-dimensional perspective that packages religious concepts into ready-made containers that broach no discussion and are subject to the oversight of religious authorities rather than being shaped by sound pedagogical principles and the needs of students.

The above-mentioned conditions place religious syllabi in a dimension outside of time and place. The courses do not meet the needs of students today or respond to contemporary challenges, and so they have no impact on the reality of society. Religious education fails to equip students with the mental, emotional, and social skills needed to fulfill themselves and to participate effectively in their countries' development.

The quality of religious education is likely to further deteriorate unless religious education becomes more than just another subject to fill classroom time. Whether students view religious instruction as interesting or boring, they are convinced that it has no relevance to their lives. Thus, between religious intolerance and hostility to religion, the door remains open to extremism and serious conflicts that threaten the stability and the fabric of society.

## The Way Forward

Considering the profound transformations that many countries must undergo, Arab ambitions for education reform must transcend building schools, modernizing curricula, improving the performance of teachers and administrators, and incorporating the latest technologies, important as these are. Efforts must aim to create education systems that enable children to acquire the cognitive, emotional, and social skills needed to thrive in a knowledge society, to participate fully in improving the quality of life, and to achieve development objectives.

### What is to be done about education policy in general?

Arab countries do not lack reform initiatives. The Gulf countries, for example, have introduced multiple reforms sharing the same aim: to develop the education system and improve its outputs. Qatar had the Education for a New Era initiative, under the auspices of the Supreme Education Council, and the Independent Schools experiment that gave schools greater autonomy to develop curricula and teaching methods. The United Arab Emirates launched the Vision 2020 Plan, which gave rise to "partnership schools," "schools of tomorrow," and "model schools." Bahrain developed the concept of "Schools of the Future" and introduced the National Project for the Development of Education and Training. Saudi Arabia unveiled the King Abdullah Project for the Development of Education in 2007, earmarking a large budget for implementation. Kuwait adopted the Education Development Strategy 2005–2025.

Despite good intentions, these reforms failed to achieve their aims. An Egyptian researcher specializing in the Gulf states observed that a bureaucratic legacy and ideological rivalries have been the primary impediments to the bold thinking needed to turn education practices around in Kuwait and Saudi Arabia. He also noted that the UAE Vision 2020 Plan, adopted in 1999 and generously funded, has come "to nothing."[35] While the situation in some other Gulf countries appears more promising, it is too early to tell what will happen. Global assessments of education quality show that despite some improvements in international rankings on technical preparedness and networked readiness, the wealthy Gulf countries still lag behind in achieving a productive education system.[36]

The Maghreb countries, particularly Algeria, Morocco, and Tunisia, have introduced numerous reforms since the 1990s, encompassing legal provisions and theoretical frames of reference, followed by changes to curricula and teaching approaches. The most meaningful change was the shift from an aims-based to a competency-based pedagogy that merges knowledge acquisition with the realities of daily life. Despite the promise of this approach and its successes elsewhere, this strategy has not improved student performance. In Tunisia, for example, which officially adopted the competency-based approach in 1999 and applied it at all levels of primary education—curriculum, textbooks, and teacher training—the generation raised on the new approach has still not attained the desired level of performance as evidenced by national and international assessments. Calls to drop the competency-based approach are growing louder by the day—not because the approach lacks validity but because the appropriate groundwork was not laid first.

What these and many other examples show is that Arab education reforms emphasize organizational and technical aspects of the education process through new technologies and curricula, while "they have never so much as dared to venture into a comprehensive educational revolution."[37] The problem reflects the capacities and economic and human resources of each country, but even more so the ability to plan and prioritize.

Arab countries can take several measures to plan and act more strategically to improve their prospects for education progress toward human and economic development (box 8.2). Among these are qualifying teachers, developing school life, and enhancing the school's relationship with the local and wider community.

**Box 8.2 The reform of education in the Arab countries: The road ahead**
Reform of education can play a central role in economic development. Education is critical to a nation's growth because it develops the minds of the young to be useful citizens. It must include teaching the young how to think for themselves and to have confidence in their knowledge. This requires highly respected and motivated teachers who are well versed in communicating with their students. Teachers must be kept abreast of new teaching methodologies, scientific breakthroughs, and literary masterpieces. They must also be motivated by awards and recognized for excellence. Thus, teacher preparation and continued training become integral parts of the necessary reforms. . . .

The problem needs to be remedied starting at the very beginning.

Preschool education, at home and kindergarten, can set the pattern. A child's perception of learning and the development of his or her personality begin at a very young age. Inquisitiveness and analytical thinking can all be implanted in the minds of young children through dialogue. More importantly, valuing knowledge and respecting its sources affect children at an early age. I can personally attest to that: my earliest recollection from childhood relates to the way my father reached for a book on his bookshelf, carried it with great care, and opened its pages with tenderness and respect.

In some countries—for example, Egypt—the information is crammed into young minds with no time allocated for discussion or reasoning, which forces an emphasis on rote learning. There are things that must be memorized, such as multiplication tables, grammar rules, or poems. But students should learn to discuss possible interpretations and understand the benefit of debate. There must be a balance between expecting obedience and encouraging innovation. Teachers should seek the participation of students in free and critical thinking, which in itself increases their interest in, and enjoyment of, the time they spend at school.

The reform of education in the Arab region will assure its political stability, economic growth, and cultural elevation. There are two prerequisites for this: first, the intellectual courage to admit that the present systems do not develop the young minds that are capable of performing the necessary tasks; second, the political will to institute the required changes. For these reasons there must be a sustained partnership between governments, the private sector, and civil society. Educators, intellectuals, and the media can work together to assure such a partnership.

There is nothing in the Arab personality that hinders growth and achievement. On the contrary, Arab/Islamic civilization lasted for eight centuries on the shoulders of scholars and innovators in every field. . . .

More than anything else, it was the quest for, the preservation of, and the increase and dissemination of knowledge that distinguished those who established and sustained Arab/Muslim civilization. To them, knowledge was to be treasured no matter where it originated, and it was considered the right of all human beings. It is imperative for us all to learn these significant lessons in order to pave the way for the new generation of Arabs to reach the dream of a better future and to contribute to modern civilization.

—Dr. Farouk El-Baz, "Reform in Arab Countries: The Role of Education," http://www.bu.edu/journalofedu-cation/files/2011/06/BUJOE-188.3El-Baz.pdf

### Qualifying teachers

Teachers are a focal point of reform around the world. The following initiatives can help empower teachers and impart the skills they need to achieve a qualitative shift in education systems:

- *Revise pre-service teacher training.* Pre-service training needs to be based on clearly delineating the qualities desired at each education level, the tasks teachers are expected to perform, and the educational and pedagogic skills they will need to perform successfully. Teacher training colleges must be revamped in light of modern advances in education theory and technology so they can equip prospective teachers with a solid theoretical and practical foundation. Countries without teacher training colleges need to establish them.

- *Develop an integrated system for monitoring, assessing, and upgrading teacher performance.* Teacher monitoring systems must go beyond routine inspections—of little use because of their censorial nature—and assume a spirit of partnership, mentoring, and guidance that reinforces teachers' confidence and encourages them to improve their performance.
- *Revise employment criteria.* Teachers who enter the classroom need the cognitive, social, and psychological skills required to perform at their best. In most Arab countries today, employment criteria still emphasize theoretical qualifications while discounting personal and psychological skills and traits (such as motivation, self-esteem, perceptions about school and the teacher's role) that can determine success or failure.
- *Develop stronger in-service training programs.* In-service training programs should do more to enhance teacher effectiveness by keeping teaching staff abreast of new findings and improving their skills. Training programs can tap into the vast potential for distance learning and training, education technologies, and modern pedagogy.
- *Devote more attention to the economic, educational, and social conditions of teachers.* Teachers who are not paid enough to ensure dignified self-sufficiency may be forced to take up private tutoring or other outside employment that siphons time and energy from teaching. To have a more balanced life and function optimally, teachers need an environment that provides space for improving their performance and comfortable working conditions that encourage them to engage fully with their students.

### Developing school life

If real and lasting education reform requires an enabling environment that imprints children with a love for knowledge and learning and helps them learn and create, a vital step is to organize the school to create a safe and stimulating learning environment. School should be a microcosm of society where children learn the rules of communal life and how to participate in public life and where they acquire the cognitive, spiritual, moral, and social values that will enable them to accommodate others and work effectively toward the common good.

Children cannot acquire such life skills by memorization. They need to experience them as a daily practice in the academic environment, through interactions with their teachers and peers and in extracurricular activities. The more democratic a school environment, the more opportunities it offers students to express themselves, the greater the freedom it gives them to voice and discuss their opinions. And the more the school environment shows students how to participate in the decisions that concern them, the greater will be the school's contribution to equipping the next generation with the tools of knowledge acquisition needed to function in a world of changes and choices and to become responsible citizens.

### Creating strategic partnerships among education stakeholders

Since children's upbringing and education are closely connected to a country's development, stability, and resilience, society must accept education and child rearing as a collective responsibility. To succeed, an education system must establish a broad network of relationships, domestic and foreign, with effective partners capable of offering intellectual, material, and technical support. Partners include education decision makers and administrators; students, parents, and guardians; civil society organizations; research centers; and vocational training and employment agencies.

National partnerships allow for consolidating channels of communication, consultation, and constructive interaction among concerned parties to establish consensus on education trends and to rally the energy to implement and develop them. Such channels also improve the fit between schools and their cultural, social, and economic environment.

Regional partnerships, by sharing diverse educational experiences, help in finding solutions to common problems. An example is the Plan for the Development of Education in the Arab Countries,[38] a joint initiative of the Arab League Educational, Cultural, and Scientific Organization, the World Bank, and the Qatar Foundation.

International partnerships can provide access to successful education experiments around the world, bringing in fresh ideas. Some Asian countries—China, Japan, the Republic of Korea, Malaysia, and Taiwan, for example—are promising potential partners. Having bet strategically on the development of education, today they are paradigms of successful, integrated, and comprehensive development. Care must be taken, however, to avoid dependency or wholesale cloning of experiences from other countries and to ensure that material aid does not dictate priorities or the nature of the funded projects.

### What is to be done for religious education in particular?

A balanced religious education is fundamental to preparing citizens who have a sound understanding of religion and its principles, providing them with a source of strength and confidence. Strong religious education helps shape a personality that is grounded in a country's historical roots and keen to preserve its identity yet ready to adopt the best manifestations of modernity. To shape such individuals, Arab societies must upgrade their religious curricula and methods of socialization to reflect authentic Arab values based on a genuine understanding of religion and, simultaneously, to absorb the developments in contemporary life. The aim is to strike a balance between Arab Islamic authenticity and the demands of globalization. Nothing in Islam prevents this approach. Consider these characteristics of Islam:

- It was founded on the injunction "Read!" and raised scholars to the status of heirs to the prophets. Islam encourages the quest for knowledge and science, which drives people toward progress and civilization.
- Its Prophet declared that his fundamental mission was to "complete the fulfillment of noble virtues." Islam, then, cannot be a source of degeneracy, violence, and terrorism; it can only be a source of moral virtue and temperate behavior.
- It calls for belief in the prophets as one of the pillars of the true faith. Such a religion cannot be a source of bigotry, discrimination, and hostility toward the other or an impediment to tolerance, peaceful coexistence, and dialogue.
- Its holy book repeats the word for 'mind' and its derivations 880 times, in addition to frequent mention of synonyms ('contemplation,' 'deliberation,' 'reflection'). Such a religion cannot be antithetical to speculative thought, the exercise of the intellect, and scientific reasoning.

Far from being a source of conflict, disintegration, and racist self-glorification, the components of Islamic cultural identity enrich and support dialogue between cultures and civilizations. When problems arise, that is frequently because these components are misinterpreted, whether by people claiming to be acting in the name of Islam or by others who have no interest in dialogue, mutual understanding, and coexistence because they are bent on conflict and force. Every call to peace and coexistence drives a wedge into such efforts.[39]

Religious events and concepts are crucial to shaping consciousness among youth of the common denominators in human experiences and to raising their awareness that religious faith presupposes a respect for others. Religious education must also teach the corollaries of this principle: a spirit of tolerance, sense of commitment, rejection of stereotypes and prejudice, awareness of the other as a natural and necessary part of our existence, and recognition of difference as a source of enrichment and completion. All religions converge on a common core of moral values that affirm goodness, justice, tolerance, brotherly love, and peaceful coexistence—values that can form a spiritual force for the benefit of the individual and society.

In *Essays on Values and Development*, four World Bank experts of different spiritual backgrounds (Christian, Hindu, Muslim, and Humanist) affirm that religion and spiritual values are the rudder that helps steer the force of science and technology (Ramgopal Agarwala) and that the world needs spiritual substance as well as material prosperity—without which efforts can bear no fruit, however good the intentions (Sven Burmester). They contend that civilization faces several global threats that cannot be confronted without a moral and spiritual platform (David Beckman). Generating such spiritual energy requires every individual and group to reform themselves first and to ground their behavior in principles emanating from moral traditions and ideals (Ismail Serageldin).[40]

Echoing such ideas, Jacques Delors, who headed the task force that prepared the UNESCO report on education for the twenty-first century, *Learning: The Treasure Within*, observed:

> The world has a longing, often unexpressed, for an ideal and for values that we shall term "moral." It is thus education's noble task to encourage each and every one, acting in accordance with their traditions and convictions and paying full respect to pluralism, to lift their minds and spirits to the plane of the universal and, in some measure, to transcend themselves. It is no exaggeration on the Commission's part to say that the survival of humanity depends thereon.[41]

From this perspective, religious education programs are indispensable for teaching children the principles of their religion, undistorted or unexploited for personal or political ends, and for exposing children to the differences and commonalities among religions (box 8.3). Children must develop respect for others' beliefs and come to realize, through practice, that difference is not an impediment to peaceful coexistence.

**Box 8.3 An interfaith school that teaches dialogue and respect for differences**

The German Diocese of Osnabrück offers a model for an interfaith school that uses religious instruction to instill in children the principles of tolerance, respect for difference, and dialogue with others. The project established a primary school for the three Abrahamic religions (Judaism, Christianity, and Islam) in cooperation with representative bodies of the three religions. Explaining how the project is meant to work, Winfried Verburg, director of the Education Department of the Episcopal Vicariate Osnabrück, said: "There will be one religious education course respectively. Approximately once every six months, a comparable topic will be covered in all three religion courses, which will then end in a Project Day on which the pupils show each other their results. In this way they'll learn to talk to each other about each other's differing religious beliefs, rituals, and customs. Our goal is to help them be capable of dialoguing with one another."

Source: www.dw.de

Arab countries need to attend to the reality of religious upbringing, identifying weak spots and determining responsibility for the intellectual complacency and apathy of youth and the erosion of principles and moral foundations that has driven some to extremism and others to ill behavior. There is a message for all Arab countries in the distortion of religion through misunderstanding and misuse, the vicious assaults and aspersions against the principles of Islam and its compatibility with contemporary life, and the accusations that Islamic religious curricula nurture extremism and terrorism. That message is the need to achieve a qualitative shift that assigns religion and spiritual and moral values the importance they merit and sets religious education on its proper course. Toward this end, the reform process must concentrate on three major contributory paths to religious upbringing—the family, academic curricula, and the media—with an eye to elevating and integrating their roles.

### Raising the intellectual level of the family

A child's first lessons in life come from the family. Within the family a child acquires the basic principles and modes of behavior needed for interaction with the community. Through interplay within the family, the child assimilates a society's culture, language, values, customs, and ways of thinking. Child rearing in most Arab environments swings between the traditional authoritarian mode and overly protective indulgence, and between the values of the past and those of the present, which are needed to prepare the child for the future. This kind of upbringing impairs a child's development, confidence, and social skills and inculcates a passive mode of knowledge acquisition.[42]

A child's first exposure to religious thought is also through the family and is shaped by the parents' cultural and social status and the intellectual climate they create. In an environment ruled by superstition and blind faith in the supernatural, a child's thinking will grow rigid, complacent, and submissive, becoming fertile ground for extremist indoctrination. Conversely, in an environment built on rational dialogue, children develop powers of free inquiry and constructive criticism that fortify them against demagoguery and ideological extremes.

There is an urgent need to empower families intellectually and to redirect misguided methods of upbringing. Some of this work can be done through organizations that engage directly with families, women, and children and through awareness-raising campaigns in the media or through cultural outreach activities in more remote areas. Such activities can bring care workers in closer contact with families, improving information dissemination and absorption.

Including educational and religious awareness-raising components as part of adult learning and literacy programs could also help effect change. The numbers of adult learners in Arab countries is rising,[43] making this segment of the population more accessible.

### Rethinking religious education curricula

The emphasis in much religious education is on sentiment and behavior—to the neglect of cognitive processes and judgment. Religious education curricula have focused on surface issues while ignoring the aspects that matter for understanding and forming moral value systems.

The content and pedagogy of religious education must be transformed to reform the intellect, develop emotional sensibility, and reshape the identity of people in the Arab region, starting from a higher religious, ethical, and cultural foundation (box 8.4). The Arab philosophical and rationalist heritage holds numerous models for inspiration, from the Mu'tazalis to Ibn Rushd (Averroës), who established the groundwork for pluralism, recognition of the other, freedom of opinion, and an appeal to rational thinking as early as the eighth to the twelfth centuries. Infusing into religious instruction an interdisciplinary dimension related to morality and human behavior would enhance student awareness that religious education is a way of thought and behavior and an avenue to a balanced social and psychological life.

---

**Box 8.4 When will the light of religious education shine?**

Religious instruction in our schools relies on giving ready-made responses to oft-repeated questions; perhaps it is hoped that the process will cut through the dark thicket of desiccated rites and rituals to extract some moral precepts, like a catechism, or, as if "explaining water with water," by reminding pupils of the commandments and the permitted and forbidden. Religious education, however, is a different thing. It seeks to expand horizons and make knowledge based on constructive criticism the foundation of every lesson. It respects students' minds and reinforces a spirit of systematic thought and analysis. What is the harm if Christian and Muslim students, sitting side by side, learn that God is one and the creator of all things? Do they not both declare that there is no god but God? Is God not merciful, revealing himself to every community in the most appropriate way, without alienating the community from its environment and culture?

Don't both religions agree on the principles of peace and justice and embrace the fight against injustice and oppression, resistance to wrongdoing, a refusal to meet evil with evil, and the proclamation of truth? Don't Islam and Christianity urge believers to aid the poor, needy, and downtrodden? Don't both religions hold the human being to be sacred? Do Muslims and Christians alike not fear God and submit to his teachings and commandments? Are not the pillars of both faiths based on justice, brotherhood, equality, prayer, and fasting? Let us then take religious education as a lamp to illuminate the dark pathways, beset by conflicts and wars, to be a factor for a strong union.

—Shalhoub 2004, 21

In 2003, the Islamic Educational, Scientific, and Cultural Organization, in cooperation with the United Nations Population Fund, prepared a handbook for teachers and designers of Islamic education curricula on integrating the concepts of reproductive health and gender into the public education curriculum for students ages six to nineteen.[44] The experiment could be expanded to include the democratic and human rights values of freedom, justice, and equality, which are compatible with the mission of religion.

But no matter how well designed the curriculum, its efficacy depends on teachers. Criteria must be developed to ensure that religious education teachers are qualified and embody the values they are assigned to impart.

### Bringing about change through the media

The influence of the media on the minds and attitudes of the young can be harnessed to spread religious values and serve as a voice of reason and moderation. A media campaign could counter the voices that distort religion and its relation to daily life. Media discourse needs to avoid the language of rebuke, intimidation, accusations of blasphemy, and emotional appeals by addressing the mind, stimulating thought, and developing humanitarian values. Tareq Suwaidan, a Kuwaiti Islamist thinker, noted that "the most important change that must occur in media discourse in general, and religious discourse in particular, is an ideological one. Religious sermonizing or emotive narrative or social discourse that is not built upon aims to change recipients' ways of thought and convictions will produce no more than an ephemeral change of limited influence."[45]

Media discourse must transcend theorizing and advance paradigms affirming that religious faith and rationalism can coexist and complement each other. Exemplars of the academic, moral, and behavioral virtues are needed to inspire youth. The Arab cultural scene is filled with role models in all fields of activity—sports, the arts, Islamic and Christian proselytizing—but role models who combine academic excellence with ideological moderation are rare. Instead, films and TV dramas frequently present an off-putting image of the superior student as unkempt and inhibited, while religious figures are presented as disapproving of modern civilization and disconnected from public life.

### A new education model

To rise to a position of global leadership, a country needs a strong educational foundation. Achieving and maintaining this base take diligence, vigilance, and creative initiatives that place the education system at the service of the country's development goals and strategic objectives.

Arab countries aspire to this goal, but despite successive education system reforms, outputs remain quantitatively and qualitatively below desired levels. To achieve development goals, Arab countries must transform their education systems from a 'factory' model to a 'company' or 'organization' one.

The factory mentality presumes the existence of an elite group of thinkers who establish policies: what will be produced, how, and according to what template. This mentality requires strict monitoring that makes teacher–workers feel simply like tools for implementing factory policy, and it instills in students ('products') a tendency toward passive consumption and dependency. The factory model is unlikely to produce active minds capable of creating and developing knowledge or producing emotionally balanced people capable of maintaining their equilibrium, interacting constructively with others, and adjusting to society in a fruitful way.

The concept of a partnership or a learning organization, by contrast, places the education of youth in the framework of a multifaceted, collective project that engages all concerned parties (family, school, research centers, employment organizations). The ways and means of learning are numerous and diverse, requiring education institutions to become centers for personal development that prepare students for the future. Teachers must be active partners in learning. Students need to understand that they are the center of attention, which enhances their motivation to acquire the knowledge and skills needed to become 'knowledge producers' and drivers of development.

A comprehensive perspective on the education system's mission would therefore call on schools to shape the spiritual, psychological, social, and cultural dimensions of students in addition to enabling learners to acquire knowledge and skills. And it would do so in a manner that allows learners to assimilate their cultural and civilizational identity and to remain open intellectually to other cultures. Reconciling the tensions between local cultural authenticity and openness to world civilization, and between tradition and modernity,[46] is not an impossible challenge but requires strategies that stimulate thought, purposeful action, and positive change.

What should concern the Arab countries is how to integrate the two frameworks—the national and historical value system, and the universal value system and global culture—without one swallowing the other. Education approaches need to transcend the habit of antithetically juxtaposing "authenticity and modernity" and "subjectivism and rationalism"[47] and turn to a more integrative outlook of productive assimilation and synthesis. Education curricula need to renounce a coerced modernity that eliminates richness and diversity and entrenches hegemony and dependence in favor of an innovative modernity that embraces local culture while coexisting with global cultures on a foundation of mutual respect. The experiences of Asian countries such as Japan and Malaysia show that modern resurgence and development can be achieved without severing peoples' ties with their culture and without invalidating indigenous national and religious institutions.

Education is the surest channel for reconciling those frameworks by developing the individual's ability to think, work, produce, and contribute to the construction of human civilization. If entry to the world of knowledge and development depends on the quality of scientific and technical education, the sustainability of such gains and their deployment for the general welfare require elevating emotional well-being and the spiritual and moral guidance as primary objectives. As the French philosopher and sociologist Edgar Morin says, "development conceived exclusively as techno-economic progress, including durable development, is in the long term unsustainable. We need a more rich and complex notion of development which is not only material but also intellectual, emotional, moral."[48]

The education system bears a vital responsibility for turning out graduates capable of pursuing development policies that draw on a positive interplay of cognitive, moral, and behavioral dimensions. The political and social environment are equally important, for they nurture the enabling conditions to create a climate of freedom, justice, and democracy that helps mold independent, well-rounded individuals.

## Notes

1   UNDP 2005a, 214.
2   UNESCO 2009.
3   ALECSO and the World Islamic Call Society 2006.
4   The four goals are universal primary education, adult literacy, gender parity, and quality of education.
5   UNESCO 2011.
6   In the 2003 round of the International Association for the Evaluation of Educational Achievement (IEA), ten Arab countries took part (Jordan, Bahrain, Tunisia, Saudi Arabia, Syria, Palestine, Lebanon, Morocco, Egypt, and Yemen); the 2007 round also included Oman, Qatar, Algeria, Kuwait, and the emirate of Dubai.

7   Overseen by the Organisation for Economic Co-operation and Development (OECD).
8   UNDP 2003a.
9   UNDP 2002b, 50.
10  MBRF (Mohamed bin Rashid Al Maktoum Foundation) and Regional Bureau for Arab States/UNDP 2009.
11  Belderrain 2003.
12  Centre international d'études pédagogiques 2004.
13  UNDP 2005a, 1.
14  MBRF (Mohamed bin Rashid Al Maktoum Foundation) and Regional Bureau for Arab States/UNDP 2009, 94.
15  MBRF (Mohamed bin Rashid Al Maktoum Foundation) and Regional Bureau for Arab States/UNDP 2009, 94.
16  Abu Sulayman 2004.
17  Abu Sulayman 2004.
18  Bokran 2007.
19  Bokran 2010.
20  Abu Zakariya 2007.
21  al-Hussayn 2003.
22  al-Shafi'i 1984.
23  The study analyzed religious education syllabi and textbooks, pedagogy, and attention to contemporary interpersonal relations for the 2010–11 academic year (Sika 2011).
24  Preface of the Curriculum of Islamic Education, Level 3.
25  Algerian Ministry of National Education (programmes.educdz.com/Arabe/Accueil.htm).
26  Sika 2011.
27  Sika 2011, background paper for the report.
28  'Atallah 2011, background paper for the report.
29  'Atrisi 2001.
30  Atallah 2011, background paper for the report.
31  Sika 2011.
32  Tunisian Ministry of Education 2006.
33  Arab Resource and Information Center for Violence against Women (www.amanjordan.org/arabic_news/wmview.php?ArtID=15601).
34  "Education and Training Efforts in the Arab Nation: Challenges and Trends" 2004.
35  Saqr 2008.
36  According to World Economic Forum 2009.
37  Malkawi and Nejadat 2007, 3.
38  ALECSO 2010.
39  al-Samadi 2008.
40  Beckman, Agarwala, Burmester, and Serageldin 2006.
41  Delors 1996, 16.

42   Suwaigh 2002.
43   World Bank 2012a.
44   IESCO 2003.
45   Suwaidan (www.suwaidan.com).
46   Delors 1996.
47   Pourtois and Desmet 2002.
48   Morin 2001, 63.

# CHAPTER 9

# The Formation of Religious Leaders and Impact of Enlightened Imams[1]

## Baqer S. Alnajjar

Religion is the foundation of Arab life, with a vital role in the public and private spheres. Its rituals, worship, and ethical orientation are important in the lives of the region's people and as the foundation for the state and society. For most Arab countries religion constitutes the core of their cultural identity and political legitimacy, and Islam is the state religion or constitutes the pillars holding the basis for the state's political structure and distribution of power.

This chapter on the contexts in which Arab devoutness and religious discourse are formed explores several questions. How does religion contribute to building and shaping society? To what extent does the role of religion reflect theory and history? How are clerics trained, and what challenges do they face? To what extent does religion express identity? What mechanisms have Muslim communities developed to preserve their identity? What role did religion play in the Arab Spring? What does the future relationship between religion and politics look like? The main issue this chapter addresses is whether the contexts that influence the formation of religious figures and ordinary people in the Arab region provide incentives that positively and effectively contribute to human development.

While many clerics are calling for religion to take on a stronger developmental and humanitarian role, the more recent texts on those issues have yet to penetrate wider circles of discourse and practice if religion is to become a tool for achieving virtue and progress. Arab society still suffers a 'text gap'—the gap between religious texts and reality.

## The Position of Religion in Society

For believers, religion lays down the guidelines that determine what is acceptable and legitimate and what is not. It is regarded as an important source of the values that regulate humanity's relationship with the world and divine will. Religion thus gives life meaning for those who practice it—the conviction that they should live to achieve a goal beyond this life. From this, people draw their identity and allow justification for their being. If the power of faith instilled by religion is used in a positive and creative manner for human well-being and the consolidation of identity, it can then empower people and set them on a path of development and progress.

Religion has brought about major changes in society, some rapidly and others gradually (box 9.1). Leaving aside the political mobilization role played by religious leaders in the Arab region since the beginning of the Arab Spring, it is important to note that such change could not have happened if religion did not serve as a positive force in changing people's attitudes.

### Box 9.1 Religion and life: The social contribution and the challenges of the relief aid ceiling

Religious institutions and groups in the Arab world appear to play a prominent role in human development, but this role is limited by two ceilings: politics and relief aid.

The state imposes two conditions on religion's role in development. The first is that the state grants religion its legitimacy. The state has allowed religion a clearly circumscribed role in development, to fill in gaps resulting from its withdrawal from public service provision under structural adjustment, privatization policies, and the move toward open markets.

The second condition is that the religious role in development must be contained within national borders unless the state's express permission is granted. This has proven a constant source of tension. For example, Islamic relief organizations in Egypt are often held up for weeks by the Egyptian authorities at the Rafah border crossing to Gaza. There have been a few exceptions. Libya was active in extending its reach into sub-Saharan Africa through aid and preaching. The Gulf states have established religious endowment funds and aid organizations, and they have played an important role in social development through extensive religious and preaching circles in Africa, Asia, and the Balkans.

The ceiling of relief aid refers to development work in response to the urgent needs of groups and individuals. Examples are the work of the Islamic Medical Organization (the health division of the Muslim Brotherhood), the many Islamic schools, and the services of the Egyptian Coptic church. The focus on health and education arises from the poor quality and underfunding of public provision of these services, but no long-term strategy is in place.

While most houses of worship have added educational services, there is little networking of associations to create pressure for change to education curricula or policies—or to try to drive state schools that offer services in mosques and churches to address the problems created by the state schools themselves. Religion's role has been limited to treating symptoms rather than fostering change. Moreover, preachers and religiously oriented social institutions rarely discuss distribution of wealth as a means of breaking the cycle of poverty.

Islamist currents, following their overwhelming success in the parliamentary elections of Egypt and Tunisia, are now expected to take on a larger role in improving conditions and moving these issues forward. The hope is, once government services properly address citizen rights, the burden will be removed from service-oriented organizations and religious institutions. This shift would allow religious institutions to focus on deepening the spiritual and moral messages that society needs in this transition phase, which seemingly will last for years. Hopes are pinned on development and aid work becoming a soft power that supports new regimes in their development, diplomatic, and humanitarian missions.

—Heba Raouf Ezzat, professor of political theory,
Cairo University

Many interpret religion as a force for organizing people's lives. For some, it embodies the spirit of community, bringing the members of a group closer in solidarity and identity through rituals. For others, it is a social, cultural, and dogmatic space that interacts and communicates with other public and private spaces—the family, the workplace, educational institutions, the political arena, and economic space. Furthermore, for some, it invigorates economic life, affirming the values of work, austerity, and saving, especially if faith is understood—as a means to salvation—to be integral to success at work and in life more broadly.

Ibn Khaldun emphasized the importance of religion in building civilization.[2] Islamic civilization is based on the association of faith and tribalism. Religion, according to Ibn Khaldun, strengthens the state by lessening the excesses of tribalism and enhancing its ethics. Building on Ibn Khaldun's concept, modern scientists write on the relationship between religion and civilization, the role of religion in achieving renaissance and *ijtihad* (independent critical reasoning applied to religious texts to derive insights into new circumstances). Some defend Islam as a model of civilization that is consistent with progress. Others call for *ijtihad* and for new concepts of faith able to forge a cultural renaissance.

Other ideas about religion center on the need to revive Islamic jurisprudence. Thinkers associated with the modern era set up the pillars of an enlightened trend in religion. They include the jurisprudence of Sayyid Jamaluddin al-Afghani (1838–97); Shaykh Abdel Rahman al-Kawakibi (1849–1902), the leader of the modern rational school; Muhammed Abdu (1849–1905); Rashid Rida (1865–1935), who combined tradition and modernity and balanced the rational and the transmitted and came to represent renewed Salafism; and Abu al-'Ala al-Mawdudi (1903–79), the founder of the largest Islamic group in the region. Both secular intellectuals and clerics contributed to this regenerative and rational trend, fighting against intellectual stagnation and fanaticism. They adhered to the foundations of Islam that preserved national identity while opening their minds to the laws of science, whose substance remains unchanged from one civilization and belief to another.

This rational strand diverged strongly from the tendency of extremism, which dominated the religious sphere in the last decades of the twentieth century and whose effects still resonate. Fundamentalist groups have proliferated, some of them adopting jihadist methods that the advocates of renewal view as contrary to the religious tenets of tolerance. Historically, even though religion was sometimes divisive, it has played a vital role in shaping human behavior and spreading the values that enable people to live together.

Religion has played a major role in the prosperity of Arab civilizations, especially in periods when it defended rational thought. According to Mohammed Abed al-Jabri and others, the Arab mind "resigned" during the long period of stagnation of the Islamic civilization (among the manifestations of this resignation was a culture of transmission, of statements instead of proofs). But in periods when the mind prevailed and when Islam fused with other civilizations, religions, and cultures in supporting principles of tolerance and peace, religion revived civilization. Open to other civilizations, the Arab Islamic mind drew from them, translated their ideas, and disseminated them widely. Moreover, Islam exhibited broad tolerance in the countries it conquered. It offered a model of diversity of cultures and coexistence, just like the time Islam ruled Andalusia.

Religion has also been instrumental in liberating people and reviving their identity following defeat. Examples are Christianity's consolidation of the Roman Empire after the fall of Rome in the fifth century; Islam's defense of Muslim lands against the crusaders in the eleventh and twelfth centuries and against the Mongol and Tatar invasions in the thirteenth century; the role of churches and monasteries in the Middle Ages in reinvigorating academic traditions and disseminating science, culture, and services; and the contribution of Islamic endowments in caring for the poor and spreading science and education. In the modern era the struggle to enlighten the mind was combined with the struggle for independence and the freeing of peoples from injustice and suffering. Religion played a key role in the decolonization of Muslim countries. Calls for independence were combined with calls for freedom from superstition. Advocates of revival defended religion's enlightening role in achieving progress.

Although some interpreters of religion turned the struggle for independence into an instrument of extremism and terrorism, religion continued to convey its sacred mission in working for development and progress. The destructive political practices associated with religion are a political co-opting of religion, diverting it from its goals of achieving the common good.

When religion contributes to the stability of society, organizes relations among its members, and perfects endeavors within a system of moral values, it contributes to community building and stability. Globalization increases the complexity of life, gives it a materialist character, and deepens manifestations of moral anxiety, alienation, and the loss of standards. In these conditions religion can restore balance by charging people with a spiritual energy that helps them meet the challenges of modern life and equips them with the moral values needed to adapt to change. Religion can become a common cultural denominator for people all the world around, enabling them to avoid bloody conflicts and wars and to achieve peace.

## Acquiring Religious Knowledge

Religion reaches people through various sources whose influence differs according to a person's age as well as social and cultural upbringing. This means that people understand Islam and Christianity in the Arab-Islamic region under numerous orientations and accents.

This reality is the source of distinctions—and perhaps contradictions—between what are termed *popular religion* and *official religion*, as well as between the religion of the intellectual elite (the clerics) and that of the masses. In addition, there is political Islam; urban Islam and desert and rural Islam; Arab Islam; and the Islam of Iranians, Indians, Turks, Africans, and westerners. Although religion may be essentially singular, the social, economic, and cultural spaces in which it is formed produce various configurations.

### Family and local community: Channels for popular piety

As children grow they begin to formulate ideas and an understanding of religion, taking cues from parents, extended families, and neighbors. This enclosed context forms the first link in the formation of an individual's knowledge of religion, not just about ritual forms of worship, values, and orientation but also about religious or sectarian identity as opposed to the local other.

Parents may begin by speaking with their children about God, the creator of the universe, his prophets, and the direction of prayer (for Muslims), as well as by teaching them to pray. Parents might take their children with them to houses of worship, introducing them to a spiritual experience that they may want to explore.[3] They may also instruct children on the qualities that religion encourages: honesty, obedience, cleanliness, order, amicability, and assistance to the less fortunate, such as the needy and the elderly. They may clarify the kinds of behavior condemned by religion, such as theft, dishonesty, ingratitude, oppression, and slander. Children may learn that acceptable and unacceptable behavior leads to rewards and punishments from God in the afterlife.[4]

Collective performance of religious rituals and duties makes them less of a choice than a custom that reinforces piety and piques interest in acquiring more knowledge from clerics and others. The way collective performance presents religion helps form the basis of an individual's cultural identity, which shapes understanding of religion, society, and life. Religious truths and doctrine are transmitted through discussions among relatives, friends, and acquaintances during and after prayer, in casual conversation, and in children's folk tales.

Religious knowledge is communicated in many forms. For Muslims these include prophetic sayings, folk tales, and stories of the prophets and the righteous narrated by parents; Friday sermons in the local neighborhood or village mosque; and stories told on religious occasions. For Christians these include Mass and sermons on Sundays and religious holidays, Sunday school, and other occasions. Different social and cultural contexts produce a range of religious expression that is typically passed down through generations.

The understanding of religion imparted by families, neighbors, and friends—commonly termed *popular religion*—is a collection of beliefs and rituals that people practice in their daily lives and through which religion serves its basic social function. These rituals, performed at celebrations, are based on beliefs that are manifested in daily life as communal laws, such as those that distinguish between permissible and prohibited foods. They include visits to holy shrines to seek assistance, thus helping people accept the fate decreed by God.[5] Some religious practices may be customs and traditions that gradually become part of a community's symbolic order. These parts of popular religion are loosely connected, evading elaboration and organization.

Although popular religion is commonly perceived to be more widespread among the working class and the poor, recent transformations in the Arab region have created a growing social demand for religion among members of the middle and upper classes, particularly by those who seek assistance with the dealings of everyday life. In addition, increasing social mobility has meant that the working class's popular culture and understanding of religion have made inroads into the middle and upper classes. And many of the new young preachers (see below) target the middle and upper classes in homes, clubs, mosques, and well-to-do neighborhoods.[6]

The class, cultural, and economic changes in the Arab region over the last three decades have made popular religion, with its limited rules, accessible to most social groups. The spontaneous and collective nature of its rituals and forms of worship allow all members of society, regardless of their social or class position, to take part. In this way popular religion is similar to popular culture, as it forms an open arena where no one is excluded.[7]

### School: The inroad of official religion

The second important source of religious knowledge is the religious curricula in public schools, state-accredited or state-funded religious schools, and private schools affiliated with independent religious institutions and groups (see chapter 8). Independent religious schools are subject to little or no official oversight.

Islam is a compulsory subject for nearly all public school students in most Arab countries. Lebanon is an exception: religion is allocated only one hour a week in state schools, and the classes are taught by instructors provided and paid by the religious sects involved.[8]

The syllabi for public school students grow more sophisticated with each year of study. Islamic textbooks focus on Qur'anic verses and prophetic sayings. Students read, interpret, recite, and memorize the texts.[9]

Teacher qualifications vary tremendously. Some teachers have university degrees in Islamic law. Others studied a mix of Arabic language and Islamic studies. Still others end up teaching by default, because of a shortage of specialist instructors. Many parents complain about the fear and horror haunting their children as a result of the dramatic images that teachers paint of hell and the tortures of the grave. Some teachers encourage students to attend extracurricular lessons provided by Islamic associations or to attend mosques for the five daily prayers.[10]

Public schools began teaching religion in the 1950s and 1960s, encouraged by Arab leaders to counter the superstitions common in popular religion, which were seen as an obstacle to modernization and development.[11] Arab leaders began to speak of an official ideology and religion that represent the "straight path," the way of the Prophet. Mixing official religion and politics along with using religion to justify mistakes by Arab politicians and decision makers has in some quarters led to a backlash against official Islam.

### The new electronic realm

The third source of religious education is the new electronic realm, whose imprint has begun to surpass the other two sources. Thanks to modern communications technology, the electronic realm has become one of the most important sources of religious knowledge (see chapter 3).

The extraordinary and unexpected expansion of the electronic realm makes it one of the most powerful—and most dangerous—influences on people's religious views; it strengthens their ideological beliefs and amplifies the voices of those urging people to join particular religious groups or engage in specific causes. Some private religious television stations broadcast programs that discuss the beliefs of other sects, often to point out perceived flaws in those religious beliefs. They aim at spotting differences with others rather than working toward greater harmony. The provocative language on some religious programs has led officials to cut off their transmission on Arab satellites, as in 2010 when the Egyptian authorities cut the transmission of some Salafi and Shi'i channels.

Because the number of channels keeps growing, there are no accurate statistics on how many broadcast from or to the Arab region. Some reports estimate that at least ninety-three religious stations broadcast in the Arab region (box 9.2).[12]

Some religious channels (as defined by their programming) have been set up simply to generate profits—for example, those that promote herbal medicine or unlicensed medical products. Some broadcast advertisements for their products.[13]

Other channels are run by religious or political groups for the purpose of issuing fatwas and discussing Islamic legal opinions. Many present hard-line opposition to the legal opinions of other schools of thought, and some even engage in virtual TV battles that fuel sectarian and doctrinal strife. These channels lean toward "a proliferation in production and dissemination of a radical religious discourse far from the language of religious tolerance."[14] In contrast, state-owned channels broadcast religious programs and host Islamic scholars with moderate views.[15]

---

**Box 9.2 Religious satellite channels in the Arab region**

18 channels on Nile Sat and Arab Sat:
  15 Sunni
  3 Shi'i
32 channels on Atlantic Bird:
  16 Sunni
  7 Shi'i
  8 Christian
  1 owned by the Ahmadiya
23 stations on Nur Sat:
  12 Shi'i
  11 Sunni
20 stations on Nile Sat only:
  15 Sunni
  5 Shi'i
3 Shi'i stations on KalafSat

*Source:* www.coptreal.com/wshowsubject.aspx?SID=39205.

Internet sites have become a source of religious knowledge. Some explain the differences between religions and sects. Others issue fatwas on request or host otherwise unpublishable religious books that address conflict between religions and sects and that use nonacademic, inflammatory language. The websites of some preachers reveal a wide range of descriptions of other groups and attacks on their beliefs.

Many preachers and shaykhs have websites to interact with their followers and those seeking fatwas. Leading shaykhs, including al-Qaradawi, al-Sayyid Fadlallah, al-'Uthaymin, al-Sayyid al-Sistani, and al-Tantawi, and popular figures, including Salman al-Ouda and Aaidh al-Qarni, all have personal websites. Many official fatwa-issuing institutions also maintain websites, which may be influenced by the views of particular religious figures.

Many religious websites—like Islam Online, established in 1999—were established to offer guidance, definitively represent religions and sects, and call people to adhere to them. This original aim has been extended to include what some call "textual fatwas," related only to people who specifically seek them and the shaykhs who issue them. These fatwas are rapidly provided, confidential, free of charge, and remain outside any oversight mechanism.[16] Islam Online has responded to seven hundred thousand fatwa requests, including those related to banks, financial transactions, and marriage.[17] Other sites include the Kuwait Fatwa Authority, the Islam Today website, the Islamic network of the Qatar Religious Endowments Ministry, the Egyptian Dar al-Ifta', and other websites not subject to any official state authority. Some countries, including Saudi Arabia recently, have tried to restrict the issuing of fatwas to members of the Council of Senior Scholars and those it licenses to do so.[18]

### Clerical Discourse and Training

Many researchers agree that Arab culture combines aspects of modernity with a flavor of patriarchal tradition in a type of forced modernization, random selectivity, and excessive consumption. This hybrid modernity has implications for thought patterns, political power, and the role of religious institutions. The new categories created by modernity (the middle classes, the working classes, modern views of women and youth) coexist with old categories (such as merchants, craftsmen, and clerics). Arab societies have not been able to resolve the contradictions between state and tribe, class and citizenship, or state and religion. Religion became an integral part of the state, engaging in political discourse and legitimizing political regimes. Clerics have played a key role in social and political life, as rulers sought the cooperation and approval of religious scholars.

This context has been favorable to the large expansion of religious education in Arab countries. New Islamic universities have been established, and pre-university religious education institutions have spread widely. The scope of religious schools, run by the state or religious groups, has increased, and Qur'anic centers, often sponsored by a village or urban mosque, have also spread. Institutions of higher education are expanding as well. For example, Egypt's al-Azhar University now includes multiple types of religious and nonreligious education.

The expansion of religious education has resulted in the formation of various groups of Islamic clerics dedicated to preaching and religious education—from preachers who perform the function of imams and teachers in religious schools to prominent religious scholars, who constitute the official religious leadership, offer religious insights and theories for life, teach Islamic jurisprudence, and preach. The number of clerics in other religions has also increased, especially Christian clerics in Egypt, Iraq, Lebanon, Palestine, and Syria, including Orthodox, Maronites (mostly in Lebanon), Evangelical Protestants, and Catholics.

Clerics are widely respected. Their work through mosques and churches gives them a direct channel of communication with the people, who turn to them for religious guidance as the problems and challenges of social life become more complex. As part of the community, clerics have become an integral part of the modernization processes that are transforming Arab societies, as they have helped affirm that religion can be consistent with modernity.

Clerics' role in establishing the compatibility of religion and modern life started early in the nineteenth century. Their defense of Islam was mixed with the defense of an Arab renaissance and of independence from colonial rule, establishing the foundations of religious engagement with modern life. Al-Azhar clerics presented Islam as a moderate religion that aims to promote human development. They issued fatwas on important matters, such as jihad (confirming that fighting is legitimate only in defending against attack, combating injustice, or ending a schism), banks (finance banks are authorized in sharia, and reasonable interest on loans is not sinful usury), and non-Muslims (who must be allowed religious freedom; attempts to impose Islamic rules on non-Muslims is not sanctioned under sharia and may even be punished).

Building on the foundations laid by these Azhari scholars and taking advantage of modern means of communication, some of the boldest and more active clerics, intellectuals, new preachers, and women preachers have spread these ideas beyond the scope of their direct influence. A resident of any Arab country can listen to Shaykh al-Qaradawi preaching from Qatar or to Shaykh Hussein Fadlallah preaching from Iraq and can read Farida Bennani writing from Morocco. The Internet, social networks, and satellite channels have provided unprecedented opportunities for clerics of all types to access a wider audience and to develop dissemination tools for religious discourse (see chapter 3).

How are clerics trained, and what challenges do they face?

### Religious leaders

The religious elite are scholars who have attained advanced religious knowledge, usually graduates of religious institutes or universities or specialists in a specific branch of religion. These religious leaders are called "shaykhs" or "men of religion." Some hold elevated ranks in the hierarchy of religious knowledge, able to issue fatwas or engage in *ijtihad*. Others hold high administrative and political office that may surpass the rank of minister in addition to their religious posts. To the state and to the public, these figures constitute a religious authority whose opinions are sought and implemented, regardless of how strict (hard-line) or lenient (flexible).

Muslim religious authorities prominent in national Arab and pan-Arab contexts include Shaykh Mahmud Shaltut, Shaykh Muhammad Ghazali, Shaykh Muhammad Sayyid Tantawi, Shaykh Ahmad al-Tayyib, Shaykh Yusuf al-Qaradawi, Shaykh Abdul Aziz bin Baz, Ayatollah al-Sayyid Hussein Fadlallah, Ayatollah al-Sayyid Ali al-Sistani, and others. Among the leading Arab Christian authorities are Pope Tawadros II and Patriarch Mar Nasrallah Safir.

Some religious leaders represent official religion through providing religious legitimacy for the decisions and policies of the ruling political regime. Many Arab regimes have relied on fatwas for political ends—for example, fatwas permitting the assistance of foreign forces in the 1990–91 war to liberate Kuwait to counter fatwas prohibiting such assistance,[19] or the fatwa issued by the Council of Senior Scholars in Saudi Arabia prohibiting demonstrations demanding political and economic reform of the kind that erupted in the Arab Spring.[20] Other religious leaders oppose the state and justify political dissent. Still others oppose any form of religious tolerance within Islam and reject international agreements that provide a wider scope for individual freedoms—particularly for women. Indeed, "an alliance between some oppressive regimes and some types of conservative religious scholars led to interpretations of Islam that serve the government but are inimical to human development, particularly the freedom of thought, the interpretation of judgments, the accountability of regimes to the people and women's participation in public life."[21]

Opposition religious leaders are also split between traditional and reformist clerics. Traditionalists oppose all new cultural forms, viewing religious reform and renewal as heretical deviations from the true religion that must be opposed. The circle of conservative clerics is represented by many scholars of the fundamentalist school, whose views reflect mainly the views of religious scholars from the Salafi school and are at times in opposition to official state positions.[22] Conservative clerics object to women driving, and some object to participating with Christians in their celebrations of Christmas and New Year's. Some even label Islamic states' celebration of independence a form of heretical innovation, forcing some countries to change "National Eid" to "National Day." The inclination of the majority of Islamic scholars in the Arab region toward conservatism is due mainly to the weak curricula in religious schools and colleges and the lack of interest of many religious scholars in ideas that fall outside the traditional religious framework—including comparative cultural studies, sociology, economics, and psychology—and newer technology, such as computers and the Internet.[23]

The reformists, though still outnumbered, are nonetheless constructing a path forward in an attempt to harmonize religion with the demands of the modern age. Examples include Shaykh Muhammad Ghazali, Shaykh Ahmad al-Tayyib, Shaykh Yusuf al-Qaradawi, and Ayatollah al-Sayyid Hussein Fadlallah. Their discourse, not restricted to matters of religious outreach (*da'wa*) and Islamic law, focuses on contemporary and development issues. Liberal engagement with the contemporary age replaces inflexibility, reliance on superstition, and attention to detail at the cost of the larger picture.

Shaykh al-Qaradawi stresses that Islam is capable of engaging with the spirit of the modern day and absorbing it in a positive way as part of the process of human development, including issues related to the environment (box 9.3), corruption, women's liberation, citizenship, the rule of law, and education reform.[24] In a book about the environment, *Environmental Protection in Islamic Law*, he outlines an advanced Islamic legal understanding of environmental protection—including deforestation, investment, and cleanliness—and calls for protection of the environment from pollution and resource depletion.[25] In a book on the position of women he criticizes the extremist view of women as creatures of lower status than men, whose uncovered face is shameful and who should be educated only in certain subjects or not at all.[26]

**Box 9.3 Protecting the environment: An Islamic point of view**

The Islamic conceptualization of the environment is based on the affirmation of a bond between mankind and the natural environment so exalted as to constitute a sort of union between them, a union with a material side and a spiritual one. But this conceptualization is expansive enough to include a metaphysical distinction in which mankind rises in worth above all other components of the environment. It is also based on the affirmation of a role for the environment in mankind's fulfillment of the mission in life for which it was created, a role the environment, in its original nature, was fashioned to carry out in accord with that mission and that is articulated in the Qur'anic concept of *taskhir*, or subjugation.

That conceptualization is based on an assessment of mankind's responsibility to the environment from the standpoint of mankind's material and moral obligation to it in terms of what each owes the other. This assessment regulates the relationship of the two parties, with responsibility for the environment on man's side, in accord with the obligation he has thanks to his faculty for reasoning, and the environment not thought of as having responsibility.

These elements in the relationship of mankind to the environment—the bond of unity between them, the subservience of the environment to mankind, and mankind's responsibility for it—should guide environmental initiatives in an altogether new direction.

—al-Najjar 1999, 150–51

## Preachers and imams

Lower in status than religious leaders, preachers work as imams in mosques, in sharia courts, as instructors in religious schools and institutes, and as presenters of religious programs on official television and radio stations. Some expound with a boldness that oversteps the more rational efforts of religious leaders. Although some hold doctoral degrees in Islamic law, they are not trained scholars credentialed to engage in *ijtihad*. Rather, they repeat the opinions of their predecessors and today's religious leaders.

Preachers have a strong presence on Arab satellite channels and in the regional press, which has helped them rise to public prominence. Some have their own websites to connect them with new audiences; others have propagated the "satellite fatwa"—a fatwa given on the air, not backed up by adequate study of the question. At times issued in haste, some of these fatwas bear no relation to honest free thought or to *ijtihad* in Islamic law.[27]

Some preachers and imams have a university education in religion; others have graduated from mid-level religious institutes; still others have attached themselves to the preaching sessions of popular religious figures in their city or village; and some have developed their religious knowledge independently. Some are officially appointed, while others meet society's demand for preachers on their own.

The discourse of these imams is usually exclusively religious and focused on the afterlife. Their teachings are textual and drawn from a vast heritage of printed and recorded religious sermons, often using published copies of what are termed "pulpit sermons" as sources of quotations and ideas. Some political leaders, to curb criticism directed at the political authorities, insist on controlling the content of sermons at Friday prayers and unifying the themes across the country. These state-controlled sermons are limited to reprimands addressing heaven and hell, the importance of worship, the life of the Prophet and his companions, and similarly uncontroversial topics.

A study of 470 sermons in Egypt found that 362 (77 percent) were religious and 108 (23 percent) addressed worldly concerns. Worshipers' relationship to God was the most frequent topic (21 percent), followed by the afterlife (18.2 percent), forms of worship (18 percent), religious rulings and admonitory fatwas (11.9 percent), Islam and the characteristics of Muslims (10.8 percent), the Qur'an (8.3 percent), and historical events (5.8 percent; figure 9.1). Sermons on temporal matters focused on five primary issues: values and role models (47.2 percent), rights (23.1 percent), general political and social issues (11.1 percent), relationship to self and others (7.4 percent), and criticism of behavior (6.5 percent; figure 9.2). Discussion of general issues and the future together occupied only 4.7 percent of the sermons' content.[28]

None of the sermons encouraged economic and social development. Conservative values are the driving force behind the appeals to individuals and groups. The values mentioned most often were social (34.1 percent); the least often mentioned were values related to work (13.2 percent).

**Figure 9.1 Religious topics (77%) of Friday sermons in Egypt, 2011 (%)**

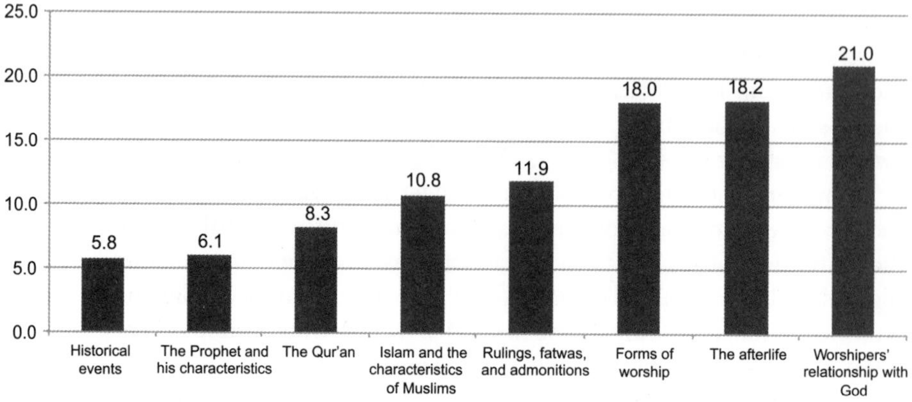

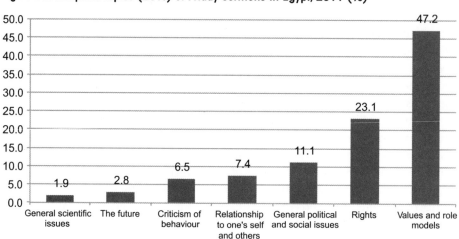

*Source:* Zayid 2011.

**Figure 9.2 Temporal topics (23%) of Friday sermons in Egypt, 2011 (%)**

*Source:* Zayid 2011.

### The intellectual *fuqaha'*

Some members of the intellectual *fuqaha'* (experts in Islamic jurisprudence) have a religious education, but they are not clerics. They may
possess extensive knowledge of religion related to business affairs, but
they do not apply their knowledge to interpret sharia or issue fatwas.
Some are asked to share their opinions on issues related to Islamic legal
cases, and some may practice religion through their academic or political positions.

Some intellectual *fuqaha'* are found among university professors of Islamic law and theology *(usul al-din)*. For some others—doctors, engineers, professionals in social and economic fields, and some professional politicians affiliated with religious political parties—religion confers legitimacy on their political role without being part of their professional life. Some may practice religion by virtue of their employment—for example, if they work for commercial religious channels or no-interest banks and other financial institutions. Their religion is a primary requirement of professional practice or political position. Being religious is a precondition for working in some of these fields.[29]

### New preachers and female preachers

The new preacher, a recent category of religious leader, is a product of the Arab region's many transformations over the last three decades, particularly society's rising demand for religious television programming. New preachers have not been trained through traditional channels (religious schools and universities) but through specializations without direct connection to preaching or religion, such as engineering, history, accounting, education, and psychology. Some were previously active in Islamic political organizations.

New preachers can be categorized into two groups: a moderate group that presents religious broadcasts that are not oriented to direct preaching or focused on Islamic law, and another group that entered preaching through politics.

The moderates have the greater presence and influence and were the first to penetrate television programming. Their shows tend to focus either on historical anecdotes related to the Prophet Muhammad and his companions, affirming values such as valor, sacrifice, generosity, pride, coexistence, and leniency in religious rulings, or on contemporary Arab social issues, such as the environment, educational and economic reform, HIV/AIDS, money laundering, and drug abuse. Coming from a non-Islamic legal background might make it easier for them to discuss content relevant to contemporary society.

This group's pleasant, often humorous style and well-groomed appearance may help them attract viewers. In contrast with the other groups of religious figures, the moderates are more interested in advancing economic and human development, protecting freedom of expression, combating terrorism, and maintaining domestic peace. Their passionate discussion has at times gone beyond religious guidance to mobilize public opinion. The best-known moderate preachers include

Amr Khaled, Tariq al-Sweidan, Nabil al-'Awadi, and al-Habib al-Jifri. Some challenge old values and tendencies that impede tolerance, acceptance of the other, social justice, and civil freedoms; and some even deal realistically with wealth. Khaled believes that the bourgeoisie plays an important role in society by accumulating wealth.[30]

For the group that entered through politics, religious authority derives from a political role for or deputization by well-known Islamic figures. While some may be referred to as "shaykh," they have not studied at religious schools, may have read but independently, or attended meetings of popular preachers. This group is defined by its hard-line political, intellectual, and religious views—rejecting political and religious differences and calling for a religious state.

Also part of the phenomenon of new preachers is the emergence of female preachers. Women first entered this arena, long a male monopoly, in Egypt. Today, female preachers are found in most Arab societies. Their discourse focuses on psychological and social guidance and discussions of social and daily life problems faced by women, including child rearing and marital relations; others focus on moral lectures.

Female preachers meet with their public in club rooms, at the offices of religious and charitable organizations, in private living rooms, and at mosques, including their adjunct halls and female-designated prayer areas, outside the five official prayer times. Most belong to the new middle class, fewer to the upper and lower classes. They may have obtained their religious education from religious universities or institutes or through specializations in the social and natural sciences and medicine. Some preach as a profession, their fees determined by the extent of their religious knowledge and the appeal of their speaking.[31]

## Islam in the world

The duties of clerics have expanded from defending Islam, affirming its compatibility with modern civilization, and issuing views and fatwas about unfolding events to dealing with the challenges of fanaticism and extremism in the interpretation of religion and religious interference in political life.

Defending Islam is important in the discourse of Islamic clerics. It initially consisted of the presentation of the truths of Islam in response to skeptics and the uninformed. But as cultural interactions with the west increased, defense of Islam began to focus on other issues:

- *Islam's contributions to western civilization.* The Qur'an emphasizes the value of knowledge and encourages learning. In the eighth and ninth centuries, Muslim philosophers and scholars revived ancient Greek science and philosophy, reintroducing them to the west in the twelfth century. Muslim scholars both preserved and enhanced the ancient learning of the Greeks, thus influencing what eventually became the western intellectual tradition.

- *Islam's capacity to engage in dialogue.* Following the events of September 11, 2001, senior clerics argued that Islam is a religion of peace. They stressed the importance of coexistence in an era of intense globalization and of renewing religious discourse to avoid conflict. They emphasized accepting the other and moving from the logic of violence and terrorism toward constructive dialogue, with a commitment to objectivity.

- *Islam's ideal image.* Clerics sought to describe the integrated model of Islam, which calls for humanity, tolerance, security, prosperity, righteousness, and piety, and to explain that Islam is not in conflict with modern life, even secular life. Important contributors include Shaykh al-Qaradawi, with a book on Islam and secularism, and Shaykh Muhammad al-Tantawi, with a book entitled "This Is Islam" condemning the events of September 11, 2001 and emphasizing Islam as a doctrine, a law, and a guide for humanity.

- *Islam's contributions to change and development.* The clerics' increased presence in the public sphere was coupled with a broader agenda for social change that emphasizes authenticity, self-reliance, and ending the human development stagnation in Arab countries through a new Arab awakening. Some clerics admit that development in Arab countries is at a standstill and have addressed the conditions needed to awaken development. The main conditions that moderate Sunnis and Shi'i agree on are banishing extremism and fanaticism in matters of religion and marshaling religion to help people build a good life and combat backwardness. Poverty occupies a central position in this discussion. Clerics emphasize a social responsibility that protects the rights of the poor, meets their needs, and preserves their dignity—not only through charity but also through jobs, so that all people can fulfill their aspirations and live a decent life.

## Schools that train Islamic clerics

The formation of clerics also requires formal education, which many religious schools, institutes, and universities provide. Religious schools are classified by religious affiliation. They can be Islamic and run by the state or its educational apparatus, belong to other religious groups and communities (such as the Salafis or the Muslim Brotherhood), or be Shi'i,

Isma'ili, Baha'i, Druze, or Christian. Some religious schools are dedicated to the memorization of the Qur'an and are often affiliated with a local mosque or school and organized by groups that seek to reach school-age youth. There are also local and foreign Christian schools and colleges, affiliated with a church that fully funds and supervises them. Some of these schools may combine modern subjects with religious education, whereas most Islamic schools teach only religious sciences.

There are no accurate statistics on the number of students in religious colleges and universities in the Arab region. Official data indicate that al-Azhar seminary school in Egypt has the most students in the Arab region studying religious law and theology, with more than 208,000, most of whom are men. Following well behind al-Azhar is Imam Muhammad ibn Saud Islamic University, with 21,745 students, the bulk of them Saudi. The number of students of religion in other Arab universities is considerably lower. For example, United Arab Emirates University had 408 students of religious sciences in 2001–2002 and only ten in 2010–11. In Kuwait, the number of students in the College of Sharia and Islamic Studies in 2010–11 was 2,201, about half of them male. Religious sciences students numbered about 26,862 in Jordan, 911 of both genders in Oman, 550 of both genders at Qatar University, and 100 at Bahrain University. Egypt and Saudi Arabia, where religion has a strong presence and national religious institutions play a big role in society, have the most religious sciences students. The student bodies studying religious sciences in the other Islamic sects, such as the Shi'i, Isma'ilis, Ibadis, and Druze, as well as among the various Christian sects, are much smaller.

Despite the changes that Islamic religious education in the Arab region has undergone, it continues to be grounded in five disciplines:

- The Qur'an and its sciences.
- Islamic law *(fiqh)* and its underpinnings.
- Prophetic traditions (Hadith) and its sciences.
- Theology *(kalam)* and its branches.
- Arabic language and its sciences.

Secondary fields taught in these universities include the biography of the Prophet Muhammad, as well as human and social sciences such as history, geography, psychology, and economics. Recently, computer science and comparative religious history have been introduced. These subjects may not carry much weight in the curricula of these universities, with their scope affected by the sincere will for change and development within the institutions.[32]

Al-Zaytuna University

Established in 737, al-Zaytuna University is one of the region's oldest education institutions (box 9.4). It has played a major role in preserving Arab-Islamic identity in Tunisia and neighboring Arab countries by conveying comprehensive cultural messages based on moderate Islamic values.

**Box 9.4 Al-Zaytuna University**

When Tunisia became independent in 1956, al-Zaytuna University consisted of the College of Theology, the College of Arabic Language, and the High Institute of Qur'anic Recitation. It also taught Arabic language and literature, Islamic legal sciences, and recitation of the Qur'an.

The scope of al-Zaytuna University subsequently diminished as it was converted into the College of Islamic Law and Theology. Marginalized, it abandoned its primary roles of developing the Islamic sciences, consolidating the Arabic language, and advancing academic research.

A presidential decree defined the university's mission as contributing to further developing human civilization by:

- Providing academic training that enables learners to learn from the values of Islam how to develop as a free and responsible person capable of reconciling commitments to religion with the need to meet the requirements of existence.
- Strengthening the understanding that Islamic thought has built on the interpretations of generations of creative and innovative scholars and seeks to expand knowledge, practice *ijtihad*, and celebrate the accomplishments of the prominent figures of this civilization.
- Reinforcing the university's transmission of the tenets of a school of thought and faith based on tolerance, religious renewal, and untiring work for the human good.
- Teaching students the value of interacting with other cultures and empowering them to enrich Islamic and human thought by reconciling innovation and heritage.

The university aims to deepen religious knowledge by offering subjects that enable an understanding of texts and an ability to read them in a way that leads to sound, independent interpretations that harmonize written texts and reality. The curriculum includes human and social sciences that engage students with other cultures and civilizations. It includes the history and sociology of religions, the history of ideas, comparative religion, the philosophy of positive law, and the history of science and art, in addition to Islamic legal science and Arabic language and other modern and ancient languages.

Graduates must engage with public life. Al-Zaytuna has thus made efforts to become a prominent, active institution. As part of the general expansion of higher education and academic research, new departments of Islamic arts and multimedia have been established.

The university aims to instill an openness to dialogue and respect for the other made possible through mutual acquaintance, intellectual interchange, and fertile partnership. Al-Zaytuna has established a consortium of universities that aim to impart sophisticated human values, including fraternity, cooperation, solidarity, and mutual benefit.

In 2010 al-Zaytuna University had 1,573 students.

—Hazem Musa,
http://ar.wikipedia.org/جامعة_الزيتونة

The author of the first Arabic encyclopedia, *al-Tifashi*, was a graduate of al-Zaytuna, as was Ibn Khaldun, the founder of sociology. Other graduates include Ibn 'Arafa al-Warghami and his students, who kept up the African school of Islamic law started by scholars of the third and fourth Islamic centuries. The school has influenced the Tunisian legal tradition, distinguished by its precise terminology and recourse to original texts and rulings. Numerous proponents of social and political reform have graduated from al-Zaytuna, including the politician Abdul Aziz al-Tha'alibi. He founded the Free Constitutional Party, which later played an important role in contemporary Tunisian history by calling for a constitution, independence, and state building.

## Islamic seminary schools

Islamic seminary schools can be classified into three main groups. Their different approaches to Islamic law are reflected in the degree of tolerance and acceptance of the sectarian and religious other.

### Al-Azhar University

The best-known Islamic seminary school is Cairo's al-Azhar, historically the destination for students from Arab and Islamic countries seeking a religious education. Al-Azhar is unique in its intellectual and religious openness toward other religions, sects, and schools of Islamic law (box 9.5). Founded in 970 or 972, al-Azhar combines religious and modern education along the lines of Egypt's other state universities.

Al-Azhar underwent reforms in the nineteenth century to become a religious educational establishment. A 1908 law split al-Azhar into three levels of study: primary, secondary, and higher, with each level lasting four years and granting passing students a degree certificate. A 1930 law split al-Azhar into five levels:

- Primary, lasting four years.
- Secondary, lasting five years.
- Followed by entrance into one of three colleges: Islamic law, theology, or Arabic language for four years.
- Followed by two years of specialized professional study in Islamic jurisprudence, the issuing of fatwas, preaching, guidance, or teaching.
- Followed again by specialized study for five years in qualification for the rank of professor.[33]

The major transformation of religious education at al-Azhar took place during the presidency of Gamal Abd al-Nasser. Law 103 of 1961 turned the university into one committee among other al-Azhar al-Sharif committees, with a remit to provide university education, and was also supported by other pre-university education institutions. This law also created the al-Azhar Supreme Council and the Islamic Research Consortium, whose role is to spread Islamic culture and heritage and manage the affairs of foreign students. The law converted al-Azhar into a modern education system that includes, alongside the colleges of Islamic law and Arabic language, specializations in medicine, dentistry, engineering, science, education, management, economics, law, foreign languages, and translation. The new bylaws stipulated that al-Azhar would be open to men and women and that all students, whatever their specialization, would study some religious sciences.[34]

## Box 9.5 From the al-Azhar Document

First, al-Azhar supports the establishment of a modern, democratic state based on a constitution drawn up with the people's consent that separates the state's powers from its legal governing institutions, specifies its governing framework, and guarantees rights and duties equitably to all its citizens. Its legislative authority is therefore in the hands of the people's representatives in accordance with the true Islamic precept, for Islam never had in its legislation or in its history what is known in other cultures as a religious state. . . . On the contrary, Islam left . . . to the people . . . to choose the mechanisms of governance and the institutions that would secure their interests, provided that the overarching principles of Islamic law, or sharia, were the source of legislation, which guaranteed followers of other revealed religions the right to be governed by their own religious precepts on issues of personal status.

Second, al-Azhar sanctions the democratic system based on free and direct elections because this is the modern formula that allows for the realization of the principles of Islamic *shura*, or consultation. These principles safeguard pluralism, the peaceful transfer of power, . . . the interests and welfare of the public as the intent of all statutes and decisions, administration of the affairs of state according to the law alone, the pursuit of corruption, the creation of complete transparency, and freedom of information and its dissemination.

Third, al-Azhar is committed to the basic freedoms of thought and opinion, with full respect for the rights of men, women, and children and emphasis on the principle of pluralism and respect for the revealed religions, with citizenship as the linchpin of responsibility in society.

Fourth, al-Azhar insists on full respect for the etiquette of dissent and the ethics of dialogue. It upholds the obligation to avoid labeling others as heretics and traitors and exploiting religion by using it to sow dissension and mutual aversion and hatred among citizens. It considers inciting sectarian strife and using racist propaganda a crime against the nation. Al-Azhar is

> committed to balanced dialogue and mutual respect and the reliance upon each of these in dealing with the different segments of society, without any discrimination between citizens in terms of rights and duties.
>
> —The al-Azhar Document on the Future of Egypt,
> 20 June 2011

In 2012 Shaykh al-Azhar Ahmad al-Tayyib's call for a review of al-Azhar's bylaws and his acceptance of direct elections to the office of Shaykh al-Azhar were important steps toward the restructuring of the institution's relationship with the Egyptian state. In general, the political changes since the January 2011 revolution have prompted renewed demands for al-Azhar's independence from the state. The revolution inspired a range of reforms that could strengthen al-Azhar's moderating role in Egypt and the Islamic world, and it could also lead to greater political independence for al-Azhar, enabling it to bring together the religious, intellectual, and political components of Egyptian society.

A review of the curricula at al-Azhar reveals the following characteristics:[35]

- Curricula in the colleges of Islamic law and theology changed considerably as new core subjects, such as computer literacy, were introduced. Although important, such changes remain limited in scope and influence.
- Islamic law and other religious topics are taught largely from traditional sources. This places them at a vast distance from contemporary life in language, terminology, writing style, argumentation, and examples, many of which are not intelligible to contemporary students.
- Outdated textbooks contain obsolete Islamic legal rulings, some of which are contradicted by modern scientific findings.
- Despite legislation enshrining the principle of equality and outlawing discrimination on the basis of sex, ethnicity, and religion, some traditional texts assigned to students espouse a contrary view.

### The Salafi school

The Salafi school in Saudi Arabia (also called the Wahhabi school) enjoys vast financial resources. Drawing students from across the Arab and Islamic worlds, its opinions have gained acceptance among new religious circles, and it has established an influential presence among other schools of thought in North Africa, Iraq, and some Asian countries. It is characterized by less openness toward other religions, schools of Islamic law, and sects of Islam. Its college of Islamic law, established in 1953, is considered the core around which Imam Muhammad ibn Saud University, one of the world's largest centers of Salafi thought, was built.

The university has expanded to eleven campuses, five in Riyadh and the others around the country. The university also has two institutes in Riyadh, one for jurisprudence and the other for Arabic as a foreign language, in addition to institutes for Islamic and Arabic sciences situated abroad in Djibouti, Indonesia, Japan, Mauritania, and the United States.[36] Imam Muhammad ibn Saud University partners with two other universities, King Faisal University and Umm al-Qura University, to offer social sciences, engineering, medicine, and other fields, in addition to specializations in Islamic law and religious studies. The two partner universities include nineteen colleges with branches in several regions; some disciplines are separated by gender.

There were 33,961 students of religious sciences at the university during the 2010–11 academic year, most of them Saudi and male. However, the university accepts women into programs in Islamic law, creed, preaching and faith, and contemporary schools.[37]

Institutes at the middle-school and high-school levels prepare students to enter one of the three Saudi Islamic universities in a religious specialization; however, they only accept men.

Religious studies classes emphasize rote learning, a focus on Islamic legal rulings (box 9.6), and the differentiation between the permitted (*halal*) and the prohibited (*haram*). The weak preparation in nonreligious curricula typically leads students toward religious education at university and entrance into professions related to religion and Islamic law after graduation.[38]

### Shi'i hawza education

*Hawza* (from the word meaning 'direction') schools are traditional religious education centers that continue to be used among Shi'i.[39] The *hawza* religious school system has historically centered in the holy city of Najaf in Iraq but has spread more recently to Lebanon and some Gulf

**Box 9.6 Stagnation of religious education**

Religious education pertaining to Islamic law remains as it has been for a thousand years. It consists of school-based Islamic legal texts that are freed of direct references and that were written long ago and memorized by students—in Hanbali law, "Zad al-mustanqa'"; in Maliki law, "Mukhtasar khalil"; in Shafi'i law, "al-Taqrib" by Abu Shuja'; and in Hanafi law, "al-Quduri." These texts were written concisely, intricately, and with condensed meanings.

Two shortcomings. First is the absence of texts from scripture and the Sunna—because the intention is to deduce them by using a legal proof and not to use them in deduction, they are devoid of signification. Second is that many of these legal opinions are taken as decisive so that any other view is worthless. This leads to excessive support for one school and being removed from the use of proof.

—Aaidh al-Qarni, *Asharq al-Awsat*, 1 November 2007

states. This geographic expansion has not diminished the centrality of Najaf, however.

The Iraqi school is characterized by quietism, whereas the Lebanese and Iranian schools mix religion with politics. A majority of Shi'i follow the Twelver school (Ja'fari). The Isma'ilis are concentrated in Syria, Saudi Arabia, India, and Pakistan; the Zaydis, numerous in northern Yemen, while also Shi'i, have their own schools.

Unlike many of the Sunni religious schools, which have modernized their religious education systems and introduced nonreligious specializations, the historic Shi'i religious schools in Najaf and Qom continue to follow the traditional *hawza* system. In attempts to update the *hawza* religious education system, some books have been slightly revised, and new readings have been added by contemporary Shi'i scholars like Muhammad Baqir al-Sadr and Muhammad Hussein Fadlallah. However, no new courses in religion and the humanities have been introduced, such as comparative religion, cultural studies, history of world civilizations, economic development in Asia and the West, and foreign languages. *Hawza* schools consist of the following education levels and curricula:

- The introductory level is the entrance to specialization in Islamic law. Students study all the Islamic sciences, including Arabic language, morphology, and logic.
- The intermediate-advanced level *(sutuh)*, which lasts three years or more, engages students in the close study of deductive Islamic law and the underpinnings of jurisprudence *(usul al-fiqh)*.
- The final level, referred to as "external research," is based on lectures reviewing a range of opinions on a single matter with the goal of selecting the correct opinion with the support of transmitted and reasoned evidence (box 9.7). Students study the philosophy of Islamic law at its constructive level.[40] They also rely on their own research and examination of exegesis, prophetic tradition, the underpinnings of Islamic jurisprudence, and other fields. This third level is the most important and includes participation by leading scholars. At this stage students may specialize in a field or conduct research in several fields. Study may result in graduation with the status of *mujtahid*, or practitioner of independent interpretative effort.[41]

There are no data on the number of students studying in Shi'i *hawza*s in the Arab region, including in Iraq.

In these schools memorization is taken as the measure of understanding and likely as the basis for promotion. Promotions take place without objective measures of students' intellectual performance or their preparedness to enter the next level. This reliance on rote learning becomes a handicap in the final level of study, when students must demonstrate an understanding of research methodology and interpretation of Islamic law. Students can find it extremely difficult to confront issues in Islamic law that they have not encountered before in their academic life.[42]

### Religious education among the Druze

Religious education among the monotheist Druze takes place in group meetings—in homes, religious sanctuaries, and special meeting places. It is limited to admitted followers, who must adhere to the sometimes strict conditions imposed by the shaykhs for clothing, social behavior, and even choice of profession. Strict requirements of appearance and inner state determine whether applicants are accepted. Group meetings take two forms: "wisdom" meetings, also referred to as "study" meetings, which are held after sunset prayers, and *dhikr* meetings, which are purely Sufi congregations.[43]

**Box 9.7 Establishing a religious basis according to Sayyid Fadlallah**

To establish a religious basis one must start with primary sources. The Qur'an is composed of sacred speech that God Almighty divinely revealed; the Messenger himself could not independently add to it or reduce it. Yet the meaning of the Qur'an is among the matters related to human understanding of a word's range of meanings according to its use and context. This is why we have witnessed commentators disagreeing over the interpretation of this or that verse. Some may have slipped into a framework of backwardness because they attempted to interpret a word on the basis of their cultural background, which may be backward in that particular regard.

So, when one studies the Sunna—the sum of the sayings of the Prophet Muhammad that the Qur'an in God Almighty's words confirms: "*And whatsoever the Messenger giveth you, take it. And whatsoever he forbiddeth, abstain [from it]*"—one must ascertain that the saying is correctly attributed to the Prophet. Many of the recorders set down in writing sayings attributed to the Prophet either for personal reasons or to acquiesce with authorities who wanted to grant themselves a certain sanctity by tying themselves to Prophetic sayings (and there are many examples of this in Islamic history).

So, one must authenticate (verify) Prophetic sayings through the chain of authorities that relayed them, as well as through the text itself with regard to its meaning (How did the Prophet use it? In what circumstances?). It is thus natural that when a text is interpreted with a limited, backward mentality, one is granted a limited, backward text that bears no relation to true exegesis. This has made religious thought questionable and the subject of debate, and in some cases even reinforces backwardness due to the narrow thinking of some people who have inherited from ignorant sources that lack cultural awareness.

Rescuing religion from cultural and ideological corruption requires immense effort to create authentic religious thought. Comprehension of religion must be open to the most exemplary rhetorical models of the Arabic language, as well as to the historical context in which a verse was revealed or a Prophetic saying originated.

*Source:* Interview with Muhammad Hussein Fadlallah by Yosri Alamir, *al-Adab* 4–5–6 (2009), www.adabmag.com/node/205

## Formation of Christian clerics

The formation of clerics among Arab Christians differs by location, whether in Egypt, Lebanon, Palestine, Syria, or Iraq, as well as by sect. Some examples:

- *The Maronite Church.* Religious students spend seven years studying before becoming parish priests. Their first year of study is preparatory and spent mostly in the Maronite Patriarchal Seminary in Ghazir, where they receive spiritual and linguistic training. During the second year students transfer to Holy Spirit University, where they undertake five years of study: two preparatory years studying philosophy followed by three years of theology. They also continue their professional education in seminary training for the priesthood. Students spend their final year at seminary school in pastoral training. Entering the seminary requires a-part-two baccalaureate or its equivalent—university graduates and professionals can enroll. In 2010 the seminary had ninety-three students; twelve to fifteen students graduate each year.
- *The Orthodox Antiochian Church.* Training for the priesthood is undertaken at the St. John of Damascus Institute of Theology in Balamand, Lebanon. Students must be at least twenty years old and spend four years at the institute undergoing theoretical (theological), applied (pastoral), and liturgical (spiritual) training. The curriculum is split into a range of fields, most of them religious, and students study the Bible, doctrine and life, church history, sacramental life and rituals, general culture, and information technology. On graduation, following consultation with their spiritual father and Balamand Institute's testimony on their behalf, students are ordained by their bishop. In keeping with the tradition of the Orthodox Church, candidates for ordination pass through the various stages of priesthood: they start as evangelical deacons, then become priests whom the bishop assigns to a parish.
- *The Evangelical Church.* Under the supervision of the Superior Evangelical Community in Syria and Lebanon, the National Evangelical Church sends students to theological colleges accredited with the Near East School of Theology, the Arab Baptist Theological Seminary, or the Mediterranean Bible College. Students spend at least three years studying in preparation for ordination, but they must also perform preparatory service.
- *The Armenian Orthodox Church.* Study in the Armenian Orthodox seminary takes eight years of full-time residency, the first four studying

the official curriculum in addition to religious subjects and Armenian language and history. In the next four years students study theology, philosophy, sacraments, ethics, hymns, and other subjects.
- *The Catholic Melkite (Greek Catholic) Church.* The St. John of Tiberias Seminary is responsible for clerical training. This patriarchal institution serves the entire Catholic Melkite Church with the aim of preparing priests. Students study humanities and spiritual, theological, and pastoral subjects.

### Issues in university-level religious education

This overview of the training of religious clerics in the Arab region presents several themes:

- Nearly all the Islamic religious colleges and universities are state-run, and some are jointly overseen by ministries of religious affairs or education. In a few cases, primarily for religious minorities, religious education is funded and overseen by institutions of a specific faith.
- The majority of religious higher education is traditional and based on transmission from teacher to student and memorization rather than reason and critique. Most teaching materials and examples date back hundreds of years, a situation incapable of producing fresh human outputs except for pioneers who depart from the traditional pattern of authority, including Muhammad Abdu, Muhammad Ghazali, and Yusuf al-Qaradawi. Some institutes and universities even continue to use the traditional language and formulations of the venerable founding fathers of Islamic law. So the openness of religious science to partnering with the social and physical sciences remains limited.[44] Most of these institutions permit only the teaching or reading of the scholars of their own sects.
- These institutes and universities rely on the rhetorical skills of teachers rather than applying modern technologies or media to teaching.
- Although the curricula of some religious universities, specifically in Egypt and Saudi Arabia, combine religious education and modern sciences, the influence of science on religion remains limited. In fact, subjecting science to the logic of Islamic law is much more common, a phenomenon referred to in the literature as the "Islamization of the sciences."
- The infrastructure capacities of some religious universities—buildings, labs, and research tools, including computers, libraries, and access to information—are inadequate for sound academic research and for teaching students advanced research skills.[45]

Today's world presents new challenges in human rights, democracy, globalization, and the media; new forms of economic advancement and political reform; and important changes in the family and social relations. And there is unprecedented friction between cultures and their values, as well as serious ethnic, religious, and sectarian strife. This context makes it ever more imperative to bring religion closer to the spirit and thinking of the age in order to help revitalize the Arab region—economically, politically, and culturally.[46]

Parts of the Arab religious education system have changed over the last few years, but the system's minimal capacity to produce new outputs that differ qualitatively from those of traditional Islamic scholars remains. And resistance to change, not limited to a particular religion or sect, continues. It is common to all dominant religions and sects in the region, if to varying degrees.

## Religion and the Arab Identity

Religion interacts with its historical circumstances and the interpretations of its believers. There is thus an overlap between religious and personal factors and even political and ideological ones. The more religion diffuses into daily life, the more it becomes expressive of the people's identity. Religion—along with the Arabic language and a shared heritage of customs, traditions, and arts—is a key component of Arab identity. But while identity has political, patrimonial, linguistic, and religious dimensions, the religious dimension has been the most influential. Also related to Arab identity is the role of women.

### Religious identity

Religion is a constant in all spheres of Arab life. Confirming one's identity through daily practices creates a cultural milieu for individuals where they feel protected from a rapidly changing, globalized society.

Both Muslims and Christians adhere to religious practices that make religion an integral part of daily life. Islamic institutions—mosques, Islamic endowments, fatwa council, universities—pervade all areas of life. Religious institutions set the beginning of the Hegira calendar and the beginning of Ramadan, and they influence policy on such contentious issues as interest on bank loans, organ and gene transplants, and cloning. While Christian institutions are also influential in the lives of Arab Christians, they have done less to shape the Arab identity.

Religious identity is also confirmed through public rituals. Examples include broadcasting prayers via satellites from Ka'ba, celebrating the Prophet's birthday, opening new radio and television stations for Qur'an and Sunna, reciting verses from the Qur'an before official ceremonies, and celebrating Christmas mass in Bethlehem (State of Palestine) and Saint Mark's Coptic Orthodox Cathedral in Cairo. Religious identity is also reinforced through the display of religious symbolism, such as wearing the hijab or growing a beard.

Religious identity is also supported by a host of organizations that circulate their views and fatwas, support development, and promote cooperation among Arab states. These organizations emerged following upheavals and transformations that highlighted the importance of religious identity, including:

- The collapse of the Islamic caliphate (in 1924) following the establishment of political systems that did not derive their legitimacy from religion, beginning with the establishment of the secular state in Turkey by Kemal Atatürk.
- Globalization's rising threat to local cultural identity.
- The emergence of immoderate religious movements, groups using religion for political purposes, and a third Sufi movement. If they clash, the Islamic Arab identity could fragment.

These organizations are both international and local. The international organizations work with government and civil society organizations to advance religion and development through education, youth empowerment, and relief to Muslims in Africa, Asia, and some Arab societies (such as in Somalia, Sudan, and Syria). The two most prominent are the Organization of Islamic Cooperation and the Muslim World League, both established in the 1960s.

The Organization of Islamic Cooperation, originating in 1969 as the Organization of the Islamic Conference, is the most influential intergovernmental organization in shaping Islamic identity. It disseminates expressions of Islamic interests, promotes international peace and cooperation, and advocates for the fulfillment of peoples' aspirations to good governance, political participation, commitment to human rights, and consolidation of the rule of law.

The Muslim World League, established in 1962, is the jurisprudence and preaching arm of the Islamic Conference. Despite being a popular civic organization, it supports the application of Islamic law (sharia). It coordinates preaching activities and organizes seminars, conferences, and relief work for victims of natural disasters. Through conferences and seminars and its development and relief work, it seeks to create space for religion in modern life, preserve the Islamic identity, and connect with other societies.

Despite the international organizations' many successes, especially in health care and education, governments have limited both their political and their development role. These organizations must limit their development activities to relief efforts that meet people's needs immediately after a disaster, and they must not intervene in sensitive issues, such as HIV/AIDS, or take a stand on social policies or wealth distribution.

While the international organizations help shape religious identity through their work in communities, local organizations have a more direct impact through actions that weave religion into every aspect of daily life. The religious foundations associated with the major mosques do this through endowments *(waqf)*, bodies of scholars (ulama), and religious references. Examples are the papers prepared by al-Azhar Mosque following the January 2011 revolution (which promoted a moderate role for religion in society and the state), a December 2012 document on women's status identifying the landmarks of religious views relating to the role of women and the importance of their participation in public life, and a January 2013 initiative calling for national reconciliation among divided political factions.

## The role of women

Although the attention given to women in Islamic discourse is longstanding, it has taken on new international and regional dimensions in the past three decades as the claims relating to women's political and social rights have expanded, especially in Islamic societies that are seen as violating women's rights. Many people believe that women in Arab countries suffer social injustice because of their low status, their absence from positions of leadership and participation in the public sphere, and the sway of patriarchal attitudes. Many see a need to adopt international conventions on women's rights, particularly in the absence of a clear Islamic vision on women's position in the world.

### The low status of women

Clerics recognize the low status of women and the marginalization of their role. Shaykh Muhammad Ghazali, for example, says that "the woman in our society does not have a cultural or a political role; she is not involved in educational programs nor in the society's systems; she has no place in the mosques' courtyards nor in the fields of jihad; mentioning her name is a disgrace; seeing her face is forbidden; her voice is an intimate part; and her first and final function is cooking and bedding!"[47] Many Arab women scholars associate this low status and negative image not with Islam itself, but with some imams' interpretations, traditions, and behavior current in the present Arab social context, a context that has to be resisted and reformed.[48]

### Women's leadership and participation

Women's participation in the public sphere is a contentious issue. Some clerics attribute women's low participation to the lack of female leaders. And they see the lack of enough qualified women as stemming from women's inability to acquire the skills necessary for political action. Women are excluded from participation and decision making and from access to senior positions in political organizations, including standing for election. Women need the same opportunities that men have to acquire skills and use them. Some Islamic scholars argue that Islam does not restrict which jobs women can hold and that jobs should be based on merit and competence.

### A male-dominated society

Arab societies are still patriarchal, and the perception persists that women are not physically or intellectually equal to men and therefore do not have the same right to engage in all spheres of productive work. Some clerics confirm this view, arguing for the superiority of men over women in power and influence. Other clerics insist on safeguards for women's work outside the home: the work must be legal, subject to the provisions of Islamic law, and not come at the expense of her work in the home, caring for her children and husband. Still other clerics defend women's rights and call on women to reject this duality and take the lead in advocating for expanded opportunities.

### Links to international conventions on women's rights

Clerics disagree about provisions in international conventions on women's rights, with some having reservations. New, however, is that these controversial issues are being discussed and debated openly. Farida Bennani and other academics who study the status of women view these reservations as baseless or even damaging. Bennani considers the reservations concerning Article VIII of the Convention to Eliminate All Forms of Discrimination against Women, which prohibits discrimination against women in national constitutions and legislations, as emptying the convention of its core principle.

## Religion and Politics after the Arab Spring

Yet another expression of religion is being shaped by political movements that combine social and political action and use religious interpretations and constructions as a façade. These practices have been adopted by political movements ranging from the extreme Salafi groups through the less extreme Muslim Brotherhood to more moderate movements. These movements are in conflict with the political regimes that were in power before the Arab Spring.

In the societies that felt the Arab Spring's power and rage, the way was paved for the rise of Islamic groups, particularly the well-organized civil society groups like the Muslim Brotherhood. These groups moved in to supply the fundamental services that the state no longer provided following privatization and restructuring policies that increased the number of people suffering from poverty. Many people in the middle class slipped into poverty, which was made worse by their awareness of the contrast between the globalized consumer culture and their deprivation. The youth of this deprived class saw the disparity between what they saw on social networks and the reality of the enormous social gap between a deprived majority and a corrupt minority seizing all the wealth.

Before the Arab Spring, the influence of religious groups had widened as they moved in to provide health care and education to the poor and assistance to unemployed young people (groups that had been abandoned by governments). The Arab Spring revolutions opened up once closed social and political spaces, and these Islamic groups moved in, transitioning from social to political action. With the absence of an alternative revolutionary leadership, the Islamic movement, with its large organizational presence, rose quickly to power, especially in Egypt, Libya, and Tunisia.

The Islamic movement's rise sparked a heated debate on the relationships between religion and politics and between religious and civil forces, the possibility of establishing a religious state, the likelihood of revolution spreading to other Arab countries, and whether the change led by the Islamic movement will be revolutionary or reformist. It is too early to answer these questions, but factors linked to religion's relationship with politics will likely shape the answers.

### Strong involvement of religion in the public space

Religion, largely a private matter before September 11, 2001, has since entered the Arab public space, where views are exchanged and political debate crystallizes public interests and enables people to reach collective agreement. Religion interacts there with other movements, both synergistically and antagonistically, and has become a key source of social capital and a drive to humanitarian action.

Since the Arab Spring revolutions, religious discourse in the public space has changed. New subjects include the relationship between religion and politics, the religious state versus the civil state, the role of Islamic law and of religious institutions in public life, and the position of non-Muslim citizens in an Islamic state. New voices are eager to become outspoken about their positions. The important questions are: To what extent will all these voices in the public space be heard in the future, and will the public space remain open?

### The civil–religious contrast

The interface between the religious and the civil is considerable in Arab policies. The rise of Islamic movements following the Arab Spring provoked a new debate over the possibility—and desirability—of separating the religious from the civil in politics. An expression of the desire for separation is the rise of parties that view themselves as wholly secular, with names such as the liberals, nationalists, civilians, and secularists. Other groups believe in greater communication and harmony between the civil and religious, seeing the civil state as resting on a foundation of religious values. Although this debate has not yet been settled, there are signs that it may lead to a clearer contrast between the religious and the civil in public and private life in Arab countries.

## The role of religion in transforming society

Several challenges prevent religion from serving an integrating role in society and from fulfilling its developmental function:

- *Continuing religious extremism.* Despite strong opposition from some quarters, religious fanaticism continues, taking new forms and spreading to new areas of the Arab world, especially among economically deprived people.
- *Rising poverty rates.* Not only does higher poverty (as high as 20 percent in some countries) mean more suffering but it also focuses religious activity more on addressing poverty today than on advancing future development.
- *Rapidly expanding religious learning.* The rapid expansion of religious learning has helped spread a type of learning that fails to resist extremism and that produces incompetent, unmotivated citizens.
- *Using religion to confer political legitimacy.* Most Arab regimes, even if they do not use religion as a ruling tool, tend to exploit religion to grant legitimacy to the regime.

- *Treating religion with hostility.* Despite relying on religion for legitimacy, many political regimes are hostile to religion and its defenders, trying to marginalize religion despite its involvement in most aspects of daily life.

There are several ways to overcome these challenges:

- Reform religious institutions and discourse to have a more positive influence on development.
- Limit and deepen religious education so that it produces strong, well-educated citizens with an integrated vision of the world.
- Train preachers, orators, and other clerics in a rational and integrated manner.
- Work on reviving rational religious diligence and draw on Arab history to re-establish value systems directed to general labor and social development.
- Separate religion from politics and end the use of religion as a tool for political and social conflict.
- Encourage charitable and developmental activity within a religious framework and work toward an integrated vision of social development.

## Notes

1   In the last stages of finalizing this chapter, UNDA asked yet again for further chapter modifications. Professor Ahmed Zayed, former dean of the Faculty of Arts at Cairo University and a well-established sociologist on the subject, came to our aid. The chapter author and the volume editor are very appreciative of his help.
2   http://ar.wikipedia.org/wiki/%D8%A7%D8%A8%D9%86_%D8%AE%D9%84%D8%AF%D9%88%D9%86.
3   Hassan 2010.
4   al-'Umran 2002.
5   Jouirou 2007a; Mundib 2006.
6   Fuad 2008.
7   Jouirou 2007b.
8   'Atallah 2011, background paper for the report.
9   Hassan 2010.
10   al-Sakran and al-Qasim 2006.
11   Jouirou 2007b.
12   www.coptreal.com/wshowsubject.aspx?SID=39205.
13   *al-Gumhuriya* 2010.
14   UNDP and Mohammed bin Rashid Al Maktoum Foundation 2009.

15  Coptreal 2010.
16  Al Mesbar Studies and Research Center 2009.
17  Al Mesbar Studies and Research Center 2009, 166.
18  arabianbusiness.com 2010.
19  Al Mesbar Studies and Research Center 2009.
20  *al-Wasat* 2011.
21  UNDP 2003b, 6–7.
22  UNDP 2006.
23  Sarush 2009a.
24  Zayid 2007.
25  al-Qaradawi 2001b.
26  al-Qaradawi 2004.
27  Qaʻu 2000.
28  Zayid 2011.
29  Fuad 2010.
30  Fuad 2010.
31  al-'Arab 2011, 259–93.
32  Al Mesbar Studies and Research Center 2010a.
33  Al Mesbar Studies and Research Center 2010b.
34  Al Mesbar Studies and Research Center 2010b.
35  Qaʻd 2000.
36  al-ʻIsa 2009.
37  Hamdan 2005.
38  al-ʻIsa 2009; al-Qasim 2011.
39  Al Mesbar Studies and Research Center 2010b.
40  Al Mesbar Studies and Research Center 2010b.
41  al-Mahrus 2009.
42  al-Mahrus 2009.
43  Anwar Abu Khuzam, in ʻAtallah 2011, 70–71.
44  Qaʻd 2000.
45  Qaʻd 2000.
46  Qaʻd 2000.
47  Ghazali 1990.
48  See the discussion by many Arab women participants, including Farida
    Bennani, professor of sharia in the Faculty of Law at Qadi Ayad
    University in Marrakesh, in "Regional Strategies for Empowering
    Women," discussions from three Amman workshops, 2–5 December
    2005, 14–17 February 2006, and 11–13 June 2006, Woodrow Wilson
    Center for Scholars (Princeton University), Middle East Program,
    www.wilsoncenter.org/sites/default/files/empoweringwomen_4.pdf.

# Part 5:
# A New History in the Making?

# CHAPTER 10

# The Birth Pangs of Transitioning from Authoritarianism:
## The Long Spring of Empowerment

Bahgat Korany

Previous analyses on Arab (mis)development—such as UNDP's well-quoted Arab Human Development Reports—addressed at least three Arab deficits in knowledge, freedom, and the status of women. In this book, we added a fourth one: a deficit in the ability to adapt. After almost four hundred pages, five hundred endnotes drawing on more than six hundred reference works, and data presented in twelve tables and fifty-three figures, what have we learned? How can these lessons help an Arab world going through the pangs of transition?

Transition is indeed painful. We felt this as both citizens and authors who have been going through it daily: at home, at work, and in the street. There is no break from this transition—even when we listen to nonpolitical programs on the radio, watch television, or follow social media. But could it be, as the Chinese proverb says, that a crisis is also an opportunity, a midwife to a new history, building on lessons of (mis)development and initiating the new era of empowerment?

This chapter builds on the book's central framework, on the previous chapters, on the growing world literature on "transitology," and on the first-hand experiences of leaders who shaped democratization elsewhere with a double objective: a) to attempt a codification of major challenges confronting an Arab world presently undergoing a painful transition; and b) to suggest a way out, to practice a form of *ijtihad*—the methodology of innovative critical thinking characteristic of some Islamic scholars.

## Meeting Current Challenges and Barriers to Empowerment

This book has focused on development-as-empowerment, viewed as the expansion of choices for Arab citizens and society, and the "Arab riddle," or the gap between Arab potential and achievement. Each chapter went beyond examining symptoms and diagnoses to focus on the most pressing question: What should be done? The book reaches three key conclusions about what the Arab countries must do to meet the current challenges.

### Renew the social contract and make it effective

A new social contract that redistributes power, reforms society, and consolidates the public sphere is needed. Despite common rhetoric about a "state governed by law and justice," the Arab world is one of the farthest removed from the culture of rule of law. Only a renewal of the social contract, through the establishment of the rule of law, can transform rhetoric into reality.

The media, which shape public awareness and engagement, must be transformed from state censor to watchdog. Rather than an arm of clientelist authority, the media should become a space for free expression. Only by acting independently, responsibly, and professionally can the media raise awareness about options for closing the gap between potential and achievement.

Performing up to potential also depends on fighting corruption. Studies closely tie greater corruption to lower achievement in health care, education, and living standards—the very bases of any development project. Ultimately, empowerment depends on political will and good governance and is linked to conflict management. In the late twentieth century Arab countries spent huge sums of money on arms and bribes; little remained for infrastructure, industry, or services.

To stanch the wasteful flow of resources and halt disempowerment will require sound conflict management—between the Arab region and the rest of the world, among countries in the Arab region, and within Arab countries. Three types of empowerment come into play: political (democratization), economic (reconstruction and regional cooperation in distributing shared resources), and preventive (managing conflict before it spirals out of control).

### Reduce social injustice and inequality

The Arab world has immense wealth. One estimate puts the Arab Gulf states' oil revenues at $1 trillion by 2015, some $200 billion more than in 2010.[1] Yet poverty is extensive and growing. And wealth is exceedingly unevenly distributed, both across and within countries; to repeat: in 2011 the income of a Qatari citizen was about fifty times that of a Yemeni citizen. Similar inequalities exist in access to education and health care.

Poverty and inequality are antithetical to empowerment. But poverty can be mitigated, and hopefully eradicated, through a new social contract that rejects apathy, alters negative attitudes toward work, and empowers individuals.

### Confront the hardships of daily life

Empowerment depends not only on narrowing the potential–achievement gap, but also on overcoming challenges and threats to happiness that wear people down and sap their energy for productive work.[2] A clean environment empowers people by protecting them from the erosion of body and spirit. Education is important for moving on, constructing identity, and developing critical thinking.

Threats to both the natural and the built environments constitute a formidable challenge in the Arab world, one that has long been ignored.[3] The ruling elites have failed to understand the severity of the problem. Environmental threats—for example, accelerating climate change, creeping desertification, worsening water scarcity, and the treatment of waste water, all of which affect food security—are directly related to the worsening problems of everyday life. These ordeals are increased by the rapidly growing number of wasteful traffic jams and accidents. The Arab region ranks first in the world in the number of traffic accidents, with more than half a million a year.[4] Solutions are available. In the United Arab Emirates, for example, stricter enforcement lowered traffic-related deaths by 10 percent in 2009.[5] Increasing the efficiency of current energy sources, developing renewable wind and solar energy, and building a regional electricity supply grid would make energy provision much cleaner, reducing its damaging environmental impact.

Education is fundamental to human development. The Arab world has made progress in constructing schools and enrolling students. But education for empowerment—the essence of development—also aims at personal development. Schools need to move beyond the factory model that turns out workers on an assembly-line basis to a model that trains creative individuals capable of using and developing knowledge and who are constructive, emotionally balanced members of society. That requires attention to religious education, which helps shape identity. But religious education in a society dominated by religious symbols and values has received fewer resources than general education, and its role in personal development and growth has been neglected. Religious education needs to be in tune with evolving social sciences, and religious rulings with the natural sciences. As religious instruction attains a modernity that is not imposed but is innovative and in harmony with identity, challenges in religious education, rather than defying solutions, will compel purposeful action and constructive change.

## The Starting Point in Empowerment:
## The Problem of Democratic Transition in the Arab World

To reiterate, the central message of this book is that change leading to empowerment must start at the center of decision making. Empowerment requires ending authoritarianism and achieving a balanced relationship between citizens and the ruling power. This book emphasizes reforming state power to achieve social justice and empowerment because state performance is society's compass, giving it direction and serving as a model for society's empowerment.

The region's obsession with (military) security at the expense of public services and wider human security has led to the collapse of the developmental state and the deterioration in living standards of people already suffering as a result of widespread corruption, poverty, unemployment, and inequality. The state typically manages the country as a private fiefdom, relying on clientelism and personal loyalties rather than competence. For some regimes this policy failure led to state failure. Two Arab countries (Somalia and Sudan) were among the world's top five failed states for four successive years on the Failed States Index (2008–11), and the position of some Arab countries with respect to this list has recently deteriorated.[6]

Although democratization has been spreading rapidly around the world—the number of democracies more than doubled from forty-four in 1985 to ninety-three in 2005[7]—Freedom House's 2010 report showed democratization in the Arab region trailing that in Latin America, Asia, and Africa. No state in the Arab region was categorized as "free" without qualification or reservation. Four Arab states were "partially free," and seventeen were "not free."[8]

As democratization spreads, the Arab region should not try to import a specific form of democratic government, because each society has its own historical and social characteristics. However, the core tenets of democracy are the same everywhere. All modes of democratic rule are based on the separation of powers, checks and balances, effective institutions of state authority and opposition parties, and an effective civil society that can confront government policies while managing difference (even within government ranks; box 10.1). At the basis is a mindset of tolerance and readiness to accept defeat and the fact that power can change hands. In such an institution-based society, everyone must adhere to practices of transparent decision making, with oversight and accountability at all levels.

### Box 10.1 Stimulating participation by civil society

Stimulating participation by civil society—in view of the diversity of interests and aspirations that it represents—is a challenge. Civil society contributed to the past decade's cumulative preparations for the Arab revolutions through rights advocacy organizations; community and mass movements; and labor, women's, and youth associations. Civil society must therefore become an effective partner in shaping the state. To perform this role, civil society needs a conducive environment. That includes laws that regulate civil society organizations (CSOs) in a manner that guarantees their right to exist and to function independent of any public authority, with the rights to freedom of expression and opinion and access to information. Laws must also guarantee the right to unrestricted and unconditional access to human and financial resources and know-how.

An environment conducive to a capable, empowered civil society lays the foundations for a balanced relationship between citizens and the ruling authority. This balance is crucial to sustaining public order, and it encourages the rise of an active and effective citizenry against a backdrop of respect for rights and duties and the sway of justice and equality. Conversely, restricting freedoms and the autonomy of the diverse components of civil society aggravates marginalization and curtails the powers of oversight and accountability.

Any discussion of civil society must address the basic standards that should apply. Civil society is a broad space, containing the social organizations, institutions, structures, and arrangements that coalesce spontaneously to defend the varied interests of a multiplicity of diverse groups and communities. These structures should show a minimum degree of commitment to standards of integrity and governance, as well as to clarity in their principles, goals, and outlooks.

In addition to advocating for the interests of diverse sectors of society, a healthy civil society also contributes to raising awareness of the concept of citizenship and to fostering social responsibility among the citizenry. Civil society performs this role by strengthening social cohesion and solidarity and by bolstering the underpinnings of communal peace in all its facets—security, political, economic, social, and cultural. CSOs committed to the causes of human rights and secular democratic principles have contributed to the formulation of appropriate policies, which help stimulate the development process and ensure its sustainability.

The chief guarantor of the fulfillment of the goals of the Arab revolutions as they forge their way to the construction of the civil state is the existence of a strong civil society capable of rejecting partial settlements and refusing to compromise on rights and principles. Real civil society is the entity best qualified to safeguard and defend people's rights. Recourse to the people has become the basis for the new era, now that citizens have broken the fear barrier and restored their confidence in their own ability to bring about change.

Realizing the above-mentioned options has become essential. We must redouble our efforts and strengthen our perseverance and determination to achieve them, for these options will lay the foundations for the future of this region. If the twenty-first century opened with a surge of protests in some states in the region, its second decade has ushered in a phase of fundamental democratic transformations. What is required is a reconsideration of the public interest so that it outweighs narrow factional interests. At that point, the region can regain its natural place on the world political and economic map. But this requires reinstating the concept of the civil democratic state, responsible citizenship, and effective public participation in making, implementing, and evaluating decisions.

—Ziad Abdel Samad, executive director, Arab NGO Network for Development (ANND)

While the Arab Spring marked a start toward democratization, the path is long, arduous, and strewn with obstacles. How can the Arab countries direct this transition? This book proposes that democratization begin with establishing a stable and peaceful means for transferring power in a state ruled by law and with codified, objective standards for decision making. Toward this end, states must pursue transparency, balanced media reporting, effective conflict management, and support for communal and individual identity. The experiences of other countries— especially those with social conditions similar to those found in the Arab world, in Asia, Latin America, or even the northern Mediterranean region—can offer some guidance in meeting these challenges, as we will see below.

Let it be said, however, that discussion of democracy in the Arab world is hardly new. In the early 1980s, for example, as a democratic wave spread across the northern Mediterranean (from Portugal and Spain to Greece), Arab intellectuals met in Cyprus to discuss their ruling regimes.[9] Democratization soon became a specialty subfield in political science. The resulting (and vast) literature identifies two phases of democratization:[10]

- Democratic transition (transitology), or the collapse of an authoritarian regime and the attempt to replace it with another system of rule.[11]
- Democratic consolidation (consolidology), which extends beyond the use of democratic practices to the deepening of democracy's roots and its expansion through society, from the factory or office to the family.

Most of the Arab region is now grappling only with the first stage: democratic transition. While the move toward democratization started even earlier, it reached a watershed moment in 2011, following the uprising in Tunisia and the ousting of Zine El Abidine Ben Ali (box 10.2), the spread of protests to Egypt and the stepping down of Hosni Mubarak in February, and the killing of Libya's Muammar Qadhafi in October. Street protests have engulfed seventeen Arab states, from Bahrain to Morocco.

## Box 10.2 The path of democratic transition in Tunisia

The Tunisian revolution against the regime of Zine El Abidine Ben Ali has paved the way for democratic transition toward a civil state with democratic institutions that express the wish of the people for freedom and dignity. This path has several stages.

*Phase 1: Downfall of head of the regime and launching change.* Muhammad Bouazizi's self-immolation on 17 December 2010 in a protest over repression and subjugation was a pivotal event on the path of democratic transition. Solidarity marches followed, expanding as they tapped into people's dissatisfaction with recent deterioration in economic, political, and living conditions, and culminating in Ben Ali's flight to Saudi Arabia on 14 January 2011. President of the Chamber of Deputies Fouad Mebazaa became acting president and began to restore Tunisia's democratic institutions until early presidential elections could be held. On 17 January Prime Minister Muhammad Ghannouchi formed a new national unity government that included members of opposition parties and civil society representatives. However, opposition figures resigned, protesting the failure to exclude supporters of Ben Ali from the government.

*Phase 2: Transition toward change.* In March 2011, with legalization of the Islamist Ennahda Movement and the announcement of the date for the first post-revolution elections, political life resumed. A new government was formed that contained no members of the former regime, and the political police and state security were disbanded—a key demand of the Tunisian revolution. A Tunisian court dissolved the Constitutional Democratic Rally, Ben Ali's party, as a symbol of one-party dictatorship.

Leading up to the Constituent Assembly elections in October 2011, a decree prohibited members of Ben Ali's regime from standing for election, and the High Independent Elections Commission was formed. Antigovernment protests began anew, prompted by concerns about the health of the democratic process and dissatisfaction with living conditions. The government used moderate force to disperse demonstrators.

*Phase 3: Building the institutions of democratic change.* The National Constituent Assembly elections of 23 October 2011 were the first free, impartial, and pluralistic elections since the founding of the republic in 1957. A diverse collection of parties emerged from the elections, with the Islamist Ennahda Movement winning the highest number of seats (eighty-nine of 217). The Constituent Assembly ratified the provisional law regulating public authorities (the "mini-constitution"), followed on 12 December 2011 by election of interim president Mohammed Moncef Marzouki, who charged the majority party (Ennahda) with forming a government.

*Phase 4: Solidifying the foundations.* In a process of consensus and political participation, the three major ideological blocs agreed to lay the groundwork for political participation. The nationalist Congress for the Republic Party gained the presidency, the leftist party Ettakatol headed the Constituent Assembly, and the Islamist Ennahda Movement led the government. This was also a period of flux, with an emphasis on the civil nature of the state and with Ennahda deciding to back exclusion of Sharia law from discussions on drafting the constitution at this stage.

*Assessment.* The tripartite ruling coalition in Tunisia has managed to maintain a peaceful society and ensure continued democratic transition. The political partnership agreement has created equilibrium among Islamists, leftists, and secularists. This political partnership has established an anchor for the democratic transition in Tunisia and has outlined the rules of political engagement for each stage. The mini-constitution that regulates general powers, rights, and responsibilities among the three leadership positions during the transition is an example of clarity of purpose and proper distribution of authority that show promise for democratic transition in Tunisia.

Nonetheless, the upcoming phase holds challenges, the most difficult being integrating the Salafists into the political process, the slow pace of economic development and social welfare, and the challenge of creating a strong, effective agreement that safeguards methodical, orderly social justice without delay.

—Larbi Sadiki, senior lecturer in Middle East politics,
University of Exeter

These movements exhibit three primary patterns, reflecting the need for an alternative, whether comprehensive or partial, for replacing a regime or cooperating with it:

- *President removal.* Street protests succeed in ousting the president, who might even be put on trial. A novel feature of modern Arab history (Lebanon excepted) is the presence of an Arab 'ex-president' who becomes an 'ex' while he is still alive.
- *Civil war.* Street protests provoke a violent response from the ruling regime, and protests spread to major urban squares, with veiled or open foreign support for one or both sides. Examples are Libya and Syria.
- *Adaptation from above.* Seeing the writing on the wall, some leaders attempt to placate protesters with long-awaited political reforms, such as constitutional measures to lessen the ruler's dominance, curb the brutality of the security forces, and grant greater powers to the legislature.[12] A loosening of restrictions on civil society organizations promotes a better balance between the ruling authority and society's ambitions—authoritarianism with a facelift. These actions forestall the economic decline, breakdown in security, and media excess that have ensued when regimes were removed—and avoid the violence of civil war. Examples include the constitutional amendments declared by Morocco's King Mohammed VI on 9 March 2011.

### Empowerment through Democratization: A Clear Path out of the Fog

People in the region who desire democratization can look to experience elsewhere for help in clarifying what an Arab roadmap to democracy might look like. That includes academic analyses and experience in other countries whose social and political contexts are relevant to the Arab region. The goal is not to imitate other parts of the world but to seek guidance, anticipate pitfalls, and see how other countries coped with similar problems.

#### Academic analyses of democratization

From the global literature on democratization over the last thirty years, we can deduce five main conclusions that are relevant to the Arab situation today:[13]

- Both the number of democracies and the rate of democratization have risen, with regimes from Latin America to southern and eastern Europe becoming more open to democracy. Thus, the Arab world is catching up with the global trend, even if it is a latecomer.[14]

- Democratization tends to face the enormous challenge of a revolution in expectations, with an outpouring of rapidly multiplying, long-simmering demands. Protesters on the streets, their patience already exhausted, call for their political, economic, and social demands to be met *immediately*.

- The cornerstone of transformation at this tense and critical time is political skill. To achieve any political stability, the ruling authority must know how to set priorities, how to get things done on a crowded agenda, and how to gain the people's confidence. Only then can political leaders tackle such difficult problems as identity, the role of religion, and the framework for political action (this may include discussions of the appropriateness of the federal model in countries with multiple ethnic and religious groups).

- To be effective, political parties and civil society groups must be able to work together. Such cooperation is particularly important in an age of global integration.

- What seems to best facilitate and protect democratization is to create national coalitions—called *pactos*, or alliances, in Latin America. Such coalitions bring together different forces and communities, sometimes including former members of the old regime. With or without transitional justice, an inclusionary rather than an exclusionary politics is the name of the game.

### First-hand experience of those who shaped democratization

How do these five analytical principles of democratization stack up against actual experience, and what guidance can that offer the Arab world about surmounting the difficulties of democratization while avoiding its pitfalls?[15]

Experience suggests four primary challenges facing democratization:

- *A revolution in expectations.* When people take to the streets in protest, productivity and economic output fall, and expectations rise. A widening gap develops between revolutionary expectations and the limited capacity to meet them. In an already charged atmosphere, this discrepancy depletes social capital and general trust, threatening to erode the legitimacy of nascent institutions.

- *The pressure of specific demands.* Some groups convert their new expectations into specific demands. For example, marginalized groups, such as poor people and youth, may demand immediate social justice. Demonstrations and sit-ins can create a sense of chaos and insecurity. When ethnic communities or regional issues are involved, the state's sovereignty and unity are themselves threatened.
- *Contradictory imperatives in dealing with the private sector.* To address some specific demands (for example, increasing employment), the government needs the private sector—itself often under fire because of corruption or greed among some leaders or because of alliances with the former regime. The government thus faces two contradictory necessities: purge the private sector of corruption to regain trust, but also restore security to the private sector to safeguard its financial contributions and its know-how. The state also needs the private sector's domestic and foreign networks if it is to work on comprehensive development with trade unions, civil society organizations, and youth groups.
- *The need for more time.* The new ruling authority may need time to meet all the demands and challenges thrust upon it, especially since its members may lack political experience. Yet time is in short supply.

These challenges of democratization can be addressed in several ways:

- *Unify rapidly.* Rapid change is needed to build unity in the ranks and with partners, especially when parties resistant to change and various counter-revolutionary elements attempt to ambush democratization and prevent the empowerment of new groups. Achieving democracy and sustainable development is an arduous process, and the pioneers of change may fall out with one another. The parties must agree to adhere to a single purpose while acknowledging the right to differ on the means for achieving democracy.[16]
- *Agree on constitutional principles.* Unity of purpose begins with agreement on constitutional principles to guide democratization—for example, guaranteeing a fair and transparent electoral process while enshrining the rule of law. Other fundamental issues concern the role of the armed forces, the relationship between civilians and the military, and the place of religion in society and politics—the debated 'civil state' issue.

- *Be inclusive.* It is vital for political actors to uphold primary values and governing principles, even while negotiating compromises on how to apply them. Negotiations should be inclusive, so that democratization starts by representing all political and social forces—even those fearful of democracy. Including youth and women may be fairly easy, with no need to wait until things calm down.[17] For example, Tunisia's "Higher Authority for Meeting the Revolution's Objectives, Political Reform, and Democratization" stipulated that political parties' electoral lists must include comparable numbers of men and women.

- *Consider transitional justice.* More difficult for a new government is dealing with remnants of the former regime. Yesterday's enemies can cause schisms in the democratization process. In South Africa, where a culture of revenge might have easily emerged, Nelson Mandela was determined to forestall its more extreme manifestations. Believing that the nation needed the financial and administrative resources of the former ruling white minority, Mandela proposed transitional justice on the principles of remorse and apology (the Truth and Reconciliation Commission), followed by amnesty. In countries where the wounds of oppressive practices have not yet healed, such transitional justice can be highly controversial. In 2005 Morocco instituted a form of transitional justice for national reconciliation, despite the human rights abuses perpetrated in the previous era.

- *Establish national alliances and coalitions.* Successful unification through national dialogue leads to national alliances or coalitions. Establishing a culture and effectuating a practice of working together might take time for opponents. Historical experience of other peoples show that *pactos* and coalition building are prerequisites for democratic transition.

- *Meet commitments and satisfy expectations.* While the preceding five steps concern mainly decisions made by ruling elites, successful democratization also requires contact between the political authority and its social base. The nascent democracy must live up to its commitments and turn slogans into achievements affecting people's daily lives. Indonesia's democratization was aided by the authorities' ability to control inflation and prevent economic decline during a seventeen-month transition. Brazil refused to implement the International Monetary Fund's recommendations to limit social spending, and instead adopted measures to protect poor families. Parallel steps were taken to reform taxation, boost export production, sign free trade agreements, and add incentives for foreign investment. A political decision limited the presidential term to four years (with the option to run for a second term), putting pressure on presidents to get things done. Confidence in democratization rose, increasing stability and leading to the continued presence of local and foreign capital.

Commitments must be balanced with sound and complementary economic measures. Marginalized groups often insist that their demands be met rapidly. When Egyptian workers demanded a higher minimum wage after President Mubarak was ousted, a flood of similar demands followed from government employees, doctors, and others. The state budget must make up for increased spending by lowering the maximum wage and by linking higher wages to higher production. Otherwise, inflation will escalate, and the poor will lose purchasing power, undermining citizens' confidence in the authorities, squandering the social capital that was so painstakingly built up, and increasing the danger of political decay. If a movement does not deliver on its commitments, supporters will abandon it.[18]

- *Ensure peace, security, and fairness.* In strengthening the political leadership of the legitimate authority, a new democracy must also ensure the integrity and behavior of the security apparatus. Violations by security personnel are a chief cause of protests in the Arab region, and addressing them is high on the list of demonstrators' demands. If the citizens demand a civilian interior minister, their voices should be heard. Further measures might include the introduction of human rights curricula in police academies, reaffirming the rule of law, and helping the security apparatus gain legitimacy.

A secure environment for democracy requires measures to uphold the rule of law and prevent the re-emergence of abuses. Even if the new government decides to grant amnesty to some members of the former regime, that should not happen before the letter of the law is applied, fairness and transparency are instituted, and the offenses of the previous regime are fully exposed. Equally important is support for the social foundations of democracy. Western liberal democracy should not be transplanted without adaptations to societies long characterized by severe injustice and exclusion.

## Peering Ahead

What is in store for the Arab uprisings in the medium term? Is this the dawn of an expanded freedom in the region that will usher in profound economic reforms, broadened human rights, social justice, and sustainable democracy? Or will there be a rise of repressive theocracies, bolstered by a general public mood opposed to the ancien régime and chaotic transitions? Will severe disturbances occur as some rulers dig in their heels and people despair at the revolution's lack of immediate political and economic payoffs? In these cases, popular grievances might follow the fault lines of sectarian and tribal divisions—plunging countries into protracted internal conflicts, lengthening the roster of impotent states, and, as legitimacy evaporates, spreading increasing chaos and threatening more state failures.

All of these scenarios could occur at once in the region, reflecting local differences. Consider the huge and peaceful turnout for the first free elections in Tunisia, held after decades of rigged, low-turnout elections. The victory of the moderate Islamist Ennahda Party represented an exercise in expanded public freedoms. And the Ennahda Party (whose leaders were known to admire the strategic successes of Turkey's Justice and Development Party) might dispel the pessimists' fear of a repressive Islamist takeover. Party leaders support gender equality, minority rights, electoral politics, a free press, and human rights, seeing these rights and principles as consistent with religious values. The party pledged to create a progressive coalition government that could win the support of investors, donors, and secularists; that would draft a new constitution to enshrine rights and freedoms; and that would respond to popular demands for jobs and social equality. The party fulfilled its campaign pledges and prepared itself to govern neither alone nor on the basis of ideology, but on the strength of its policies and programs and its ability to get things done.

The Tunisian political system's openness to real alternatives demonstrated that moderate Islamists can help formulate a political pact as the cornerstone of a comprehensive social contract. Tunisia has avoided the splintering caused by excluding identities based on certain beliefs. As in Turkey, a group that expressed the spiritual values of the majority was able to form a sustainable government.

In Egypt, by contrast, peaceful protests soon gave way to renewed threats of violence. Rather than rewrite the constitution, the Supreme Council of the Armed Forces opted to amend it, putting proposed changes to a referendum on 19 March 2011. The amendments limited presidents to two terms, relaxed the criteria for nomination to the presidency, and restored full judicial supervision of the polls. The amendments also provided for the possibility of a new constitution after the elections and restricted the power to declare or renew a state of emergency—the widely loathed power that had enabled a state of emergency to remain in effect for twenty-nine years, which was finally lifted in May 2012. A decree also extended military rule well beyond the scheduled parliamentary elections. Violent clashes broke out as popular disapproval mounted over nebulous plans to release power to civilians. Demonstrators demanded a rapid end to military rule, while the authorities were increasingly willing to use force. The military's treatment of women and minorities stirred open suspicion.

The short time frame before parliamentary elections in Egypt gave the smaller and less-well-known political parties little time to organize, providing a critical advantage to more established groups, such as the Muslim Brotherhood. The results of the People's Assembly elections, announced on 21 January 2012, handed the Muslim Brotherhood's Freedom and Justice Party 47 percent of the seats in parliament (238 of 498). The Salafist Islamist Nur Party came in second, at 25 percent. The new ruling party, which pledged "consensual" policies,[19] soon found its stewardship strongly framed by popular expectations focusing on employment, income distribution, participation, and rapid transition to civil rule—not on religious beliefs. But Islamists failed in coalition building and, for various reasons, mismanaged the transition.[20] Mass protests followed on the first annual anniversary of the presidential election in June 2013, the army intervened and deposed the elected civilian president, and polarization prevails at the time of writing. After almost thirty years with one president and more than forty years with one constitution, Egypt had two presidents in less than two years and is preparing for a third, and the people voted three times in constitutional referendums within the last three years.

Meanwhile, in Libya, Syria, and Yemen, brutal, vengeful actions by regimes have foreclosed the possibility of a peaceful transition. Despite brief celebration in Libya of the prospect of national reconciliation after Qadhafi, it soon became apparent that any new leadership would inherit a tribal society torn by old rivalries as well as by the recent conflict. Building coalitions to bridge these differences is a crucial challenge—perhaps more urgent than national elections, which have not yet been organized.

In Syria, after years of violent repression and mass sectarian murder, hopes for a political solution are still dim. When the regime held a popular referendum in February 2012 to replace the Ba'th Party's monopoly on power with a multiparty system, followed by parliamentary elections in May 2012, opposition groups saw only a hollow gesture. With the regime almost totally isolated in the Arab world, and the UN Secretary-General using such terms as "crimes against humanity,"[21] Syria's wounds will take many years to heal.

In short, the Arab uprisings of 2011 have had different outcomes depending on the context. In wealthy oil-producing countries, political circumstances may be ripe for protest while economic circumstances are not. Those countries have the means to alleviate economic grievances, provide safety nets, and keep their people's protests well below the boiling point. That gives them a little time for enacting political reforms to broaden public representation and participation (box 10.3). In contrast, non-oil-producers—especially those with sharply climbing youth unemployment and income inequality—face much starker choices. The time for coercive rule is probably coming to an end, meaning that the authorities must act to transfer power to representative institutions. In societies torn by conflict, the danger is that the winds of political change will fan the flames of old sectarian and tribal disputes: the absence of a socialization in managing differences and a pluralistic framework leaves these various identity groups thirsting for power and resources in their own country and eager to see their peers in other countries attain the same.

New leaders and governments will rise to power in some Arab countries over the next ten years following their transition into nascent democracy. Every new leadership group and coalition will face questions about how to govern. They will need to know how to assess underlying democratic change, how to give that change constitutional and legal force, how to fine-tune political balances that promote pluralism, and how to keep people participating in democratic processes while building alliances to steer the transition across contested political spaces. Finally, the new leaders will need to address how to build a new official memory by acknowledging and confronting the past.

*Arab policymakers must make these choices at a time of crisis in the model to which they have aspired—democracy in a market economy.* Widening income disparities, rising unemployment, and the personal debt crisis, especially in the United States, prompted people from all walks of life to take to the streets in protest against injustice—the rising so-called "Wall Street" contention. Huge bailouts costing billions of dollars or euros—though they probably averted collapse of the international monetary order—alienated ordinary citizens who footed the bill only to see the banks rewarding themselves with the first gains from the crisis. In the United States the traditional two-party system has been infected by

### Box 10.3 The Gulf countries and the Arab Spring

The events of the Arab Spring came as a great surprise to most countries of the Gulf—as they did to other countries in the region and the world—and their repercussions were reflected in both official and popular reactions. Initially, Gulf governments were hesitant to take a position on these events, whose nature they were unable to understand and whose course they were unable to predict.

Gulf diplomacy succeeded in achieving a political settlement to the Yemeni crisis, mediating the agreement to hand over power, the removal of the Yemeni regime, and introduction of political and constitutional changes. As the events of the Libyan revolution escalated, the Gulf countries ratcheted up their efforts to support the Arab Spring revolutions in order to take the lead in the international diplomatic drive. The Gulf countries propelled the UN Security Council to adopt resolutions to protect the Libyan people.

At the outset of the Syrian revolution, the Gulf countries took a position similar to the one they adopted toward the Libyan revolution. Again, the Gulf Cooperation Council (GCC) countries spearheaded Arab diplomacy and contributed to international efforts to protect the Syrian people and support their revolution.

In general, the Arab Spring imposed huge financial obligations on the Gulf states to ease the process of change. Gulf countries played a pioneering role in steering diplomatic efforts in the Arab region and exerted considerable influence on regional and international diplomacy.

As a direct consequence of the impact of the Arab Spring, Bahrain and Oman faced the challenge of popular protests at home, while popular pressure mounted in the other Gulf countries.

In Bahrain, grassroots reform protests escalated dangerously, challenging the legitimacy of the regime and the ruling family. Violent clashes between security forces and demonstrators ensued. The official position in the Gulf was to stress that this protest movement was tainted by sectarian motives and foreign intervention. Ultimately, the security situation was brought under control with the help of military assistance from the GCC's Peninsula Shield Force. While the Bahraini leadership promised multiple reforms, the government continues to contend with numerous challenges that could reignite popular protest.

In Oman, which experienced more limited popular protests, the leadership restored calm by meeting many of the protesters' demands. Senior officials charged with corruption were removed from their posts, constitutional reforms were introduced, and a social security system for the unemployed was announced alongside job creation measures.

Qatar and the United Arab Emirates witnessed limited calls for political reform, mainly emanating from social networking websites. Security authorities arrested several leaders of the opposition and stripped a number of people of their citizenship. Kuwait experienced a surge of protests by stateless persons demanding citizenship rights, as well as political and media campaigns criticizing the performance of the ruling family and insisting that its members be subject to constitutional checks and accountability. The crisis culminated with the dismissal of the prime minister, the dissolution of parliament, and the holding of new elections, which gave various opposition forces a majority.

In Saudi Arabia there were attempts—mostly through social networking media—to mobilize mass protests demanding political, economic, and social reforms. The government responded by allocating enormous sums of money to meet citizen demands for salary increases, bonuses, and other measures to alleviate the economic burden on citizens. It also introduced a social security program for the unemployed and took action to provide new job opportunities for young people. On the whole, measures were restricted to the economic dimension and to short-term remedies. There was little progress in meeting demands for political reform. The situation remained calm, however, apart from some disturbances in the eastern part of the country where members of the Shi'a minority staged demonstrations demanding freedom to practice their religion and to exercise their rights as citizens to equality and justice. The authorities handled the protests using political and security methods and generally succeeded in restoring calm.

On the whole, the Arab Spring has had limited impact on the Gulf countries, largely due to the features that distinguish these countries from the others in the Arab region. Foremost among them is the long-established legitimacy of the ruling families. The hereditary monarchies have demonstrated their ability to preserve this legitimacy and, simultaneously, their ability to adjust to popular demands and changing circumstances. The economic factor is not a major source of anxiety for most citizens of the Gulf countries, whose financial and economic abundance enables high standards of living and the availability of essential services.

The governments of the Gulf countries nonetheless sense the mounting pressure of popular demands for political and economic reforms—to expand popular participation in decision making, fight corruption and abuse of authority, provide transparency and accountability, and make the members of ruling families legally accountable.

—Abdulaziz Sager, chairman, Gulf Research Center (GRC)

the politics of anger, reflecting a growing gulf between people and their elected representatives. In the Eurozone, harsh austerity measures intended to cap the exploding debt crisis have exposed the fragility of what was formerly hailed as the model of regional integration—and informed the Greeks, Irish, Portuguese, and Spanish that their standard of living comes second to an economic union that seems to favor its more powerful members. With mature democracies in confusion and the Arab people calling on governments to follow the same model, Arab elites find themselves trapped.

The majority of lessons in democratization for Arab countries are from the previous century. An earlier wave of democratization affected Spain, Portugal, and Greece in the mid-1970s; dismantled the former Soviet Union in 1989–91 (box 10.4); and then swept Latin America, East Asia, and Africa—bypassing the Arab world. Yet its lessons on transitional phases remain pertinent. Democratization is an arduous process, vulnerable to setbacks, disruptions, and disappointments. Not a single country in this wave of democratization was transformed without pain, and most still face profound challenges. Egypt, Tunisia, Libya, and others will have a similarly disorderly experience. Even if the results of change do not initially seem to differ much from past conditions, the governments that finally emerge will be built—for the first time in many decades—on the legitimate mandate of empowered citizens.

**Box 10.4 The Arab revolutions and the experiences of Eastern Europe**
The revolutions of the Arab Spring in Tunisia, Egypt, Libya, Yemen, and Syria, and the movement toward revolutions in other Arab countries, including Algeria, Morocco, Bahrain, and Sudan, were influenced by the rapid and astonishing developments and changes that the world is witnessing. The Arab people have woken up just to see how poor a share of freedom, democracy, and dignity they have. And they revolted. This experience is somewhat similar to the spring that swept throughout Eastern Europe after the downfall of the Soviet Union. The birth of democracies in Eastern Europe has been difficult, and victory emerged only after bitter struggle against the existing systems. Similarly, the Arab world is witnessing the birth of a new world that tyrants and unjust rulers strive to oppose, but in the end, this new world will inevitably emerge.
—Tawakkol Karman, 2011 Nobel Peace Prize laureate, www.nobelprize.org/nobel_prizes/peace/laureates/2011/karman -lecture_en.html

### Learning to Adapt and to Engage in Dialogue

The Arab world is at a watershed moment and in a race against time.[22] Focusing on challenges to empowerment, this book suggests ways to meet them: from rotating power, establishing the rule of law, promoting a balanced media, and ensuring transparency to combating corruption and poverty, promoting sound conflict management, and tackling environmental problems. Also essential is progress toward an education system in tune with contemporary knowledge that also protects and supports Arab identity.

Alarm bells are ringing louder and louder. Most regimes are cracking at the top, while people's revolution of expectations keeps streets and *midan*s boiling. Without institutionalized adaptation, more and more Arab countries will hemorrhage social capital and suffer political decay, swelling the ranks of failing or failed states—or extreme disempowerment.

Yet the crises in the Arab world did not begin with the Arab Spring. Rather, the Arab Spring comes at the end of a prolonged period of crisis. By 2010 poverty and deprivation had risen to 40 percent in some Arab countries.[23] Between 2000 and 2010, plans to create 90 million new jobs in the Arab economies fell short, at just 60 million jobs. A generation of young people has been unable to find work or has been compelled to work in unregulated sectors, stuck between poverty and the fear of greater poverty.[24] It is hardly surprising that so many Arab societies have now exploded. Bouazizi's self-immolation was not an individual reaction, but a reflection of a sociopolitical crisis. This is why it sparked protests and brought down four authoritarian presidents.

Democratization, whether revolutionary or reformist, was inevitable—not simply because the region lagged so far behind global trends, but also because of domestic factors. The sluggish pace of democratization in the Arab region is part of a much larger problem: call it the "adaptation deficit." A key challenge for government authorities, for many opposition parties, and for civil society groups, the Arab adaptation deficit also afflicts regional organizations—in particular the Arab League (as affirmed by some of the league's most ardent defenders and even by its recently elected secretary-general).[25]

Of marked importance to the Arab Spring has been the generation gap between an ailing, geriatric political leadership and an enthusiastic, active youth base—the majority of the population in most Arab countries.[26] A marked difference appears in the ability to recognize change and adapt to it. Leaders in most Arab countries could not comprehend what was taking place in the street, could not grasp the seriousness of the protests.

How to begin adapting? While acknowledging that change and adaptation are continuous processes occurring throughout society, this book has insisted that changes in a system of governance must begin with political authority at the top. Participation, coordination, power redistribution, and elite-rotation must replace control and the securocracy mindset that put itself above public scrutiny.

A fundamental requirement for transformation is ongoing communication between the pinnacle and the base. Such dialogue has been taking place for some time: in Lebanon (whose history abounds with examples of national dialogue), Saudi Arabia (where King Abdullah established the King Abdulaziz Center for National Dialogue in 2003), and Yemen (where then-president Ali Abdullah Saleh announced a dialogue with the Joint Meeting Parties in May 2009). During a crisis such dialogues become more urgent and widespread: they came to Egypt on 22 May 2011, to Bahrain on 2 July 2011, and to Syria on 6 July 2011.

Yet experience shows that holding national dialogues is not enough. Circumstances need to be conducive to their success. Most dialogues fail either because they are a pure façade, adopted as a reflexive means to contain citizen anger, or because they are held under improper conditions—for example, during confrontations between protesters and security forces in Syria and in Yemen. Inappropriate settings, whether tactically chosen or not, often lead opposition forces to boycott national dialogues. The street eventually loses its faith in national dialogue, regarding it as a ruse to perpetuate rule and control.

A credible national dialogue is almost the only way for multiple political and social groups (governmental and nongovernmental) to progress toward democracy, by learning how to adapt to others' demands and avoid polarization—which leads to government rupture and paralysis.

Participatory collective management can empower the Arab future. It can help forestall "Somalization"—the snowballing effects of institutional erosion and political disintegration that produce failed states. Most important, participatory collective management can link Arab democratization with the social justice that was so rousingly demanded in the Arab streets early in 2011.[27]

## Notes

1  Gulf Research Center 2011.
2  The personal happiness of Arab citizens as a basis for empowerment and enthusiasm for sustainable development, whether in terms of the quality of nutrition or other material and moral obstacles to daily performance, continues to be ignored (see the background papers by Abdullah and Salah Benjelloun).

Among fifty countries surveyed for *World Happiness Report 2012*, the United Arab Emirates ranked seventeenth (first in the Arab world); Saudi Arabia, twenty-sixth; Kuwait, twenty-ninth; and Qatar, thirty-first. Denmark placed first. The United States ranked eleventh. The report draws attention to the fact that wealth is not necessarily the key to happiness;

other criteria are involved, such as good health, job security, and family stability (*al-Hayat* 2012b).

3   AHDR 2009.

4   WHO 2009. These accidents caused 36,000 deaths and 400,000 injuries, in addition to enormous economic losses, in Arab countries; about five people are killed in road accidents every hour. The report warned that traffic accidents would become the fifth major cause of death by 2030, responsible for 3.6 percent of all deaths. In a statement for Arab Traffic Week in May 2010, the Arab Road Safety Organization observed that traffic accidents are one of the most serious problems depleting Arab societies' resources. And according to an article in *al-Hayat* in December 2011, the Saudi Arabian traffic authority reported that 6,485 people were killed in more than 485,000 traffic accidents in the kingdom during 2008—an average of seventeen lives each day.

5   A December 2011 Booz & Company report showed how hazardous it was to use cell phones (voice, reading, text) while driving (*al-Hayat* 2012a).

6   These measures were developed and applied by *Foreign Policy* magazine and the Fund for Peace 2011.

7   Dorrenspleet 2005.

8   See the Freedom House website, www.freedomhouse.org, which includes the organization's annual reports and index indicators. A recent World Bank report agreed on this low ranking for the status of democracy in the Arab region: Ross, Kaiser, and Mazaberi 2011.

9   This academic conference—one that most Arab states refused to host— was planned by the Center for Arab Unity Studies in Beirut. See the early, pioneering anthology *Azmat al-dimuqratiya fi al-watan al-'arabi*, 1984.

10  The list of such studies—even in Arabic—has now grown extensive, but at its forefront is the research program organized by Ali Khalifa al-Kawari and Raghid al-Sulh, which has held an annual conference in Oxford since the 1990s (www.arabsfordemocracy.org). The program has now published seven volumes. See, for example, al-Kawari 2007; al-Kawari et al. 2009; Sadiqi 2007; Salamé 1994; Korany et al. 1998, Routledge Studies in the Middle East 2011; al-Badawi and al-Maqdisi 2011.

11  In the 1999 book she edited, *Transition to Democracy*, Lisa Anderson considers an early, pioneering article on this issue (Rustow 1970).

12  Placation has taken the form of absolving eighty thousand Moroccan farmers of their debt (*al-Shuruq* 2011) and of Saudi King Abdullah bin Abdel Aziz's allocating $36 billion to meet various social needs. These "acts of generosity" extend to some social and political dimensions, such as the release of prisoners, the granting of citizenship, and proposals for constitutional amendments. Merrill Lynch (2011) reported that Gulf Cooperation Council countries raised their social spending in the first half of 2011 by $150 billion.

13  This review of the abundant literature of the last thirty years relied on papers and discussions from the conference organized by the American University in Cairo in June 2011. It also benefited from conversations with some of the leading authors of this literature, notably the Swiss-American Philippe Schmitter, whose book *Transitions from Authoritarian Rule* (1986), cowritten with Guillermo O'Donnell, is considered a milestone in the research and analysis in this field.

This literature, while valuable, has some serious shortcomings. Above all, it overlooks the Arab world (which it refers to as the "Arab exception") in analyses of how the world is changing. On criticisms of the Arab exception even before the Arab Spring, see Korany 2010.

14  Bernhage 2009.

15  This section draws on the documents and presentations of the conference organized by the UNDP in Cairo from 5 to 7 June 2011. Many of these testimonies came from those who led processes of democratization, such as former presidents, political party leaders, and other prominent figures from Brazil, Chile, Indonesia, Mexico, and South Africa. Former Egyptian prime minister Essam Sharaf called on his colleagues who have undergone democratization to step forward with information and advice, helping his country overcome its difficulties as fast as possible and at the least possible cost.

16  The number of revolutionary groups active in Egypt during July 2011 was between 168 and 216, in addition to the familiar groups and parties (Said 2011).

17  In the summer of 2011, Egypt's minister of local development, Muhammad Attiya, stated, "The nature of the critical stage that the country is passing through is the reason for excluding youth and women" (*al-Shuruq* 2011).

18  On 6 August 2011, the *New York Times*, as well as the Arabic-language online journal *Elaph*, published a photograph of unemployed vagrants in Sidi Bouzid, the hometown of Bouazizi, the young man whose self-immolation sparked the Tunisian revolution. It appears that angry people removed his portrait from the pictured square following news that his family had moved to a comfortable house in La Marsa, a wealthy suburb near the Tunisian capital.

19  Rabie 2012.

20  Korany 2013.

21  News & Media United Nations Radio 2012.

22  Even after the situation stabilizes, the ordeals of some of these societies (particularly Libya, Yemen, and Syria) will be similar to those of post-conflict societies, which have to heal wounds in order to move forward. The increasing research on the condition of such societies has become so prolific that it is impossible to discuss in the space available here.

23  UNDP 2011a, 2011b.

24 Carnegie Middle East 2011.

25 The late Salama Ahmed Salama, former editor in chief of the Egyptian newspaper *Madrasat al-Hukm al-Sharqi*, recently drew attention to this clear and growing deficit, noting that "resisting change has become a school in Middle Eastern governance" (Salama 2011). This deficit is not limited to political authority but extends to the very foundation of society: the family. Thanks to the communications revolution, the young have begun to instruct the old, and the image of the head of the family has been transformed from teacher to learner (see, for example, Hafni 2013). Yet enabling ruling authorities to deal with change remains essential (Luciani 2013).

26 See the minutes of the Youth Forum held in Beirut in September 2011, in the framework of discussions on the ideas of this book.

27 Those concerned with this region, whether from here or from abroad, might seriously consider analyzing the democratization experiences of the past century and the democratic revolutions of the nineteenth century, and even before, in order to take a penetrating look at democratic theory itself and to assess its priorities. In the process, they should ask themselves whether it is even remotely feasible, under the Arabs' current conditions, to establish a social contract that not only sets transparency, accountability, and the rotation of power among its highest priorities, but that, above all, sets the social foundation of all these demands. This means making social justice—in its wider sense that goes beyond correcting inequitable distribution of income—the highest priority of all.

# Bibliography

AAI (Arab Archives Institute). 2007. *Against Corruption: The Role of Arab Civil Society in Fighting Corruption.* Amman: Arab Archives Institute.

Abdel-Gadir, A. 2007. "al-Faqr: mu'ashirat al-qiyas wa-l-siyasat." Arab Planning Institute in Kuwait. Kuwait City: Bridge Development Series.

———. 2009. "al-Numuw al-iqtisadi al-muhabi li-l-fuqara'." Arab Planning Institute in Kuwait. Bridge Development Series no. 82. Kuwait City: Arab Planning Institute in Kuwait.

Abdel Gelil, I. 2008. *Framework for Solar Thermal Energy Use in the Southern Mediterranean Countries.* Berlin: SOLATERM, GTZ.

Abdel-Ghafar, M.A. 2003. *Fadd al-niza'at fi-l-fikr wa-l-mumarasa al-gharbiya.* Algeria: Dar Houma.

Abdul-Jabbar, F. 2010. *al-Imama wa-l-afandi: susiyulujiyat khitab wa-harakat al-ihtijaj al-dini.* Beirut: Manshurat al-Jamal.

Abdullah, B. 2010. In Ba 'Amir, Y. 2010. "Suyul al-Su'udiya takshif al-fasad al-mali." Aljazeera.net. 10 May. http://www.aljazeera.net/nr/exeres/774638c1-bab6-4133-a639-3a7a34810b96.htm.

Abdullah, M. 2010. "al-Sa'ada al-nafsiya lada al-muwatinin al-'arab." Background paper for the 2012 Arab Human Development Report. Cairo.

'Abdul-Latif, 'A. 2004. "al-Fasad ka-zahira 'arabiya wa aliyat dabtiha: itar li-fahm al-fasad fi-l-watan al-'arabi wa mu'alajatihi." *al-Mustaqbal al-'arabi,* no. 309. Beirut. http://www.acrli.org/publicationansListing_ar.aspx?categoryID=4&postingID=390.

'Abdul-Rahman, N. 2001. "al-Fasad wa-l-tanmiya, al-tahaddi wa-l-istijaba." *al-Idari*, no. 86.

al-'Abidi, K. *'Aqabat amam al-huriyat bi-l-mintaqa al-'arabiya.*

Abou-Hadid, A.F. 2006. *Assessment of Impacts, Adaptation and Vulnerability to Climate Change in North Africa: Food Production and Water Resources.* Washington, DC: Assessment of Impacts and Adaptations to Climate Change.

Abu 'Arja, T. 2003. *al-I'lam wa-l-thaqafa al-'arabiya: al-mawqif wa-l-risala.* Amman: Majdalawi House.

Abu-Fadil, M. 2004. "Straddling Cultures: Arab Women Journalists at Home and Abroad." In *Women and Media in the Middle East: Power through Self-expression,* edited by N. Sakr, 180–202. London: I.B. Tauris.

Abu-Isma'il, K., J. Ahmad, and R. Ramadan. 2010. "al-Faqr fi al-buldan al-'arabiya wa-l-manatiq al-namiya." New York: UNDP.

Abu-Nimer, M. 1996. "Conflict Resolution in an Arabic Context: Some Conceptual Questions." *Peace and Change* 21, no. 1 (January): 22–40.

Abu Sulayman, A. 2004. *Azmat al-irada wa-l-wijdan al-muslim: al-bu'd al-gha'ib fi mashru' islah al-umma.* Damascus: Dar al-Fikr. http://maghress.com/almassae/117386

Abu Zakariya, Y. 2007. "Bayn al-ta'lim al-dini wa-l-hawiya." http://nashiri.net/component/content/article/3143.html.

Achy, L. 2010. "Morocco's Experience with Poverty Reduction: Lessons for the Arab World." Carnegie Endowment for International Peace, http://carnegieendowment.org/files/morocco_poverty1.pdf.

ACIAC (The Anti-Corruption and Integrity in Arab Countries Project). www.undp.pogar.org/anticorruption.

ACSAD (Arab Center for the Study of Arid Zones and Drylands). 1997. "Water Resources and Their Utilization in the Arab World." Second Water Resources Seminar, Kuwait, 8–10 March.

Adli, H. 2005. "Fa'aliyat mu'assasat al-mujtama' al-madani wa ta'thiruha 'ala balwarat siyasat infaq li-l-khadamat al-ijtima'iya." Paper presented during a seminar on the Social Welfare State at the Swedish Institute in Alexandria. Center for Arab Unity Studies.

Adly, A. 2012. *The Politics of Development: A Comparison of Turkey and Egypt.* London and New York: Routledge.

AFED (Arab Forum for Environment and Development). 2008. *Annual Report: Arab Environment, Future Challenges.* Edited by M.K. Tolba and N. Saab. Beirut. http://www.afedonline.org/en/inner.aspx?contentID=347.

———. 2009. *Annual Report: Arab Environment, Climate Change: Impact of Climate Change on the Arab Countries.* Edited by N. Saab and M.K. Tolba. Beirut. http://www.afedonline.org/afedreport/Full%20English%20Report.pdf.

———. 2010. *Annual Report: Arab Environment, Water: Sustainable Management of a Scarce Resource.* Edited by M. El-Ashry, N. Saab, and B. Zeitoon. Beirut. http://www.afedonline.org/Report2010/main.asp.

El-Affendi, A. 2004. "al-Tariq ila al-khuruj min dawlat al-thaqb al-aswad." Background paper for the 2004 AHDR. New York: UNDP.

AHDR. 2009. *Challenges to Human Security in the Arab Countries.* Arab Human Development Report. New York: UNDP.

ALESCO (Arab League Educational, Cultural, and Scientific Organization). 2010. *Khuttat tatwir al-ta'lim fi al-'alam al-'arabi.* Tunis: ALESCO Publications.

ALESCO and the World Islamic Call Society. 2006. "Istratijiyat tatwir al-tarbiya al-'arabiya (al-istratijiya al-muhadaththa)." http://www.alecso.org.tn/index.php?option=com_content&task=view&id=640&Itemid=557&lang=ar.

Algerian Ministry of National Education. n.d. "Minhaj al-tarbiya al-islamiya." National Office of Scholastic Publications. http://programmes.educdz.com/Arabe/Accueil.htm.

al-'Alimi, R. 2000. "Les procédures de justice tribale dans la société yéménite." *Chroniques yéménites.* August. http://cy.revues.org/6.

Almasude, A. 1999. "The New Mass Media and the Shaping of Amazigh Identity." In *Revitalizing Indigenous Languages*, edited by J. Reyhner, G. Cantoni, R.N. St. Clair, and E. Parsons-Yazzie, 117–28. Flagstaff, AZ: Northern Arizona University.

Alnajjar, B. 2010. "al-Fada' al-sibarni wa tahawwulat al-quwa: muqaraba 'arabiya". *Majallat al-mustaqbal al-'arabi.* December.

al-'Alwani, T.J. 2004. *al-Harakat al-islamiya al-mu'asara.* Cairo: al-Ma'had al-'Alami li-l-Fikr al-Islami.

———. *La ikrah fi al-din.* Cairo: Maktabat al-Shuruq al-Duwali.

Anan, Kofi. 2004. "Introduction to UNCAC." New York: United Nations.

ANND (Arab NGO Network for Development). 2004. *The Annual Report for 2004.* Beirut: Arab NGO Network for Development.

Anwar, W.A. 2003. "Environmental Health in Egypt." *International Journal of Hygiene and Environmental Health* 206, no. 4/5: 339–50.

AOAD (Arab Organization for Agriculture Development). 2007. "al-Taqrir al-sanawi li-l-tanmiya al-zira'iya fi al-'alam al-'arabi." http://www.aoad.org/devreport2007.pdf

———. 2008. "Taqrir awda' al-amn al-ghiza'i al-'arabi." http://www.aoad.org/Foodsec2007.pdf.

al-'Arab, M.I. 2011. "al-Da'iyat al-jadida: al-zahira wa-l-tahaddiyat." In *al-Du'a al-judad: 'asranat al-tadayyun wa bi' al-da'wa*, 259–329. Al Mesbar Studies and Research Center.

Arab Advisors Group. 2009. *E-government Initiatives in the Arab World 2009.* Amman.

Arab Anti-Corruption Center. 2006. *International Projects for Fighting Corruption and the Call for Political and Economic Reform in Arab Countries.* Beirut: Center for Arab Unity Studies.

Arab Barometer. 2006. "Results of the Arab Barometer Surveys for 2006." www.arabbarometer.org/reports/countryreports/comparisonresutls06.html.

Arab Center for Policy and Research Studies, Doha. 2011. *Arab Opinion Index 2011*. http://www.dohainstitute.org/portal.

Arab Convention on the Suppression of Terrorism. http://www.anhri.net/docs/undocs/aact.shtml2011/06/06.

Arab Election Watch. 2010–11. www.arabew.org.

Arab Forum for Environment and Development. 2008. *Arab Environment: Future Challenges*. http://www.afedonline.org/afedreport/.

Arabic Network for Human Rights Information. 2010. 21 October. www.anhri.net.

Al Arabiya. 2010. "1,100 qana tilifisyuniya natiqa bi-l-'arabiya tunafis bi-quwa 'ala al-mushahidin." 23 October. http://www.alarabiya.net/articles/2010/10/23/123345.html.

Arab Labour Organization. 2010. *The Second Arab Report on Employment and Unemployment in Arab States*.

Arab League. 2010. *The 2010 Joint Arab Economic Report*. Abu Dhabi, UAE: Arab Monetary Fund.

Arab League and UNDP. 2010. *Third Arab Report on the Millennium Development Goals*. New York and Cairo: UNDP.

Arab Monetary Fund. 2010. *The Unified Arab Economic Report for 2010*. Abu Dhabi: Arab Monetary Fund.

Arab Organization for Agricultural Development. 2009. Report.

Arab Organization for Human Rights. 2010a. *Annual Report: Human Rights in the Arab World*. Center for Arab Unity Studies.

———. 2010b. *al-Taqrir al-sanawi: huquq al-insan fi al-watan al-'arabi*.

Arab Reform Initiative. 2011. *Annual Report 2009–10*. Paris and Beirut: Arab Reform Initiative. http://www.arab-reform.net/country-reports

Arab Resource and Information Center for Violence against Women. n.d. http://www.amanjordan.org/arabic_news/wmview.php?ArtID=15601

Arima, Ben C. 2010. "The Face of Urban Poverty: Explaining the Prevalence of Slums in Developing Countries." United Nations University: World Institute for Development Economic Research (UNU-WIDER) Working Paper no. 2010/30. http://www.wider.unu.edu/stc/repec/pdfs/wp2010/wp2010-30.pdf.

'Ashour, S. 2008. "Mukafahat al-fasad li-da'm al-tanmiya." http://www.pogar.org/publications/agfd/GfDII/corruption/deadsea/ahma dashour-ar.pdf

'Atallah, T. 2011. "al-Qiyam wa-l-ta'lim al-dini fi Lubnan min khilal al-tarbiya al-madrasiya wa-l-ta'lim al-'ali li-l-a'ima wa-l-kahana." Background paper.

'Atrisi, T. 2001. "al-Qiyam fi kutub al-ta'lim al-dini." In *al-Masadir al-diniya li-huquq al-insan: tashkiliya wa namadhij fi-l-takamul wa-l-insijam*. Beirut: Middle East Council of Churches.

Ayish, M. 2010. "Arab State Broadcasting Systems in Transition: The Promise of the Public Service Broadcasting Model." *Middle East Journal of Culture and Communication* 3 (1): 9–25.

*Azmat al-dimuqratiya fi al-watan al-'arabi.* 1984. Beirut: Center for Arab Unity Studies.

Bahjat, Q. 1987. "Wafida, mutagharriba, lakinaha baqiya: tanaqudat al-duwal al-'arabiya al-qutriya." *Majallat al-mustaqbal al-'arabi,* no. 105, November.

Bakir, A., et al. 2010. *Turkiya bayna tahaddiyat al-dakhil wa rahanat al-kharij.* Beirut: Arab Scientific Publishers.

Baqir, M. 2007. "Qiyas al-faqr fi-l-tatbiq." Background paper for the 2009 Arab Human Development Report. New York: UNDP.

Barakat, H. 2000. *al-Mujtama' al-'arabi fi-l-qarn al-'ishrin: bahth fi taghayur al-ahwal wa-l-'alaqat.* Beirut: Center for Arab Unity Studies.

Barilari, A. 2000. *L'Etat de droit: réflexions sur les limites du juridisme.* Rome: La librarie juridique de référence en ligne.

Al-Basir, H. 1998. "al-I'lam al-'arabi wa 'asr al-khaskhasa." In *Dur wasa'il al-i'lam al-'arabiya fi da'm thaqafat al-mujtama' al-madani,* edited by Saad Eddin Ibrahim, 63–72. Cairo: Ibn Khaldun Center for Development Studies.

Bassiouni, M.S. 2003. *al-Watha'iq al-dawliya al-ma'niya bi huquq al-insan, al-mujallad al-thamin: al-watha'iq al-islamiya wa-l-iqlimiya.* Cairo: Shuruq.

Bassiouny, H. "al-'Alaqa bayna al-i'lamiyin wa-l-siyasiyin fi al-watan al-'arabi." *Majallat 'alam al-fikr* 23, nos. 1–2.

BBC News. 2009a. "Flood Deaths in Saudi Arabia Rise to around 100." http://news.bbc.co.uk/2/hi/8384832.stm.

———. 2009b. "Press Alarm at Egypt–Algeria Football Violence." 18 November. http://news.bbc.co.uk/2/hi/8366340.stm.

Beckman, D., R. Agarwala, S. Burmester, and I. Serageldin. 1991. *Friday Morning Reflections at the World Bank: Essays on Values and Development.* Washington DC: Seven Locks Press.

———. 2006. *al-Tanmiya wa-l-qiyam: munaqashat hurra li nukhba min khubara' al-Bank al-Dawli.* Cairo: Supreme Council of Culture Publications.

Beetham, D. 2006. *Parliament and Democracy in the Twenty-first Century: A Guide to Good Practice.* Inter-Parliamentary Union.

Belderrain, J.-E. 2003. "Interprétation des évolutions mondiales du point de vue de la société multiculturelle latino-américaine." *Perspectives* 33, no. 2. http://www.ibe.unesco.org/publications/Prospects/ProspectsPdf/126f/belf.pdf.

Benjelloun, A. 2008. "al-Faqr wa-l-badana fi al-buldan al-'arabiya: dirasat al-'alaqa baynahuma." Background paper for the 2009 Arab Human Development Report. New York: UNDP.

———. 2011. "Poverty and Obesity in the Arab World." Background paper for the Tenth Anniversary Arab Human Development Report, *Arab Empowerment.* New York: UNDP. Also available on AUC Forum website: www.aucegypt.edu/ResearchatAUC/rc/aucforum

Bernardi, C. 2010. "Saudi Bloggers, Women's Issues and NGOs." *Arab Media & Society* 11 (Summer). www.arabmediasociety.com/?article=757.

Bernhage, P. 2009. "Measuring Democracy and Democratization." In *Democratization,* edited by Christian Haerpfer et al., 24–40. Oxford and New York: Oxford University Press.

Böckenförde, E.W. 2000. *Le droit, l'état et la constitution démocratique.* Rome: La librarie juridique de référence en ligne.

Bokran, M. 2007. "al-Tifl wa-l-din." http://www.maghress.com/hespress/15216.

———. 2010. "Tadris al-'aqida li-l-atfal: al-'aqida al-ash'ariya anmudhajan." http://maghress.com/almassae/117386.

Bouhaha, A-R. 2009. *Tuqus al-'ubur.* Beirut: al-Intishar al-'Arabi.

Boulet, D. 1991. *Vers l'état de droit: La théorie de l'état et l'état de droit.* Paris: Editions l'Harmattan.

Bouthoul, G. 2007. *Le Phénomène-Guerre.* Trans. Elie Nassar. Beirut: Dar al-Tanwir.

Bowen, S. 2013. *Learning from Iraq: A Final Report from the Special Inspector General for Iraq Reconstruction.* http://www.sigir.mil/learningfromiraq/index.html.

Brahimi, L. 2000. "Rapport du groupe d'études sur les opérations de paix." http://www.operationsdepaix.net/Rapport-Brahimi.

———. 2011. Paper delivered at the international forum on "The Arab World in Turmoil: Uprisings or Revolutions?" Algeria, 27–30 October.

Brandolino, J., and D. Luna. 2008. "Addressing Corruption through International Treaties and Commitments." December 2006. IIP Digital.

Brinkerhoff, D.W. 1999. "Identifying and Assessing Political Will for Anti-Corruption Efforts." USAID's Implementing Policy Change Project. Working paper no. 13. http://www.usaid.gov/our_work/democracy_and_governance/publications/ipc/wp-13-ms.pdf.

B'Tselem. 2011. "Statistics on Settlements and Settler Population." http://www.btselem.org/settlements/statistics.

Burgat, F. 2008. "Le règlement des conflits tribaux au Yémen." *Égypte/Monde arabe.* 3rd series: Le shaykh et le procureur. 8 July: 101–26. http://ema.revues.org/index1042.html.

Bu Taleb, M.N. 2011. "al-Ab'ad al-siyasiya li-l-zahira al-qibliya fi-l-mujtama'at al-'arabiya: muqaraba susiyulujiya li-l-thawratayn al-tunisiya wa-l-libiya." www.dohainstitute.org.

Cadart, J. 1990. *Institutions politiques et droit constitutionnel.* Paris: Editions Economica.

CAMP (Cambridge Arab Media Project) and CIS (Prince Alwaleed Bin Talal Centre of Islamic Studies). 2010. *Religious Broadcasting in the Middle East. Islamic, Christian, and Jewish Channels: Programmes and Discourses.* Report for a conference at Cambridge University, 30–31 January, Cambridge, UK.

"Carnegie Middle East Center in Beirut Symposium." 2011. *al-Hayat.* 6 November.

Catusse, M., B. Destremau, and E. Verdier. 2009. *L'Etat face aux débordements du social au Maghreb: Formation, travail et protection sociale.* Paris: Editions Karthala.

Center for Studies and Research of Developing Countries. 1999. *Corruption and Development.* Development Issues vol. 14. Cairo: Center for Studies and Research of Developing Countries.

Centre international d'études pédagogiques. 2004. "Ecole et religion." *Revue Internationale d'éducation Sèvres* 36 (October). http://www.ciep.fr/ries/ries36b.php.

Chamber of Deputies. *Wathiqat al-Ta'if.* Republic of Lebanon. http://www.lp.gov.lb/SecondaryAr.Aspx?id=13.

Chedid, R., and F. Chaaban. 2003. "Renewable-energy Developments in Arab Countries: A Regional Perspective." *Applied Energy* 74: 211–20.

Chen, K.S., Y.T. Ho, C.H. Lai, and Y.A. Tsai. 2004. "Trends in Concentration of Ground Level Ozone and Meteorological Conditions during High Ozone Episodes in the Kao King Airshed, Taiwan." *Journal of Air Waste Management* 54: 36–48.

Chevallier, J. 1999. *La mondialisation de l'état de droit.* Mélanges Ardant. Rome: La librarie juridique de référence en ligne.

———. 2010. *L'Etat de droit.* Paris: Editions Montchrestien.

Coronel, S.S. 2003. "The Role of the Media in Deepening Democraçy." http://unpan1.un.org/intradoc/groups/public/documents/UN/UNPAN01 0194.pdf.

Côté, G.-S. 2006. "La coopération environnementale internationale est-elle possible sans puissance hégémonique? L'approche institutionnaliste de Robert O Keohane." http://www.cpsa-acsp.ca/papers-2006/C%C3%B4t%C3%A9.pdf.

al-Dageli, W. 2010. "Towards an Integration of Electrical Projects in the Arab Countries: Potentials and Considerations—The Need for Arab Markets for Electrical Energy." Workshop on Impact of Climate Change in the Arab Region: Towards a Sustainable Renewable Energy—Opportunities and Challenges. Manama, Bahrain: UNDP and Arab League.

Daycock, C., R. Desjardins, and S. Fennell. 2004. "Generation Cost Forecasting Using On-line Thermodynamic Models." *Proceedings of Electric Power.* Baltimore, MD. March. http://www.etapro.com/resources/EP2004GenCostForecasting.pdf.

Deane, J., K. Dixit, N. Mue, F. Banda, and S. Waisbord. 2003. "The Other Information Revolution: Media and Empowerment in Developing Countries." In *Communicating in the Information Society*, edited by B. Girard and S. Ó Siochrú, 65–100. Geneva: United Nations Research Institute for Social Development.

Delors, J. 1996. *L'éducation, un trésor est caché dedans.* Report to UNESCO, International Commission on Education for the Twenty-first Century. Paris: Odile Jacob.

Deutsche Welle.
http://www.dw.de/%D9%85%D8%AF%D8%B1%D8%B3%D8%A9-%D8%A7%D9%84%D8%AF%D9%8A%D8%A7%D9%86%D8%A7%D8%AA-%D8%A7%D9%84%D8%A5%D8%A8%D8%B1%D8%A7%D9%87%D9%8A %D9%85%D9%8A%D8%A9%D8%AA%D8%AC%D8%B1%D8%A8%D8%A9-%D8%A3%D9%84%D9%85%D8%A7

%D9%86%D9%8A%D8%A9-%D8%B1%D8%A7%D8%A6%D8%AF
%D8%A9-%D9%81%D9%8A-%D8%AF%D8%B9%D9%85-%D8
%AD%D9%88%D8%A7%D8%B1-%D8%A7%D9%84%D8%A3%D8
%AF%D9%8A%D8%A7%D9%86/a-5256091
Development Network (Shabakat Tanmia). n.d. "Azmat qita' al-qurud al-
sughra fi-l-Maghrib: al-asbab al-maskut 'anha."
http://www.tanmia.ma/article.php3?id_article=25749&lang=ar.
al-Dhawadi, Z. 2010. *al-Khuruj min nasaq al-dawla al-diniya*. Beirut: al-Intishar
al-'Arabi.
Dorrenspleet, R. 2005. *Exploring the Structural Sources of the Fourth Wave*.
Boulder, CO: Lynne Rienner.
Dregne, H.E., and N.T. Chou. 1992. "Global Desertification Dimensions and
Costs." In *Degradation and Restoration of Arid Lands*, edited by H.E.
Dregne. Lubbock: Texas Tech University Press.
http://www.ciesin.org/docs/002-186/002-186.html.
Dris-Aït Hamadouche, L., and Y. Zoubir. 2013. *Global Security Watch—The
Maghreb: Algeria, Libya, Morocco, and Tunisia*. Santa Barbara: Praeger.
Dubai Press Club. 2009. "Arab Media Outlook." Dubai.
www.dpc.org.ae/UserFiles/AMO%20Eng%20combined.pdf.
Ebi, K., and G. McGregor. 2008. "Climate Change, Tropospheric Ozone and
Particulate Matter, and Health Impacts." *Environmental Health Perspectives*
116: 1449–55.
http://ehp03.niehs.nih.gov/article/fetchArticle.action?articleURI=info:doi
/10.1289/ehp.11463.
"Education and Training Efforts in the Arab Nation: Challenges and Trends."
2004. Paper presented to the forty-seventh session of the International
Education Conference, Geneva.
EEHC (Egyptian Electric Holding Company). 2008. *Annual Report*. Cairo.
http://www.moee.gov.eg/English/Electric%20eng%202010.pdf.
Egyptian Ministry of Media. 2008. *Mithaq al-sharaf al-i'lami al-'arabi*.
http://www.moinfo.gov.eg/AR_Agrements.aspx.
Eid, H.M., and N.M. el-Mowelhi. 1998. "Impact of Climate Change on Field
Crops and Water Needs in Egypt." African International Environmental
Conference. Cairo.
Elbadawi, I., and S. Makdisi. 2012. *Why the Arab Democratic Deficit*. London
and New York: Routledge.
ESCWA (Economic and Social Commission for Western Asia). 2005.
"Urbanization and the Changing Character of the Arab City."
http://www.escwa.un.org/information/publications/edit/upload/sdd-05-1-
e.pdf.
———. 2007a. "A Critical Review of Successful Experiments in Integrated
Social Policy." ESCWA Working Paper. New York: United Nations.
———. 2007b. "Youth in the ESCWA Region: A Study of Reality and the
Effects of Development Policies." No. 4. New York: United Nations.

———. 2008. "Integrated Social Policy: From Concept to Practice." ESCWA. New York: United Nations.

———. 2009. "Multidimensional Poverty: Definitions and Measurement Methodologies." Working Paper Presented during the Experts' Meeting on the Measurement of Poverty. ESCWA. Beirut: UN Economic and Social Council.

———. 2010a. "The Education for All Global Monitoring Report on University Education: The Way to Achieve Fairness for the Deprived. A Regional Overview of Arab States." New York: UNESCO Publications.

———. 2010b. *Food Security and Conflict in the ESCWA Region.* New York: United Nations.

———. 2010c. "Promoting Large-scale Renewable Energy Applications in the Arab Region: An Approach for Climate Change Mitigation." http://www.escwa.un.org/information/publications/edit/upload/SDPD-10-WP-2.pdf.

———. 2010d. *The Third Arab Report on the Millennium Development Goals 2010 and the Impact of the Global Economic Crisis.* New York and Beirut: United Nations.

Failed States Index. 2013a. "Foreign Policy." http://ffp.statesindex.org/rankings-2013-sortable

———. 2013b. "Fund for Peace and Foreign Policy." January. http://foreignpolicy.com/failedstates

Faiz, Ra'id. 2009. *The Rural Poverty in Arab Countries and the Role of the Arab Organization for Agriculture in Reducing Its Impact.* Arab League and Arab Organization for Agriculture Development.

al-Fanik, F. 1998. "Sulukiyat al-sahafa al-dimuqratiya." In *Dur wasa'il al-i'lam al-'arabiya fi da'm thaqafat al-mujtama' al-madani*, edited by Saad Eddin Ibrahim, 37–51. Cairo: Ibn Khaldun Center for Development Studies.

FAO (Food and Agriculture Organization). 2008a. "Climate Change Adaptation and Mitigation: Challenges and Opportunities for Food Security." Information Document HLC/08/INF/2, High-Level Conference on World Food Security: The Challenges of Climate Change and Bio-energy. Rome. 3–5 June. ftp://ftp.fao.org/docrep/fao/meeting/013/k2545e.pdf.

———. 2008b. FAOSTAT Databases. http://faostat.fao.org.

———. 2010. "The State of Food Insecurity in the World: Addressing Food Insecurity in Protracted Crises." Rome. http://www.fao.org/docrep/013/i1683e/i1683e.pdf

Farahat, M.N. 2009. "Hudud al-himaya al-qanuniya li-l-fard fi al-nuzum al-'arabiya." Background paper for the 2009 AHDR. New York: UNDP.

al-Faris, A. 2001. *al-Faqr wa tawzi' al-dakhl fi-l-buldan al-'arabiya.* Beirut: Center for Arab Unity Studies.

Federation of Arab Journalists. 2009. *Press Freedom in the Arab World.*

The Foundation Coalition. *Understanding Conflicts and Conflict Management.* http://foundationcoalition.org/publications/brochures/conflict.pdf.

Freedom House. 2009. "Freedom of the Press 2009."
www.freedomhouse.org/template.cfm?page=251&year=2009.
———. 2011. "Freedom of the Press Survey, Global Press Freedom Rankings."
http://freedomhouse.org/images/File/fop/2011/FOTP2011GLobalRegio
nalTables.pdf.
Freeman, M., and D. Marotine. 2007. *Qu'est-ce que la justice transitionnelle?*
International Center for Transitional Justice.
http://www.ictj.org/images/content/7/5/752.pdf.
Freund, J. 1976. "Guerre et politique: de Karl von Clausewitz à Raymond
Aron." *Revue française de sociologie* 17, no. 4: 643–51.
http://www.persee.fr/web/revues/home/prescript/article/rfsoc_0035-
2969_1976_num_17_4_4894.
Fuad, W. 2008. *al-Tadayyun al-jadid: muhawala li-fahm al-zahira*. Beirut: Arab
Scientific Publishers.
Gates, S., H. Hegre, H.M. Nygård, and H. Strand. 2010. "Consequences of
Armed Conflict." Center for the Study of Civil War. University of Oslo,
Norwegian University of Science and Technology.
Gemayel, S. *L'Etat de droit*. www.kateeb.org.
Geneva Center for the Democratic Control of Armed Forces. 2003.
*Parliamentary Oversight of the Security Sector: Principles, Mechanisms, and
Practices.* Arabic translation by Hanan Wali, 2004. Geneva: Inter-
parliamentary Union, Geneva Centre for the Democratic Control of Armed
Forces.
German Agency for Technical Cooperation (GTZ). 2004. "Corruption and
Gender: Approaches and Recommendations for TA." Eschoborn,
Germany: Deutsche Gesellschaft für Zusammenarbeit (GTZ).
Ghanim, G. 1997. *al-Qawanin wa-l-nuzum 'abr al-tarikh*. Beirut: Sadir Press.
———. 2005. *Hukm al-qanun*. Beirut: UNDP–Arab Center for the
Development of the Rule and Law and Integrity.
Ghazali, M. 1990. *Qadaya al-mar'a bayn al-taqalid al-rakida wa-l-wafida*. Cairo:
Dar al-Shuruq.
———. 1991. *Turathuna al-fikri fi mizan al-shara' wa-l-'aql*. Cairo: Dar al-Shuruq.
———. 2000. *al-Ta'assub wa-l-tasamuh bayn al-masihiya wa-l-islam*. Cairo:
Nahdat Misr.
———. 2010. *Raka'iz al-iman bayn al-'aql wa-l-qalb*. Cairo: Dar al-Shuruq.
Giddens, A. 1989. *Sociology*. Oxford: Polity.
Global Arab Network. 2011. *al-Thawra al-suriya: al-farq bayna Lawna al-Shibl
wa Rula Ibrahim*. http://www.globalarabnetwork.com/opinion/4325-2011-
05-28-17-14-08.
GMMP (Global Media Monitoring Project). 2010. *Who Makes the News*.
www.whomakesthenews.org/images/stories/restricted/regional/Middle_%
20East.pdf.
El Gody, A. 2007. "New Media, New Audience, New Topics, and New Forms
of Censorship in the Middle East." In *New Media and the New Middle*

*East*, edited by P. Seib, 213–34. New York: Palgrave Macmillan.

Goodman, E., and J. Shapiro. 2009. "From Broadcast to Broadband: Redesigning Public Media for the 21st Century." Lecture at Harvard University. 3 November. Summary available online at http://cyber.law.harvard.edu/events/luncheon/2009/11/Shapiro.

Greenberg, T.S., L.M. Samuel, W. Grant, and L. Gray. 2009. *Stolen Asset Recovery: A Good Practices Guide for Non-conviction-based Asset Forfeiture*. Washington, DC: World Bank. http://www.coe.int/t/dghl/monitoring/moneyval/web_ressources/IBRDWB_Guidassetrecovery.pdf

Gulf Research Center. 2011. 13 December. *The Gulf Yearbook*. Jedda and Dubai.

*al-Gumhuriya*. 2010. "Fawdat al-qanawat al-fada'iya al-diniya: Li-maslahat man?" www.coptreal.com/wshowsubject.aspx?SID=39205.

Habib, R. 1991. *al-Ihya' al-dini*. Cairo: al-Dar al-'Arabiya.

Haéri, P. 2008. *De la guerre à la paix: Pacification et stabilisation post-conflit*. Paris: Economica.

Haffar, M. 2004. "Impact of Transport on Current Air Pollution in Syria and Mitigation Strategies." Seminar on Clean Fuels and Vehicles in Western Asia and North Africa. Beirut. 17–19 March.

Hafni, Q. n.d. "Muwajahat al-usra al-'arabiya li-l-tahaddiyat al-mu'asira." Background paper for the 2012 Arab Human Development Report.

Al-Hail, A. 2000. "The Age of New Media: The Role of Al-Jazeera Satellite TV in Developing Aspects of Civil Society in Qatar." *Transnational Broadcasting Studies* 4 (Spring). www.tbsjournal.com/Archives/Spring00/Articles4/Ali/Al-Hail/al-hail.html.

Hamdan, A. 2005. "Women and Education in Saudi Arabia: Challenges and Achievements." *International Education Journal* 6: 42–64.

Hammami, N. 2006. *Islam al-fuqaha'*. Beirut: Dar al-Tali'.

Hamzawy, A. 2010. "Azmat al-sharia: qira'a fi waqa'i' wa nata'ij al-intikhabat al-barlamanyia al-misriya." Washington DC: Carnegie Endowment for International Peace.

Hassan, M.S. 2010. *Marja'iyat al-jami'at*. Beirut: al-Intishar al-'Arabi.

*al-Hayat*. 2012a. 10 October.

———. 2012b. 10 April, p. 24.

Henderson, K. 2005. "A Regional Strategy for Promoting a Free Media and Freedom of Expression in the Middle East and North Africa: Decriminalizing Defamation and Insult Laws against Journalists and the Media through Legislative Reforms, Executive Decrees, and Prioritized Law Enforcement Policy Statements." IFES Rule of Law White Paper Series. International Foundation for Electoral Systems, Washington, DC. www.ifes.org/publication/1157b03c64072655b2490a18963fae1a/WhitePaper_7_Freedom_of_press_MENA.pdf.

Hilal, A.D., and M. Nafin. 2000. *al-Nuzum al-siyasiya al-'arabiya: qadaya al-istimrar wa-l-taghyir*. Beirut: Center for Arab Unity Studies.

Hobeika, L. 2010. "Review Economic Policies after Results." *al-Sharq*, 22

December 2010. http://www.al-sharq.com/news/details/175624

Hofheinz, A. 2005. "The Internet in the Arab World: Playground for Political Liberalization." *International Politics and Society* 3: 78–96.

Human Rights Watch. 2010. "Elections in Egypt: State of Permanent Emergency Incompatible with Free and Fair Vote." November. New York: Human Rights Watch. www.hrw.org/sites/default/files/Reports/Egypt-1110 Web for Posting.pdf

Huntington, S. 1991. *The Third Wave: Democratization in the Late Twentieth Century*. Norman: University of Oklahoma Press.

al-Hussayn, A. 2003. "Asbab al-'unf wa-l-irhab wa-l-tatarruf." Electronic Library of the Forum for Handicapped Research and Studies. http://www.assakina.com/book/book19/index.1.html.

ICG (International Crisis Group). 2012. *Policy Briefing on Syria*. 5 March. Damascus and Brussels: Middle East Briefing.

IEA (International Association for the Evaluation of Educational Achievement). 2008a. "TIMSS 2007 International Mathematics Report: Findings from IEA's Trends in International Mathematics and Science Study at the Fourth and Eighth Grades." http://timss.bc.edu/TIMSS2007/mathreport.html.

———. 2008b. "TIMSS 2007 International Science Report: Findings from IEA's Trends in International Mathematics and Science Study at the Fourth and Eighth Grades." http://timss.bc.edu/TIMSS2007/sciencereport.html.

IEA (International Energy Agency). 2010. *Key World Energy Statistics*. http://www.iea.org/textbase/nppdf/free/2010/key_stats_2010.pdf.

ILO. 2010. *World of Work Report 2010: From One Crisis to the Next?* Geneva: International Institute for Labour Studies. http://www.ilo.org/public/portugue/region/eurpro/lisbon/pdf/worldwork_2010.pdf

———. 2013. *Global Employment Trends*. Geneva: International Institute for Labour Studies.

ILO and UNDP. 2012. *Rethinking Economic Growth: Towards Productive and Inclusive Arab Societies*. Geneva: International Institute for Labour Studies.

El Imam, M. 2010. "Crossing the Minefield." In *Viewpoints*, special ed. State of the Arts, Volume 6: Creative Arab Women, 20–21. Washington, DC: Middle East Institute.

Institut Panos Paris. 2011. *PSB Newsletter*. 9 March.

International Institute for Democracy and Electoral Assistance (IDEA). 2011. *Constitution Building after Conflict: External Support to a Sovereign Process*. Sweden: International IDEA.

International Islamic Federation of Student Organizations. "al-Zaytuna: jam'iyat al-ulama wa-l-muslihin." www.iifso.com/ar/?p=84.

International Organization for Migration and League of Arab States. 2004. *Arab Migration in a Globalized World*. Geneva: International Organization for Migration/League of Arab States.

Internet World Stats. 2010. "Middle East."
www.Internetworldstats.com/middle.htm.

IPCC (Intergovernmental Panel on Climate Change). 2007. *Climate Change
2007: Impacts, Adaptation and Vulnerability.* Contribution of Working
Group II for the Fourth Assessment Report.
http://www.ipcc.ch/publications_and_data/ar4/wg2/en/contents.html.

Irani, G.E., and N.C. Funk. 1998. "Rituals of Reconciliation: Arab–Islamic
perspectives." *Arab Studies Quarterly* 20, no. 4 (Fall): 2–34.

Iraq Body Count. http://www.iraqbodycount.org.

al-'Isa, A. 2009. *Islah al-ta'lim fi-l-Su'udiya.* Beirut: Dar al-Saqi.

ISESCO (Islamic Educational, Scientific, and Cultural Organization). 2003.
"Dalil al-isisku li-idmaj mafahim al-sihha al-injabiya wa-l-naw' al-ijtima'i
fi minhaj al-tarbiya al-islamiya." Morocco: ISESCO Publications.

Al Jazeera. 2011. Numerous articles.

Al Jazeera Center for Studies. 2010. "al-Intikhabat al-barlamaniya al-misriya:
al-waqi wa ihtimalat al-mustaqbal." www.aljazeera.net.

Jordanian Ministry of Education. "Adillat al-mu'allimin li-jami' al-sufuf."
Bureau of Academic Curricula and Textbooks.
http://eduwave.elearning.jo/datapool/qrc/Adellah-Index.htm.

Jouirou, Z. 2007a. *al-Islam al-sha'bi.* Beirut: Dar al-Tali'.

———. 2007b. *al-Qisas fi-l-nusus al-muqaddasa.* Tunis: Dar al-Ma'arif li-l-
Nashr.

al-Juhni, E.I.M. "al-Faqr wa qad istawtana diyar al-'arab?"
www.alarabiya.net/save_pdf.php?cont_id=62878.

Kaldor, M. 1999. *New and Old Wars: Organized Violence in a Global Era.*
Stanford CA: Stanford University Press.

al-Karaghouli, A. 2004. "Current Status of Renewable Energies in the Middle
East and North African Region." UNEP/POWA conference, organized
by the government of Germany.

al-Kawari, A.K. 2007. *Nahw mafhum jami' yu'azziz al-intiqal ila al-dimuqratiya
fi al-bilad al-'arabiya.* January 24. http://www.arabsfordemocracy.org.

al-Kawari, A.K., and A.-F. Madi. 2009. *Tansiq wa-tahrir: limadha intaqal al-
akhirun ila al-dimuqratiya wa ta'akhur al-'arab.* Beirut: Center for Arab
Unity Studies.

Kebabjian, G. 1996. "Théorie de la stabilité hégémonique ou théories des
régimes?" *Economies et sociétiés* 30, no. 6.

Khairallah, D. 2004. "al-Fasad ka-zahira 'alamiya wa aliyat dabtiha." *al-
Mustaqbal al-'arabi*, no. 309. Beirut.

Khalayfi, A. 2007. *al-Islam al-'arabi.* Beirut: Dar al-Tali'.

Khalifa, M. 2011. "Redefining Slums in Egypt: Unplanned versus Unsafe
Areas." *Habitat International* 35, no. 1: 40–49.

al-Khamri, H. 2008. "Saudi Women Journalists Are Coming Out of the
Closet." Menassat. www.menassat.com/?q=en/news-articles/2671-saudi-

women-journalists-are-coming-out-closet.

Khatib, L. 2009. "Satellite Television and Political Conflict in the Arab World: A Critical Assessment." In *Spaces of Security and Insecurity: Geographies of the War on Terror*, edited by K. Dodds and A. Ingram, 205–20. Aldershot, UK: Ashgate Publishing.

al-Khayyat, 'A. 2005. "al-Hukm al-salih shart li-mukafahat al-fasad." *al-Hayat*, 30 October.

———. 2010. "Mukafahat al-fasad, al-ishkaliyat wa-l-mu'awwiqat wa-l-fajawat." Presented at conference, "Arab-Anti-Corruption Organization," 3–5 July. Cairo.

al-Khayyun, R. 2005. *al-Adyan wa-l-madhahib fi al-'Iraq*. Beirut: Dar al-Jamal.

al-Khidr, A.-A. 2010. *al-Su'udiya: sirat dawla wa mujtama'*. Beirut: al-Shabaka al-'Arabiya li-l-Abhath wa-l-Nashr.

Korany, B. 1994. "Arab Democratization: A Poor Cousin." *Politics and Society* 27, no. 3: 34–37.

Korany, B., ed. 2010. *The Changing Middle East: A New Look at Regional Dynamics*. Cairo: American University in Cairo Press.

Korany, B., R. Brynen, and P. Noble, eds. 1998. *Political Liberalization and Democratization in the Arab World*. Vol. 2, *Comparative Cases*. Boulder, CO: Lynne Rienner.

Krichen, M. 2011. "al-Fasad wa-l-rashwa fi Tunis." Al Jazeera TV. 18 November.

Landau, A. 2006. *Théorie et pratique de la politique internationale*. Paris: L'Harmattan.

League of Arab States. 2004. *I'lan Tunis*. Issued by the Summit Meeting, 16th session, 22–23 May. Tunia: League of Arab States.

"League of Islamic Universities in Doha Creates the First Project to Use Technology to Modernize Arabic Language Instruction Programs." 2011. *al-Ahram*. 24 November.

Leclerq, C. 1994. *Libertés publiques*. Paris: Litec.

Legatum Institute. 2011. *Prosperity Index 2011*. http://www.prosperity.com/prosperiscope.

Leung, J. "The Rule of Law and Its Relevance to the HKSAR." www.jasononline.com/law/ruleoflaw.htm.

Limam, M.H. 2011a. *Zahirat al-fasad al-siyasi fi al-Jaza'ir: al-asbab wa-l-athar wa-l-islah*. Issue 391. Algier: al-Mustaqbal al-'Arabi.

———. 2011b. *Zahirat al-fasad al-siyasi fi al-Jaza'ir*. Beirut: Center for Arab Unity Studies.

Lomborg, B., ed. 2004. *Global Crises, Global Solutions*. Cambridge UK: Cambridge University Press.

Luciani, G. n.d. "The Post-rentier State." Background paper for the 2012 Arab Human Development Report. New York: UNDP.

Mahiou, A. 1997. *L'Etat de droit dans le monde arabe*. Paris: Editions CNRS.

Mahmoud, Y. 2005. "Baramij al-takyif al-iqtisadi wifqan li-l-munazzamat al-dawliya wa 'atharuha 'ala al-duwal al-namiya." *Majallat Jami'at Tishrin li-l-Dirasat wa-l-Buhuth al-'Ilmiya* 27, no. 2.

Mahmud, A.-H. 2000. *Manhaj al-islah al-islami fi al-mujtama'*. Cairo: Dar al-Rashad.

al-Mahrus, K. 2009. *Manahij al-dirasat al-diniya*. Beirut: Dar al-Mahajja al-Bayda'.

Malkawi, N., and A. Nejadat. 2007. "Tahaddiyat al-tarbiya al-'arabiya fi-l-qarn al-hadi wa-l-'ishrin wa atharuha fi tahdid dawr mu'allim al-mustaqbal." *University of Sharjah Journal for Humanities and Social Sciences* 4, no. 2 (June): 143–58.

Malki, A., et al. 2009. *al-Raqaba al-maliya fi al-aqtar al-'arabiya*. Workshop of the Arab Anti-Corruption Organization.

Malki, M. 2004. *al-Dimuqratiya dakhil al-ahzab fi al-buldan al-'arabiya*. Beirut: Center for Arab Unity Studies.

———. 2007a. "al-Barlaman fi al-Maghrib." In *al-Barlaman fi al-duwal al-'arabiya*. Beirut: Arab Center for the Development of the Rule of Law and Integrity and UNDP.

———. 2007b. "al-Dustur al-ta'aqudi wa-l-dasatir fi al-bilad al-'arabiya." In *al-Dimuqratiya wa al-taharrukat al-rahina fi al-shari' al-'arabi*. Beirut: Center for Arab Unity Studies.

———. 2008. "al-Intikhabat al-maghribiya fi zill al-hakkama al-intikhabiya." In *al-Nazaha fi al-intikhabat al-barlamaniya*. Beirut: Arab Anti-Corruption Organization and the Center for Arab Unity Studies.

———. 2010a. *al-Muwatana wa-l-wihda al-wataniya fi al-watan al-'arabi*. Marrakech: Arab Political Science Association and Laboratory for Constitutional and Political Studies.

———. 2010b. *al-Raqaba al-barlamaniya fi al-dasatir wa-l-anzima al-dakhiliya li-l-barlamanat al-'arabiya*. Parliamentary Development Initiative in the Arab Region and UNDP. http://www.arabparliaments.org/arabic/groups/oversight.asp.

Marchal, R. 2010. "Le Sud peut vivre sans le Nord, pas l'inverse." *Jeune Afrique*. 22 October.

MBRF (Mohamed bin Rashid Al Maktoum Foundation) and Regional Bureau for Arab States/UNDP. 2009. *Arab Knowledge Report: Toward Productive Intercommunication for Knowledge*. Dubai: Al Ghurair Printing and Publishing House.

Medany, M.A., and S.M. Attaher. 2007. "Climate Change and Irrigation in the Mediterranean Region." *Proceedings of the International Conference on Climate Change and Their Impacts on Coastal Zones and River Deltas*. Alexandria, Egypt. 23–25 April.

Merrill Lynch. 2011. September 8. http://www.barrick.com/files/doc_presentations/2011/Barrick-MerrillLynch-Sept2011.pdf

Al Mesbar Studies and Research Center. 2009. *al-Mu'assasat al-diniya*. No. 30. al-Shariqa, United Arab Emirates: al-Mesbar.

———. 2010a. *al-Ta'lim al-dini: al-tahlil*. No. 40. al-Shariqa, United Arab Emirates.

———. 2010b. *al-Ta'lim al-dini: al-tawsif*. No. 39. al-Shariqa, United Arab Emirates.

el-Mikawy, N. 2004. "The Media and Civil Society." *Magazine for Development and Cooperation 7*.

Mirkin, B. 2010. "Demographic Levels: The Arab Region's Trends and Policies." Series of papers on the Human Development Report. New York: UNDP.

al-Misawi, S. 2010. *Islam al-sasa*. Beirut: Dar al-Tali'.

Mockle, D. 1995. "L'Etat de droit et la théorie de la rule of law." *Cahiers de droit 35*, no. 4 823–904.

Montesquieu. 2001. *The Spirit of the Laws*. Translated by Thomas Nugent. Kitchener, Ontario: Batoche Books.

Moody-Stuart, G. 1999. *The Cost of Corruption*. The Center for Private International Projects. www.cipe-arabia.org/pdfhelp.asp.

Morin, E. 2001. *Seven Complex Lessons in Education for the Future*. Paris: UNESCO.

Morris, B. 1987. *Anthropological Studies of Religion*. Cambridge, UK: Cambridge University Press.

Mossaad, N. 2009. "Tanawu' al-hawiyat fi al-watan al-'arabi." Background paper for UNDP, AHDR 2008.

Muhsin, Y. 2010. "Kharitat al-fasad fi-l-Yaman, atrafuhu al-nafidha." San'a, Yemen: Observatory for Human Rights.

al-Mukhadimi, A. 2004. *Niza'at al-hudud al-'arabiya*. al-Fajr.

Mundib, A-G. 2006. *al-Din wa-l-mujtama'*. Casablanca, Morocco: Afriqiya al-Sharq.

al-Murabit, F. 2010. *al-Sulta al-tanfidhiya fi buldan al-maghrib al-'arabi: dirasa qanuniya muqarina*. Beirut: Center for Arab Unity Studies.

Murden, S. 2002. *Islam, the Middle East and the New Global Hegemony*. Boulder, CO: Lynne Rienner.

al-Musa, E.S. 2003. *al-I'lam wa-l-mujtama': dirasat fi al-i'lam al-urduni wa-l-'arabi wa-l-duwali*. Amman: Ministry of Culture.

al-Mutlaq, L. 2008. "Musahamat kubra wa mu'assasat al-qita' al-khass wa kibar rijal al-a'mal fi baramij al-tanmiya wa-l-tashghil." Paper presented to the Arab Forum on the New Role of the Private Sector in Development and Employment. New York and Cairo: UNIFEM/Arab League.

al-Nabulsi, S. and 'A. al-Shalabi. 2009. "Anzimat al-tamwil al-saghir al-mula'ima li-tatwir al-mujtma' al-mahali." Paper presented at the Second Regional Conference on Creativity and Initiatives of Development in Arab Cities. New York: UN Habitat.

Naeas, H. 2008. "Report on Air Pollution as a Result of Vehicles and Transport in Damascus City." Damascus: Damascus University Geography Department.

Nagano, T., K. Hoshikawa, S. Donma, T. Kume, S. Őnder, B. Őzekici, R. Kanber, and T. Watanabe. 2007. "Assessing Adaptive Capacity of Large

Irrigation Districts towards Climate Change and Social Change with Irrigation Management Performance Model." In *Water Saving in Mediterranean Agriculture and Future Research Needs*, edited by N. Lamaddalena, C. Boglitti, M. Todorovic, and A. Scardigno, 293–302. Proceedings of the International Conference of WASAMED Project. Valenzano, Italy. 14–17 February. http://ressources.ciheam.org/om/pdf/b56_1/00800120.pdf.

al-Nahdy, S. 2007. "Cyclone Gonu's Winds Blast Oman Coast." Associated Press Writer (Fox News Online). www.foxnews.com/printer_friendly_wires/2007Jun05/0,4675,Cyclone Gonu,00.html

al-Najjar, A.-M.O. 1999. *Qadaya al-bi'a min manzur islami*. Doha: Endowment of Shaykh Ali bin Abdullah Al al-Thani for Information and Research.

Nasrallah, R. 2007. *al-Amn al-i'lami al-'arabi: ishkaliyat al-dur wa-l-huwiya*. Beirut: Riyad al-Rais.

National Consortium for the Study of Terrorism and Responses to Terrorism. 2012. *Global Terrorism Database*. http://www.start.umd.edu/gtd/.

National Democratic Institute for International Affairs. 2007. *Yemen: Tribal Conflict Management Program*. Research Report. March.

Nazario, O. 2007. "A Strategy against Corruption: CARICOM Conference on the Caribbean. A 20/20 Vision." Washington, DC, 19–21 June. http://webcache.googleusercontent.com/search?q=cache:50ewMQUXjHA J:www.cpahq.org/CPAHQ/CMDownload.aspx%3FContentKey%3Defd36 893-8265-4a69-9370-350130278795%26ContentItemKey%3D08be8177-d8d4-454c-a4db-916395dc3078+&cd=1&hl=en&ct=clnk&gl=sa

News and Media United Nations Radio. 2012.

Nicholson, S. 2005. "On the Question of the 'Recovery' of the Rain in the West African Sahel." *Arid Environment* 63: 615–41. http://www.met.fsu.edu/people/nicholson/papers/recovery_JAE_05.pdf.

Nilsson, E.D., Ü. Rannik, M. Kulmala, G. Buzorius, and C.D. O'Dowd. 2001. "Effects of Continental Boundary Layer Evolution, Convection, Turbulence and Entrainment, on Aerosol Formation." *Tellus Series B: Chemical and Physical Meteorology* 53: 441–61. http://www.tellusb.net/index.php/tellusb/article/view/16617.

OAPEC (Organization of the Arab Petroleum Exporting Countries). 2009. *Annual Statistical Reports: Kuwait*. http://www.oapecorg.org/ARPubl/ASR/ASR2009.pdf.

OECD (Organisation for Economic Co-operation and Development). n.d. "Benchmark Report on Improving Transparency in Government Procurement Procedures in Iraq." http://www.oecd.org/document/44/0,3746,en_2649_34135_44736108_1_1_1_1,00.html.

———. 2007. PISA 2006 Science Competencies for Tomorrow's World. OECD Programme for International Student Assessment (PISA).

http://www.oecd.org/dataoecd/15/13/39725224.pdf.

———. 2009. "Joint Learning Study on Morocco: Enhancing Integrity in Public Procurement." http://www.oecd.org/document/35/0,3746,en_2649_34135_41548899_1_1_1_1,00.html.

———. 2010. "Progress in Public Management in the Middle East and North Africa: Case Studies on Policy Reform." http://www.oecd.org/document/5/0,3746,en_34645207_34645555_45695557_1_1_1_1,00.html.

Ofcom 2011. "What is Ofcom?" www.ofcome.uk/about/what-is-ofcom/.

Okot-Uma, R.W. 2000. *Electronic Governance: Re-inventing Good Governance.* American Society for Public Administration. http://citeseerx.ist.psu.edu/viewdoc/summary?doi=10.1.1.122.2101.

Owen, R. 2013. *The End of Arab Presidents for Life.* Cambridge, MA: Harvard University Press.

Patlitzianas, K.D., H. Doukas, and J. Psarras. 2006. "Enhancing Renewable Energy in the Arab States of the Gulf: Constraints and Efforts." *Energy Policy* 34: 3719–26. http://ipac.kacst.edu.sa/edoc/2009/176313_1.pdf.

Peters, B. 2010. "The Future of Journalism and Challenges for Media Development." *Journalism Practice* 4 (3): 268–73.

Pies, J. 2008. "Agents of Change? Journalism Ethics in Lebanese and Jordanian Journalism Education." In *Arab Media: Power and Weakness,* edited by Kai Hafez. New York: Continuum.

Pinfari, M. 2009. *Nothing But Failure? The Arab League and the Gulf Cooperation Council as Mediators in Middle Eastern Conflicts.* Crisis States Research Center, Working Paper no. 45.

Pourtois, J.-P., and H. Desmet. 2002. *L'éducation post-moderne.* Arabic translation by Sasi Nur al-Din, edited by Sola Abdallah. Tunis: ALESCO Publications.

Qaisi, I., and F. Sha'ban. 2011. "al-Naql wa-l-muwasalat: zahma wa talwith wa takhalluf." *al-Hayat.* 4 December. http://www.daralhayat.com/internationalarticle/325345.

al-Qaradawi, Y. 2001a. *Dawr al-qiyam wa-l-akhlaq fi al-iqtisad al-islami.* Cairo: Maktabat Wahba.

———. 2001b. *Ra'ayat al-bi'a fi shari'at al-islam.* Cairo: Dar al-Shuruq.

———. 2004. *Khitabuna al-islami fi 'asr al-'awlama.* Cairo: Dar al-Shuruq.

———. 2010. "al-Dimuqratiya wa ittifaquha ma'ruh al-islam."

Qaram, G. 2007. *al-Mas'ala al-diniya fi-l-qarn al-wahid wa-l-'ishrin.* Beirut: al-Farabi.

Qarni, B. 1987. "Wafida, mutagharriba, lakinaha baqiya: tanaqudat al-dawla al-'arabiya al-qutriya." *al-Mustaqbal al-'arabi,* no. 105.

al-Qasim, A.-A., ed. 2011. *Manahij al-'ulum al-shara'iya fi al-ta'lim al-su'udi.* Beirut: al-Shabakat al-'Arabiya li-l-Abhath wa-l-Nashar.

Qa'ud, 'A. 2000. *Nahw islah 'ulum al-din: al-ta'lim al-azhari numudhajan.*

Cairo: Cairo Institute for Human Rights Studies.

"al-Quwwat al-'askariya al-'arabiya tatajahhaz li-muwajahat duwal al-jiwar wa laysa Isra'il: al-sira'at al-hududiya bayna duwal al-khalij wa jiwariha hurub jahiza." 2010. *Damon News*. 14 August.

Rabie, A.H., ed. 2012. *The 25 January Revolution: A Documentary Analysis*. Cairo: Al-Ahram Center for Political and Strategic Studies.

Rahbani, L. 2010. "Women in Arab Media: Present but Not Heard." Presentation at Stanford University, 16 February, Stanford, CA.

Rahhal, H. 2010. *Muhammad Mahdi Shams al-Din: ru'ya fi ru'ahu al-islahiya*. Beirut: Markaz al-Hadara li-Tanmiyat al-Fikr al-Dini.

Reinisch, L. 2010. "Environmental Journalism in the UAE." *Arab Media & Society* 11 (Summer). www.arabmediasociety.com/countries/index.php?c_article=234.

Reporters without Borders. 2008. *Press Freedom Index*. Paris.

———. 2010a. Freedom of Press Index 2010. http://en.rsf.org/press-freedom-index-2010,1034.html.

———. 2010b. Press Freedom Index. Paris.

Rodinson, M. 1966. *Islam and Capitalism*. London: Penguin.

Ross, M., K. Kaiser, and N. Mazaheri. 2011. The "Resource Curse in MENA?" World Bank Policy Research Working Paper 5742. Washington, DC: World Bank.

Rustow, D. 1970. "Transitions to Democracy." *Comparative Politics* 2, no. 3: 337–63.

Sadiqi, 'A. 2007. *al-Bahth 'an dimuqratiya 'arabiya: al-khitab wa-l-khitab al-muqabil*. Beirut: Center for Arab Unity Studies.

Saghiya, H. 2010. *Nawasib wa-rawafid: munaza'at al-Sunna wa-l-Shi'a fi al-'alam al-islami al-yawm*. Beirut: Dar al-Saqi.

Sa'id, A.K.Q. 2008. "Fa'iliyat al-aliyat al-madaniya fi hall al-niza'at." *al-Watan*, 26 December.

Said, A.M. 2011. "Hayra thawriya." *al-Ahram*. 28 July.

Sakr, N. 2007. *Arab Television Today*. London: I.B. Tauris.

Sakr, N., ed. 2004. *Women and Media in the Middle East: Power through Self-expression*. London: I.B. Tauris.

al-Sakran, I., and A.-A. al-Qasim. 2006. *al-Muqarrarat al-diniya: ayn al-khalal?* Paper presented to Second National Dialogue Forum, Mecca, Saudi Arabia. Mecca: Bin Jama'a. www.muslimdiversity.net

Salah, I. 2003. *al-Fasad wa-l-islah*. Damascus: Publications of the Arab Writers Union.

Salama, S.A. 2011. "Madrasa al-hakim al-shuruq." *al-Shuruq*. 15 August. http://www.shorouknews.com/columns/view.aspx

Salamé, G. 1994. *Démocraties sans démocrates*. Paris: Fayard.

Salem, H. 2003. *al-Sahafa al-misriya wa qadaya al-fasad*. Cairo: Misr al-Mahrousa.

Salih, N. 2008. "al-Fasad fi-l-'alam al-'arabi: ma'nahu, dawafi'uhu wa asbabuhu, nata'ijuhu wa 'ilajuhu." *al-Hiwar al-mutamaddin*, no. 2201, 24 February.

al-Samadi, K. 2008. *al-Qiyam al-islamiya fi al-manzuma al-tarbawiya: dirasa li-l-qiyam al-islamiya wa aliyat ta'ziziha*. Morocco: ISESCO Publications.

al-Samadi, K., and A.-R. Halali. 2007. *Azmat al-ta'lim al-dini fi al-'alam al-islami*. Damascus: Dar al-Fikr.

Saqr, A. 2008a. "Mubadarat tatwir al-ta'lim." http://www.carnegieendowment.org/arb/?fa=show&article=20580&lang=ar.

———. 2008b. "GCC States Competing in Educational Reform." http://www.carnegieendowment.org/2008/08/12/gcc-states-competing-in-educational-reform/48y.

Sarush, A.-K. 2009a. *al-Siratat al-mustaqima*. Beirut: al-Intishar al-'Arabi.

———. 2009b. *al-Siyasa wa-l-tadayyun*. Beirut: al-Intishar al-'Arabi.

al-Sayyid, R. 1993. *Mafahim al-jama'at fi-l-islam*. Beirut: Dar al-Muntakhib al-'Arabi.

Schech, S. 2002. "Wired for Change: The Links between ICTs and Development Discourses." *Journal of International Development* 14: 13–23.

Schmitter, P., and G. O'Donnell. 1986. *Transitions from Authoritarian Rule*. Baltimore: Johns Hopkins University Press.

Semien, D. 2009. 'Alerte précoce': Réseau francophone de recherche sur les opérations de maintien de la paix." 16 March. http://www.operationspaix.net/Alerte-precoce.

Seurin, J.L. 1984. *La constitutionnalisation aujourd'hui*. Paris: Editions Economica.

al-Shafi'i, Ibrahim. 1984. "Asbab zahirat insiraf al-tulab 'an dirasat al-tarbiya al-islamiya." Al-Ezz Cultural Forums (Studies and Research in Islamic Education). http://www.al3ez.net/vb/showthread.php?7184.

Shalhoub, G. 2004. "al-Shabab al-lubnani wa-l-tarbiya al-diniya: al-tarbiya al-diniya mata yanbalij nuruhu?" *al-Nahar*, 11 November, p. 21.

Shaqir, Y. 2001. *al-Huriyat al-sahafiya fi-l-Urdun: dirasa muqarina fi al-tashri'at*. Amman: The Jordanian Journalists' Syndicate.

Sheuya, S. 2008. "Improving the Health and Lives of People Living in Slums." *Annals of the New York Academy of Science* 1136: 298–306.

Shobaki, A. 2006. "al-Idara al-hizbiya li-l-intikhabat al-tashri'iya wa-l-ra'isiya." In *Nuzum idarat al-intikhabat fi Misr ma' al-muqarana bi-halat buldan ukhra*, edited by Amr Shobaki and Hisham Rabie. Cairo: Center for Political and Strategic Studies.

*al-Shuruq*. 2011. 23 June; 6 August.

Sika, N. 2011. "al-Tarbiya al-diniya fi al-'alam al-'arabi." Background paper.

"Somalie: La Ligue Arabe est totalement absente." 2007. *Alternatives Internationales*. 13 January. http://www.alterinter.org/article534.html.

Stowasser, B.F., ed. 1987. *The Islamic Impulse*. Washington, DC: Center for Contemporary Arab Studies, Georgetown University.

Suwaidan, T. 2013. "al-Taghyir fi al-khitab al-i'lami al-dini." 15 May. http://www.suwaidan.com.

Suwaigh, S. 2002. "al-Tanshi'a al-ijtima'iya li-l-tifl al-'arabi wa 'alaqatuha bi tanmiyat al-ma'rifa: dirasa tahliliya." Paper presented at the seminar "Early Childhood: Its Specific Features and Requirements," Kingdom of Saudi Arabia.

Tangui, C. 1985. *Le droit sans l'état*. Paris: Editions PUF.

al-Tanir, S. 2009. *al-Faqr wa-l-fasad fi-l-'alam al-'arabi*. 1st ed. Beirut: Dar al-Saqi.

*al-Taqrir al-sanawi li-l-lajna al-'ulya li-l-tansiq bayn al-qanawat al-fada'iya al-'arabiya*. 2010.

Tardy, T. 2009. *Gestion de crise, maintien et consolidation de la paix: Acteurs, activités et défis*. Brussels: Editions de Boeck Université.

Thai, E. 2010. "Alternate Viewpoints: Counter-hegemony in the Transnational Age." *Arab Media and Society* 11 (Summer).

Al-Thawr, S. n.d. "The Poverty Map in the Arab World."

———. 2010. "Dirasat aswat al-fuqara': taqyim al-khitta al-khumasiya al-thalitha li-l-tanmiya al-iqtisadiya wa-l-ijtima'iya wa-l-takhfif min al-faqr 2006–2010." Ministry of Planning and International Cooperation in the Yemeni Republic.

Transparency International. 2005. *Corruption Perceptions Index, 2005*. http://www.transparency.org/policy_research/surveys_indices/cpi/2005.

———. 2007. *Corruption Perceptions Index, 2007*. http://www.transparency.org/policy_research/surveys_indices/cpi/2007.

———. 2008. *Corruption Perceptions Index, 2008*. http://www.transparency.org/policy_research/surveys_indices/cpi/2008.

———. 2009. *Corruption Perceptions Index, 2009*. http://www.transparency.org/policy_research/surveys_indices/cpi/2009.

———. 2010. *Corruption Perceptions Index, 2010*. http://www.transparency.org/policy_research/surveys_indices/cpi/2010.

———. 2011a. *Bribe Payers Index*. http://www.pogar.org/publications/agfd/GfDII/corruption/deadsea/ahmadashour-ar.pdf.

———. 2011b. *Corruption Perceptions Index, 2011*. http://cpi.transparency.org/cpi2011/results/.

———. 2012. *Corruption Perception Index 2012*.

Troper, M. 1992. "Le concept d'état de droit." *Droits* 15: 51–63.

Tunisian Ministry of Education. 2006. "al-Baramij al-jadida li-l-tarbiya al-islamiya." Bureau of Academic Programmes and Textbooks. Tunis: Centre National Pédagogique.

Turner, B. 1974. *Weber and Islam*. London: Routledge & Kegan.

———. 1991. *Religion and Social Theory*. London: Sage.

U4/Anti-Corruption Resource Center. 2011. Website operated by CNI: CHR Michelsen Institute: www.u4.no.

al-'Umran, J. 2002. "Tanmiyat al-qiyam al-sulukiya lada talamidh al-marhala al-ibtida'iya." *Majallat al-Tufula*, no. 7. Bahraini Association for Child Development.

UN (United Nations). 2004. United Nations Convention against Corruption.

http://www.unodc.org/documents/treaties/UNCAC/Publications/Convention/
08-50024_A.pdf. English: http://www.unodc.org/documents/treaties/
UNCAC/Publications/Convention/08-50026_E.pdf]

———. 2008. *UN E-government Survey 2008: From E-government to Connected Governance.* New York: United Nations.

———. 2009. "Secretary-General, Message for International Anti-Corruption Day, 7 December 2009."
http://www.un.org/News/Press/docs/2009/sgsm12660.doc.htm

———. 2010. *UN E-government Survey 2010: Leveraging E-government at a Time of Financial and Economic Crisis.* New York: United Nations.

UNDEF News. 2009.
www.equalaccess.org/up_content/uploads/media/undef_update_1.PDF

UNDP (United Nations Development Programme). 1998. "Fighting Corruption to Improve Governance." http://www.undp-pogar.org/publications/finances/anticor/fightingcorruption98a.pdf.

———. 2002a. *AHDR (Arab Human Development Report): Creating Opportunities for Future Generations.* Regional Bureau for Arab States.
www.arab-hdr.org/publications/other/ahdr/ahdr2002e.pdf

———. 2002b. *Arab Human Development Report, 2002: Creating Opportunities for Future Generations.* Regional Bureau for Arab States, UNDP. New York and Amman: UNDP.

———. 2002c. *Taqrir al-tanmiya al-insaniya al-'arabiya li-l-'am 2002: khalq al-furas li-l-ajyal al-qadima.* Amman: Regional Bureau for Arab States, United Nations Development Programme.

———. 2003a. *Arab Human Development Report 2003: Building a Knowledge Society.* New York and Amman: United Nations Regional Office, UNDP.

———. 2003b. *Taqrir al-tanmiya al-insaniya al-'arabiya li-l-'am 2003: nahw iqamat mujtama' al-ma'rifa.* Amman: Regional Bureau for Arab States, United Nations Development Programme.

———. 2004a. *Arab Human Development Report 2004: Toward Freedom in the Arab World.* New York and Amman: UNDP Regional Bureau of Arab States.

———. 2004b. *Taqrir al-tanmiya al-insaniya al-'arabiya li-l-'am 2004: nahw al-huriya fi al-'alam al-'arabi.* Amman: Regional Bureau for Arab States.

———. 2005a. *Arab Human Development Report 2005: Toward the Rise of Women in the Arab Countries.* New York and Amman: United Nations Regional Office, UNDP.

———. 2005b. *Taqrir al-tanmiya al-insaniya al-'arabiya li-l-'am 2004: nahw al-huriya fi-l-'alam al-'arabi.* Amman: Regional Bureau for Arab States, United Nations Development Programme.

———. 2006a. *Communication for Empowerment: Developing Media Strategies in Support of Vulnerable Groups.* Practical Guidance Note. New York: United Nations.
www.amarc.org/documents/articles/Communication_for_Empowerment.pdf.

———. 2006b. *Taqrir al-tanmiya al-insaniya al-'arabiya li-l-'am 2005: nahw nuhud al-mar'a.* Amman: Regional Bureau for Arab States, United

Nations Development Programme.

———. 2007. *al-Qada' fi al-duwal al-'arabiya*. Beirut: Arab Center for the Development of the Rule of Law and Integrity and UNDP-POGAR.

———. 2008a. *Corruption and Development*. Democratic Governance Team. New York: UNDP.

———. 2008b. *A Users' Guide to Measuring Corruption*. Oslo Governance Center. New York: UNDP.

———. 2009a. *AHDR (Arab Human Development Report): Challenges to Human Security in the Arab Countries*. Regional Bureau for Arab States. http://www.arab-hdr.org/publications/other/ahdr/ahdr2009e.pdf

———. 2009b. *Arab Human Development Report 2009: Challenges to Human Security in the Arab Countries*. New York and Amman: UNDP Regional Bureau of Arab States.

———. 2009c. *The Arab Knowledge Report 2009: Toward Productive Intercommunication for Knowledge*. New York: United Nations.

———. 2009d. *Taqrir al-tanmiya al-insaniya al-'arabiya li-l-'am 2009: tahadiyat amn al-insan fi-l-buldan al-'arabiya*. Beirut: Regional Bureau for Arab States, United Nations Development Programme.

———. 2010a. *Egypt Human Development Report 2010*. New York: UNDP.

———. 2010b. *Guidance Note: UNCAC Self Assessments—Going beyond the Minimum*. New York: UNDP.

———. 2010c. *Human Development Report 2010: The Real Wealth of Nations: Pathways to Human Development*. New York and Amman: UNDP Regional Bureau of Arab States.

———. 2010d. "Population Levels, Trends and Policies in the Arab Region: Challenges and Opportunities." AHDR Research Paper Series.

———. 2010e. Programme of the Conference on Building Strategic Anti-Corruption Partnerships in the Arab Region. 26–27 October. Regional Bureau for Arab States, Amman: UNDP.

———. 2010f. *The Third Arab Report on Millennium Goals*. New York and Cairo: United Nations, League of Arab States.

———. 2011a. *Human Development Report 2011: Sustainability and Equity—A Better Future for All*. New York: UNDP.

———. 2011b. Proceedings from conference "Transitions to Democracy." Cairo, 5–7 June.

UNDP (United Nations Development Programme) and the Arab League. 2009a. "Development Challenges in Arab States." Part 1.

———. 2009b. "Development Challenges in Arab States." Part 2. New York: UNDP.

———. 2009c. *Improving Food Security in Arab Countries*. Washington DC: World Bank.

UNDP and the Mohammed bin Rashid Al Maktoum Foundation. 2009. *Taqrir al-ma'rifa al-'arabi li-l-'am 2009: nahw tawasul ma'rifi muntij*. Dubai, United Arab Emirates: Regional Bureau for Arab States.

UNDP-PACDE. 2011. "Global Thematic Programme on Anti-Corruption for Development Effectiveness." *PACDE*: 2008–11.

UNDP (United Nations Development Programme) and Regional Bureau for Arab States. n.d. Programme on Governance in the Arab Region (POGAR). www.pogar.org.

UNEP (United Nations Environment Programme) and Regional Office for West Asia. 2006. "Air Quality and Atmospheric Pollution in the Arab Region." Ed. M. El-Raey. ESCWA/League of Arab States/UNEP, Regional Office for West Asia Report. http://www.un.org/esa/sustdev/csd/csd14/escwaRIM_bp1.pdf

———. 2007. "Current Status of Renewable Energies in the Middle East and North African Region." http://www.unep.org/publications/search/pub_details_s.asp?ID=3975.

UNESCO (United Nations Educational, Scientific, and Cultural Organization). 1996. Declaration of Sana'a. http://portal.unesco.org/ci/en//ev.php-URL_ID=5351&URL_DO=DO=TOPIC&URL_SECTION=201.html.

———. 2009. *Overcoming Inequality: Why Governance Matters*. EFA Global Monitoring Report 2009. http://www.unesco.org/new/en/education/themes/leading-the-international-agenda/efareport/reports/2009-governance/.

———. 2011. *The Hidden Crisis: Armed Conflict and Education*. EFA Global Monitoring Report 2011. http://www.unesco.org/new/en/education/themes/leading-the-international-agenda/efareport/reports/2011-conflict/.

UNFCCC (United Nations Framework Convention on Climate Change). 2007. The National Communications Documents. http://unfccc.int/meetings/cop_13/items/4049.php.

UN-Habitat (United Nations Human Settlements Program). 2003. *The Challenges of Slums: Global Report on Human Settlements*. London: Earthscan Publications. http://www.unhabitat.org/downloads/docs/GRHS.2003.0.pdf.

———. 2009. *Urban World Innovative Cities: Why Learning Is the Key to Urban Development*. http://mirror.unhabitat.org/pmss/listItemDetails.aspx?publicationID=2784.

———. 2012. Urban Planning for City Leaders. 2nd ed. http://mirror.unhabitat.org/pmss/listItemDetails.aspx?publicationID=3385.

UNIFEM (United Nations Development Fund for Women). 2006. *Women's Development Report*. New York: United Nations.

United Nations General Assembly. 2005. Resolution 60/147, adopted 16 December. http://www.ohchr.org/french/law/reparation.htm.

United Nations Office for the Coordination of Humanitarian Affairs. 2001. "Algeria: Floods OCHA Situation Report No. 7." http://reliefweb.int/node/90714.

United Nations Public Administration Programme. 2012.

www.unpan.org/egovkb

United Nations Relief and Works Agency.
http://www.unrwa.org/etemplate.php?id=253.

Wahba, H. 2010. "Khubara' al-i'lam wa 'ulama' din yuhadhirun min qanawat al-fitna al-madhhabiya." *al-Tawafuq* 3 August.

*al-Wasat*. 2011. "al-Su'udiya tatba' 1.5 milyun nuskha min fatwat tahrim al-tazahur." 29 March.

Waslekar, S., and I. Futehaly. 2009. *Cost of Conflict in the Middle East*. Mumbai: Strategic Foresight Group.

WHO (World Health Organization). 2005. *Air Quality Guidelines for Particulate Matter, Ozone, Nitrogen Dioxide and Sulphur Dioxide: Global Update 2005. Summary of Risk Assessment.*
http://whqlibdoc.who.int/hq/2006/WHO_SDE_PHE_OEH_06.02_eng.pdf.

———. 2009. *Road Safety Report*. Geneva: World Health Organization.

Wood, J. 2010. "Lebanon Cracks Down on Internet Freedom." *New York Times*. 4 November. http://www.nytimes.com/2010/11/04/world/middleeast/04iht-m04m1leblog.html?_r=1.

World Association of Newspapers. 2010. *Middle East and North Africa Media Guide*.

World Bank. 2000. *Business Environment and Enterprise Performance Surveys 2000.*
http://web.worldbank.org/WBSITE/EXTERNAL/COUNTRIES/ECAE
XT/EXTECAREGTOPANTCOR/0,,contentMDK:20720934~pagePK:3
4004173~piPK:34003707~theSitePK:704666,00.html.

———. 2004. "Cost of Corruption."
http://web.worldbank.org/WBSITE/EXTERNAL/NEWS/0,,contentM
DK:20190187~menuPK:34457~pagePK:34370~piPK:34424~theSitePK:4
607,00.html.

———. 2007a. "Making the Most of Water Scarcity: Accountability for Better Water Management Results in the Middle East and North Africa."
http://siteresources.worldbank.org/INTMENA/Resources/Water_Scarcit
y_Full.pdf.

———. 2007b. *The Road Not Travelled: Educational Reform in the Middle East and North Africa*. Executive Summary of the Report on Development of Middle East and North Africa. Washington, DC: World Bank.

———. 2008. *Regional Summary on the Middle East and North Africa*. Washington DC: World Bank.

———. 2010a. *Databank of Global Governance Indicators, 2010.*
http://databank.worldbank.org/ddp/home.do.

———. 2010b. *World Governance Indicators 2010.*
http://databank.worldbank.org/ddp/home.do.

———. 2011a. *Reducing Conflict Risk: Conflict, Fragility and Development in the Middle East and North Africa*. World Bank.

———. 2011b. *The World Development Report: Conflict, Security, and Development*. http://wdr2011.worldbank.org/fulltext.

————. 2011c. *The World Development Report: Conflict, Security, and Development.* Overview. wdr2011.worldbank.org/sites/default/files/WDR2011_Overview.pdf.

————. 2012a. *Knowledge Assessment Methodology.* http://info.worldbank.org/etools/kam2/KAM_page5.asp.

————. 2012b. *World Development Indicators.* http://databank.worldbank.org/ddp/home.do.

————. 2013. *World Bank Publications: World Development Indicators.* http://data.worldbank.org/data-catalog/world-development-indicators/wdi-2013

World Bank Data. 2010. *Global Development Indicators.* http://databank.worldbank.org/ddp/home.do.

*World Development Indicators.* 2012. Washington, DC: World Bank.

World Economic Forum. 2009. *Global Information Technology Report, 2008–2009.* Geneva: SRO-Kundig.

World Justice Project. 2011. Rulĕ of Law Index. http://worldjusticeproject.org/rule-of-law-index/.

World of Work Report. 2010. "From One Crisis to the Next." Switzerland: International Institute for Labour Studies.

Yemeni Ministry of Education. 2009. "Islamic Studies Syllabi, 2009–2010." Curricula and Guidance Department. http://www.yemenmoe.net/Course.aspx

————. 2009–10. "Scholastic Requirements for Islamic Education." Department of Curricula and Guidance. http://www.yemenmoe.net/Course.aspx

Yom, S. 2005. "Civil Society and Democratization in the Arab World." *Middle East Review of International Affairs* 9 (4):15.

Yusuf, M., and 'A. al-Din. 2008. *al-Shabab wa thaqafat al-islah.* Alexandria: Library of Alexandria.

Zaidah, S. 2010. "Education: Bedrock for Social Change." In *Viewpoints,* special ed. State of the Arts, Volume 6: Creative Arab Women. Washington, DC: Middle East Institute.

Zaki, M. 2007. *Civil Society and Democratization in the Arab World.* Cairo: Ibn Khaldun Center for Development Studies. www.glp.net/c/document_library/get_file?p_l_id=10413&folderId=12858 &name=DLFE-1901.pdf.

Zayani, M., ed. 2005. *The Al Jazeera Phenomenon: Critical Perspectives on New Arab Media.* London: Paradigm Press.

Zayid, A. 2007. *Suwar min al-khitab al-dini.* Cairo: Dar al-'Ayn li-l-Nashr.

————. 2011. *Qiyam al-tanmiya fi al-khitab al-dini al-mu'asir.* Cairo: Egyptian Cabinet Information and Decision Support Center.

Zayid, A., and 'A. al-Zubayr, eds. 2005. *al-Nukhab al-ijtima'iya: halat al-Jaza'ir wa Misr.* Cairo: Maktabat Madbuli.

# Index